THE VIKINGS IN I

Manchester University Press

MANCHESTER MEDIEVAL STUDIES

SERIES EDITOR   Professor S. H. Rigby

SERIES ADVISORS   Professor John Hatcher
Professor J. H. Moran Cruz

The study of medieval Europe is being transformed as old ortho-doxies are challenged, new methods embraced and fresh fields of inquiry opened up. The adoption of interdisciplinary perspectives and the challenge of economic, social and cultural theory are forcing medievalists to ask new questions and to see familiar topics in a fresh light.

The aim of this series is to combine the scholarship traditionally associated with medieval studies with an awareness of more recent issues and approaches in a form accessible to the non-specialist reader.

MANCHESTER MEDIEVAL STUDIES

THE VIKINGS IN ENGLAND
SETTLEMENT, SOCIETY
AND CULTURE

D. M. Hadley

Manchester University Press

Manchester and New York

distributed exclusively in the USA by Palgrave

Published by Manchester University Press
Oxford Road, Manchester M13 9NR, UK
and Room 400, 175 Fifth Avenue, New York, NY 10010, USA
www.manchesteruniversitypress.co.uk

Distributed in the United States exclusively by
Palgrave Macmillan, 175 Fifth Avenue,
New York, NY 10010, USA

Distributed in Canada exclusively by
UBC Press, University of British Columbia, 2029 West Mall,
Vancouver, BC, Canada V6T 1Z2

British Library Cataloguing-in-Publication Data is available

Library of Congress Cataloging-in-Publication Data is available

ISBN 978 0 7190 5982 7 paperback

First published by Manchester University Press in hardback 2006

First reprinted 2006

Printed by Lightning Source

CONTENTS

LIST OF ILLUSTRATIONS   *page*   vii
ACKNOWLEDGEMENTS   xi
LIST OF ABBREVIATIONS   xiii
PREFACE   xv

1 The Scandinavian settlements: the development of a debate   1
2 Anglo–Scandinavian political accommodation   28
3 Scandinavian rural settlement   81
4 Scandinavians in the urban environment   145
5 Churches and the Scandinavians: chaos, conversion and change   192
6 Burial practices: ethnicity, gender and social status   237
   Epilogue   272

SELECT BIBLIOGRAPHY   282
INDEX   291

LIST OF ILLUSTRATIONS

1 Scandinavian place-names in England. Drawn by Colin Merrony after J. D. Richards, *Viking Age England* (2nd edn, Stroud, 2000).

2 Excavations at Repton (Derbys). Drawn by Oliver Jessop after M. Biddle and B. Kjølbye-Biddle, 'Repton and the "great heathen army", 873-4', in J. Graham-Campbell, R. A. Hall, J. Jesch and D. Parsons (eds), *Vikings and the Danelaw. Select papers from the proceedings of the Thirteenth Viking Congress* (Oxford, 2001), pp. 45-96, fig. 4.5.

3 Imitation 'Alfred' coin. Reproduced by permission of Mark Blackburn and the Fitzwilliam Museum.

4 Coin of Guthrum. Reproduced by permission of Mark Blackburn and the Fitzwilliam Museum.

5 St Edmund penny. Reproduced by permission of Mark Blackburn and the Fitzwilliam Museum.

6 The estates of St Cuthbert. Drawn by Oliver Jessop after C. D. Morris, 'Viking and native in northern England: a case-study', in H. Bekker-Nielsen, P. Foote and O. Olsen (eds), *Proceedings of the Eighth Viking Congress* (Odense, 1981), pp. 223-44, fig. 2.

7 Coins minted in York in c.895-905. Reproduced by permission of Mark Blackburn and the Fitzwilliam Museum.

8 Coins minted in York in the early tenth century. Reproduced by permission of Mark Blackburn and the Fitzwilliam Museum.

9 Die for the minting of the St Peter's coinage. Reproduced by permission of York Archaeological Trust.

10 Stone sculpture at York Minster. Reproduced by permission of English Heritage.

11 Places referred to in the text. Drawn by Oliver Jessop.

12 An artist's reconstruction of the farmstead at Ribblehead (Yorks). Reproduced by permission of York Museums Trust (Yorkshire Museum).

13 Scandinavian trefoil brooch from Stallingborough (Lincs). Reproduced by permission of Kevin Leahy and North Lincolnshire Museum.

14 Scandinavian quadrangular brooch from Elsham (Lincs). Reproduced by permission of Kevin Leahy and North Lincolnshire Museum.

15 Scandinavian convex disc-brooch from Heckingham (Norf). From S. Margeson, *The Vikings in Norfolk* (Norwich, 1997), p. 21, drawn by

D. Fox. Reproduced by permission of Norwich Castle Museum and Art Gallery.

16 Anglo–Scandinavian flat disc-brooch from Norwich (Norf). Drawn by Ryszard Hajdul, and reproduced by permission of Norfolk Archaeological Unit.

17 Scandinavian strap-end from Walsingham (Norf). From S. Margeson, *The Vikings in Norfolk* (Norwich, 1997), p. 22, drawn by S. White. Reproduced by permission of Norwich Castle Museum and Art Gallery.

18 Anglo–Scandinavian trefoil brooch from Cranwell (Lincs). Reproduced by permission of Kevin Leahy and North Lincolnshire Museum.

19 Plan of York. Drawn by Oliver Jessop after R. A. Hall, *Viking Age York* (London, 1994), fig. 6.

20 Excavations at Coppergate in York. Reproduced by permission of York Archaeological Trust.

21 A copper-alloy strap-end from York, decorated with Borre-style ring chain ornament. Reproduced by permission of York Museums Trust (Yorkshire Museum).

22 Anglo–Scandinavian flat disc-brooch from York. Reproduced by permission of York Archaeological Trust.

23 Ninth-century sarcophagus from Derby. Photograph by Phil Sidebottom.

24 Plan of Nottingham. Drawn by Oliver Jessop, after R. A. Hall, 'The Five Boroughs of the Danelaw: a review of present knowledge', *ASE*, 18 (1989), 149–206, fig. 7.

25 Plan of Stamford. Drawn by Oliver Jessop, after C. Mahany, A. Burchard and G. Simpson, *Excavations in Stamford, Lincolnshire 1963–1969* (London, 1982), fig. 6.

26 Plan of Lincoln. Drawn by Oliver Jessop, after R. A. Hall, 'The Five Boroughs of the Danelaw: a review of present knowledge', *ASE*, 18 (1989), 149–206, fig. 6.

27 Coin minted in Leicester in the late ninth century. Reproduced by permission of Mark Blackburn and the Fitzwilliam Museum.

28 Torksey-type ware storage vessel from Coppergate in York. Reproduced by permission of York Archaeological Trust.

29 Sculpture at Lindisfarne (Northumb). Copyright: Department of Archaeology, University of Durham. Photographer: Tom Middlemass.

30 Sculpture at Nunburnholme (Yorks). Copyright: Department of Archaeology, University of Durham. Photographer: Tom Middlemass.

31 Sculpture at Gosforth (Cumb). Reproduced from W. G. Collingwood, *Northumbrian Crosses of the Pre-Norman Age* (London, 1927), fig. 184.

32 Sculpture at Kirklevington (Yorks). Drawn by Alex Norman.

33 Sculptures with warrior and heroic images. Drawn by Oliver Jessop.

34 Hogback sculptures at Brompton (Yorks). Drawn by Alex Norman after a photograph in J. D. Richards, *Viking Age England* (2nd edn, Stroud, 2000), fig. 73.

35 Map of Scandinavian burials. Drawn by Oliver Jessop after J. D. Richards, *Viking Age England* (2nd edn, Stroud, 2000), fig. 63, with the addition of recently discovered sites.

36 Plan of the cremation mounds at Heath Wood, Ingleby (Derbys). Reproduced by permission of English Heritage.

37 Mound 50 at Heath Wood, Ingleby (Derbys) during excavation. Reproduced by permission of Julian Richards.

38 Grave goods excavated at Hesket-in-the-Forest (Cumb). Reproduced from *Archaeologia Aeliana*, 2 (1832).

39 Burials at Cumwhitton (Cumb). Drawn by Oliver Jessop, after M. Pitts, 'Cumbrian heritage', *British Archaeology*, 79 (2004), 28–31.

40 Locations of burials and sculpture in later Anglo-Saxon Lincolnshire. Drawn by Oliver Jessop.

41 Sculpture at Weston (Yorks). Drawn by Oliver Jessop.

ACKNOWLEDGEMENTS

I have benefited enormously from discussions with friends and colleagues during the writing of this book, especially Julian Richards, David Stocker, Paul Everson, Kevin Leahy, Lesley Abrams, Paul Blinkhorn, John Blair, Gabor Thomas and Andrew Reynolds. I am also grateful to Julian Richards, David Stocker, John Blair and Mark Blackburn for making their work available to me in advance of publication. For permission to reproduce illustrations, I am grateful to English Heritage; Kevin Leahy and the North Lincolnshire Museum; Tim Pestell and the Norwich Castle Museum and Art Gallery; The Yorkshire Museum; the British Academy Corpus of Stone Sculpture at the University of Durham; York Archaeological Trust; Norfolk Archaeological Unit; Mark Blackburn and the Fitzwilliam Museum; and Phil Sidebottom and Julian Richards. I would also like to thank Christine Kyriacou, Alice Lyons, Katy Whitaker, Derek Craig, Melanie Baldwin, Tim Pestell, Mark Blackburn and Kevin Leahy for help with tracking down illustrations. Mark Bennet at Lincoln Historic Environment Record, and Mike Hemblade at North Lincolnshire Sites and Monuments Record, were both enormously helpful with the research for this book. I am grateful to Alex Norman, Colin Merrony and, especially, to Oliver Jessop for preparing original drawings, and to Hugh Willmott and Shane Eales for assistance with manipulating digital images. My colleagues Hugh Willmott and Oliver Jessop kindly read drafts of parts of this book and made many valuable suggestions, and I am also grateful to Janet Nelson and Matthew Innes for feedback on the original proposal for the book, and to Steve Rigby and an anonymous reviewer for comments on the final draft. I would also like to thank Jonathan Bevan at MUP for his support and forbearance. Finally, I owe the greatest debt to my family who provided endless encouragement and support during the preparation of this book, and it is to Olly and Isabelle that this book is dedicated.

ACKNOWLEDGEMENTS

LIST OF ABBREVIATIONS

AgHR	*Agricultural History Review*
ANS	*Anglo-Norman Studies*
Antiq. J.	*Antiquaries Journal*
Arch. J.	*Archaeological Journal*
ASE	*Anglo-Saxon England*
ASSAH	*Anglo-Saxon Studies in Archaeology and History*
BAJ	*Bedfordshire Archaeological Journal*
BAR	British Archaeological Reports
BNJ	*British Numismatic Journal*
Brit. Ser.	British Series
CBA	Council for British Archaeology
Curr. Arch.	*Current Archaeology*
DAJ	*Derbyshire Archaeological Journal*
DB	*Domesday Book* (the most accessible edition is the series edited by J. Morris (Phillimore))
EAA	East Anglian Archaeology
EETS	Early English Text Society
EHD I	*English Historical Documents, vol. I, c.500–1042*, ed. D. Whitelock (2nd edn, London, 1979)
EHR	*English Historical Review*
EME	*Early Medieval Europe*
Hist. Today	*History Today*
IBGT	*Institute of British Geographers Transactions*
Int. Ser.	International Series
JBAA	*Journal of the British Archaeological Association*
J. Brit. Stud.	*Journal of British Studies*
JDANHS	*Journal of the Derbyshire Archaeological and Natural History Society*
JHG	*Journal of Historical Geography*
LAHST	*Leicestershire Archaeological and Historical Society Transactions*
Land. Hist.	*Landscape History*
LHA	*Lincolnshire History and Archaeology*
Med. Arch.	*Medieval Archaeology*

Med. Hist.	*Medieval History*
Mid. Hist.	*Midland History*
North. Hist.	*Northern History*
Oxford J. of Arch.	*Oxford Journal of Archaeology*
PCAS	*Proceedings of the Cambridge Antiquarian Society*
PDAS	*Proceedings of the Devon Archaeological Society*
PHFCAS	*Proceedings of the Hampshire Field Club and Archaeological Society*
PSAS	*Proceedings of the Society of Antiquaries of Scotland*
S	P. H. Sawyer (ed.), *Anglo-Saxon Charters: an annotated list and bibliography* (London, 1968) [documents cited by number]
TLAHS	*Transactions of the Leicestershire Archaeological and Historical Society*
TRHS	*Transactions of the Royal Historical Society*
TTS	*Transactions of the Thoroton Society*
YAJ	*Yorkshire Archaeological Journal*
WANHM	*Wiltshire Archaeological and Natural History Magazine*

PREFACE

This study offers a new interdisciplinary perspective on the Scandinavian impact on England during the ninth and tenth centuries. It focuses on the ways in which Scandinavians took control and settled in parts of northern and eastern England; the responses of the settlers and indigenous populations to each other; and the processes by which the settlers were eventually integrated into local society and culture. Documentary, archaeological, art-historical and linguistic evidence are examined to provide the fullest picture possible of the Scandinavian settlements. Much ink has been expended over the apparently contradictory impressions of the Scandinavian impact provided by these diverse forms of evidence, with scholars often becoming entrenched in their positions as they privilege the evidence with which they are most familiar. Yet, as we shall see, apparent discrepancies between our sources often relate to the social, geographical and chronological contexts from which the evidence derives, and many of the apparent inconsistencies have much to reveal about the diverse range of responses among both the Scandinavians and the indigenous populations to the circumstances of settlement.

In a recent review of the development of the debates about the Scandinavian settlement in England, Julian Richards and I observed that the subject has long been placed within a rigid set of parameters, resulting in a fixation with a particular set of questions, perspectives and data.[1] How many vikings were there? Where, precisely, did they settle? Why is there so little evidence for pagan activity? Why is there so little evidence for Scandinavian influence in the archaeology of rural settlements, given that the linguistic and place-name evidence appears to betoken mass settlement? Why are there so few Scandinavian burials? What was the Danish contribution to the so-called Danelaw? What were the relative levels of continuity and change in the wake of the Scandinavian settlements? And so on. We concluded that some of these questions which underpin traditional approaches to the subject, especially those relating to the numerical impact, are fundamentally unanswerable, and that it is unlikely that the retrieval of new data, most obviously archaeological, will allow us to answer them in the future. Other questions, especially those concerned with the identification of Scandinavian burials and settlements, betray an approach restricted to a very narrow body of evidence, while some of the consternation expressed about the seemingly contradictory impressions of Scandinavian settlement seems to derive from an expectation that the Scandinavian impact should be consistently measurable in a diverse range of evidence. The fact that debate on the Scandinavian settlements has stagnated has become a common refrain in recent reviews of the subject. Yet, while it is certainly true that a familiar set of enquiries have informed many discussions of the Scandinavian impact, scholars working on various aspects of early medieval documentary, archaeological, artefactual, onomastic and linguistic evidence have in fact found many new and exciting things to say about material from the regions of Scandinavian settlement in recent years. Unfortunately, much of this work has not, as yet, filtered through to mainstream literature on the Scandinavian impact on England, while at the same time scholars in one field often seem ignorant of – or at least fail to incorporate – developments in other fields. A major aim, then, for this book, is to re-examine the Scandinavian settlement in England in the light of new research into early medieval social organisation and, in producing a new work of synthesis, to open up fresh dialogue between the specialists in the broad field of viking studies.

Chapter 1 provides an overview of previous studies of the Scandinavian settlements. There have been many studies in recent years, providing useful overviews of the development of scholarship on the impact of the Scandinavians on England, and it is not necessary to rehearse these old arguments at length.[2] Furthermore, it is neither particularly useful nor fair to criticise earlier work that was necessarily a product of its time. Thus, the opening chapter briefly reviews previous approaches to the available evidence, and then highlights recent research that potentially paves the way for interdisciplinary dialogue. A discussion of the background to the Scandinavian settlements then follows, including consideration of the possible causes of the departure of so many Scandinavian from their homelands from the late eighth century onwards. Subsequent chapters take a thematic approach to the Scandinavian settlement. Chapter 2 examines the political dimensions of Scandinavian settlement, focusing on the relationships forged between Scandinavian and indigenous lords, and the ways in which power structures and the material culture of lordship were modified to take account of the newcomers. In Chapter 3, the broader circumstances of rural settlement are addressed, and evidence for the adaptation of existing estate and administrative organisation is explored, while linguistic change and examples of everyday material culture are scrutinised for the information that they contain about Anglo–Scandinavian interaction. In Chapter 4, the urban environment of Scandinavian settlement is discussed. Chapter 5 considers the fate of the Church in the wake of Scandinavian settlement, and the processes of conversion and Christianisation of the settlers, while Chapter 6 examines the burial strategies employed in northern and eastern England during the turbulent times of the ninth and tenth centuries. The final chapter (Epilogue) draws together the main themes of the book, and compares the Scandinavian impact on England with other regions of north-west Europe.

Notes

1 D. M. Hadley and J. D. Richards, 'Introduction: interdisciplinary approaches to the Scandinavian settlement', in D. M. Hadley and J. D. Richards (eds), *Cultures in Contact: Scandinavian settlement in England in the ninth and tenth centuries* (Turnhout, 2000), pp. 3–15, at 3–4.

2 See, for example, P. Wormald, 'The ninth century', in J. Campbell (ed.), *The Anglo-Saxons* (London, 1982), pp. 132–57; *idem*, 'Viking studies: whence and whither', in R. T. Farrell (ed.), *The Vikings* (Chichester, 1982), pp. 128–53; P. A. S. Stafford, 'The Danes and the Danelaw', *Hist. Today*, 36 (1986), 17–23; J. Graham-Campbell, 'Pagans and Christians', *Hist. Today*, 36 (1986), 24–8; D. M. Hadley, ' "And they proceeded to plough and to support themselves": the Scandinavian settlement of England', *Anglo-Norman Studies*, hereafter: *ANS*, 19 (1997), 69–96; S. Keynes, 'The vikings in England, c.790–1016', in P. H. Sawyer (ed.), *The Oxford Illustrated History of the Vikings* (Oxford, 1997), pp. 48–82; S. Trafford, 'Ethnicity, migration theory and the historiography of the Scandinavian settlement of England', in Hadley and Richards (eds), *Cultures in Contact*, pp. 17–39; B. Crawford, 'The Vikings', in W. Davies (ed.), *From the Vikings to the Normans* (Oxford, 2003), pp. 41–71.

1

The Scandinavian settlements:
the development of a debate

And that year [876] Halfdan shared out the land of the Northumbrians,
and they proceeded to plough and to support themselves . . . Then in
the harvest season [877] the army went away into Mercia and shared out
some of it, and gave some to Ceolwulf . . . In this year [880] the army
went from Cirencester into East Anglia, and settled there and shared out
the land.[1]

The impact of the Scandinavian settlements of the ninth and tenth
centuries on English society has long been a controversial subject.
For historians, much of the controversy stems from the paucity of
written sources, while for all scholars the difficulties of understanding the
Scandinavian impact are compounded by the need to integrate a diverse
range of historical, archaeological, material–cultural and linguistic evidence. The tendency of scholars to privilege one source of evidence over
another, while understandable enough, often frustrates attempts to produce a meaningful synthesis of the available sources. In attempting such a
synthesis, what are the challenges? Although the *Anglo-Saxon Chronicle*
helpfully informs us that in the 870s and 880s Scandinavian armies began
to settle, the sources are unfortunately silent about the scale of the settlement and have little to say about how it occurred. Written sources rarely,
if ever, comment on whether, or how often, the Scandinavian settlers
forcibly seized land, bought land, or were granted land. Equally unclear
from the written record is whether they settled in previously unoccupied
land or alternatively in long-settled districts, and, if the latter, whether they
drove out the existing inhabitants or came to some sort of accommodation
with them. The processes by which the Scandinavians took control in
parts of northern and eastern England, and the nature of their subsequent

interaction with the existing population of those regions, are, thus, largely unrecorded. Although, then, there are clear limitations on the use of documentary sources for understanding the progress, extent and nature of Scandinavian settlement, many studies have, nonetheless, deduced that the Scandinavian impact on northern and eastern England was profound, and extended to distinctive forms of tenurial organisation, social structure and local administration, language, place-names, personal names, stone sculpture, coinage and jewellery. However, although each perceived peculiarity of the society and culture of northern and eastern England has at some point been ascribed to Scandinavian influence, few of these categories of evidence are amenable to close dating, and many of the apparent Scandinavian traits are difficult to distinguish from their Anglo-Saxon counterparts. Accordingly, there has been considerable debate about what this evidence reveals about the scale and character of the Scandinavian settlement.[2]

Outline of the debate

Over the last sixty years a diverse range of opinions about the Scandinavian settlements have been expressed, and it is apparent that particular disciplines have tended to incline towards very different approaches and interpretations. For example, linguists and place-names scholars have traditionally tended to argue for settlement on a massive scale, given the extent of Scandinavian impact on language and names (fig.1). This is, perhaps, not surprising, given that the avowed aims of the English Place-Names Society, which published its first volume in 1924, were to use toponymic evidence to throw light on the Anglo-Saxon and Scandinavian settlements by establishing the proportions of names given by the settlers and indigenous peoples in each case.[3] Some historians have also inclined towards this view of a large-scale Scandinavian settlement. Sir Frank Stenton, who incidentally was also a leading light in early place-names studies, long ago argued that the Danish influence on northern and eastern England was extensive, and maintained that it was no coincidence that 'a social organisation to which there is no parallel elsewhere in England occurs in the one part of the country in which the regular development of native institutions had been interrupted by a foreign settlement'.[4] For Stenton, the Scandinavians not only seized political control of those regions, but were also responsible for a wholesale transformation of social and economic organisation.

By contrast, in the mid-1950s R. H. C. Davis presented a different perspective, as he rejected the idea that the plethora of Danish personal

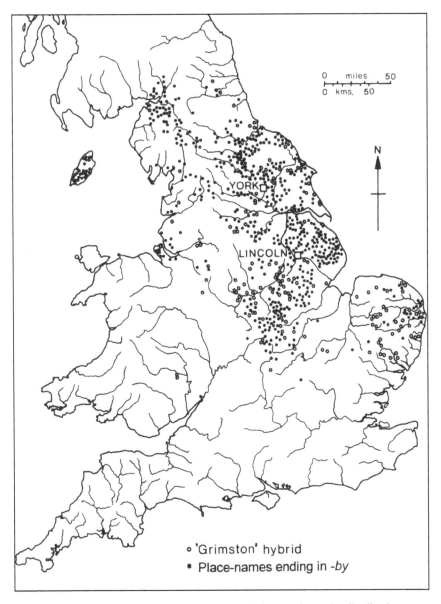

1   Scandinavian place-names in England. This map shows the distribution
of place-names formed with the Scandinavian element -*by*, and also place-
names formed from an Old Norse and Old English element (often known as
'Grimston hybrids').

names recorded in East Anglia in the tenth to twelfth centuries betokened the invasion of large numbers of Danes; in the same way that the Normans were to do later, the Danes had merely started a new fashion in names. He also queried whether the distinctive social organisation of eastern England should be attributed to Scandinavian influence, given similarities with regions unaffected by the settlers.[5] A few years later, fellow historian Peter Sawyer published a short paper entitled 'The Density of the Danish Settlement in England' in which he argued that the case for a large-scale migration had been overstated.[6] In his subsequent book, *The Age of the Vikings*, first published in 1962, he questioned the reliability of contemporary sources, suggesting that they may have exaggerated the numbers of Scandinavian ships involved in raiding England. This belief, combined with his view that the ships may have contained only thirty or so men, led him to propose that the Scandinavian armies may have consisted of hundreds rather than thousands.[7] In the second edition of his book, Sawyer went so far as to conclude that 'apart from their settlements and their influence on the language . . . and on some of the terminology of law and administration, the Scandinavians do not seem to have made a distinctive mark on England'.[8] Moreover, he queried the belief that the peculiarities of the regions of Scandinavian settlement, largely recorded in Domesday Book over two centuries after settlement began, must necessarily have resulted from the influx of large numbers of settlers, suggesting, rather, that 'the Danish colonisation of England . . . was, in fact, the work of the "armies" themselves'.[9]

Sawyer's work proved controversial, and many parts of his argument were subsequently rejected. Place-names scholars, for example, found it impossible to accept that anything other than settlement on a massive scale could account for the linguistic impact of the Scandinavians. Accordingly, Kenneth Cameron suggested that if the armies really were much smaller than had been supposed, then there must have been an undocumented 'secondary migration' following in the wake of the military conquest of northern and eastern England.[10] Nicholas Brooks later argued that the *Anglo-Saxon Chronicle* probably did not exaggerate the numbers of ships involved in the viking raids, since both the *Chronicle* and contemporary continental sources are remarkably consistent. For example, the army led by Sigefrid that was besieged on the River Meuse in 882, was said by a continental chronicle to have numbered 200 ships, and when this same army subsequently crossed the Channel the *Anglo-Saxon Chronicle* similarly estimated it at 200 or 250 ships.[11] Sawyer's estimation of the numbers carried by individual ships has also been questioned, as have some of his views on the unreliability of monastic sources.[12] Yet despite these objections to aspects of his thesis, there was increased tendency in the light of Sawyer's work to highlight the similarities between the regions of Scandinavian settlement in northern and eastern England and other parts of Anglo-Saxon England. Many of the peculiarities of the region were subsequently attributed to semantic, rather than actual, change.[13] Moreover, despite the arguments of Sawyer's detractors, one fact remains undisputable: for over forty years his work (recently described as 'calculating and devastating iconoclasm') has shaped the terms of the debate over the Scandinavian impact on England.[14]

Archaeologists have contributed less to the discussion of Scandinavian settlement than have historians and linguists, in marked contrast to the contributions archaeologists have made to our understanding of the earlier Germanic invasions of Britain.[15] This has arguably been because of the comparative rarity of finds of what are believed to be Scandinavian settlements or burials. For example, supposedly Scandinavian burials, identified on the basis of grave goods and the cremation rite, have been found in England at fewer than thirty sites, most of which consist of only a few burials.[16] Meanwhile, discussion of Scandinavian rural settlement has typically been limited to just a handful of sites, none of which displays much that is deemed to be diagnostic of Scandinavian settlement.[17] This lack of archaeological evidence for Scandinavian settlement has always appeared anomalous in the face of arguments for a mass invasion of Scandinavians, but has rarely been addressed by the proponents of the maximalist case. It has, however, tended to provide supporting evidence to those who maintained that the Scandinavian impact was a more limited conquest. Ironically, even though excavations at York in the 1970s and 1980s produced a huge volume of material from the period of documented Scandinavian control of the city, the evidence emerged at a time when archaeologists were generally sceptical of attributing transformations in the archaeological record to waves of migrants, and these excavations indirectly contributed to the minimalist case.[18] Traditionally, then, archaeological evidence has either been harnessed to the varying interpretations offered by historians, or has been discussed by archaeologists little interested in the scale of the settlement. Over the last few years, however, the case for mass settlement has received new vigour from some archaeologists, as reports of the recovery of large amounts of Scandinavian-style metalwork in eastern England have begun to appear in print.[19]

In a recent paper, Simon Trafford stated that the study of the Scandinavian settlements in England 'has been effectively stalled' on the issue of the scale of the settlement, which has limited all subsequent debate. He further observed that:

The implication seems to be that if the numbers of 'Danes' and 'English' could somehow be determined precisely, then all other pieces of the Danelaw jigsaw would instantly fall into place, and the baffling complexities of the linguistic, toponymic, and material evidence would resolve themselves into a comprehensible picture of the history of eastern England in the ninth to eleventh centuries.[20]

Certainly, the scale of the settlement has been the focus of often quite ferocious debate, although in recent studies by historians there has been a tendency to avoid the issue of scale entirely, given the dearth of evidence that would allow the matter to be settled conclusively.[21] If the impression given is that debate over the Scandinavian settlements has 'stalled', then this is at once both dispiriting for those involved in the debate and also a matter of presentation. On the contrary, it can be suggested that the study of the Scandinavian settlements in England has not stalled, but what has happened is that the inclination to attempt a synthesis of the diversity of evidence, which was a major virtue of Peter Sawyer's work, has diminished. It is to this challenge that the present study addresses itself.

Recent work on the Scandinavian settlements

The foregoing outline of debates about the Scandinavian settlements is well known, and has been discussed in greater detail on many occasions.[22] Yet the study of the Scandinavian impact is broader and more nuanced than many chapter-length, or even book-length, reviews often suggest, and two of the main aims of the present volume are to bring this research to wider attention and to suggest ways in which these newer approaches may be integrated. A brief review of some of the recent research that focuses on debates other than the scale of the settlements indicates the potential new directions for students of the Scandinavian settlements.

In the field of historical linguistics and onomastics (the study of naming practices), Gillian Fellows-Jensen, John Insley, the late Cecily Clark and David Parsons, for example, have identified something of the context in which place-names and personal names were formed, allowing this evidence to throw light on issues other than simply the scale of settlement.[23] John Hines and Matthew Townend have discussed ways of using linguistic and place-name evidence to inform us of relationships between the settlers and the indigenous peoples. Hines has demonstrated the value of combining historical, archaeological and linguistic evidence, and has, for example, suggested that language was as susceptible to manipulation for the purposes of displaying ethnic or political allegiance as were items of material culture.[24] Townend, meanwhile, has commented on the importance of distinguishing between the circumstances in which place-names were created and the contexts in which they were recorded. He has also concluded that different names for the same place may have circulated locally, and that this implies the existence of two separate speech communities.[25] Attention has been paid recently to the circumstances in which languages change as speakers of different languages come into contact, and much has been made of analogous, and better-recorded, examples of language change.[26]

Patrick Wormald observed in 1982 that it was striking that students of the Viking Age had said very little about the leaders of the raiders and settlers, which was in marked contrast to studies of other early medieval societies.[27] Since then, several studies have specifically addressed the issue of lordship in the wake of the Scandinavian settlement, and have focused on the political implications of the Scandinavian conquest of parts of England, and the ways in which this event was dealt with in subsequent decades after the country was unified under a single king.[28] Evidence not usually employed in such debates has recently been re-evaluated in this light. For example, stone sculpture, which used to be discussed as a marker of the precise locations of Scandinavian settlement and occasionally as an indication of its scale, has more recently been discussed in the context of tenth-century lordship. David Stocker and Paul Everson have, for example, examined the ways in which sculptural styles may have been adopted according to the prevailing political climate in a region. They have also commented on the proliferation of sculpture in urban centres, where it may have been used as a medium for competitive social display among the merchant classes.[29]

The fate of the Church in the wake of the Scandinavian settlements remains a matter for great debate.[30] However, in addition to debate about the fates of individual churches, discussion has recently broadened to explore the mechanisms by which the conversion of the settlers to Christianity may have been achieved, and the processes by which Scandinavian settlers and their ways of life were Christianised.[31] The roles of churches, churchmen and their patrons in local society have been analysed, especially in the comparatively better-documented regions of East Anglia in the tenth century.[32] The evidence provided by stone sculpture for ecclesiastical fortunes has also been addressed, and Richard Bailey and the late James Lang have written about sculpture as a medium in which competing religious concepts were made mutually comprehensible.[33]

Sculptures have also been analysed in the context of the burial practices of the settlers, since many, if not most, were grave markers displayed in churchyards. Such studies make it clear that there is more evidence for Scandinavian funerary practices than has traditionally been thought, and that the burial record is not the only medium in which the funerary behaviour of Scandinavian settlers may be traced.[34] In the last two decades many new cemeteries of ninth- to eleventh-century date have been excavated, yet the amount of Scandinavian material recovered from graves has not increased significantly. This has encouraged archaeologists to seek new ways of exploring the Scandinavian influence, and has increased the conviction of some archaeologists that the settlers may be identified through a diverse and much wider range of funerary practices than was hitherto believed. That the settlers quickly adopted indigenous funerary behaviour now seems likely.[35]

In recent years there have been many excavations of both rural and urban settlements of the ninth to eleventh centuries in the regions of Scandinavian settlement. While the imprint of the settlers remains elusive, and little that is diagnostic of Scandinavian influence has been detected in the study of settlement location and layout or in the form of buildings, nonetheless, such excavations reveal much about the transformations in rural and urban society to which both the settlers and indigenous populations contributed.[36] Moreover, although rarely recovered from excavated settlements, examples of the material culture that the settlers both brought with them and made following settlement have increased significantly over the last decade. Collaboration with metal-detectorists, particularly in East Anglia, Lincolnshire and eastern Yorkshire, has permitted the recording of hundreds of dress-fittings and items of jewellery that date to between the ninth and eleventh centuries. Some of the artefacts were manufactured in Scandinavia, but many others were made in Britain and incorporate both Scandinavian and indigenous characterstics. Studies of this evidence are now asking questions about the nature of interaction between the settlers and local people, and about the ways in which such personal items of material culture may have contributed to displays of ethnicity and other forms of social identity.[37] Numismatic evidence continues to increase, throwing important light on the economy and administrative structure of northern and eastern England in the wake of the Scandinavian conquest, and about the political aspirations of the settlers.[38] There has also been extensive research into the pottery manufactured and traded particularly in eastern England in the later Anglo-Saxon centuries, and this has revealed much about the economy and settlement hierarchies of those regions, and also about the social implications of pottery production and exchange.[39]

Archaeologists now regularly stress that the available evidence does not help us to determine the scale of the Scandinavian settlement or to trace its progress, and that it is inadequate to present the distribution of artefacts of Scandinavian manufacture or bearing Scandinavian-style ornamentation, as simply an index of Scandinavian settlement and impact.[40] They have also argued that there need be no direct relationship between the distribution of certain forms and styles of material culture and the locations of particular ethnic groups, observing that ethnic identities were not simply passively reflected in the archaeological record. Instead, archaeologists have recently explored the ways in which material culture was used in the construction of aspects of social, political and ethnic identities.[41]

The documentary evidence has also recently been subject to critical review. For example, historians have drawn attention to similarities between the society and institutions of northern and eastern England, the so-called 'Danelaw', and those found in other parts of early medieval Britain. Most studies of ecclesiastical organisation, estate structure, lordship, land-holding and peasant status would now accept that there are basic similarities in local organisation and society across early medieval Britain, and attribute regional variations discernible in northern and eastern England to a range of factors. The Scandinavian settlements are now widely thought to have affected the development of native institutions rather than to have imported entirely novel modes of organisation.[42] The use of the terms 'Dane' and 'Danelaw' in contemporary documents has recently been re-evaluated to take account of the ways in which ethnic identities were constructed in the early medieval period.[43] It is now recognised that ethnic allegiance was not the only, or even necessarily the most important, aspect of social identity among early medieval peoples, and that, moreover, ethnic identity may only be expressed or be relevant to daily life in certain circumstances. Furthermore, historians have demonstrated that ethnic identities were mutable, that they were especially liable to be transformed in the face of contact with new peoples, as social circumstances changed and the political tide turned, and that they were not invariably expressed through a standard set of characteristics.[44] In sum, new questions, new debates and new sources of evidence have emerged in individual studies over the last few years, which together offer the potential to reinvigorate the study of the Scandinavian impact on English society.

9

The background to Scandinavian settlement in England: the raids

In order to place the settlements, which form the focus of this study, in context it is necessary to review the preceding period of raiding.[45] The earliest documented raids occurred in the late eighth century, and include attacks on the church at Lindisfarne (Northumb) in 793, and on other islands around Britain where major religious communities were located, such as Iona, Skye (Scotland) and Rathlin (Irish Republic) in 795.[46] While raiding in Britain and also Frankia is recorded in the early years of the ninth century, it is not until the 830s and 840s that further raids on England are recorded in the *Anglo-Saxon Chronicle*. These were largely in southern England, although raids on Lindsey and East Anglia are noted in 841, and according to Roger of Wendover's thirteenth-century account King Rædwulf and one of his ealdormen were killed during a raid on Northumbria in 844.[47] The nature of the raids changed shortly afterwards, as the *Chronicle* records that in 851 'for the first time, heathen men stayed through the winter on Thanet [Kent]', thus extending the length of the raiding campaigns.[48]

The raiding appears to have intensified in 865 with the arrival of the great army ('*micel here*') under the leadership of Ivarr and Halfdan, which was apparently much larger than any of the previous raiding bands.[49] During the 860s and 870s successive raids are recorded, and the political landscape was transformed as the kingdoms of Northumbria, East Anglia and Mercia succumbed to the Scandinavian raiders. This series of developments occurred not only because of the great size of the raiding army, and its apparent ability to move quickly, but also because of internecine disputes and the capacity of the army to exploit this situation. Over the following few years there are indications that the great army established new English rulers in Northumbria, Mercia and East Anglia. It is not certain that there was an intention to settle permanently at this stage, but the involvement of the raiders in the internal politics of three Anglo-Saxon kingdoms marked a change in tactics from the hit-and-run raids of earlier periods and paved the way for subsequent Scandinavian rule and settlement in parts of northern and eastern England.

In 867 the great army went to York, where King Osbert had been driven out, according to the *Anglo-Saxon Chronicle*, in favour of 'a king with no hereditary right', Ælla. It is probable that the army was taking advantage of divisions among the Northumbrians. Indeed, the *Chronicle* observes, 'there was great civil strife going on in that people'.[50] It is not impossible that they had been actively sought out by some party or other, and later sources reveal that after capturing York, the army established a local man, Egbert, as king, although the situation in York itself is unclear as some of these sources state that he was only king north of the River Tyne.[51] Little is known of Egbert, but he clearly forged some sort of alliance with Archbishop Wulfhere of York, and the two fled together from Northumbria in 872 – according to one late source, seeking refuge at the court of King Burgred of Mercia.[52] The viking army briefly returned to Northumbria, and then withdrew to spend the winter at Torksey (Lincs) having failed, if indeed this was the plan, to reinstate Egbert.[53] Egbert died in exile and was replaced by another local man, Ricsige, who similarly may have ruled only north of the Tyne, and Archbishop Wulfhere was subsequently recalled to his see. Although this event does not seem to have been at the behest of the viking army, it seems plausible that the army may have played a part in paving the way for the Archbishop's return, and Ricsige, while not appointed by the army, may have owed his position to collaboration with it.[54]

In 869 the army went into East Anglia, where the forces of King Edmund fought against them unsuccessfully and the king was killed. Towards the end of the tenth century, Abbo of Fleury, who had previously taught at Ramsey Abbey (Hunts), wrote a hagiographical text about King Edmund, alleging that he was martyred in gruesome fashion (he was apparently whipped, had spears thrown at him and was subsequently beheaded) by the viking army. Although the more lurid details of Abbo's account are debatable, it is possible that the king was put to death after defeat on the battlefield.[55] Two kings who ruled in East Anglia after the death of King Edmund, Æthelred and Oswald, are known only from their coinage.[56] They may have been Scandinavian appointees, as it seems unlikely that after the great army had killed King Edmund and 'conquered all the land' they would not have retained some control over East Anglia. Indeed, Abbo of Fleury's account of the death of King Edmund implies that it occurred because he refused to submit to the leader of the great army, perhaps indicating that the army was seeking to establish a 'puppet' ruler in this kingdom.[57] An element of institutional continuity is certainly suggested by the similarity of one of the coins in the name of King Æthelred to those issued for King Edmund, which was minted by one of the latter's moneyers, Sigered.[58] Both Æthelred and Oswald also used the moneyer Beornheah, who had earlier minted coins for Edmund. The coinage of Æthelred and Oswald shares the characteristics of coins known to have been minted under Scandinavian rule, including blundered inscriptions, and it is modelled on Frankish coinage of the early 860s, with which the great army may have been familiar before it came to England.

Thus, Mark Blackburn has suggested that this numismatic evidence offers strong support to the argument that Æthelred and Oswald were Scandinavian appointees.[59] The name of Æthelred is also intriguing, as it has similarities with the names of Edmund's two predecessors, Æthelstan (who ruled at some point between c.830 and 845) and Æthelweard (who ruled some time between c.845 and 855), and it may suggest some continuity with the earlier regime.[60]

Unquestionably a Scandinavian appointee was Ceolwulf of Mercia, who was established as king by the great army when it overwintered at Repton (Derbys) 873-4:

> And drove King Burgred across the sea . . . And they conquered all that
> land. And he went to Rome and settled there . . . And the same year they
> gave the kingdom of the Mercians to be held by Ceolwulf, a foolish
> king's thegn; and he swore oaths to them and gave hostages, that it
> should be ready for them on whatever day they wished to have it, and he
> would be ready, himself and all who would follow him, at the enemy's
> service.[61]

The written record provides little information on this first stage of involvement of the great army in English politics, but a combination of evidence from Mercia illuminates the impact of the raiders and infers that they were politically astute in their actions, and were, perhaps, preparing the way for settlement. The events set in motion during the winter of 873-4 can be illuminated by consideration of a diverse range of evidence, and this multidisciplinary case-study sets the scene for the approaches taken throughout this book. Despite his description as 'a foolish king's thegn', Ceolwulf was acceptable enough for the Mercian bishops and at least some of Burgred's leading nobles to attend his councils and to witness the charters issued at these gatherings.[62] Numismatic evidence reveals that Ceolwulf was also sufficiently acceptable for the London mint to issue coins in his name, and perhaps also for King Alfred of Wessex to be prepared to embark with him on a reform of the coinage, even though Ceolwulf had replaced his brother-in-law as king of Mercia.[63] Irrespective of the *Chronicle*'s assessment, it seems likely that Ceolwulf was a member of one of the rival Mercian royal lines, perhaps, given his name, a descendant of the Mercian kings Cenwulf (796-821) and Ceolwulf I (821-3), and the events at Repton may have represented the involvement of a raiding army in internecine disputes.[64]

Archaeological investigations have thrown further light on the impact of the army on Repton and Mercia. Excavation revealed sections of a

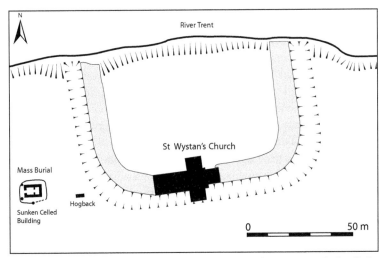

2 Excavations at Repton (Derbys). Excavation and survey revealed a ditch running from the banks of the River Trent to either side of the church. The remains of at least 264 individuals were excavated in a sunken mausoleum to the west of the church.

V-shaped ditch abutting the east end of the crypt and chancel of the church of St Wystan, and a resistivity survey suggested that the ditch curved northwards and extended to the banks of the River Trent, while a magnetometer survey and subsequent excavation indicated that there was a similar ditch on the west side of the church (fig. 2). Excavation to the east of the church suggested that the ditch had been backfilled from the north side, implying that there was once a bank on the inside of the ditched enclosure. The ditch dates to between a phase of burial of the eighth and ninth centuries and the resumption of burial in the early tenth century, when a number of burials were cut into the fill of the ditch.[65] This ditched enclosure (of 1.46 ha) has been interpreted as a short-lived defensive earthwork incorporating the church into its line, with the latter perhaps serving as a 'gatehouse', and has been linked directly to the events of 873-4.[66] A number of burials accompanied by weapons in the vicinity of the church may date to the same period and have interred members of the army; indeed, one of these burials includes coins from the mid-870s.[67]

The disarticulated remains of at least 264 individuals found within a former mausoleum to the west of the church have also been associated with the events of 873–4, although there has been considerable debate about the significance of this deposit. The skeletal population, consisting over-whelmingly of males, has been described as 'physically robust', and it may have included members of either the monastery at Repton or the great army, although the general lack of wound trauma suggests that they were not the murdered monastic community or the battle dead of the winter of 873–4. Indeed, recently acquired radiocarbon dates from the skeletal mate-rial, ranging from the seventh to the late ninth century, indicate that the deposit does not derive from a single event, rather that the bodies represent the dead of many generations. This is an interpretation reinforced by the artefacts recovered from among the disarticulated remains from diverse time periods, including precious metalwork of the seventh and eighth centuries and five silver pennies, of which four were no earlier than c.872 and the other dated to 873–4.[68] The composition of the deposit indicates that many of the skeletons had been brought to the mausoleum from their original resting-places, after the bodies had decayed, given that the small bones of the hands and feet are almost completely absent. Evidence that many of the bones were once stacked up around the walls of the eastern compartment reinforces the impression that much of the deposit was in a disarticulated state. Excavation revealed an orderly stack of bones in the north-east corner, and a labourer alleged to a passing early eighteenth-century antiquarian that he had dug into the mausoleum some years earlier and seen a large skeleton in a stone coffin in the centre of the compartment and 'round it lay one hundred humane skeletons, with their feet pointing to the stone coffin' suggesting that more bones had been stacked in an orderly fashion before being disturbed by the labourer. The labourer also reported that above the burials were stones set on timber joists, while exca-vation revealed that the whole building was sealed with a low stone cairn, which was covered by a low pebble mound and topped with a stone kerb, and that a layer of red Keuper marl had been spread on the floor before the bones were placed in the eastern compartment. A final part of the puzzle is presented by a multiple burial of four young people at the south-west corner of the mound.[69]

The excavators, Martin Biddle and Birthe Kjølbye-Biddle, have argued that the deposit relates directly to the events of 873–4. They suggest that the remains were largely those of members of the great army, whose sur-vivors may have gone to great lengths to bring together their deceased from wherever they had previously been buried, although, given the radio-carbon dates, the deposit must also have included remains from earlier burials at Repton – perhaps members of the religious community or the

Mercian royal house.[70] The central burial reportedly seen in the seventeenth century is interpreted as that of a king, perhaps accompanied by some of the artefacts found in the mound, including fragments of a sword, an iron axe, two large and seven small seaxes, knives, a chisel and a barrel-padlock key. The excavators have suggested that this may have been the burial of Iguuar, said by the chronicler Æthelweard to have been one of the leaders of the 'great army', and who, according to Irish sources, died in c.873. This may be the same man as the Ivar *beinlausi*, or 'boneless', who is said by saga tradition to have died and been buried in England, according to some sources in a mound.[71] The excavators construe the multiple burial as a sacrifice associated with the closing of the mound.[72] This interpretation of the archaeological evidence at Repton implies a dramatic series of events over the winter of 873-4.

Of course, other interpretations of the archaeological record are possible. For example, Julian Richards has suggested that the army may have added its own dead to an existing charnel deposit. He reminds us that when the great army gained control of Mercia they did so not by its destruction but by placing their own candidate on the throne, and it is worth adding that the army had made peace with the Mercians after taking up winter quarters at Torksey (Lincs) in 872-3, and the events at Repton may, as we have seen, have involved the army in an internecine dispute, assisting a rival for the throne.[73] We should also note that in 877 the army in Mercia 'shared out some of it, and gave some to Ceolwulf', implying that the mutually beneficial relationship between the army and the new king continued.[74] Was this really a context in which a major Mercian centre would be destroyed? The charnel deposit was, in fact, placed in a mausoleum that was in a state of disrepair, to judge from the presence of fallen stucco, and the western compartment may have been in use as a workshop, given the debris of animal bones, broken bone objects and charcoal.[75] Thus the army may have reused a building that had formerly, but no longer, served a religious function. Richards suggests that the charnel deposit, sealed beneath a mound, may have been a highly visible symbol of the great army's occupation of a major Mercian royal and cult centre, reflecting a degree of accommodation with the existing order, in which the new order was, in the words of the prehistorian Richard Bradley, 'invested with the authority of the past'.[76] Whichever way the archaeological evidence is interpreted, and in advance of final publication any interpretation must remain provisional, there is no doubt that the army had a major impact on both Repton and Mercia, and that its intentions to remain a major influence in the kingdom must have been clear.

Background to the raids

Why did the viking raids on other parts of Europe begin, and why, later in the ninth century, did raiding turn to settlement? Although this enormous subject is beyond the scope of this volume, nonetheless, a brief outline of the range of possible causes of raiding and settlement is a useful reminder of the broader context in which the Scandinavian impact on English society is located.

Viking Age Scandinavian societies did not produce written accounts of contemporary events, with the exception of runestones, which mostly date from the later tenth and eleventh centuries, and which throw little light on raiding and settlement overseas. Therefore, we have to draw on the testimony of written sources produced outside of Scandinavia, or those produced within Scandinavian society at a much later date, and on archaeological evidence.[77] Contemporary western European sources commonly assign the Scandinavian raids to divine punishment. Alcuin, a Northumbrian scholar at the court of Charlemagne, reflected on the attacks on Lindisfarne as follows:

> Consider carefully, brothers, and examine diligently, lest perchance this unaccustomed and unheard-of evil was merited by some unheard-of evil practice . . . from the days of King Ælfwold fornications, adulteries and incest have poured over the land, so that these sins have been committed without any shame and even against the handmaids dedicated to God. What may I say about avarice, robbery, violent judgments? – when it is clearer than day how much these crimes have increased everywhere, and a despoiled people testifies to it.[78]

Writing in the late ninth century, King Alfred of Wessex also wrote of the viking invasions as punishments 'when we neither loved wisdom ourselves nor allowed it to other men; we possessed only the name of Christians, and very few possessed the virtues'.[79] One reason why there may have been a strong belief in divine retribution among churchpeople was that the Prophet Jeremiah (writing near Jerusalem in the late sixth century BC) had foretold that divine punishment for the chosen people would eventually come from the North. And it is notable that many ecclesiastical commentators, especially in Frankia, referred to the raiders as 'Northmen', thus identifying the raiders with prophetic claims.[80]

In seeking more historical explanations for the viking raids, some historians and archaeologists have suggested that one factor may have been an increase in population in Scandinavia, leading to a shortage of land.

However, there is little evidence to support this suggestion, and the earliest people to leave Scandinavia appear to have been concerned with raiding, trading and amassing wealth, rather than with settlement.[81] Another explanation for the Viking Age commonly offered in textbooks is improvements in Scandinavian sailing ships. To judge from archaeological finds of boats and from depictions of boats with oarsmen on the picture stones from the island of Gotland, the Scandinavians appear to have relied on oar power up until the seventh century, and only began to use ships with sails in the eighth century. It is thought that this form of construction was imported from western Europe, probably as a result of trading contacts. However, while this may explain why the Scandinavians were such mobile raiders, it does not explain why they chose to raid in the first place.[82]

Economic factors almost certainly played a part in prompting the viking raids. The eighth century saw increased trade around the North Sea and the Baltic, leading to the development of trading centres at places such as Dorestad (Netherlands) on the Rhine, *Quentovic* near Boulogne (France), at *Hamwic* (Southampton, Hants), Fordwich (near Canterbury, Kent), London, Ipswich (Suff), York, Ribe (Denmark), Hedeby (Germany), Kaupang (Norway), Birka (Sweden) and Staraja Ladoga (Russia). A visitor from northern Scandinavia to the court of King Alfred of Wessex in the late ninth century revealed something of the goods traded around Scandinavia. Ohthere observed that the tribute paid by the Lapps to the Norwegians 'consists of the skins of beasts, the feathers of birds, whale-bone, and ship-ropes made from walrus hide and sealskin', and although the destination of the tribute is not stated, it is likely that much of it made its way into various trading communities in Scandinavia and eventually western Europe.[83] Indeed, there is archaeological evidence revealing that produce from the Baltic, in particular amber and whetstones, was traded into western markets. This trade may have been a prompt for the emergence of more permanent trading centres in and around the Baltic during the late eighth century, to replace what had previously been seasonal market-places.[84] Some leaders emerged in Scandinavia who were particularly well-placed to exploit this situation formally, for example through tribute-taking and taxation. According to the *Frankish Royal Annals*, the Danish king Godfred removed merchants from *Reric* (possibly Groß Strömkendorf, Germany) in Slavic territory, to Hedeby in 808, suggesting that royal control was exerted over trading activities.[85] Moreover, recent archaeological investigation of trading sites shows that not only did the previously short-lived marketing centres become more fixed and of increased scale during the eighth and ninth centuries, but that the range of goods being manufactured and traded around the Baltic became more standardised, which may suggest some form of centralised control over them.[86] In contrast, it has been suggested that others who were not in a position to benefit from this increasing trade may have resorted to piracy, and that it was perhaps inevitable that this should spill over into western Europe, whose riches would have become increasingly apparent.[87] There is also evidence that the supply of silver into the Baltic from territories to the east had dried up by the tenth century – another factor which may have prompted raids westwards.[88]

The archaeologist Björn Myrhe has argued that there may have been significant contact between Scandinavia and Britain many decades before the traditional start date of the Viking Age in the last years of the eighth century. There are, indeed, a number of eighth-century artefacts from Britain found in Scandinavia, especially in graves, such as an Irish reliquary and a book mount adapted to become a brooch.[89] These are usually regarded as having been brought into Scandinavia well into the ninth century, but Myrhe argues that there are no archaeological grounds to prevent the graves containing eighth-century British artefacts from actually being eighth-century graves.[90] In seeking an explanation for why such contacts spilled over into violence, he identifies the growing power of Charlemagne's kingdom and the fact that it was an expansionist polity with a different ideological system, in the form of Christianity, from that of the regions of Scandinavia. Indeed, unlike some other scholars he does not think that the raids on places like Lindisfarne and Iona were simply aimed at looting wealth, arguing instead that they may have been driven by ideological concerns, prompted by a perceived threat to the Scandinavian political and social order and from the political regimes with which it was associated.[91] This controversial thesis by Myrhe proposes that the Scandinavian assaults on western Europe were 'deliberately planned . . . they were not ignorant barbarians; they knew well the military and ideological pressure they were facing'.

Finally, both archaeologists and historians working on different types of evidence have suggested that changes in political structure, involving both rising royal power and challenges to ruling dynasties, may have prompted the raids and settlements overseas. Both contemporary Frankish sources and the later Scandinavian sagas suggest that in the ninth and tenth centuries royal authority and succession were subject to many challenges in various parts of Scandinavia. When Denmark is first mentioned in continental written sources in the late eighth century, it is perceived as having powerful kings, an impression confirmed by archaeological evidence for complex earthwork features such as the Danevirke across the neck of the Jutland peninsula; gold hoards including bracteates modelled on Roman medallions and regarded as symbols of office; participation in long-distance trading networks (e.g. at Lundeberg, Fyn); and the central role in the production of animal art.[92] During the ninth and tenth centuries, however, this royal power was subject to dynastic conflicts and challenges, which are arguably reflected in the emergence of richly furnished burials in the tenth century.[93] In 810, for example, King Godfred was murdered by his nephew, Hemming, after which succession disputes became common. Unsuccessful challengers for the Danish throne often subsequently made their way into Frankia. For example, when the sons of King Godfred drove out yet another challenger, Harald, he went to the Frankish emperor, Louis the Pious, who attempted to help restore him to the Danish throne, which was eventually achieved in 819. The following year, raiders plagued Frankia, and it is possible that the losers in a dynastic dispute were involved.[94] Rootless war-bands were useful allies for those competing for positions of authority, both within Scandinavia and elsewhere. The ninth-century *Life of St Anskar* recounts the exiled king of the Swedes, Anound, seeking recruits among the Danes to help him regain his former position, offering them in return access to Birka with its rich merchants and large amounts of goods and money.[95] In Frankia the eldest of the rebellious sons of Louis the Pious, Lothar, persuaded Harald, whom Louis had previously championed, to raid Frisia in 833 and so compound the difficulties faced by the emperor. At a later date, Charles the Bald was inclined to recruit one raiding party to use against others, as he did in 860 when a certain Weland, based with his forces on the River Somme, agreed to attack another viking army on the River Seine in return for a handsome payment.[96] Later Scandinavian sources, such as *Egil's Saga* and the *Heimskringla* ('The Circle of the World'), allege that in the ninth and tenth centuries emergent royal leaders in Norway established their position by demoting local kings to the status of earls, prompting many of the latter to set off overseas, typically heading for northern Britain or Iceland. These sources also suggest that feuds within the royal dynasties themselves led to some members of Norwegian royal families seeking their fortunes elsewhere.[97]

These recent interpretations of the archaeological and documentary evidence suggest that internal factors within Scandinavia were important in bringing about the Viking Age. Moreover, this focus on social and political developments within Scandinavia does more than account for raids; it also begins to make sense of why so many Scandinavians settled overseas. As Patrick Wormald has put it, 'Not just the lure of western wealth, but profound changes in what had hitherto been a fairly "traditional" society, sent increasing numbers careering out of their environment, and gave them leaders of regal status, who, if they were not to reign at home, would seek to do so elsewhere'. This approach presents a different perspective from that offered by Peter Sawyer's argument that the Age of the Vikings could be accounted for by considering it to be 'an extension of normal Dark Age activity, made possible and profitable by special circumstances', in particular by economic developments. In contrast, Wormald suggests that 'what we are seeing is an *abnormal crisis* in Scandinavian society'.[98]

One final issue that we should mention in seeking to explain the Scandinavian raids on, and settlement in, other parts of Europe relates to the impact that previous generations of Scandinavian settlers may have had. The raids and settlement went on over many decades, and later raiders and settlers may have been attracted by increasing familiarity with what other parts of Europe had to offer. There is also evidence that they became increasingly involved in domestic politics and disputes within various parts of north-western Europe, and that decisions about where to raid or settle may have been determined by knowledge of the political situation in various parts of Europe.[99]

Conclusions

The time is ripe for a new approach to the impact of the Scandinavian settlements on Anglo-Saxon England, one that not only returns to the well-known and extensively studied evidence with fresh perspectives, but which draws on the wide range of newly recovered archaeological evidence that has yet to make an impact on more general studies. It is important to pay close attention to the context of the available evidence. Although there is an understandable temptation to extrapolate broad conclusions from a small body of evidence specific to a particular context, this must only be attempted with caution. Rather than assisting our understanding of the Scandinavian impact on England, the aggregation of diverse evidence often obscures the picture. By exploring the diversity of evidence and high-lighting the range of interaction between the settlers and the indigenous population, we can begin to appreciate the Scandinavian settlers not simply as Scandinavians, but also as kings, lords, peasants, merchants, craft-workers, men, women and members of families. As we shall see, the problem with which we are confronted is not lack of evidence; there is ample evidence for the Scandinavian impact. Rather, the challenges that we face include the difficulties of interpreting a broad range of evidence, which often appears to present conflicting impressions of the Scandinavian impact. Our evidence suggests a diversity of forms of Anglo–Scandinavian interaction, and it is only through an interdisciplinary approach that we can come close to understanding the complexity of the Scandinavian impact on England.

Notes

1 *English Historical Documents, vol. I, c.500–1042*, ed. D. Whitelock (2nd edn, London, 1979), hereafter *EHD I*, pp. 195–6.

2 F. M. Stenton, *Anglo-Saxon England* (3rd edn, Oxford, 1971), pp. 502–25; P. H. Sawyer, *The Age of the Vikings* (2nd edn, London, 1971), pp. 152–76.

3 E. Ekwall, 'The Celtic element', in A. Mawer and F. M. Stenton (eds), *Introduction to the Survey of English Place-Names*, vol. 1 (1) (Oxford, 1924), pp. 15–35, at 17; *idem*, 'The Scandinavian element', in *ibid.*, pp. 55–92, at 56; this is a point also made recently in S. Trafford, 'Ethnicity, migration theory and the historiography of the Scandinavian settlement of England', in D. M. Hadley and J. D. Richards (eds), *Cultures in Contact: Scandinavian settlement in England in the ninth and tenth centuries* (Turnhout, 2000), pp. 17–39, at 31.

4 Stenton, *Anglo-Saxon England*, p. 519.

5 R. H. C. Davis, 'East Anglia and the Danelaw', *Transactions of the Royal Historical Society*, hereafter *TRHS*, 5th ser., 5 (1955), 23–39, at 29–30; *idem*, *The Kalendar of Abbot Samson of Bury St Edmunds and Related Documents*, Camden Soc., 3rd ser., 84 (1954), xxxii–xlvii.

6 P. H. Sawyer, 'The density of the Danish settlement in England', *University of Birmingham Historical J.*, 6 (1) (1958), 1–17.

7 Sawyer, *The Age of the Vikings*, pp. 172–3.

8 *Ibid.*, pp. 124–31, 168–73.

9 Sawyer, 'The density of the Danish settlement', p. 11; *idem*, *The Age of the Vikings*, pp. 168–9.

10 The point was made in H. Loyn, *Anglo-Saxon England and the Norman Conquest* (London, 1962), p. 54, and expanded on by Kenneth Cameron in his three papers on the place-names of the territory of the Five Boroughs: *Scandinavian Settlement in the Territory of the Five Boroughs: the place-name evidence* (Nottingham, 1965); 'Scandinavian settlement in the territory of the Five Boroughs: the place-name evidence, part II, place-names in thorp', *Mediaeval Scandinavia*, III (1970), 35–49; and Cameron, 'Scandinavian settlement in the territory of the Five Boroughs: the place-name evidence, part III, the Grimston-hybrids', in P. Clemoes and K. Hughes (eds) *England Before the Conquest: studies in primary sources presented to Dorothy Whitelock* (Cambridge, 1971), pp. 147–63.

11 N. P. Brooks, 'England in the ninth century: the crucible of defeat', *TRHS*, 5th ser., 29 (1979), 1–20, at 3–8.

12 A. L. Binns, 'The navigation of Viking ships around the British Isles in Old English and Old Norse sources', in B. Niclasen (ed.), *The Fifth Viking Congress* (Tórshavn, 1968), pp. 107–8; P. Wormald, 'Viking studies: whence and whither', in R. T. Farrell (ed.), *The Vikings* (Chichester, 1982), pp. 128–53, at 129.

13 O. Fenger, 'The Danelaw and the Danish law', *Scandinavian Studies in Law*, 16 (1972), 85–96; P. A. Stafford, 'The Danes and the Danelaw', *History Today*, hereafter: *Hist. Today*, 36 (1986), 17–23.

14 Trafford, 'Ethnicity, migration theory', p. 18.

15 See, for example, H. Hamerow, 'Migration theory and the migration period', in B. Vyner (ed.), *Building on the Past* (London, 1994), pp. 164–77; J. Hines, 'The becoming of the English: identity, material culture and language in early Anglo-Saxon England', *Anglo-Saxon Studies in Archaeology and History*, hereafter: *ASSAH*, 7 (1994), 45–59; J. Chapman and H. Hamerow, 'On the move again – migrations and invasions in archaeological explanation', in J. Chapman and H. Hamerow (eds), *Migrations and Invasions in Archaeological Explanation*, British Archaeological Reports, International Series, hereafter: BAR Int. Ser., 664 (Oxford, 1997), pp. 1–10; H. Hamerow, 'Migration theory and the Anglo-Saxon "identity crisis" ', in *ibid.*, pp. 33–44; Trafford, 'Ethnicity, migration theory', pp. 23–8.

16 For recent reviews, see J. Graham-Campbell, 'Pagan Scandinavian burial in the central and southern Danelaw', in J. Graham-Campbell, R. A. Hall, J. Jesch and D. Parsons (eds), *Vikings and the Danelaw: select papers from the proceedings of the Thirteenth Viking Congress* (Oxford, 2001), pp. 105–23; J. D. Richards, 'The case of the missing Vikings: Scandinavian burial in the Danelaw', in S. Lucy and A. Reynolds (eds), *Burial in Early Medieval England and Wales* (London, 2002), pp. 156–70.

17 The evidence has been reviewed recently in J. D. Richards, 'Identifying Anglo-Scandinavian settlements', in Hadley and Richards (eds), *Cultures in Contact*, pp. 295–309.

18 R. A. Hall, *The Viking Dig* (London, 1984); Trafford, 'Ethnicity, migration theory', pp. 30–1.

19 S. Margeson, 'Viking settlement in Norfolk: a study of new evidence', in S. Margeson, B. Ayres and S. Heywood (eds), *A Festival of Norfolk Archaeology* (Hunstanton, 1996), pp. 47–57; *idem, The Vikings in Norfolk* (Norwich, 1997); K. Leahy and C. Paterson, 'New light on the Viking presence in Lincolnshire: the artefactual evidence', in Graham-Campbell, Hall, Jesch and Parsons (eds), *Vikings and the Danelaw*, pp. 181–202.

20 Trafford, 'Ethnicity, migration theory', p. 19.

21 For example, the scale of the settlement is not discussed in S. Keynes, 'The Vikings in England, c.790–1016', in P. H. Sawyer (ed.), *The Oxford Illustrated History of the Vikings* (Oxford, 1997), pp. 48–82, or D. M. Hadley, ' "And they proceeded to plough and to support themselves": the Scandinavian settlement of England', *ANS*, 19 (1997), 69–96.

22 See preface, n. 2.

23 G. Fellows-Jensen 'Scandinavian settlement in Yorkshire – through the rear-view mirror', in B. E. Crawford (ed.), *Scandinavian Settlement in Northern Britain* (London, 1995), pp. 170–86; C. Clark, 'Clark's first three laws of Applied Anthroponymics', *Nomina*, 3 (1979), 13–19, at 17–18; D. Parsons, 'How long did the Scandinavian language survive in England? Again', in Graham-Campbell, Hall, Jesch and Parsons (eds), *Vikings and the Danelaw*, pp. 299–312.

24 J. Hines, 'Scandinavian English: a creole in context', in P. S. Ureland and G. Broderick (eds), *Language Contact in the British Isles* (Tübingen, 1991), pp. 403–27, at 418; *idem*, 'Focus and boundary in linguistic varieties in the northwest Germanic continuum', in V. Faltings, A. Walker and O. Wilts (eds), *Friesische Studien II* (Odense, 1995), pp. 35–62, at 58.

25 M. Townend, 'Viking Age England as a bilingual society', in Hadley and Richards (eds), *Cultures in Contact*, pp. 89–105; *idem*, *Language and History in Viking Age England. Linguistic relations between speakers of Old Norse and Old English* (Turnhout, 2002).

26 M. Barnes, 'Norse in the British Isles', in A. Faulkes and R. Perkins (eds), *Viking Revaluations* (London, 1993), pp. 65–84, at 81.

27 Wormald, 'Viking studies', p. 144. The main exception to this generalisation, and discussed by Wormald in his paper, was the work of Alfred Smyth: *Scandinavian York and Dublin. The history and archaeology of two related Viking kingdoms*, 2 vols (Dublin, 1975–8); *Scandinavian Kings in the British Isles, 850–880* (Oxford, 1977).

28 Keynes, 'The Vikings in England', pp. 63–73; P. Kershaw, 'The Alfred–Guthrum treaty: scripting accommodation and interaction in Viking Age England', in Hadley and Richards (eds), *Cultures in Contact*, pp. 43–64; M. Innes, 'Danelaw identities: ethnicity, regionalism and political allegiance', in *ibid.*, pp. 65–88; D. M. Hadley, ' "Hamlet and the princes of Denmark": lordship in the Danelaw, c.860–954', in *ibid.*, pp. 107–32; *idem*, 'Viking and native: rethinking identity in the Danelaw', *Early Medieval Europe*, hereafter: *EME*, 11 (1) (2002), 45–70.

29 P. Everson and D. Stocker, *Corpus of Anglo-Saxon Stone Sculpture, Vol. 5. Lincolnshire* (Oxford, 1999), pp. 80–7; D. Stocker, 'Monuments and merchants: irregularities in the distribution of stone sculpture in Lincolnshire and Yorkshire in the tenth century', in Hadley and Richards (eds), *Cultures in Contact*, pp. 179–212; see also P. Sidebottom, 'Viking Age stone monuments and social identity', in *ibid.*, pp. 213–35; D. Stocker and P. Everson, 'Five towns funerals: decoding diversity in Danelaw stone sculpture', in Graham-Campbell, Hall, Jesch and Parsons (eds), *Vikings and the Danelaw*, pp. 223–43.

30 S. Foot, 'Violence against Christians', *Medieval History*, hereafter: *Med. Hist.* 1 (1991), 3–16; G. Halsall, 'Playing by whose rules? The Vikings and the Church in ninth-century England', *Med. Hist.*, 2 (1992), 2–12; A. Smyth, 'The effect of Scandinavian raiders on the English and Irish churches: a preliminary reassessment', in B. Smith (ed.), *Britain and Ireland 900–1300. Insular responses to medieval European change* (Cambridge, 1999), pp. 1–38.

31 L. Abrams, 'The conversion of the Danelaw', in Graham-Campbell, Hall, Jesch and Parsons (eds), *Vikings and the Danelaw*, pp. 31–44; *idem*, 'Conversion and assimilation', in Hadley and Richards (eds), *Cultures in Contact*, pp. 135–53.

32 J. Barrow, 'Survival and mutation: ecclesiastical institutions in the Danelaw in the ninth and tenth centuries', in Hadley and Richards (eds), *Cultures in Contact*, pp. 155–76.

33 R. N. Bailey, *Viking Age Sculpture in northern England* (London, 1980), pp. 101–75; *idem*, *England's Earliest Sculptors* (Toronto, 1997), pp. 80–94; J. T. Lang,

'Sigurd and Weland in pre-Conquest carving from northern England', *Yorkshire Archaeological Journal*, hereafter: *YAJ*, 48 (1976), 83–94.

34 D. M. Hadley, 'Burial practices in the Northern Danelaw, c.650–1100', *Northern History*, hereafter: *North. Hist.*, 36 (2) (2000), 199–216, at 212–15.

35 *Ibid.*: Richards, 'The missing Vikings: Scandinavian burial in the Danelaw'.

36 For recent reviews, see Richards, 'Identifying Anglo–Scandinavian settlements'; R. A. Hall, 'Anglo–Scandinavian attitudes: archaeological ambiguities in late ninth- to mid-eleventh-century York', in Hadley and Richards (eds), *Cultures in Contact*, pp. 311–24; R. A. Hall (ed.), *Aspects of Anglo–Scandinavian York*, The Archaeology of York, 8 (York, 2004); A. Vince, 'The new town: Lincoln in the high medieval era (c.900 to c.1350)', in D. Stocker (ed.), *The City by the Pool. Assessing the Archaeology of the City of Lincoln* (Oxford, 2003), pp. 159–296.

37 G. Thomas, 'Anglo–Scandinavian metalwork from the Danelaw: exploring social and cultural interaction', in Hadley and Richards (eds), *Cultures in Contact*, pp. 237–55.

38 C. E. Blunt, B. H. I. H. Stewart and C. S. S. Lyon, *Coinage in Tenth-Century England: from Edward the Elder to Edgar's Reform* (Oxford, 1989); M. A. S. Blackburn, 'Expansion and control: aspects of Anglo–Scandinavian minting south of the Humber', in Graham-Campbell, Hall, Jesch and Parsons (eds), *Vikings and the Danelaw*, pp. 125–42; *idem*, 'The coinage of Scandinavian York', in Hall (ed.), *Aspects of Anglo–Scandinavian York*, pp. 325–49; *idem*, 'Currency under the Vikings. Part 1. Guthrum and the earliest Danelaw coinages' (forthcoming) *British Numismatic Journal*, hereafter: *BNJ*.

39 See, for example, A. Vince, 'Lincoln in the early medieval era, between the 5th and 9th centuries', in Stocker (ed.), *The City by the Pool*, pp. 141–56; *idem*, 'Lincoln in the high medieval era'; L. Symonds, *Landscape and Social Practice: the production and consumption of pottery in 10th-century Lincolnshire*, British Archaeological Reports, hereafter: BAR Brit. Ser., 345 (Oxford, 2003); *idem*, 'Territories in transition: the construction of boundaries in Anglo–Scandinavian Lincolnshire', in D. Griffiths, A. Reynolds and S. Semple (eds), *Boundaries in Early Medieval Britain* (Oxford, 2003), pp. 28–37.

40 Hadley, ' "And they proceeded to plough and support themselves": the Scandinavian settlement of England', 82–93; Hadley and Richards, 'Introduction', pp. 9–12 in Hadley and Richards (eds), *Cultures in Contact*, pp. 3–15; Richards, 'Identifying Anglo–Scandinavian settlements', pp. 297–303; Hall, *Aspects of Anglo–Scandinavian York*, pp. 317–21; Thomas, 'Anglo–Scandinavian metalwork', pp. 240–1; G. Halsall, 'The Viking presence in England? The burial evidence reconsidered', in Hadley and Richards (eds), *Cultures in Contact*, pp. 259–76, at 268–9.

41 Thomas, 'Anglo–Scandinavian metalwork', pp. 240–1, 252; Hall, *Aspects of Anglo–Scandinavian York*, pp. 319–21.

42 Wormald, 'The ninth century', p. 164; this is a major theme in D. M. Hadley, *The Northern Danelaw: its social structure, c.800–1100* (London, 2000).

43 Innes, 'Danelaw identities'; Hadley, 'Viking and native'.

44 See, for example, H. Wolfram, *The Goths* (Berkeley, trans. 1988); H. Wolfram and W. Pohl, *Typen der Ethnogenese unter besonderer Berücksichtigung der Bayern*

(Vienna, 1990); P. Geary, 'Ethnic identity as a situational construct in the early Middle Ages', *Mitteilungen der Anthropologischen Gesellschaft in Wien*, 113 (1983), 15–26; S. Reynolds, 'What do we mean by "Anglo-Saxon" and "Anglo-Saxons"?', *Journal of British Studies*, hereafter: *J. Brit. Stud.*, 24 (1985), 395–414; P. Amory, 'The meaning and purpose of ethnic terminology in the Burgundian Laws', *EME*, 2 (1) (1993), 1–28; *idem*, 'Names, ethnic identity and community in fifth- and sixth-century Burgundy', *Viator*, 25 (1994), 1–30; P. Heather, *The Goths* (Oxford, 1996); W. Pohl and H. Reimitz, *Strategies of Distinction: the construction of ethnic communities* (Leiden, 1998).

45 It should, of course, be noted that raiding carried on once settlement had commenced.

46 Frankia was not immune at this time, and there was also a raid on the monastery of St Philibert on Normoutier near the estuary of the Loire (France) in 799. Overviews of the course of events are provided in G. Jones, *A History of the Vikings* (2nd edn, Oxford, 1984), pp. 145–240; D. Ó Corráin, 'Ireland, Wales, Man and the Hebrides', in Sawyer (ed.), *History of the Vikings*, pp. 83–109; J. L. Nelson, 'The Frankish Empire', in *ibid.*, pp. 19–47; J. Graham-Campbell (ed.), *Cultural Atlas of the Viking World* (New York, 1994), pp. 122–63.

47 The existence of King Rædwulf is recorded only by Roger of Wendover, but his account is corroborated by the survival of a number of coins bearing Rædwulf's name: J. J. North, *English Hammered Coinage, I, Early Anglo-Saxon to Henry III, c.650–1272* (London, 1994), p. 72.

48 *EHD I*, p. 188.

49 A. Campbell (ed.), *The Chronicle of Æthelweard* (Edinburgh, 1962), p. 35; *EHD I*, p. 191 and n. 5; Stenton, *Anglo-Saxon England*, p. 246, and n. 2.

50 *EHD I*, p. 191.

51 D. W. Rollason, *Sources for York History to AD 1100*, The Archaeology of York, 1 (York, 1998), p. 63.

52 *EHD I*, p. 194 and n. 1, 282; Rollason, *Sources for York History*, p. 63.

53 *EHD I*, p. 194, 282–3.

54 *Ibid.*, p. 283.

55 *Ibid.*, p. 192; M. Winterbottom (ed.), *Three Lives of English Saints* (Toronto, 1972), pp. 65–87.

56 P. Grierson and M. A. S. Blackburn, *Medieval European Coinage 1: the early Middle Ages (5th–10th centuries)* (Cambridge, 1986), p. 294.

57 D. N. Dumville, *Wessex and England from Alfred to Edgar* (Woodbridge, 1992), p. 6, n. 28.

58 Blackburn, 'Expansion and control of aspects of Anglo–Scandinavian minting', p. 127.

59 Blackburn, 'Currency under the Vikings'.

60 These kings are known only from their coinage: J. Campbell (ed.), *The Anglo-Saxons* (Harmondsworth, 1982), p. 135. That Æthelred may have been the King of Wessex of this name has been suggested, but this king had died by 871 and the coinage appears to extend later than this date, while the use of an earlier East Anglian moneyer and some of the blundered inscriptions combine to make it

certain that this Æthelred was not the King of Wessex: Blackburn, 'Currency under the Vikings'.

61 *EHD I*, p. 194.

62 P. H. Sawyer (ed.), *Anglo-Saxon Charters: an annotated list and bibliography* (London, 1968), [documents cited by number], hereafter: S 215 and 216.

63 S. Keynes, 'King Alfred and the Mercians', in M. A. S. Blackburn and D. N. Dumville (eds), *Kings, Currency and Alliances. History and coinage of southern England in the ninth century* (Woodbridge, 1998), pp. 1–45, at 12–19. Burgred was married to Alfred's sister, Æthelswith.

64 Wormald, 'The ninth century', in J. Campbell (ed.), *The Anglo-Saxons* (London, 1982), pp. 132–57.

65 This date is consistent with the small number of finds recovered from the fill of the ditch, including pottery of the late ninth or tenth century, a copper-alloy pin, human bone and iron coffin-fittings: M. Biddle and B. Kjølbye-Biddle, 'Repton and the "great heathen army", 873–4', in Graham-Campbell, Hall, Jesch and Parsons (eds), *Vikings and the Danelaw*, pp. 45–96, at 57–9.

66 *Ibid.*, pp. 46, 58–9.

67 *Ibid.*, pp. 60–5.

68 *Ibid.*, 68–9.

69 *Ibid.*, 67–74.

70 *Ibid.*, pp. 78–9; D. W. Rollason, *The Mildrith Legend: a Study in Early Medieval Hagiography* (Leicester, 1982), pp. 26, 77, 81, 93; *EHD I*, p. 176; *idem*, 'The cults of murdered royal saints in Anglo-Saxon England', *Anglo-Saxon England*, hereafter: *ASE*, 11 (1983), 1–22, at 5–9.

71 Biddle and Kjølbye-Biddle, 'Repton and the "great heathen army"', pp. 81–4.

72 *Ibid.*, p. 74.

73 *EHD I*, p. 194.

74 *Ibid.*, p. 195.

75 Biddle and Kjølbye-Biddle, 'Repton and the "great heathen army"', p. 72.

76 J. D. Richards, 'Boundaries and cult centres: viking burial in Derbyshire', in Graham-Campbell, Hall, Jesch and Parsons (eds), *Vikings and the Danelaw*, pp. 97–104, at 100–1, citing R. Bradley, *Altering the Earth: the origins of monuments in Britain and continental Europe* (Edinburgh, 1993), p. 116. See also, J. D. Richards, 'Excavations at the Viking barrow cemetery at Heath Wood, Ingleby, Derbyshire', *Antiq. J.*, 84 (2004), 23–116. There is no evidence that those interred in the multiple burial had been ritually sacrificed, and the form of the grave has parallels in execution cemeteries: see chapter 6, p. 000.

77 On the available evidence see Graham-Campbell, *Cultural Atlas of the Viking World*, pp. 38–120; B. Sawyer and P. H. Sawyer, *Medieval Scandinavia from Conversion to Reformation, c.800–1500* (Minnesota, 1993), pp. 1–26.

78 *EHD I*, p. 843.

79 S. Keynes and M. Lapidge, *Alfred the Great. Asser's* Life of King Alfred *and Other Contemporary Sources* (Harmondsworth, 1983), p. 125.

80 Nelson, 'The Frankish Empire', p. 19.

81 P. H. Sawyer, 'The causes of the Viking Age', in Farrell (ed.), *The Vikings*, pp. 1–7, at 1–2; *idem*, 'The Age of the Vikings, and before', in Sawyer (ed.), *History of the Vikings*, pp. 1–18, at 3–8.

82 Sawyer, 'The causes of the Viking Age', pp. 5–6; J. Bill, 'Ships and seamanship', in Sawyer (ed.), *History of the Vikings*, pp. 182–201.

83 Sawyer, 'The causes of the Viking Age', p. 2.

84 Sawyer, 'The causes of the Viking Age', pp. 2–4; J. Callmer, 'Urbanization in Scandinavia and the Baltic region c.AD 700–100: trading places, centres and early urban sites', in B. Ambrosiani and H. Clarke (eds), *Developments around the Baltic and North Sea in the Viking Age* (Stockholm, 1994), pp. 50–90.

85 Sawyer, 'The causes of the Viking Age', p. 3.

85 *Ibid.*, pp. 3–5; Callmer, 'Urbanization in Scandinavia', pp. 60–5; M. Müller-Wille and A. Tummscheit, 'Viking Age proto-urban centres and their hinterlands: some examples from the Baltic area', in J. Hines, A. Lane and M. Redknap (eds), *Land, Sea and Home* (Leeds, 2004), pp. 27–39, at 36–9.

86 Callmer, 'Urbanization in Scandinavia', pp. 60–5.

87 Sawyer, 'The causes of the Viking Age', pp. 3–4, 7.

88 Sawyer, *The Age of the Vikings*, pp. 196–200.

89 J. Graham-Campbell and D. Kidd, *The Vikings* (London 1980), pp. 34–5.

90 B. Myrhe, 'The beginning of the Viking Age – some current archaeological problems', in A. Faulkes and R. Perkins (eds), *Viking Revaluations* (London, 1993), pp. 182–216, at 188–92, 195–9.

91 *Ibid.*, pp. 194–8.

92 L. Hedeager, 'Kingdoms, ethnicity and material culture: Denmark in a European perspective', in M. Carver (ed.), *The Age of Sutton Hoo* (Woodbridge, 1992), pp. 279–300, at 282–3, 293–300.

93 *Ibid.*, pp. 297–8; A. Pedersen, 'Similar finds – different meanings? Some preliminary thoughts on the Viking-age burials with riding equipment in Scandinavia', in C. K. Jensen and K. H. Nielsen (eds), *Burial and Society* (Aarhus, 1997), pp. 171–83, at 173–80.

94 Nelson, 'The Frankish Empire', pp. 21–3.

95 Sawyer, 'The causes of the Viking Age', pp. 4–5.

96 Nelson, 'The Frankish Empire', pp. 23–4, 36.

97 Wormald, 'Viking studies', p. 147.

98 *Ibid.*, pp. 147–8; Sawyer, *The Age of the Vikings*, pp. 202–3.

99 Nelson, 'The Frankish Empire', pp. 24–30.

2

Anglo–Scandinavian political accommodation

The political implications of the Scandinavian conquests and settlement of parts of northern and eastern England in the late ninth and tenth centuries were immense. The ruling dynasties of the Mercian, East Anglian and Northumbrian kingdoms were dislodged in the 860s and 870s (see pp. 10–15), after which part or all of these kingdoms came under Scandinavian control. Yet despite these profound changes, the manner in which the Scandinavians ruled has not received the attention it merits. How did Scandinavian leaders take control in parts of northern and eastern England, and by what means did they maintain their power? Did the conquerors rule in a uniform fashion, or did they adopt diverse strategies, and if so, why? What impact did the Scandinavian conquest have on the indigenous secular and ecclesiastical elite of northern and eastern England, and how did the latter respond to the settlers? To what extent did the regional traditions of northern and eastern England continue to resonate in the political sphere following Scandinavian conquest, and how did the West Saxon kings deal with this following their conquest of the Scandinavian-controlled territories over the course of the tenth century? Discussion of the political impact of the Scandinavian conquest routinely rests on analysis of the accounts provided in the *Anglo-Saxon Chronicle* and a small number of other written sources. Yet it is apparent that the superficially straightforward events that they record are likely to have been considerably more complex. Moreover, while we are often informed of *what* happened, little is said of *how* or *why*. The written record also typically focuses on specific places and individual people, with the *Chronicle* prioritising the actions of successive West Saxon kings, while the wider implications of actions and events are left undisclosed. For this reason, the following discussion also draws on numismatic, sculptural and archaeological evidence, which can illuminate political strategies adopted by successive rulers in the so-called Danelaw, and which have the advantage of providing a broader perspective than the written record, albeit one that is rarely as chronologically precise. Anglo–Scandinavian political relationships have recently been described as 'overwhelmingly obscure',[1] yet although the challenges of studying Anglo–Scandinavian political relationships in regions that yield up little contemporary documentation are considerable, there are grounds, as we shall see, for greater optimism.

Guthrum, Alfred and Anglo–Scandinavian relations in East Anglia in the late ninth century

It is instructive to begin with discussion of the most extensively documented example of Anglo–Scandinavian diplomacy, that between Alfred, king of Wessex, and Guthrum, leader of a Scandinavian army that settled in East Anglia in 880. Numismatic evidence also throws light on Anglo–Scandinavian relations in East Anglia during the later ninth century, revealing that while the focus of the written sources is on the initiatives of Alfred, both Guthrum and the East Anglian elite made distinctive contributions to the political scene in East Anglia. In 878 the armies of King Alfred and Guthrum met at Edington (Wilts), and the West Saxons prevailed. Following this defeat, Guthrum and thirty of his leading men were baptised into Christianity, in a protracted ceremony that began near Athelney (Som), and was completed at Wedmore (Som). The events are mentioned in the *Anglo-Saxon Chronicle*, and described in more detail by Asser in his *Life of King Alfred*:

> Guthrum, their king, promised to accept Christianity and to receive baptism at King Alfred's hand; all of which he and his men fulfilled as they had promised. For three weeks later Guthrum, the king of the pagans, with thirty of the best men from his army, came to King Alfred at a place called Aller, near Athelney. King Alfred raised him from the holy font of baptism, receiving him as his adoptive son; the unbinding of the chrisom on the eighth day took place at a royal estate called Wedmore. Guthrum remained with the king for twelve nights after he had been baptised, and the king freely bestowed many excellent treasures on him and all his men.[2]

The practice of one ruler standing sponsor to another at their baptism or confirmation was widely known in England from the seventh century onwards, and commonly preceded political negotiation between Christian and pagan leaders.[3] The events of 878 provide the earliest recorded example of an English king standing sponsor to a Scandinavian leader, although royal involvement in the baptism of Scandinavians is recorded earlier in Frankia, when, for example, King Charles the Bald arranged the conditions for the baptism of Scandinavian raiders in 873, following a precedent set by his father, Louis the Pious, when he stood as godfather to the Danish King Harald and his wife in 826.[4]

Although neither Asser nor the *Anglo-Saxon Chronicle* mention it in their accounts of the events of 878, a later *Chronicle* entry reveals that Guthrum was given the baptismal name of Æthelstan.[5] The influence of Alfred can perhaps be seen in this choice of name, as Æthelstan had been the name of his eldest brother, and a name with such familial and royal associations may have been deemed by Alfred to be an appropriate choice to symbolise the personal but formal arrangement that standing sponsor to an individual at baptism represented.[6] The name had also been borne by an earlier king of East Anglia, who reigned c.830–45, although it may be a mere coincidence that the new Æthelstan subsequently became the king of East Anglia.[7] In 878, Guthrum had, as yet, no specific known associations with East Anglia, but given that parts of the army had already settled in eastern Mercia and Northumbria, it is likely that Guthrum intended to settle somewhere. Guthrum and his army did not immediately proceed towards East Anglia after his baptism, leaving their base at Chippenham (Wilts) for Cirencester (Gloucs) in Mercia where they stayed for a year.[8] The events of 878–9 roughly coincide with the end of the reign of the Mercian king Ceolwulf II, who had been appointed in 873–4 by the 'great army' of which Guthrum's forces had been a part (see p. 12), and the year that Guthrum spent at Cirencester may, as David Dumville has suggested, have been while new political arrangements for Mercia were being deliberated.[9] Thus, relatively brief accounts of events provided by Asser and the *Chronicle* hint at considerably more complex political manoeuvring.

In 880 the *Anglo-Saxon Chronicle* records that Guthrum and his army left Cirencester and went to East Anglia 'and settled there and shared out the land'.[10] The political context of this event is unclear, as it is uncertain who the ruler(s) of this region currently were, although, as we have seen (see pp. 11–12), it is likely that the region was already under some form of Scandinavian control. Given the dearth of written evidence for East Anglian history in the late ninth century, most discussions of Guthrum's reign begin, and sometimes end, with examination of his continuing relations with King Alfred. Preserved in a late eleventh- or early twelfth-century collection of Anglo-Saxon legal texts is a record of a peace (*frið*) forged between Guthrum and Alfred. The treaty begins as follows:

> This is the peace which King Alfred and King Guthrum and the councillors of all the English race and all the people who are in East Anglia have all agreed on and confirmed with oaths, for themselves and for their subjects, both for the living and for the unborn, who care to have God's favours or ours.[11]

The treaty then defines a boundary between the areas of jurisdiction of the two kings running 'up the Thames, and then up the Lea, and along the Lea to its source, then in a straight line to Bedford, then up the Ouse to Watling Street'. The remainder of the treaty is concerned with compensation payments (*wergilds*) in the events of the death of various classes of person, and with the regulation of relations between the followers of Alfred and Guthrum, with respect to trade, legal disputes, and the movement of people between the two areas of jurisdiction.[12]

Interpretation of the significance of this treaty is far from straightforward, and even its date is uncertain. Since it associates Guthrum with East Anglia, it is unlikely to date to before 880 when the *Chronicle* says that Guthrum settled there, and the treaty must have been drawn up before 890 when Guthrum died. Some scholars have argued that it must date to 886 or later, because this is when Alfred is believed to have captured London, which is on the 'English' side of the boundary recorded in the treaty.[13] Furthermore, it has been argued that the contrast evident in the treaty between, on the one hand, Guthrum and 'all the people in East Anglia' and, on the other, Alfred and 'the councillors of all the English [*ealles Angelcynnes witan*]' could not have been conceived of before the events of 886, when, according to the *Anglo-Saxon Chronicle*, King Alfred received in London the submission of 'all the English (*Angelcyn*) that were not under subjection to the Danes'.[14] However, after recent evaluation of the coinage minted there in the late 870s and early 880s, Mark Blackburn has concluded that London was not under Scandinavian control at this time, and that this removes a major obstacle to dating the treaty to earlier than 886.[15] In any case, as David Dumville has observed, after the demise of Northumbria, East Anglia and Mercia as independent kingdoms between 867 and 874, it may have been quite reasonable for Alfred, as the last independent English king, to regard himself as commanding the counsel of all the English long before 886.[16] Whatever the date, and the context, of the agreement between the two rulers, the written text clearly emanated from the Alfredian court circle and it may even be the earliest known legislative statement from Alfred.[17]

Some have regarded this treaty between Alfred and Guthrum as representing the foundation of the so-called Danelaw, and there has been considerable debate about the nature of the boundary. For example, why does it stop at Watling Street? Was it intended to run along the Roman road, as many modern maps would have it? We should remember, however, that there is no evidence that what was later to be known as the Danelaw was conceived of as a political entity at this early date, and the boundary appears to have been short-lived.[18] Most discussions of the treaty focus on its definition of separate spheres of authority, division of territory and regulations for the avoidance of disputes between the followers of Alfred and Guthrum. However, Paul Kershaw has recently argued that the terms of this treaty are also concerned with the integration of Guthrum into ninth-century English politics, of Guthrum's followers into the legal, social and economic structure of local society, and of the territories to the east of Wessex into Alfred's realm.[19] The signing of treaties between rulers in early medieval western Europe was common, but this tradition of treaty-making was not practised in Scandinavia, and thus, more broadly, the treaty represented the drawing of a Scandinavian leader into a western European tradition of diplomacy.[20]

The treaty notes that Alfred was supported by the *witan* ('king's council') of the *Angelcynn*, while Guthrum is described as having agreed upon the peace with 'all the people (*þeod*) in East Anglia', but both of these phrases mask a complex reality. The latter phrase probably indicates both settlers and pre-existing inhabitants of East Anglia, many of whom may have submitted to Guthrum, as those in the vicinity of his base at Chippenham had done early in 878. It perhaps also signifies a lack of certainty on the part of those who drew up the treaty about the political structure of the Scandinavians in contrast to that of the West Saxons.[21] The role of Alfred as ruler of the English was a new concept, and this treaty may have provided Alfred with an opportunity to present himself as the representative of territories beyond Wessex and 'to breathe life into the notion of Englishness'.[22] Later in the treaty, reference is made to Danes, but Guthrum's army may not have consisted exclusively of men who identified themselves in this way; indeed, the presence of continental names among Guthrum's moneyers suggests that some, at least, of his followers were not even from Scandinavia. Thus, the treaty arguably represents part of the process by which the settlers, whatever their background, were labelled as Danes for legal purposes.[23] As Kershaw has argued, this treaty did not simply reflect existing ethnic identities, but played an active role in creating them, in the realms of both Guthrum and Alfred.[24]

The treaty can also be seen as part of the process by which Alfred and Guthrum tried to make sense of each other's society, although in the process some simplification of social reality may be expected, especially in - attempts to draw parallels between various strata of English and Scandinavian society.[25] The treaty was one means by which the co-existence of the Scandinavians and the indigenous populations was managed, although we should not assume that such strategies of accommodation at the level of idealised, prescriptive law directly affected the lives of the wider population, or that its terms were universally accepted. Nonetheless, the fact that Guthrum allowed himself to be presented in the guise of an English king must have played a part in establishing Guthrum and his followers as permanent features in the society of East Anglia. The treaty presents Guthrum as a Christian king, and as a legislator in the Christian, western European tradition, and, while Scandinavian notions of kingship may have been rather different from those of Alfred, all the recoverable evidence suggests that this is how Guthrum wished to present himself and conduct his kingship.

That this relatively new perspective on the treaty has merit is indicated by the coinage minted in East Anglia during Guthrum's rule, which reinforces the notion that Guthrum intended to rule in the manner of a Christian, English king. Until recently, it was thought that earlier East Anglian moneyers, coin designs and expertise in die-cutting had not survived into Guthrum's reign, but more recently Mark Blackburn has identified an early issue by Guthrum that is similar to those coins minted for Æthelred and Oswald in the years after the demise of King Edmund (see p. 11). This coinage, minted in Guthrum's baptismal name, is similarly based on a Carolingian prototype featuring a temple, and the reverses of two of the coins incorporate the mint name of Quentovic, and they may have been official dies taken from the trading centre, providing another indication of the importance of continental moneyers in the early Danelaw coinage.[26] The minting of coins by a Scandinavian king is especially striking, since coins were rarely minted in Scandinavia at this time.[27] The next coins minted in Guthrum's realm were imitative of contemporary issues of King Alfred, bearing Alfred's name and sometimes even the names of his moneyers, and they were minted at a number of sites in both East Anglia and the east midlands (fig. 3). These imitations, often displaying poor literacy, were lighter than the coins of Alfred, and it has long been thought that they were simply crude and inferior copies. However, more recently, Blackburn has analysed the weights of a large number of coins and, having shown that the imitations are consistently lighter (around 1.35 g) than the Alfredian

3 Imitation 'Alfred' coin. This imitative phase of minting lasted from the early 880s until the mid- to late 890s. The coins were copies of a range of Alfred's coins, including those minted at London, Canterbury and Oxford, and were struck at a number of mints in East Anglia and the east midlands. These coins were lighter than the original Alfredian coins.

prototypes (1.6 g), has argued that the imitations were deliberately minted at this lighter weight standard. Significantly, this was the traditional Anglo-Saxon weight standard, in contrast to the heavier Alfredian coins, which were the product of a reform of the coinage in c.880. Thus, far from producing simply a pale imitation of contemporary West Saxon coins, Guthrum's moneyers, some of whom appear to have been continental newcomers, copied the style of Alfred's coins but adopted the weight standard of the pre-reform coinage. This, and the uniformity of the hoards recovered from East Anglia, indicates that by c.895 the East Anglian coinage was relatively homogeneous and largely excluded non-local coins, implying that it was 'quite a respectable monetary system'.[28] It is also notable that the earlier coins of Æthelred and Oswald and the earliest issue of Guthrum did not adhere to the weight standard (1.75 g) of the Carolingian prototypes on which they were based, but were also struck at the traditional East Anglian weight standard. In sum, this monetary system suggests that at least this aspect of Guthrum's reign was partly forged in the style of Alfred but it was also shaped by local East Anglian demands.

In this respect, it is worth considering whether enigmatic entries in the *Anglo-Saxon Chronicle*, hinting at developments beyond our ability to reconstruct in detail, may reveal the continuing significance of ancient East Anglian concerns. For example, the entry for 885 records that 'King Alfred sent a naval force from Kent into East Anglia' and into the mouth of the River Stour, and this suggests not only a probable breach of the peace with Guthrum's realm, but some dispute involving Essex, since this river was the ancient boundary between the East Angles and East Saxons.[29] The recovery of Essex by the West Saxons (it had been part of its 'eastern kingdom' since 825) is obscure, but had seemingly begun by the 890s, given that an Ealdorman of Essex is noted on the West Saxon side in 896. Yet, a viking raiding force periodically used Essex as a base from 893, and during this time it received military assistance from East Anglia, where its

4   Coin of Guthrum. This coin was minted in
Guthrum's baptismal name of Æthelstan.

women were placed in safety in 895.[30] Thus, while Guthrum and his followers were now firmly established in East Anglian society, they were not
averse to causing problems for the West Saxons, something which may
have been influenced by the interests of the native East Anglians and the
people of Essex.

Guthrum's reign was also shaped by the dominant Christian culture in
East Anglia. For example, a number of coins minted in East Anglia were
overtly issues of the new king, issued in his baptismal name, Æthelstan,
and marked with a cross (fig. 4).[31] Since there should be little doubt that
Guthrum himself dictated the presentation of his name, this coinage suggests that in at least some circumstances his baptismal name was a means
by which he presented himself in the guise of an Anglicised king, and infers
a continuing commitment to Christianity.[32] Indeed, when the *Anglo-Saxon
Chronicle* records his death in 890, it describes him as 'the northern king,
Guthrum, whose baptismal name was Æthelstan', and notes that he was
Alfred's godson.[33] The terms of Guthrum's treaty with Alfred imply that
he had pretensions as a ruler on a national, if not international, scale, and
that he may have thought of his realm as a member of the wider community
of western European Christian states, and his coins reflect such ambitions.
We do not know whether Guthrum was a patron of the East Anglian
Church, but this combination of documentary and numismatic evidence
provides a context in which churches may have survived, if not prospered
(see pp. 212–14).

We do not know who ruled East Anglia following the death of
Guthrum.[34] Yet while the written record is not forthcoming, the coinage
issued from the latter years of the ninth century has much to reveal about
the political scene in the region. The early imitative phase of coinage and
the Guthrum/Æthelstan coins were succeeded by an anonymous coinage
in the name of the murdered King Edmund, which commenced in c.895
(fig. 5). That Guthrum's unknown successors as ruler in East Anglia

5 St Edmund penny. Coins in the name of the murdered King Edmund of East Anglia began to be minted in c.895.

should issue an even more overtly Christian coinage than his Æthelstan series indicates that the promotion of Christianity was official policy, and implies that the Church was important to the secular administration in late ninth-century East Anglia.[35] It seems likely that this coinage was struck at a number of mints in both East Anglia and the east midlands. For example, the obverse of one coin bears the inscription NORDVICO, which has been interpreted as Norwich, while the moneyer Gundbert was probably operating at *Sceldfor*, probably Shelford (Cambs), where he had earlier minted coins in the name of Earl Sihtric. Some of the St Edmund moneyers later minted coins for King Edward the Elder in a style that has been attributed to the north-east midlands, possibly Stamford (Lincs), and a few coins bearing the mint name of York are also considered to have been struck in the east midlands.[36] This St Edmund coinage implies a tolerance of Christianity, if not its promotion. The anonymity of the Edmund coins makes it difficult to know who was responsible for them, and this anonymity may reflect a multiplicity of Scandinavian rulers (?kings) at this time in East Anglia and the east midlands, but the intended audience for the Christian symbolism may be surmised to have included the indigenous lords of East Anglia and the east midlands and also the wider local population, who together may have influenced both the use of Christian symbolism and the weight standard of the coinage. Those responsible for the coinage may arguably have been attempting to convince the kings of other realms, including Wessex and Frankia, 'that they were within the civilised community of Christian states'.[37]

The career of Guthrum and the St Edmund coinage provide valuable insight into Anglo–Scandinavian relations in East Anglia, but we must remember that the political history of late ninth-century East Anglia is largely hidden from view. In drawing attention to this issue, James Campbell has recently commented on the notable cluster of Scandinavian place-names on the east coast of Norfolk in the hundreds of East and West

Flegg. This district appears to have been an island in the Anglo-Saxon period, the extent of which is indicated by the silt and clay soils that now surround the district. Campbell suggests that the distinctive cluster of place-names may indicate that Flegg was a 'viking island base settlement', perhaps corresponding to the periodic Scandinavian occupation of the island of Walcheren off the Frisian coast in the ninth century.[38] Although this suggestion gives rise to questions about how the Scandinavian place-names were perpetuated, which can only have been achieved through more extensive and enduring settlement than a temporary military base, it does, as Campbell observes, present the possibility of some major event in the history of East Anglia of which we are otherwise ignorant. Whether it relates to the 870s when East Anglia was apparently ruled by Scandinavian appointees (see p. 11) is an issue for future research to consider, and recent excavations at Repton (Derbys) (pp. 12–15) indicate the potential for archaeological evidence to illuminate the politics of a particular period.[39]

Although the evidence for Guthrum's reign in East Anglian society and for his integration into the Anglo-Saxon political structure is limited to a few references in the *Anglo-Saxon Chronicle* and Asser's *Life of King Alfred*; the treaty with Alfred; and the coinage minted in East Anglia during the 880s, it is, as we have seen, possible to discern much about the style of his kingship and the complexity of his relationships with the English elite. Moreover, the treaty between Guthrum and Alfred set a precedent of documenting and legislating for relations between the Scandinavians and indigenous society, and the integration of Scandinavian settlers into the English legal system was, as we shall see, a recurrent theme in tenth- and eleventh-century law-codes.[40]

Guthred and the community of St Cuthbert

There is only one other well-documented account of a ninth-century Scandinavian ruler forming a working relationship with local rulers, and this concerns Guthred, the leader of a Scandinavian army based in northern England, who apparently became king at the behest of the religious community of St Cuthbert. While it may not be an entirely typical account, it does provide important insights into the ways in which a religious community coped with the turbulent military and political situation of the later ninth century.

In 875 the community had left the island of Lindisfarne with the body of St Cuthbert and embarked on wanderings that lasted seven years.

Eventually, the monks, along with Bishop Eardwulf and Abbot Eadred of Carlisle, came to Chester-le-Street (Dur) where the community was to reside for over a century. An important written source for these events is the anonymous *History of Saint Cuthbert*, the earliest surviving manuscript of which dates to the eleventh century, although much of the text was probably first compiled in the mid-tenth century.[41] According to this text, when the community reached Chester-le-Street, St Cuthbert appeared to Abbot Eadred, and instructed him as follows:

> 'Go', he said, 'over the Tyne to the Danish army and tell them that, if they wish to obey me, they should show you a certain boy called Guthred, son of Hardacnut, who is the slave of a certain widow, and in the early morning you and the whole army are to give the widow the price for him. Give the price at the third hour and at the sixth hour lead him before the multitude so that they may elect him king. At the ninth hour lead him with the whole army on to the hill called *Oswigesdune* and there place a gold armlet on his right arm and thus they are all to constitute him king. Say also to him that after he has been made king he should give to me all the land between the Tyne and the Wear . . . Resolved as a result of this vision . . . the holy abbot hastened to the heathen army; and being honourably received by it, he faithfully carried out in order what had been enjoined on him. For he both found and redeemed the boy, and made him king by the goodwill of the whole multitude . . . Then Bishop Eardwulf brought to the army and to the hill the body of St Cuthbert, and over it the king himself and the whole army swore peace and fidelity, for as long as they lived; and they kept this oath well.[42]

Although distinguishing fact from fictionalised version of reality is difficult in what is clearly a miracle-story, there seems little reason to doubt that the *History of Saint Cuthbert* preserves a tradition of real interaction between a raiding army and the community. The background to St Cuthbert's intervention in local politics can be traced through both the *History* and later sources from Durham. However, determining the political motivations of both Guthred and the community is challenging. For example, the written sources claim that the saint's community was impoverished and few in number, but it can be inferred that the community was rather more robust than this, given the sheer volume of material that they took with them, including the relics of Aidan, Oswald and successive bishops of Lindisfarne; manuscripts including the Lindisfarne gospels; various treasures; and, according to Symeon of Durham writing in the twelfth century, a stone cross.[43] Moreover, the impression conveyed of the community wandering haphazardly around northern England should be tempered by the recognition that the places the community visited, including Carlisle (Cumb) and Crayke (Yorks), were in regions where the community possessed land. Thus, David Rollason has suggested that the community may have been taking an opportunity to visit its outlying estates, and to strengthen links with its tenants through the strategic translation of the saint. The body of the saint was effectively the title deed to the lands granted to the community, and by visiting its estates and displaying the saint the community was asserting its political influence.[44]

Following Rollason's reinterpretation of the wanderings of the community around the north of England as strategic rather than pitiful, Eric Cambridge has suggested that the arrival of the community at Chester-le-Street may have represented not the occupation of a site new to the community, but a return to a place that had periodically accommodated the community over many years.[45] The relocation of the community may have been determined less by the dangers posed to the community from staying in Lindisfarne – where there is archaeological evidence to suggest continued occupation and religious activity, including the display of stone sculpture into the tenth century – than by a perceived need to protect the community's lands further south.[46] This would provide an explanation of why, during turbulent times, the community moved *towards* the areas of Scandinavian settlement rather than away from them. The prolonged stay at Chester-le-Street may have been encouraged by increased Scots domination to the north of the River Tweed; the flow of land to the community from further south, especially in the vicinity of Durham to where the community eventually moved in 995; and perhaps also the opportunities presented by the demise of the see of Hexham (Northumb), which had disappeared from the historical record in the earlier ninth century.[47]

If the actions of the community may be interpreted in this way, then they appear to have been largely successful, as the majority of the lands possessed by the community prior to 875 still belonged to it in the eleventh century. Moreover, the community also seems to have acquired additional lands during the later ninth and earlier tenth centuries; possibly in some cases at the expense of other religious communities, since some of these lands were in the vicinity of Hexham, Monkwearmouth and Jarrow (Northumb).[48] In this context the support offered to Guthred seems to have been politically motivated, and the community was rewarded with a substantial endowment between the Tyne and the

Wear.[49] Peaceful interaction with Guthred apparently continued, as Abbot Eadred subsequently purchased additional lands from him at Monk Hesleden, Horden, Little and Castle Eden, Hulam, Hutton Henry and Willington (Dur) and bestowed them on the community.[50] It has been argued that when describing the events of the 870s and 880s, later writers would have disproved of such worldly interest in landed estates, not to mention the willingness to forge a political alliance with a heathen army, and that this may account for the subsequent presentation of the relevant events concerning the wanderings of the community in rather more pathetic terms.[51]

The dealings of the community of St Cuthbert with local Scandinavians may chiefly have been prompted by the potential threat that the army posed, but it may also have been a move designed to acquire a powerful ally against other Scandinavian groups and perhaps also local lords. Certainly, the community's lands had not been immune to secular ambition in preceding years. For example, in the 860s, kings Osbert and Ælla had both taken lands from St Cuthbert's community, and the *History of Saint Cuthbert* attributes their subsequent death at the hands of a viking army to the intervention of the saint, which was a warning to other kings and princes that they should not steal the lands of the saint.[52] In turn, Guthred and his followers presumably benefited from the legitimation that the community and its saint accorded them. This must have proved useful in a region in which rival groups of Scandinavians appear to have been operating, and where English lords also vied for power, including the lords of Bamburgh and a King Egbert who was said to have been ruling 'the Northumbrians' while Guthred ruled in York.[53] The degree of accommodation between the community and the army is reflected in the ceremony that Guthred underwent, which may have contained both Christian and pagan elements. It involved the exchange of vows in the presence of the relics of the saint, and the giving of a gold armlet, which was presumably a Scandinavian – perhaps pagan – symbol of authority.[54] The hill at which the ceremony took place was linked to a seventh-century Northumbrian king, Oswiu (d. 670), which was doubtless intended to add the credence of history and of earlier regnal traditions to the legitimacy of the events of 883.[55]

The *History of Saint Cuthbert* has little to say about the nature and extent of Guthred's kingship, but more can be deduced from other sources. Although, it is not certain from the account of his accession that he was converted to Christianity, it is, nonetheless, likely that Guthred was converted at some point. The later tenth-century chronicler Æthelweard records that 'Guthfrith, king of the Northumbrians' was buried in York Minster in 895, and assuming, as seems likely, that he is the same man as the Guthred of the *History of Saint Cuthbert*, it is improbable that the Archbishop would have permitted his burial at the Minster if he had not converted.[56] This tale also implies that Guthred/Guthfrith exercised some level of authority in York, which may have been prompted by the fact that the community of St Cuthbert had previously held lands there, and it would be consistent with the wider strategies of the community to seek to secure or reacquire such land.[57] A coin from a hoard found at Ashton (Essex) bears the name of Guthfrith and appears to have been struck south of the Humber, suggesting that he even exercised some authority far to the south of York, as later Scandinavian kings of York were to do.[58] Certainly, at least one ruler in York exercised authority south of the Humber in the 890s, since Æthelweard alleges that King Alfred of Wessex sent an ambassador to York in 894 to negotiate over land to the west of Stamford. It is not certain that Alfred's ambassador was dispatched to meet Guthfrith, but a Scandinavian king supported by the community of St Cuthbert may have appeared to a West Saxon king as a ruler worthy of, and susceptible to, diplomatic activity.[59]

The intervention of the community of St Cuthbert into local politics proved beneficial to their landed interests, and also appears to have assisted in the integration of at least one group of raiders into local society in northern England. Although the written record states that the community suffered – and we should not doubt that these were dark days – at the same time we can infer that the community was tenacious in protecting its landed interests, demonstrating an ability to respond proactively to changed circumstances and to innovate in its interactions with the raiders. For his part, Guthred acquired an influential ally, and this may have contributed to his success in gaining a foothold in York and ultimately exercising some influence south of the Humber.

Ragnall, Northumbrian lords and the community of St Cuthbert

The *History of Saint Cuthbert* also provides an important insight into the processes of Scandinavian conquest and settlement in northern England in the early tenth century, but in this case the raiders were more inclined to make allies among the laity, to the detriment of the community of St Cuthbert. According to the *History*, c.914 Ragnall, who is said by other sources to have been a grandson of Ivarr, one of the leaders of the great army, occupied the land of Ealdred, son of Eadwulf the reeve of Bamburgh

(Northumb). Ealdred sought the support of the Scots and entered into battle with the invader, who subsequently defeated the Bernicians and Scots at Corbridge (Northumb). Following the battle, Alfred, one of the tenants of St Cuthbert's community, fled, and Ragnall took his land and divided it between two of his followers, Onlafbal and Scula (fig. 6).[60] In the following years Ragnall was active in the Isle of Man and Ireland, but at least some of his followers remained in Northumbria.[61] Ragnall returned in c.918 and according to the *History of Saint Cuthbert* fought a second battle at Corbridge.[62] Subsequently, Ragnall is said to have divided out the land that he had won in battle from another of the community's tenants, Eadred, and the recipients were his son, Esbrid, and Ealdorman Ælstan.[63] This turn of events reveals that Scandinavian conquerors were not averse to endowing land on local men, although in this case it is not apparent whether this was to reward their support in battle or to placate the vanquished.

Ragnall died in either 920 or 921, and the *History of Saint Cuthbert* notes that he died 'taking nothing with him of what he had stolen from St Cuthbert except his sin'.[64] Much of the land that Ragnall took from the community and endowed on Onlafbal was, indeed, returned to it. The *History* recounts how the community succeeded in regaining the lands granted to Onlafbal, although the precise means are hidden behind the moralising tones of its account of Onlafbal's fate when he entered their church at Chester-le-Street: 'when he had put one foot outside the threshold, he felt as if iron were deeply fixed in the other foot. With this pain piercing his diabolical heart, he fell, and the devil thrust his sinful soul into hell. And St Cuthbert, as was right, received his land'.[65] However, other estates were seemingly not recovered until the eleventh century, while clusters of Scandinavian place-names in County Durham infer Scandinavian settlement in this district, indicating that the *History of Saint Cuthbert* may have been simplifying the situation in its account of Ragnall's demise and the subsequent fate of its landed possessions.[66]

While Scandinavian lordship north of the Tees was short-lived, there are grounds for suggesting some continuing Scandinavian influence, and additional insight into the relationships of the community of St Cuthbert and its tenants with local Scandinavians is provided by tenth-century stone sculptures. Those at Chester-le-Street are rather different from the sculptures produced at Lindisfarne in the eighth and ninth centuries, as the community adopted the new Scandinavian artistic influences. Secular influence on sculptural production is indicated by a cross-shaft at Chester-le-Street depicting an armed man on horseback, above which

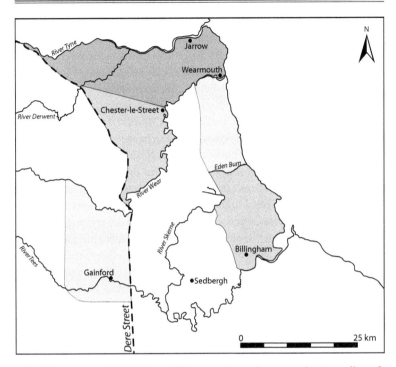

6 The estates of St Cuthbert. This map shows the approximate outline of
estates acquired by and taken from the community in the later ninth and
tenth centuries. The estate between the Eden Burn and the River Wear was
granted to Onlafbal by Ragnall in the early tenth century, while the estate
between the Eden Burn and the River Tees was granted to Scula. Together
these estates correspond with the lands granted to Alfred, who had
previously fled from the 'pirates' in the west, and sought the protection of the
community. The Gainford estate and the estate bounded by the River Wear,
Dere Street and Chester-le-Street had been held from the community by
Eadred, who was killed in the second battle of Corbridge, and whose lands
were also redistributed by Ragnall. The estate between the Tyne and the
Wear was acquired by the community in c.883 from Guthred, and appears to
correspond with the endowment of the community of
Monkwearmouth–Jarrow.

there is an inscription recording the name Eadmund, who may have been
commemorated by the cross-shaft, either when it was made or later, since
the inscription may have been a secondary addition.[67] Sculpture in the
church at Gainford (Dur) also incorporates Scandinavian motifs, despite

43

a seemingly unbroken succession of English lords, albeit sometimes, as in the case of Esbrid and Ealdorman Ælstan, owing their position to the raiders. [68] The later tenth-century sculptures nearby at Aycliffe (Dur) also combine indigenous styles and overtly ecclesiastical images (such as the Crucifixions of Christ and St Peter, and ecclesiastics with books and crosses) with Scandinavian styles. In this respect it may be significant that Aycliffe was given to the community of St Cuthbert in 930 by Scott, who was probably the son of Ealdorman Ælstan, suggesting the influence of family connections on the introduction of Scandinavian influence into this region. [69] It should, however, be noted that the Aycliffe sculptures are later in date than those from Gainford. Following the recorded events surrounding Ragnall's arrival in the region, little more is known of the existence, let alone the fate, of Scandinavian settlers in the region between the Tees and the Tyne, yet the sculptural evidence reveals a merging of native and Scandinavian traditions, suggesting that Scandinavian settlers continued to have a cultural influence on the region, and that churches were focal points for lordly display at which the Scandinavian influence was expressed and modified in an indigenous medium. [70] Intriguingly, the Scandinavian influence visible on some sculptures, such as at Gainford, is similar to that discernible on sculptures produced at York, implying that while the lands between the Tees and the Tyne were dominated by the community of St Cuthbert throughout the later ninth and tenth centuries, there were, nonetheless, cultural, and perhaps also ecclesiastical, links, to the south. [71]

The continuing importance of a Christian culture of lordship and the assimilation of the Scandinavian elite to this emerge from the evidence for this region. Thus, although Ragnall clearly caused problems for the community of St Cuthbert, it is equally apparent that the community succeeded in retaining its prominent position between the Tyne and the Tees. [72]

The archbishops and the Scandinavian kings of York

It is apparent that at least some of the Scandinavian conquerors relied on ecclesiastical support and Christian symbolism to establish and underpin their authority. Such support was doubtless offered as a matter of expediency as ecclesiastics fought to sustain their way of life and the Christian faith, and to protect their landed endowments. Yet other factors were clearly crucial, including the intention of the conquerors to rule in the manner of Anglo-Saxon kings, and the desire of indigenous lords, both lay as well as ecclesiastical, to maintain something of the ruling status quo and

to foster the regional identities of northern and eastern England in the face
not only of Scandinavian conquest but also of the West Saxon dynasty.
Nowhere are these factors more in evidence than in York.

Although the history of York in the late ninth and early tenth centuries
is scarcely documented, accommodation between the archbishops of York
and Scandinavian rulers can be discerned, primarily in the numismatic
record. The Scandinavians reintroduced a silver coinage into
Northumbria following a period of debasement, when the penny (the
styca) was no longer minted in silver but in pure brass, and an eventual cessation of minting, possibly as early as the 850s. Many of the coins minted
in the names of two otherwise unknown Scandinavian kings, Siefrid and
Cnut (c.895–905), bore liturgical inscriptions, including DNS DS REX
(*Dominus Deus Rex*, 'The Lord God (is) King'), DNS DS O REX (*Dominus
Deus Omnipotens Rex*, 'The Lord God Almighty (is) King') and *Mirabilia
fecit* ('He has done marvellous things', from Psalm 98) (fig. 7).[73] These
coins also incorporated various types of crosses into the design, and
around forty different combinations of obverse and reverse designs are
known among this coinage. With their innovative style, these coins have
been described as 'implying the presence of a highly literate and innovative person or group of people behind the designs', and as displaying
'remarkable imagination and intellectual vigour'.[74] This was, then, a
highly competent first foray into the minting of coins in York in the name
of new Scandinavian rulers. Coins of Charles the Simple, who ruled in
western Frankia from 897 to 922, influenced the design for two types of the
Cnut coins, and it has been suggested that the use of a *Karolus* monogram
may indicate that Cnut was one of the vikings on the Seine who accepted
baptism from Charles in 897, and perhaps even that Charles was his baptismal name. If so, such a move would mirror Guthrum's use of his baptismal name on coins (see pp. 33, 35), and may reflect a Scandinavian ruler
in York flagging both his Christian credentials and also his associations
with the Frankish realm.[75]

There has been debate about whether the coinage of the late ninth
century was primarily an ecclesiastical issue or whether the Scandinavian
rulers were the main influence on the design of, and messages conveyed by,
the coins.[76] It would be unusual for a coinage to be an entirely ecclesiastical issue (see p. 49), and, indeed, lapses in literacy on the coins infer
that control over the coinage was ultimately in the hands of the
Scandinavians.[77] Nonetheless, the Archbishop of York, Wulfhere for much
of this period, must have played an important role in fostering both
Anglo–Scandinavian relations and the overt use of Christianity to support

45

7 Coins minted in York in c.895–905. Coins 1–5 were minted for King Siefrid, and coins 6 and 7 were minted for King Cnut, with the latter bearing a *Karolus* monogram. Coins 8 and 9 incorporate the inscription *Mirabilia fecit* ('He has done marvellous things'), which on the latter is paired with DNS DS O REX (*Dominus Deus Omnipotens Rex*, 'The Lord God Almighty (is) King'). Coin 9 was minted for ALVVALDVS, probably King Alfred's nephew Æthelwold.

the new regime. This coinage shows familiarity with Anglo-Saxon and Carolingian designs, yet was also innovative in its inscriptions, including both the liturgical phrases and the depiction of the mint name (*Ebraice civitas*). Accordingly, Mark Blackburn has argued that it would have conveyed a number of contemporary messages: independence from Wessex, Mercia and also other areas of Scandinavian control; the royal status of the Scandinavian rulers, something that was unusual among coins minted in the east midlands and East Anglia; the administrative ability of those issuing the new coinage; and the importance of Christianity to the kings,

8   Coins minted in York in the early tenth century. Coins 1, 4 and 5 are St
Peter coins: the latter two with a sword and a sword and mallet, respectively.
Coins 2 and 3 were minted for Ragnall. Coin 2 has a bust of the king, while
coin 3 incorporates a bow and a hammer.

who appear to have been 'not only militarily powerful, but also politically
and diplomatically astute, and who came to recognise the political benefits
the church could offer to a newly established kingdom'.[78]

By c.905 a coinage in the name of St Peter emerged, perhaps influenced
by the St Edmund coinage of East Anglia first minted a decade earlier,
although the form of the inscription (SCI PETRI MO, 'St Peter's
mint/money') is closer to Carolingian prototypes. The St Peter's coinage
was minted for around twenty years, and later coins incorporated swords
on the obverse, and Thor's hammers or crosses on the reverse (fig. 8).[79]
The St Peter coinage was briefly interrupted by a coinage in the name of
Ragnall after he captured York c.919.[80] Ragnall's earliest penny has a head
on the reverse, the only such depiction on a coin struck for a Scandinavian
ruler in England, and it appears to have been modelled on Edward the
Elder's portrait coinage.[81] The second type of Ragnall coin incorporates
a hand or glove on the obverse, which may have been a pagan symbol of
the god Thor, but it may equally have been influenced by the *Manus Dei*
('Hand of God') issue of Edward the Elder, while the third type displayed
a hammer and a bow and arrow – as much secular as pagan images
(fig. 8).[82] It has been noted that this coinage is also derived from
Carolingian prototypes, and the resumption of a *Karolus* monogram may
not only have been intended to draw on an earlier York coinage, but may
also have been directly influenced by the coinage of Charles the Simple,
providing, perhaps, another indication of the international contexts in

47

which Scandinavian conquerors operated and perhaps also aspired to rule.[83] It is possible that Ragnall had been active in Frankia, and it has been suggested that Charles may have been a baptismal name, as it had perhaps been earlier for Cnut. Alternatively, the adoption of the *Karolus* monogram may have been a political move, in the face of the advance of Edward the Elder, to advertise some connection, whether personal or political, with the Frankish king.[84]

Ragnall was succeeded by a kinsman, Sihtric Caoch, who left Ireland in 920 (see p. 64), and whose rule appears to have seen the continuation of the combination of Anglo-Saxon and Scandinavian motifs on coins introduced by Ragnall. The sword St Peter coinage appears to have continued to be minted during his reign, while the small number of coins minted in Sihtric's name appear to have been struck at various sites south of the Humber, including Lincoln, and some of these coins incorporated swords, with either a cross or a hammer on the reverse.[85] In the LVDO SITRIC inscription on one of the cross-type coins, *Ludo* may have been an unknown title, but it has alternatively been suggested that it may have been an abbreviation of a baptismal name, *Ludovicus*.[86]

After Sihtric's death York was possibly ruled briefly by his kinsman Guthfrith, of whom no coins are known, and was then seized by the West Saxon king Athelstan (see p. 64). Following the death of Athelstan in 939, York was intermittently under the control of Norse kings until c.954, and the coinage issued at this time in York is very varied, and has sometimes been interpreted as having been overtly pagan and therefore as marking a change of tactics among the Scandinavian kings of York. A coinage minted for Olaf Guthfrithson incorporated a raven, while coins minted for Olaf Sihtricson, nicknamed Cuarán ('of the sandal') (941–4, 949–52), Sihtric (possibly a brother of Olaf Cuarán) and Ragnall Guthfrithson (943–4) incorporated a tri-lobed ornament (known as a triquetra) on the obverse, and a triangular standard on the reverse. Yet, although the raven, standard and the triquetra may, indeed, have been Scandinavian and pagan images, Christian parallels can also be found. For example, the raven was associated with St Oswald of Northumbria (d. 642), and the triquetra was used to represent the Trinity in seventh- and eighth-century art; moreover, the standard was topped with a cross, and crosses occur on many of the coins produced in York at this time. Perhaps the coinage was appealing to a dual audience, as Blackburn suggests, and it is notable that while Olaf Guthfrithson was an innovator, his reign also witnessed a return to the weight standard of the St Peter's coinage, after it had been increased by Athelstan's moneyers.[87]

It is improbable that a coinage could reflect anything other than official policy, and the imagery and inscriptions used on the coinage that has just been outlined must have been deliberate. The use of Christian symbolism and inscriptions and the fact that the name of the King is normally presented in Latin (as REX) must have been due to ecclesiastical influence, doubtless that of the archbishops, who may have been the prime instigators behind such developments. That this was undertaken in collaboration with the Scandinavian rulers is certain, since, as Mark Blackburn has commented, it would be unprecedented for an early medieval secular ruler to hand over all control over coinage, and the profits derived from it, to an ecclesiastic.[88] The discovery of a die for striking the later St Peter's coins in the Coppergate area, well away from the Minster, perhaps strengthens the argument that this was not exclusively an ecclesiastical issue (fig. 9), as does the increasingly poor literacy observable on the coins (with, for example, the mint name EBORACE becoming BORACE, BRACE, RACE, IIACE, BORAI); nonetheless, the influence of St Peter's and the Archbishop in York society must have been considerable.[89] The combination of Christian and pagan symbols in some of the earlier tenth-century coinage, and the fact that the earliest York coinage and that of Olaf Guthfrithson adopted the earlier Northumbrian weight standard and not the heavier weight standard of contemporary Anglo-Saxon coins, represents a complex stage of Anglo–Scandinavian accommodation, in which Christian and pagan, Northumbrian and Norse influences were negotiated.

9   Die for the minting of the St Peter's coinage. This iron coin die was found during excavations at Coppergate, and was produced for minting the later sword St Peter coins.

The inscriptions on the coins are largely in Latin, if sometimes garbled, and they serve to present successive Scandinavian rulers and kings in the guise of Christian, English kings, albeit on occasions with the addition of motifs uncommon to English coins, such as swords. This reveals that although the Scandinavians had a runic script and their own language, it was not employed for their coinage, presumably in part because of their reliance on moneyers accustomed to the Roman alphabet and Latin. There is, however, a rare exception to this among some of the coins minted in York, and also Derby, for Olaf Guthfrithson, on which Olaf is presented in Norse as CUNUNC (ON *konungr*) rather than Latin REX.[90] This is a striking and rare non-runic example of the writing of Old Norse (see chapter 3). The context for the coinage is the period after the death of King Athelstan, when Olaf regained Scandinavian control of York from the West Saxons and subsequently extended his authority to the south. Accordingly, this issue has been described by Richard Hall as 'propaganda coinage', and the combination of the legend and the depiction of a raven, the bird of battle, suggests to Alfred Smyth that it was a 'victory-coinage celebrating the return to power of Ivarr's descendants at York'.[91] This may have been a period of defiance of the Christian West Saxons, and Matthew Townend has described the coin-legend as 'a linguistic articulation of political identity'.[92] If so – and even if the message was pagan and Olaf himself remained pagan – his coinage was seemingly part of a strategy that also resonated within Northumbria; the coinage was notably returned to the pre-Athelstan weight standard and he was supported in some of his activities at this time by Archbishop Wulfstan (see p. 65).[93]

The mint at York, where coins were struck for a succession of rulers of diverse backgrounds from the late ninth century onwards, has been described by Michael Dolley as 'one of the most apolitical mints of all times', showing little difficulty in adapting itself to the changing political situation.[94] Alternatively, one could view the mint and the influence over it of successive archbishops, not as apolitical, but as driven by attempts to serve the interests of Northumbria, a deduction that can be borne out by consideration of the career of Archbishop Wulfstan (931–56). He allied himself with a succession of leaders in York, and this may have been more than expediency as the political tide turned, and may represent the Archbishop playing a leading role in periodic exertions of Northumbrian independence from West Saxon control. Presumably, King Athelstan (924–39) had sanctioned his appointment in 931, as by that time the West Saxon king had control of York. The Archbishop witnessed all of the King's charters between 931 and 935, implying that he was a significant figure at the royal court, and was the recipient of a large grant of territory in the north-west early in his career (see p. 62).[95] However, Wulfstan is suspiciously absent from the witness lists of royal charters from 936 to 941, which may imply that he was involved in opposition to Athelstan and his successor, Edmund (939–46). Perhaps he supported Olaf Guthfrithson against Athelstan at the battle of *Brunanburh* in 937, and he may also have played a part in receiving Olaf at York upon his return to England in 939, as the two certainly campaigned together in Mercia in the following year.[96]

Following Olaf's death and Edmund's capture of the north midlands in 942, Wulfstan reappears on the witness lists of royal charters.[97] Notably, Edmund came to some arrangement with the new rulers in York, as he stood as sponsor to the confirmation and baptism, respectively, of Olaf Cuaràn and Ragnall Guthfrithson – events in which the Archbishop must have played a part.[98] After Olaf and Ragnall were driven out of York (by Edmund, according to the *Anglo-Saxon Chronicle*) Wulfstan was a regular attendee at the West Saxon court until 947. He was present at the coronation of King Eadred (946–55) in 946, and came to an agreement with the new king at Tanshelf (Yorks) along with the Northumbrian councillors in 947.[99] It may, then, be significant that Wulfstan appears not to have attended meetings of royal councillors once Eric Bloodaxe had been accepted as king by the Northumbrians – contrary to their pledge of allegiance to Eadred, although it is difficult to determine whether Wulfstan was actively involved in this decision or whether his desertion of southern court politics was an expedient measure to protect his position in York.[100] That Eadred was angry with Wulfstan may be reflected in his army's burning of the major Northumbrian church at Ripon (Yorks) in 948. Subsequently, following a great slaughter of Eadred's army, the king 'became so angry that he wished to march back into the land and destroy it utterly', and this prompted the Northumbrians to desert Eric.[101] Wulfstan once again attended Eadred's court at least until 950, when the Northumbrians took first Olaf Cuaràn and then Eric as their king.[102] In 952 Eadred's patience wore out and he 'ordered Archbishop Wulfstan to be taken into the fortress of *Iudanbyrig* [possibly Castle Gotha, Cornwall], because accusations had often been made to the king against him'.[103] Wulfstan seems to have been released by 953, but when the *Chronicle* records in 954 that he received a bishopric, it is not entirely clear that he was reinstated in York, and while absences from court prior to his death in December 956 may have been related to the political situation in northern England, his failing health may equally have been a factor.[104]

It is difficult to discern the motivations of Wulfstan from the entries in the *Anglo-Saxon Chronicle* and his attestation of royal charters, but this evidence reveals that Wulfstan could not be relied upon to remain loyal to southern English kings. Support for Scandinavian kings was more than passive, extending, as we have seen, to influencing the forms of coins which were arguably the most visible paraphernalia of their kingship. This support was presumably offered in the interests of Northumbrian independence from southern rule, and it is likely that Wulfstan's position would have been strengthened by the political flux in York, rendering him a potent symbol, and facilitator, of continuity.[105]

The political activities of successive archbishops can be traced through the documentary and numismatic evidence, but far less attention has, however, been paid to the archaeological evidence for their strategies. In particular, the funerary sculptures produced and displayed in York in the earlier tenth century demonstrate a willingness to incorporate Scandinavian styles and iconography. For example, at the Minster cemetery, one grave-slab depicts a figure wielding his sword against a serpent, a headless torso, and a human figure with its hand raised to its mouth, which have been interpreted as scenes from the Sigurd legend (fig. 10), while the winged figure on a cross-shaft is probably Weland, the flying smith.[106] Other York sculptures incorporated Scandinavian zoomorphic designs, and there are also examples of the so-called hogback grave-covers and ring-headed crosses typical of western Britain, which are believed to have been adopted in Northumbria under Scandinavian influence.[107] At the Minster cemetery, at least, it is unlikely that such sculptures could have been displayed without the acquiescence of the archbishops. The diversity and elaboration of sculptures, grave furniture and grave structure suggests that the elite were buried in the Minster cemetery.[108] With its mixture of – on the one hand – indigenous practice, continuing local stylistic influence and even evidence that some earlier monuments were reworked as header or foot stones, and, on the other, Scandinavian-influence, the sculpture suggests a willingness for the elite, whether of Northumbrian or Scandinavian stock, to bury their dead in the same cemetery and to tolerate, if not adopt, aspects of each other's culture.[109]

In a recent study of stone sculpture in Yorkshire and Lincolnshire, David Stocker and Paul Everson observed that in the earlier part of the tenth century many sculptures in both Yorkshire and Lincolnshire were carved on stone acquired from York, including examples of reused Roman masonry. Aside from indicating that York was a centre of sculptural production, they have suggested that the wide distribution of sculptures on

10   Stone sculpture at York Minster. A number of sculptures were excavated
in situ above graves in a cemetery beneath York Minster. This grave-slab
depicts a dragon-like creature and a human figure wielding a sword, which
has been interpreted as the heroic figure Sigurd slaying the dragon. On the
top of the slab is another dragon-like creature, adjacent to which stands a
human figure with its hand raised to its mouth, taken to be a depiction of the
heart-roasting scene, and also a headless torso, believed to represent the
decapitation of Sigurd's treacherous stepfather Reginn.
Length of sculpture is 1.30m

York stone reflects the Archbishop exercising a direct involvement in the
foundation of local churches and their equipment with sculptures.[110]
Stocker has also suggested that the sculptures in York and elsewhere in
Northumbria, attest to a new and self-confident identity, forged from an
amalgamation of Christian and Scandinavian imagery.[111] While they certainly suffered at the hands of Scandinavian raiders and settlers, this sculptural evidence suggests that, nonetheless, churches played an important
role in expressions of regional identity in the early tenth century, and that
the role of the archbishops of York was crucial to this.

From at least the last decade of the ninth century, Scandinavian rule in
Northumbria depended on the support of the archbishops of York. At the

same time, references in the *Chronicle* to the actions of 'the Northumbrians' may reflect the fact that the local aristocracy continued to exert some influence in the political affairs of York and Northumbria more broadly. Consequently, David Rollason has recently concluded that the Scandinavian political impact on Northumbria may not have been as great as at first appears, with the archbishops and the aristocracy continuing to be influential even though the ruling royal dynasties had been removed.[112] While this argument has merit, the numismatic evidence, revealing a diversity of Scandinavian, Northumbrian, West Saxon and continental influences and a dynamism that might not be expected had the Archbishop been in sole charge of its production, implies that the Scandinavians were the dominant political power in York. Yet this dominance doubtless would not have been possible without the active support of the archbishops and the Northumbrian aristocracy.

Anglo–Scandinavian relations in the north and east midlands and East Anglia, c.900–24

Following the Scandinavian conquest of eastern Mercia the *Anglo-Saxon Chronicle* has little to say about how the north and east midlands were organised and ruled. The impression conveyed by numismatic evidence of the late ninth and early tenth century and the *Chronicle* account of the later West Saxon conquest of the region, is that it was divided into a number of territories administered from fortified centres (*burhs*). Once the West Saxon conquest of the Scandinavian-controlled regions commenced, the *Chronicle* implies a relentless and systematic campaign during which the *burhs* and their surrounding territories were captured one after another over the course of around a decade. However, consideration of a wider range of evidence and recent re-examination of aspects of the *Chronicle* account reveals considerably more about the nature of Scandinavian control, the complexity of the challenge faced by the West Saxons and the accommodation forged between West Saxon kings and the ruling classes in the north and east midlands, including those of Scandinavian descent.

Following the death of King Alfred in 899, his successor, Edward the Elder, was challenged from within the West Saxon royal family, from which ensued a series of events that demonstrated the dangers presented by the presence of Scandinavian-controlled territories to the north and east. In 900, Alfred's nephew, Æthelwold, seized royal residences at Wimborne (Wilts) and *Twinham* (at Christchurch, Hants) in an act of rebellion against the new king.[113] He subsequently went to Northumbria, where he was received by the army. According to the C version of the *Chronicle* they 'accepted him as king', although this information is notably not provided in the A version, which has the most West Saxon perspective of all of the versions of the *Chronicle*, and which would scarcely have been inclined to accord Æthelwold regal status.[114] His authority in York is inferred by coins minted there, almost certainly for Æthelwold, in the name of 'ALVVALDVS' (fig. 7).[115] His movements over the following year are uncertain, but in late 901 or early 902 Æthelwold arrived in Essex with a fleet, mustered from an unknown location, where submission was made to him.[116] Essex appears to have remained, or subsequently become, part of Wessex following the Scandinavian settlement of East Anglia, since an Ealdorman Beorhtwulf is noted in the *Chronicle* entry for 896, and Æthelwold may have been preparing to wrest control of Wessex by securing the easterly parts, and the region most difficult for Edward to defend.[117] In the following year, Æthelwold 'induced the army in East Anglia to break the peace' and they raided as far as Cricklade and Braydon (Wilts). Returning eastwards, Æthelwold's army was overtaken by the army of Edward the Elder, and in the *Anglo-Saxon Chronicle*'s account of the battle that ensued, Æthelwold is said to have died alongside the otherwise unknown King Eohric, and 'Brihtsige, son of the *atheling* Beornoth'.[118] The title *atheling* ('throneworthy') and the personal names of these two men suggest that Beornoth and Brihtsige were descendants of one of the royal houses of Mercia, which at this time was under the control of Ealdorman Æthelred and his wife Æthelflaed, daughter of King Alfred.[119] If we are right about their ancestry, this entry in the *Chronicle* suggests that members of two of the royal houses of England were prepared to side with a viking army in pursuit of dynastic ambition.

The account in the *Anglo-Saxon Chronicle* of the West Saxon conquest of the territories controlled by the Scandinavians reveals a little about the political structure in the north and east midlands. In 909, Edward the Elder dispatched an army comprised of West Saxons and Mercians into 'the territory of the northern army', perhaps as a punitive measure, and in 910, after the army in Northumbria 'had broken the peace and raided into Mercia', Edward's forces defeated this army at Tettenhall (Staffs), during which three kings (Eowils, Ivar and Halfdan) and several of their leading followers were killed. Since they are not referred to elsewhere in the documentary record and no coins appear to have been minted in their names, it is not known where they ruled, and they may have been rulers local to the north midlands rather than kings in Northumbria.[120] There is, indeed, other evidence to suggest that control over the north and east midlands was fragmented. For example, coins were minted at various locations in those regions in the late ninth and early tenth century, for a variety of rulers. Examples include the coins minted for an otherwise unknown king, Halfdan, somewhere in the north-east midlands c.900, and, as we have already seen (see p. 36), coins were also minted briefly for Earl Sihtric at Shelford in the late ninth century, while the anonymous St Edmund coins were minted at various places in the east midlands, perhaps indicating that those regions were ruled by a variety of individuals.[121] By at least the second decade of the tenth century, control over these regions was divided among a group of men below the rank of king, such as *jarls* and *holds*, who seem to have been local commanders based in the *burhs*. That, at least, is the implication of references in the *Anglo-Saxon Chronicle* to the armies of Edward the Elder winning the submission of Jarl Thurcytel and 'all the *holds* and the principal men who belonged to Bedford' in 914, and Jarl Thurferth and the *holds* and 'all the army which belonged to Northampton' in 917.[122]

Although the *Chronicle* does not tell us this, it is apparent that the capture and construction of *burhs* in the north and east midlands by Edward and Æthelflaed in the second decade of the tenth century was not the first stage of their expansion, which in turn reveals something of the ways in which Scandinavian settlers interacted with indigenous lords.[123] A charter issued by King Athelstan in 926 confirmed to a certain Uhtred 60 *manentes* of land at Hope and Ashford (Derbys), which he had bought from the heathen at the command of King Edward and Ealdorman Æthelred. This purchase of land must date to some time between the start of Edward's reign in 899 and the death of Ealdorman Æthelred in 911. In another charter of 926, Athelstan again confirmed to an English lord that land that had been purchased from the heathen at the behest of Edward and Æthelred, in this case five *manentes* of land in Chalgrave and Tebworth (Beds) acquired by the thegn Ealdred. This acquisition of land probably followed the peace established in 905 between King Edward and the army of the East Angles and the Northumbrians a little over five miles away at Tiddingford (Bucks).[124] These two charters suggest that before military campaigns in the areas of Scandinavian control were attempted, the West Saxons encouraged supporters to acquire land in those regions.[125] Given that Derby to the south was not captured by Æthelflaed until 917, it appears that for several years Uhtred possessed land within an area of Scandinavian control, although on what terms is unclear. Uhtred was probably a lord from Bernicia, where he also periodically took on Scandinavian raiders (see p. 58). In the period of Scandinavian control of the north and east midlands there were, then, at least some English lords of various allegiances holding land.

In 912 Edward had *burhs* constructed at Hertford, one on either side of the River Lea, and Witham (Essex), and, in 914, *burhs* were constructed on either side of the River Ouse at Buckingham, and in due course Bedford (915), Derby, Towcester (Northants), Tempsford (Beds), Huntingdon, Colchester (Essex) (917), Leicester and Stamford (Lincs) (918) fell to Edward or Æthelflaed.[126] What followed the construction and capture of the *burhs* in Scandinavian-controlled territory is scarcely described by the *Chronicle*, but matters were probably not as straightforward as it generally infers. It is, for example, apparent that Edward was faced not only with the Scandinavian threat, but also with the challenge of controlling Mercia. In 918, when Æthelflaed, who had been ruling in Mercia, died, Edward dealt with any possible challenge from within Mercia by removing Æthelflaed's daughter to a southern monastery. He also received the submission of 'all the nation in the land of the Mercians' at Tamworth (Staffs), and subsequently went to Nottingham where 'all the people who had been settled in Mercia, both Danish and English, submitted to him'.[127] In the following year, Edward ordered new *burhs* to be built at Thelwall (Ches) and Manchester, and in 920 he went to Nottingham and had a second *burh* built on the south side of the River Trent – undertakings which may have had as much to do with securing his authority in Mercia as with the Scandinavian threat.[128] The meagre details provided by the *Chronicle* about the peace negotiations that followed the capture of *burhs* from Scandinavian control imply a succession of formal agreements, although, if they were underpinned by the signing of peace treaties, none of the latter survive. Following the submissions to Edward, arrangements must have been made concerning the staffing and administration of both the *burhs* and their surrounding territories, but few details are recorded. One exception occurs in the *Chronicle* account of Edward's capture of the *burh* at Nottingham in 918, after which he 'ordered it to be repaired and manned both with Englishmen and Danes'.[129] Presumably these Englishmen included followers of Edward left at Nottingham to help secure the *burh*, although they may also have included local men. By this time few of the army involved in the conquest of eastern Mercia in the 870s would have still been alive, and it is likely that those labelled as 'Danes' were a combination of more recent arrivals and the descendants of the original army, and the latter must have included a fair number of sons born to English wives and concubines.

Numismatic evidence reveals that Edward the Elder retained moneyers already operating in various *burhs* under Scandinavian influence. While they may not have been Scandinavians themselves, since many bore continental personal names, their survival owes something to Edward's willingness to retain elements of the existing administrative system. Coins minted in the north-east midlands soon after Edward's conquest adopted the West Saxon weight standard, emphasising the absorption of the mints into the West Saxon administrative machinery. However, coins minted later in Edward's reign bear blundered inscriptions, which, according to Mark Blackburn, is typical of Scandinavian-controlled mints, implying that the *Anglo-Saxon Chronicle* account of Edward's unfaltering conquest of the north and east midlands was not the whole story, as does an anonymous issue from the north-east midlands featuring a hammer and a sword – similar to the sword St Peter coins.[130]

With such reservations about the written record in mind, it is worth scrutinising the *Chronicle* account of Edward's apparent success in establishing his overlordship in various regions in 920:

> Then he [Edward] went from there into the Peak District to Bakewell and ordered a *burh* to be built in the neighbourhood and manned. And then the king of the Scots and all the people of the Scots, and Ragnall, and the sons of Eadwulf and all who live in Northumbria, both English and Danish, Norsemen and others, and also the king of the Strathclyde Welsh and all the Strathclyde Welsh, chose him as father and lord.[131]

This has usually been regarded as relatively straightforward evidence for the submission of the named rulers to Edward the Elder, but more recently Michael Davidson has suggested that the reality may have been more complex – involving peacemaking and the need for these various rulers to gain from their contemporaries recognition of their, often newly won, spheres of influence.[132] We must remember that Edward had only recently begun the conquest of the north midlands, and he appears to have had some concerns about his capacity to control Mercia. Meanwhile, Ragnall had been establishing his position in Northumbria over at least six years, but not without struggle, and had only recently gained control of York. In previous years he had fought in battle at Corbridge against Ealdred and Uhtred, 'the sons of Eadwulf', who were rulers in Bernicia, where they may have been recognised as kings, and against Constantin, king of the Scots.[133] That Ragnall, nevertheless, considered himself Edward's equal may be reflected in his copying of Edward's portrait coinage shortly before this meeting (see p. 47). The relationship between the kings of the Scots and of the Strathclyde Welsh is poorly documented, but the latter appear to have been in a position of subordination to the former.[134] Davidson also notes that there is no supporting evidence for Edward's supposed overlordship, unlike the evidence of coinage and charters from a later date to demonstrate the reality of the *Chronicle*'s comment that his son, Athelstan, 'brought under his rule all the kings that were in this island' in 927 (see p. 64). It is not even certain that all of the named rulers appeared together before Edward. While this new reading of the *Chronicle* entry for 920 is conjectural, it does have the merit of prompting consideration of the likelihood that Edward was really in a position to command such subordination from other rulers, and it raises the possibility that what has been regarded as a relatively straightforward *Chronicle* account masks complex political negotiation.[135] We must remember that the *Chronicle* not only recorded, but also created, history.

The fate of Lindsey (northern Lincolnshire) is undocumented, but it is unlikely that Edward advanced that far, as the region appears to have been under the political control of kings in York. The links between early tenth-century sculptures from Lindsey and York and its hinterland have already been discussed (see p. 52). The influence of the York mint on coins produced in Lincoln in the 920s is identifiable in a coinage in the name of St Martin, which has similarities with the St Peter's coinage, and also in coins almost certainly minted in Lincoln for the York king Sihtric Caoch.[136] In East Anglia the progress of the expansion of Edward's authority is also undocumented, but unlike in the north and east midlands *burhs* do not appear to have been constructed. The St Edmund coinage was replaced by one in Edward's name late in his reign, but these were copies of coins minted in London, often with blundered inscriptions, and were struck, probably at Norwich, to the lighter Anglo–Scandinavian weight standard typical of East Anglian coinage.[137] On numismatic grounds, it is thus considered unlikely that the mint at Norwich ever came under Edward's control.[138] This, and similar numismatic evidence from the north and east midlands (see p. 58), either suggests limitations on the extension of Edward's administrative machinery, or reflects his cultivation of local elites. Either way, the existing Anglo–Scandinavian elite of those regions continued to play an important part in local administration after they had submitted to Edward.

The processes by which Edward secured control over the territories around the *burhs* listed in the *Chronicle* are unclear, but must have involved rewarding followers with land. Unfortunately, there is a dearth of charter material for the second half of Edward's reign. Recently, David Dumville has suggested that this may be more than a mere accident of survival, and that Edward may have deliberately refrained from issuing new land-books, thus avoiding alienating from royal control any further land in the heartlands of his kingdom. Given that it is unreasonable to suppose that Edward did not endow at least some of his most loyal supporters with land, Dumville suggests that Edward may have been rewarding them with land grants in the north and east midlands, and that it may not be accidental that the apparent cessation in the issuing of charters coincides with the beginning of West Saxon conquest of Scandinavian-controlled regions.[139] Indeed, a twelfth-century record (*Liber Eliensis*) of the lands of the monks of Ely (Cambs) alleges that after Edward the Elder captured Huntingdon in 917, he acquired land in the vicinity on a massive scale, and while some of this remained in royal hands, other lands must have been distributed to Edward's followers.[140] What sort of documentation may have followed from the granting of land acquired from Scandinavian lords is, however, unknown, and it does not survive.[141] Many Scandinavian landholders must have fallen in battle, and others were doubtless removed because of the threat to peace that they posed, but others probably retained their land.[142] An indication of how this may have occurred in practice is provided by the *Liber Eliensis*, which incorporates a Latin translation of a lost late tenth-century Old English source recording, among other matters, the history of land at Bluntisham (Hunts). This land had been acquired by Bishop Æthelwold during the reign of King Edgar, but after the king's death the sons of a man called Boga of Hemingford attempted to claim it. They maintained that their uncle, named Tope, was the heir to this land in Bluntisham through the action of his grandmother who had submitted to Edward the Elder at Cambridge earlier in the tenth century. The case of the sons of Boga was judged spurious, because of mistaken claims about when the submission had occurred, nonetheless the account does seem to confirm that voluntary submission to the English king would lead to acknowledgement of property rights, and that at least some Scandinavian landholders retained their lands following the West Saxon conquest.[143]

Some Scandinavians who accepted West Saxon overlordship also retained aspects of their political power. For example, Thurferth, who submitted to Edward in 917, subsequently attested royal charters as *dux* and may have retained some administrative authority in the vicinity of Northampton, while Athelstan's charters were witnessed by others with Scandinavian names, who had presumably also retained some form of local authority in East Anglia or the east midlands, such as Halfdene, who possessed lands in Hertfordshire and Bedfordshire; Scule, who appears to have held lands in Suffolk; and Haddr who appears in the witness lists next to Scule so frequently as to suggest that he, too, was from East Anglia.[144]

Other Scandinavians, however, chose to leave after the West Saxon advance, such as Jarl Thurcytel and 'those men who wanted to follow him' who went across the sea to the land of the Franks 'with the peace and help of King Edward', and it is possible that Edward provided money to facilitate this departure.[145]

There is, then, evidence that reveals Scandinavian control of the north and east midlands to have been fragmented, while some parts of these regions were periodically under the authority of rulers in York or East Anglia, to judge from numismatic evidence. However, the extent of the direct authority of rulers at York and in East Anglia over the east midlands may have been limited by local lords, who appear to have had some freedom of action – at least where the minting of coins, the sale of land and submission to invading powers were concerned. There is also some evidence for English lords holding land in these regions during the period of Scandinavian control. Given the limited range of sources of any type at our disposal for the north and east midlands in the late ninth and early tenth centuries, it is inevitable that we have to approach the period of Scandinavian control largely via the more detailed evidence in the *Anglo-Saxon Chronicle* for subsequent West Saxon conquest. Yet our understanding of the extent of West Saxon authority during Edward's reign, and the means by which control was established, depends on examination of a wide range of sources, on reconsidering the apparently straightforward entries in the *Chronicle* and, in the case of charters, perhaps also requires us to be sensitive to the significance of absence of evidence. The impression that emerges is of regional identities remaining relevant after West Saxon conquest, and of compromise between Edward and his representatives and the local elites, who were of both local and Scandinavian descent.

Anglo–Scandinavian relations in the north-west, c.902–45

Much of the impact of Scandinavians on the north-west of England is undocumented. The region appears to have escaped the attentions of the 'great army' in the 860s and 870s, but it was certainly raided and settled by Scandinavians, probably both via Ireland and also from the eastern part of Northumbria, to judge from the place-name evidence, and Scandinavian and Irish influences on stone sculpture and other forms of material culture, including jewellery.[146] The *Annals of Ulster* record that a group of Scandinavian raiders were driven from their base on the River Liffey in 902, and this is believed to be the group led by one Ingimund, which, according to another Irish source, 'The Three Fragments of Irish Annals', failed in an attempt to land in Wales and then proceeded to Chester. Æthelflaed is said to have made peace and granted Ingimund land, and the concentration of Scandinavian place-names in the Wirral peninsula has been taken as evidence for the location of this endowment.[147] Ingimund subsequently attempted to take Chester, but was repulsed by the Mercians, and two Welsh chronicles (*Annales Cambriae* and *Brut y Tywysogion*) record the defeat of the forces of 'Ogmundr', believed to be the same man as Ingimund, in a battle in 905 at a place called *Ros Melion*, probably on Anglesey. Æthelflaed's repair of the defences at Chester in 907 is often regarded as a response to the actions of Ingimund, although the Welsh dimension should not be overlooked, and conflict with the Welsh may have been a factor prompting the subsequent construction of other *burhs* in the area, including Eddisbury (914), Runcorn (915), Thelwall (919), Manchester (919) and *Cledemutha*, believed to be Rhuddlan (Flints) (921).[148]

One of the few written accounts of raids on the north-west concerns a certain Alfred who, according to the *History of Saint Cuthbert*, 'came over the mountains in the west . . . fleeing pirates' and sought the protection of the community of St Cuthbert.[149] Presumably he lost his lands in the process. Another possible example of Scandinavian expropriation is suggested by King Athelstan's purchase of land at Amounderness (Lancs) in the 930s, as it is declared that 'I bought [it] with no little money of my own' in a charter granting this land to the Archbishop of York, while in a later version of the charter in the *Chronicle of the Archbishops of York* it is added that the land was bought 'from the pagans', perhaps from the 'Agmundr *hold*' whose name and title were incorporated in the place-name.[150] Further north, a dynasty referred to as the kings of Cumbria emerged in the tenth century. It used to be thought that this referred to the kings of Strathclyde, who themselves had been a cadet branch of the kings of the Scots since 889 when a viking sack of Dumbarton had ended the native dynasty of Strathclyde. However, more recently it has been argued that the kings of Cumbria may have emerged from among the local elite in the wake of the collapse of the Northumbrian dynasty. According to this interpretation, the British place-names in the far north-west were not reintroduced by the kings of Strathclyde, but were survivals from the pre-English period in this region. In this respect, the kings of Cumbria may be the counterparts to the earls of Bamburgh in the north-eastern part of Northumbria, with both reflecting the re-emergence of a native ruling dynasty in the wake of the political disruptions of the later ninth century.[151]

Sculptures from the north-west not only combine Anglo-Saxon and Christian imagery with Scandinavian styles and motifs, but are also often influenced by Irish art. For example, the head of the Gosforth (Cumb) cross has a 'Celtic' form, and many other crosses, in Cumbria and Cheshire in particular, are wheel-headed in the Irish fashion (fig. 31).[152] David Griffiths has recently argued that such displays were prompted by a desire for Scandinavian lords to create a new forward-looking statement of authority in tandem with indigenous symbols of power. He has contrasted this form of display with the elaborate mound burials of the region, which he suggests represent the Scandinavian elite making more conservative statements about their Norwegian background, arguing that they were broadly contemporary responses to a fast-changing political and settlement context. These statements were created within the context of an Irish Sea cultural zone, and parallel statements can be found in Ireland and the Isle of Man.[153]

The progress of West Saxon conquest of the north-west of England is scarcely known. The submission of various northern rulers to King Athelstan at Eamont Bridge (Cumb) in 927 (see p. 64), and the King's purchase of land at Amounderness, may have been defensive strategies rather than the first stage of an attempt to conquer the north-west. Athelstan may have adapted a policy initiated by his father of bolstering West Saxon conquest of Scandinavian-ruled territories by purchases of large landed estates, and this land may have been intended as a buffer zone against Norse raids from the west.[154] That the region was hostile to the West Saxons, not simply because of its Scandinavian contingent, is indicated by the presence of King Owain of Cumbria among those defeated in battle by Athelstan at the unidentified *Brunanburh* in 937.[155] In 945, according to the *Anglo-Saxon Chronicle*, King Edmund 'ravaged all Cumberland', using the land conquered to seal an alliance with King Malcolm of the Scots; while, according to Roger of Wendover, the sons of King Dunmail of the Cumbrians were blinded.[156] Beyond this, there is little to indicate that the north-west was brought within the realm of the West Saxon kings, and significantly, perhaps, even by the time of Domesday Book, the administrative system of the English kings does not appear to have been fully extended into this region.[157] It is apparent that the Scandinavian influence was but one of the factors that shaped political developments in this region.[158]

Anglo–Scandinavian relations in the east midlands, East Anglia and the Kingdom of York, c.924–54

Upon his death in 924, Edward the Elder was succeeded by his younger son Ælfweard in Wessex and in Mercia by his eldest son Athlestan, but within a month Ælfweard was dead and Athelstan succeeded to the whole of his father's realm.[159] Meanwhile, Ragnall had been succeeded as king in York in 920 or 921 by his kinsman Sihtric Caoch from Dublin. In 926 Sihtric and Athelstan met at Tamworth, and the West Saxon king gave his sister in marriage to the northern king, in a diplomatic strategy adopted by Athelstan on several other occasions in his dealings with fellow rulers.[160] Roger of Wendover's thirteenth-century version of the *Chronicle* records that Sihtric was baptised, and it is not unreasonable to believe that this would have been a minimum requirement for Athelstan to sanction the marriage of his sister to Sihtric. Roger also alleges that neither the conversion nor the marriage were long-lived.[161] Following the death of Sihtric in 927, Athelstan asserted influence over the north, when he 'brought under his rule' the kings of the Scots, the West Welsh, Strathclyde and Gwent and the lord of Bamburgh, Ealdred. Peace was established with pledges and oaths at Eamont, and the rulers also 'renounced all idolatry' – a curious phrase which may have referred to the relationship between Constantin, king of the Scots, and Guthfrith, then ruling in Dublin – the latter being was the most obvious candidate to be referred to as an idolator.[162] Indeed, the *Anglo-Saxon Chronicle* records that Athelstan subsequently expelled King Guthfrith, who, according to a later source, was then in Strathclyde. It is possible that he was the brother of Sihtric Caoch, and later sources indicate that after his expulsion Athelstan took control of York, implying that Guthfrith's rule was centred on York.[163]

Athelstan's involvement in the north extended beyond York, and he made a number of substantial grants of land to northern churches. The *History of Saint Cuthbert* preserves a record of Athelstan's gifts to the community of St Cuthbert in 934 – including a large estate at South Wearmouth (Northumb), in addition to books, vestments, and precious ornaments. Association with St Cuthbert also provided useful support for Athelstan's rule in southern England, and the king had a collection of hagiographical and liturgical manuscripts in honour of the saint compiled for use in Wessex.[164] The strength of Athelstan's claim to authority over the various rulers of Britain is reflected in the subscription of various *subreguli* and men with Scandinavian names to his charters, and in the imperial titles adopted in his charters and on his coins. Athelstan's control over York was emphasised by the minting of coins in his name there in which he was styled, as on most mints to the south and west of Watling Street, as *rex to(tius) Brit(anniae)*.[165] It is, however, worth noting that moneyers in Mercia and Northumbria eschewed the depiction of the king's head that was common on coins minted in Wessex, which may be a reflection of the political sensibilities of these districts.[166] Nonetheless, during Athelstan's reign the weight standard of the York coinage was gradually increased, to bring it in line with West Saxon coinage.[167] At this time the practice of naming the moneyers at York was introduced. Most had Frankish names (such as Regnald, Durant, Rernart and Wadter) implying that Scandinavian rulers in York had brought in continental moneyers to set up the mints, as in the east midlands and East Anglia where such names appear from the 880s, and also that they continued to work for their new rulers.[168] Athelstan appears to have ruled York until his death in 939, although his authority was briefly challenged by Olaf, the son of Guthfrith, who had allied himself with King Constantin of the Scots and possibly married his daughter. However, Olaf and his allies were decisively defeated in battle by Athelstan in 937 at *Brunanburh*.[169]

From c.932, East Anglia was under the control of Ealdorman Athelstan, a son of one of the late ninth-century sub-ealdormen of Mercia, Æthelfrith. The area of jurisdiction of Athelstan, known in later sources as 'Half-King', appears to have extended beyond Norfolk and Suffolk into Northamptonshire, Cambridgeshire, Huntingdonshire and the fenland of Lincolnshire. He was assisted by numerous men with Scandinavian names, who were either newly arrived settlers or the sons of earlier settlers, indicating that the administration of this part of King Athelstan's realm was an Anglo–Scandinavian affair.[170] The impact of Athelstan 'Half-King' may be reflected in the quality and consistency of the coinage minted at Norwich, where all the coins depict the royal bust of Athelstan crowned. These 'highly competent products' replaced the less-accomplished workmanship of coins minted in the name of Edward and also the later St Edmund coins, both of which were characterised by blundered inscriptions.[171]

Upon the death of King Athelstan in 939, Olaf returned from Dublin and took York, and, as we have seen (see p. 51), in 940 he raided the midlands as far south as Northampton, accompanied by Archbishop Wulfstan. Returning northwards he was met at Leicester by the army of Athelstan's successor, his brother Edmund. Battle was averted by the archbishops of York and Canterbury who arranged a peace, following which Olaf was given the territory between Watling Street and Northumbria, and coins were subsequently minted in his name in the territory of the Five Boroughs.[172] The following year, Olaf died and was replaced by a kinsman, Olaf Cuarán, who in 942 lost to Edmund the lands won in 940. Peace was subsequently made with Edmund, but it was not a long-lived arrangement, as Olaf, and another ruler, Ragnall Guthfrithson, were driven out of York in 944 and Edmund 'reduced all Northumbria under his rule'.[173]

Like his brother before him, Edmund also sought to secure his authority in his newly won territories by endowing land on individuals and institutions from whom he could reasonably expect support. In 942 he granted a group of estates in the middle Trent valley to Wulfsige the Black, probably a member of a leading Mercian family. This was a strategically important grant straddling the River Trent and the main access road between Derby and Nottingham to the north and Lichfield and Tamworth to the south. This grant was presumably made after the capture of the Five Boroughs in the same year, but Edmund's control over this region cannot have been well established, and the grant should be seen as a measure to exert royal authority in new territories through the efforts of local lords rewarded with substantial landed properties.[174] Edmund also patronised the community of St Cuthbert, and it has been suggested that the growing links between the community and the house of Wessex may have prompted the incorporation of a passage on King Alfred into the *History of Saint Cuthbert*. The passage in question provides an account of the miracles that St Cuthbert allegedly performed for the king while he was in hiding from viking raiders in the Somerset marshlands in 878, and it states that St Cuthbert assured Alfred that he and his descendants would in future rule over all Britain. Although once thought to have been an eleventh-century interpolation, more recently Luisella Simpson has suggested that the Alfred passage may have been composed in the wake of Edmund's visit to Chester-le-Street, probably in 944 or 945, when he commended himself and his men to God and the community, and offered sixty pounds, two gold bracelets and two Greek pallia. Contemporary political circumstances meant that the community was important to underpinning West Saxon royal authority in northern England, and it may, as David Rollason has observed, have been an important counterbalance to the rebellious church in York.[175] The rewards offered to the community may have been the context in which it sought to extend back in time its links with Wessex.[176]

Following Edmund's death in 946, he was succeeded by his brother Eadred, who secured pledges and oaths from the Northumbrians. This was not necessarily an act of submission to Eadred, and it may be that the King was forced to come to terms with the northern elite, as it is notable that the meeting between the two sides occurred at Tanshelf near what was probably a territorial frontier.[177] Moreover, the Northumbrians were soon 'false to it all', and accepted as their king, Eric Blood-axe, son of King Harold Fairhair of Norway. King Eadred then ravaged Northumbria, although part of his army was defeated at Castleford (Yorks). His threat to return to Northumbria and 'destroy it utterly' prompted the councillors of the Northumbrians to desert Eric, as we have seen (see p. 51). The events of the following years are confused, but Olaf Cuarán appears to have returned to Northumbria in 949, only to be driven out upon the return of Eric in 952. Eric ruled the Northumbrians until he was expelled by them two years later, and Eadred succeeded to the kingdom of Northumbria.[178] Roger of Wendover states that Eric was betrayed by Earl Oswulf, lord of Bamburgh, and killed by one Earl Maccus, an otherwise unknown character, suggesting that the eventual capture of York by the West Saxons may have had much to do with political rivalry within Northumbria.[179] It may not have been immediately apparent, but the expulsion of Eric effectively brought the age of viking rule in northern England to an end, and from this point onwards Northumbria was governed by earls appointed by the West Saxons, now kings of England.[180]

Ethnic identities: the political and legal framework of England in the later tenth and early eleventh centuries

From the very earliest stages of conquest and settlement, there was a need for indigenous rulers to devise strategies to facilitate the incorporation of the settlers into the social, political and legal structure of England. Although the treaty between Alfred and Guthrum is a sole surviving example of the written diplomacy between a ninth-century Scandinavian lord and an English ruler, it is clear, as we have seen, that diplomatic negotiations between Scandinavian and English lords were common, and Anglo–Scandinavian relations were sometimes enshrined in written codes. For example, Edward the Elder's Exeter law-code (presumably pre-dating his capture of the east midlands) refers to the lost 'written peace settlements' (friðgewritu) addressing legal matters outside his 'own kingdom . . . in the east or in the north'.[181] The incorporation into the English kingdom of successive generations of Scandinavian settlers and their descendants was accompanied by a need to handle the regional identities of various parts of England, and Matthew Innes has recently argued that these two identities were brought together in successive legislation issued in the tenth and eleventh centuries.[182] Edgar, for example, legislated in his fourth law-code (possibly of the 970s) that 'secular rights should be in force among the Danes according to such good laws as they best decide on'.[183] Any argument that he was encouraging the settlers and their descendants to live under separate legal codes from the indigenous stock is difficult to sustain: how, for example, would the descendants of earlier generations have been identifiable after a century of social mixing and intermarriage?[184]

Accordingly, more recent interpretations have looked to the political context of the legislation. It is, for example, apparent that the political and legal activities of all southern kings from the mid-tenth century were tempered by regional interests. This was reflected in the frequent appointment of men to positions of authority in northern England, i.e. men who had landed interests both in the North or north midlands and also further south, in order to ensure both their loyalty and the acceptance of the appointment by the northern lords. At the same time, the archbishopric of York was held in plurality with a see further south for much of the mid- to late tenth century, doubtless to militate against any Archbishop behaving in the manner of Wulfstan.[185] Edgar's code was addressed to the ealdormen of East Anglia, Northumbria and Mercia, and was apparently intended as a companion code to one outlining the measures for the rest of England, and the separate provision for 'the Danes' may have been intended to help maintain a semblance of political unity by recognition of regional legal traditions, and it may also have been intended to foster good relations with the northern part of the kingdom, where Edgar had reigned for two years from 957, while his brother, Eadwig, ruled in Wessex.[186] The use of ethnic terminology in Edgar's law-code may have been prompted by the recent history of the region and the background of some of its elite, and perhaps also by the more recent arrival of Danish merchants or mercenaries. Indeed, an early eleventh-century panegyric added to the *Anglo-Saxon Chronicle* complained that Edgar 'attracted hither foreigners and enticed harmful people to this country'.[187] It is notable, however, that while he was ruling in the North, Edgar's conception of this territory, as expressed in the terms of one of his charters, was that it consisted of 'the Mercians, Northumbrians and Britons'; in that context, at least, 'the Danes' were not identified as a separate part of his kingdom.[188]

While the West Saxon rule of the former areas of Scandinavian control in the later tenth century does not form a central theme of the present volume, and neither do the subsequent Scandinavian raids or the eventual accession of the Danish King Cnut to the English throne in 1016, it is nonetheless important to consider aspects of these events in order to establish the long-term political impact of the earlier Scandinavian conquests. Æthelred II legislated for the areas of earlier Scandinavian settlement, when he issued a law-code at Wantage (Berks), probably in 997, which concerned the territory of the Five Boroughs.[189] This code incorporates much Scandinavian terminology, in contrast to a broadly contemporary code issued at Woodstock (Oxon), said to be 'according to the laws of the English'. However, the Wantage code does not provide evidence for a kingdom riven by ethnic difference, which could be recognised by the king in objective, legal terms. As Patrick Wormald has observed, 'no West Saxon king or council could have produced a code so thoroughly Scandinavian in form and content', and he has concluded that the code must have been drawn up by men familiar with the situation in northern England, and have been heavily influenced by regional interests and preoccupations. While it was royal law, intent on introducing some rules and practices from Wessex into the territory of the Five Boroughs and perhaps elsewhere in northern England, in its execution it was also effectively a local product created by men from that region. Thus, the Wantage code reveals the need to legislate separately for this region, and exposes the influence of local men on the expression of regional legal provision, but the form and content of this law-code does not support the case for ethnic separatism within parts of northern England.[190]

The practice of recognising the distinctive legal traditions of northern and eastern England was continued into the eleventh century, when a series of law-codes associated with Archbishop Wulfstan II of York follow the precedent set by Edgar of acknowledging these traditions as Danish. In c.1008 Wulfstan first made use of the term *Dena lagu* ('the law of the Danes', although it is usually rendered as 'Danelaw' by modern commentators), which was intended to distinguish the legal traditions in northern and eastern England from those of Mercia and Wessex.[191] Wulfstan legislated for both Æthelred and Cnut, and the conquest by the latter and the presence of his followers among the court elite provided a new and pressing dimension for the expression of the duality of Danes and English within the laws of the kingdom. Moreover, Wulfstan consciously looked to the past for the basis of this legal provision. For example, in the so-called 'Laws of Edward and Guthrum' (which, while purporting to be an agreement between Alfred, Edward the Elder and the viking leader Guthrum, was drawn up by Wulfstan) the Archbishop looked back to the days 'when the English and the Danes unreservedly entered into relationships of peace and friendship'.[192] What emerges from the legislation associated with Wulfstan, as Innes argues, is acknowledgement that the law of the kingdom was based on accommodation between the Danes and the English, and this came to be the template for political organisation and negotiation between the regional elite and the kings of England.[193] When, on his accession to the throne, Cnut declared that the laws of Edgar would be observed, he was looking back to the reign of a not only glorious king, but also one renowned for bringing foreigners into his realm.[194] Thus, the use of the Danish label in legal contexts was as likely to have been influenced by regional interests, political pressures and perhaps by the renewed Scandinavian threat as by the weight of numbers of Scandinavian settlers of several generations earlier.

Conclusions

Throughout this discussion, a diverse range of evidence has been adduced, and an important conclusion to emerge is that, whatever the merits of the case made, there is ample evidence with which to discuss Anglo–Scandinavian political interaction and accommodation in most regions of northern and eastern England. Although it is difficult to determine the intent of the viking raiders on England from the available evidence, on the basis of their actions it appears that a major concern was to take control of various parts of England and to establish themselves as rulers. This marked a distinct change of policy, and in doing so a succession of Scandinavian leaders of war-bands quickly adopted a style of rule similar to that of indigenous rulers, and they sometimes even looked to the broader international context, drawing on influences from Frankia and Ireland, as we have seen. Once removed from their background, and as they sought to establish themselves in an unstable environment, it is perhaps not surprising that these rulers should have come so quickly to adopt the trappings of lordship prevalent in England, including the issuing of coinage, reliance on the support of the Church, and the use of literacy, and to have found ways to interact with local rulers. That some Scandinavian leaders were described as kings in Anglo-Saxon sources suggests, as Patrick Wormald has put it, that the term 'was used consciously, because it expressed a quality which set some viking leaders apart from others, and which was recognisably royal in European terms'.[195] In this respect it is difficult to escape the conclusion that collaboration with ecclesiastics was a major factor prompting this contemporary perception. Furthermore, the minting of coins in many regions of Scandinavian conquest reflects, as Simon Keynes has commented, the desire of these new rulers 'to furnish themselves with the trappings of respectable royal government'.[196]

Periodically, however, Scandinavian rulers made statements referring to their Scandinavian, pagan background, including, for example, the use of Old Norse on the coins of Olaf Guthfrithson, the display of pagan motifs on stone sculptures (see pp. 215–19), and short-lived elaborate funerary displays (discussed in chapter 6). This was arguably more than a passive display of Scandinavian-ness, and appears to have been prompted by the occasional need to make statements of group identity. Yet such displays were also influenced by the internal politics of England. We can, for example, locate Olaf Guthfrithson's Old Norse expression of kingship on his coins within the context of rivalry between Northumbria and Wessex, while elaborate funerary displays under mounds in the north-west may owe much to the Irish Sea context, which was clearly influential on this region long before, as well as during, the Scandinavian settlements.[197] It is apparent that despite the Scandinavian conquests and settlement, the regional identities of many parts of England either survived more-or-less intact, or were rejuvenated. In Northumbria, for example, the kingdom became fragmented, with the Scandinavian kings based at York apparently ruling only in southern Northumbria; while north-eastern Northumbria was ruled by the earls of Bamburgh, who may have been descended from the earlier kings of Bernicia, one of the kingdoms of which Northumbria was comprised; and in north-western Northumbria the shadowy kings of Cumbria emerged, who may have been descendants of earlier British rulers. Regional politics and the relationship of various regions to the crown remained important, and were not superseded, so much as compli-cated, by responses to the Scandinavian settlement.[198] Thus, when dis-cussing the Scandinavian impact and ensuing Anglo–Scandinavian political relations, we cannot think solely in terms of a single indigenous response. Similarly, the ways in which the Scandinavian conquerors ruled their new territories varied greatly, both across England and over time. A recent discussion of the Scandinavians in the north-west concluded, in a statement that is also applicable more broadly to the political scene in northern and eastern England in the late ninth and earlier tenth centuries, that this was 'truly a place where the binary concept of "native" and "immi-grant" are wholly inadequate to explain the complexity of the situation'.[199]

Notes

1 L. Abrams and D. N. Parsons, 'Place-names and the history of Scandinavian set-tlement in England', in J. Hines, A. Lane and M. Redknap (eds), *Land, Sea and Home* (London, 2004), pp. 379–431, at 388.

2 S. Keynes and M. Lapidge, *Alfred the Great. Asser's Life of King Alfred and Other Contemporary Sources* (Harmondsworth, 1983), p. 85; *EHD I*, p. 196.

3 Keynes and Lapidge, *Alfred the Great*, p. 249; C. Thomas-Edwards, 'Alliances, godfathers, treaties and boundaries', in M. A. S. Blackburn and D. N. Dumville (eds), *Kings, Currency and Alliances. History and coinage of southern England in the ninth century* (Woodbridge, 1998), pp. 47–62.

4 J. L. Nelson, *The Annals of St-Bertin* (Manchester, 1991), p. 185; *idem*, 'The Frankish Empire', in P. H. Sawyer (ed.), *The Oxford Illustrated History of the Vikings* (Oxford, 1997), pp. 19–47, at 23, 33. Harald was not at that point raiding

Frankia, and Louis had been championing his cause against rivals in the Danish territories.

5   *EHD I*, p. 200.

6   Æthelstan had ruled the eastern part of the West Saxon domains (roughly Sussex, Surrey, Kent and Essex) under his father, King Æthelwulf: Keynes and Lapidge, *Alfred the Great*, pp. 231–2

7   This king is known only from his coins: P. Wormald, 'The ninth century', in J. Campbell (ed.), *The Anglo-Saxons* (London, 1982), pp. 132–57, at 135.

8   *EHD I*, p. 196.

9   D. N. Dumville, *Wessex and England from Alfred to Edgar* (Woodbridge, 1992), p. 7, n. 37.

10 *EHD I*, p. 196.

11 There are two slightly different Old English versions of the treaty surviving in this collection (Corpus Christi College, Cambridge MS 383): Keynes and Lapidge, *Alfred the Great*, pp. 171–2, 311–13.

12 R. H. C. Davis, 'East Anglia and the Danelaw', *TRHS*, 5th ser., 5 (1955), 23–39, at 33–7.

13 Various attempts to date the treaty are discussed in Dumville, *Wessex and England*, pp. 13–18.

14 *EHD I*, p. 199; F. M. Stenton, *Anglo-Saxon England* (3rd edn, Oxford, 1971), p. 260.

15 M. A. S. Blackburn, 'The London mint in the reign of Alfred', in Blackburn and Dumville (eds), *Kings, Currency and Alliances*, pp. 105–25.

16 Dumville, *Wessex and England*, pp. 19–20.

17 P. Wormald, *The Making of English Law: King Alfred to the twelfth century* (Oxford, 1999), p. 286; P. Kershaw, 'The Alfred–Guthrum treaty: scripting accommodation and interaction in Viking Age England', in D. M. Hadley and J. D. Richards (eds), *Cultures in Contact: Scandinavian settlement in England in the ninth and tenth centuries* (Turnhout, 2000), pp. 43–64, at 48–50.

18 Discussed in *ibid.*, pp. 46–7; see also Dumville, *Wessex and England*, pp. 18–19; D. H. Hill, *An Atlas of Anglo-Saxon England* (Oxford, 1981), pp. 43–7, 97–8.

19 Kershaw, 'The Alfred–Guthrum treaty', p. 58.

20 *Ibid.*, pp. 48, 51–2, 58.

21 Dumville, *Wessex and England*, p. 20, n. 97; Kershaw, 'The Alfred–Guthrum treaty', p. 57; Keynes and Lapidge, *Alfred the Great*, p. 83.

22 Kershaw, 'The Alfred–Guthrum treaty', pp. 57–8

23 *Ibid.*, p. 58; see also M. Innes, 'Danelaw identities: ethnicity, regionalism and political allegiance', in Hadley and Richards (eds), *Cultures in Contact*, pp. 65–88.

24 Kershaw, 'The Alfred–Guthrum treaty', pp. 58–9.

25 *Ibid.*, pp. 55–6.

26 M. A. S. Blackburn, 'Expansion and control: aspects of Anglo-Scandinavian minting south of the Humber', in J. Graham-Campbell, R. A. Hall, J. Jesch and D. Parsons (eds), *Vikings and the Danelaw. Select papers from the proceedings of the Thirteenth Viking Congress* (Oxford, 2001), pp. 125–42, at 127–8; *idem*,

'Currency under the Vikings. Part 1. Guthrum and the earliest Danelaw coinages' (*British Numismatic Journal*, hereafter: *BNJ*, forthcoming).

27 The few coins that are known to have been minted in Scandinavia are found in the trading centres of the region and are largely copies of continental coins: J. Graham-Campbell (ed.), *Cultural Atlas of the Vikings* (New York, 1994), pp. 81–2.

28 Blackburn, 'Expansion and control', pp. 128–30; on the moneyers' names, see V. Smart, 'Scandinavians, Celts and Germans in Anglo-Saxon England: the evidence of moneyers' names', in M. A. S. Blackburn (ed.), *Anglo-Saxon Monetary History* (Leicester, 1986), pp. 171–84, at 175–6.

29 *EHD I*, p. 198; discussed in Dumville, *Wessex and England*, p. 8. Given the disputes over the dating of the treaty between Alfred and Guthrum, it is uncertain whether this naval encounter occurred before or after the treaty was created.

30 *EHD I*, pp. 202–5; Dumville, *Wessex and England*, pp. 8–9.

31 Blackburn, 'Expansion and control', pp. 126–8.

32 *Ibid.*, p. 136.

33 *EHD I*, p. 200.

34 King Eohric, who was killed in battle in 904 fighting on the side of Alfred's nephew Æthelwold (see p. 55), was not necessarily the King of East Anglia, as is assumed in *EHD I*, p. 208 and n. 11; see Dumville, *Wessex and England*, p. 8, n. 41.

35 Blackburn, 'Expansion and control', pp. 135–6.

36 C. E. Blunt, B. H. I. H. Stewart and C. S. S. Lyon, *Coinage in Tenth-Century England. From Edward the Elder to Edgar's reform* (Oxford, 1989), pp. 100–2; Blackburn, 'Expansion and control', pp. 132–3.

37 *Ibid.*, p. 136.

38 J. Campbell, 'What is not known about the reign of Edward the Elder', in N. J. Higham and D. H. Hill (eds), *Edward the Elder 899–924* (Manchester, 2001), pp. 12–24, at 18–21; this evidence is also discussed in Abrams and Parsons, 'Place-names', pp. 415–21.

39 M. Biddle and B. Kjølbye-Biddle, 'Repton and the "great heathen army", 873–4', in Graham-Campbell, Hall, Jesch and Parsons (eds), *Vikings and the Danelaw*, pp. 45–96; J. D. Richards, 'Boundaries and cult centres: Viking burial in Derbyshire', in *ibid.* pp. 97–104.

40 Kershaw, 'The Alfred–Guthrum treaty', pp. 44–5.

41 E. Craster, 'The patrimony of St Cuthbert', *English Historical Review*, hereafter: *EHR*, 69 (1954), 177–99; L. Simpson, 'The King Alfred/St Cuthbert episode in the *Historia de Sancto Cuthberto*: its significance for mid-tenth-century English history', in G. Bonner, D. Rollason and C. Stancliffe (eds), *St Cuthbert, His Cult and His Community to AD 1200* (Woodbridge, 1989), pp. 397–411; D. W. Rollason, *Sources for York History to AD 1100*, The Archaeology of York, 1 (York, 1998), p. 22. More recently, it has been suggested that it was compiled for the first time in the eleventh century, but drawing on earlier texts: T. J. South, *Historia de Sancto Cuthberto. A history of Saint Cuthbert and a record of his patrimony* (Cambridge, 2002), pp. 25–36. On the seven years' wanderings, see *ibid.*, pp. 59, 96–101.

42 *Ibid.*, p. 53; D. W. Rollason, 'The wanderings of St Cuthbert', in D. W. Rollason (ed.), *Cuthbert, Saint and Patron* (Durham, 1987), pp. 45–59, at 47.

43 *Ibid.*, pp. 46–50; E. Cambridge, 'Why did the community of St Cuthbert settle at Chester-le-Street?', in Bonner, Stancliffe and Rollason (eds), *St Cuthbert*, pp. 367–86, at 378, n. 43.

44 Rollason, 'The wanderings of St Cuthbert', pp. 50, 54–7.

45 Cambridge, 'Why did the community of St Cuthbert settle at Chester-le-Street?', p. 385.

46 The evidence for continuity at Lindisfarne is discussed in chapter 5, pp. 196–9.

47 Cambridge, 'Why did the community of St Cuthbert settle at Chester-le-Street?', pp. 385–6; D. W. Rollason, *Northumbria 500–1100: creation and destruction of a kingdom* (Cambridge, 2003), pp. 246–7.

48 South, *Historia de Sancto Cuthberto*, pp. 53, 59–63, 89, 95; W. M. Aird, *St Cuthbert and the Normans* (Woodbridge, 1998), p. 36.

49 South, *Historia de Sancto Cuthberto*, p. 53; Rollason, *Northumbria*, p. 246.

50 South, *Historia de Sancto Cuthberto*, pp. 59, 95.

51 Aird, *St Cuthbert and the Normans*, p. 35.

52 South, *Historia de Sancto Cuthberto*, p. 51.

53 Rollason, *Sources for York History*, pp. 63–4.

54 The ring may have been similar to that with which viking raiders made peace with King Alfred in 876 when they 'swore him oaths on the sacred ring': *EHD I*, p. 194; Rollason, *Northumbria 500–1100*, p. 246.

55 Innes, 'Danelaw identities', p. 79; L. Abrams, 'The conversion of the Danelaw', in Graham-Campbell, Hall, Jesch and Parsons (eds), *Vikings and the Danelaw*, pp. 31–44, at 37.

56 A. Campbell, *The Chronicle of Æthelweard* (Edinburgh, 1962), p. 51. The twelfth-century *History of the Kings* gives the date of Guthred's death as 894, and the similarity of the date to that offered by Æthelweard for the death of Guthfrith increases the likelihood that Guthred and Guthfrith are the same person: Rollason, *Sources for York History*, p. 64.

57 This strategy was at some point successful, as land in York was recorded among the possessions of the Bishop of Durham in the Domesday Book: Aird, *St Cuthbert and the Normans*, pp. 18–19. It is likely that the Cnut and Siefrid known only from their coinage succeeded Guthred/Guthfrith in York, rather than ruling contemporaneously: M. Dolley, 'The Anglo-Danish and Anglo-Norse coinages of York', in R. A. Hall (ed.), *Viking Age York and the North*, CBA Research Rep., 27 (London, 1978), pp. 26–31, at 26; Rollason, *Sources for York History*, pp. 63, 65, 177–8.

58 M. A. S. Blackburn, 'The Ashton hoard and the currency of the southern Danelaw in the late ninth century', *BNJ*, 59 (1989), 13–38, at 18–20.

59 Campbell, *The Chronicle of Æthelweard*, p. 51. Alfred's interest may have been connected with claims to the traditional dowry-land of the Mercian queens, given that his daughter was married to the Mercian ruler, Æthelred: P. A. Stafford, *The East Midlands in the Early Middle Ages* (Leicester, 1985), pp. 112–14.

60 South, *Historia de Sancto Cuthberto*, pp. 61, 105–6; on Ragnall's career, see Rollason, *Sources for York History*, p. 66.

61 South, *Historia de Sancto Cuthberto*, pp. 63, 107.

62   Although the *History of Saint Cuthbert* provides two accounts of Ragnall fighting
     at Corbridge, it is possible that there was only a single battle, of which the text gives
     two accounts. Indeed, Irish sources refer to a single battle at Corbridge, occurring
     in 918, although Bishop Cuthheard, said to have encountered Onlafbal after the
     battle at Corbridge, is believed to have died in 915: South, *Historia de Sancto
     Cuthberto*, pp. 105–9.

63   *Ibid.*, pp. 63, 106, where it is noted that the wording of the text makes it unclear
     whether Ælstan was the brother of Esbrid or Eadred. The distribution of land by
     Ragnall is discussed in chapter 3, pp. 84–5.

64   South, *Historia de Sancto Cuthberto*, p. 63.

65   *Ibid.*, pp. 61–2.

66   *Ibid.*, pp. 107–8.

67   R. Cramp, *Corpus of Anglo-Saxon Stone Sculpture, Vol. 1. County Durham and
     Northumberland* (Oxford, 1984), pp. 31–2, 53–9.

68   *Ibid.*, pp. 80–90.

69   C. D. Morris, 'Aspects of Scandinavian settlement in northern England: a review',
     North. Hist., 20 (1984), 1–22, at 8.

70   C. D. Morris, 'Viking and native in northern England: a case-study', in H. Bekker-
     Nielsen, P. Foote and O. Olsen (eds), *Proceedings of the Eighth Viking Congress*
     (Odense, 1981), pp. 223–44, at 229–33.

71   Cramp, *County Durham and Northumberland*, pp. 29, 81, 87.

72   See also Rollason, *Northumbria 500–1100*, p. 255.

73   Dolley, 'The Anglo–Danish and Anglo–Norse coinages of York', p. 26; M. A. S.
     Blackburn, 'The coinage of Scandinavian York', in R. A. Hall (ed.), *Aspects of
     Anglo–Scandinavian York*, The Archaeology of York, 8 (4) (York, 2004),
     pp. 325–49, at 329.

74   *Ibid.*

75   *Ibid.*, pp. 330–1.

76   Compare Rollason, *Northumbria 500–1100*, pp. 224–8 with Blackburn, 'The
     coinage of Scandinavian York', pp. 331–2.

77   *Ibid.*

78   *Ibid.*

79   Blunt, Stewart and Lyon, *Coinage in Tenth-Century England*, pp. 103–6;
     Blackburn, 'The coinage of Scandinavian York', pp. 332–5.

80   Although the historical sources give contradictory information about when
     Ragnall captured York, and there has also been debate about the date when coins
     began to be minted there for Ragnall, most commentators now concur that both
     events occurred in c.919: *EHD I*, p. 218; Rollason, *Sources for York History*, p. 66;
     for contrasting views on the inception of the coinage of Ragnall, see A. P. Smyth,
     *Scandinavian York and Dublin. The history and archaeology of two related Viking
     kingdoms*, 2 vols (Dublin, 1975–8), I, pp. 103–6; Dolley, 'The Anglo–Danish and
     Anglo–Norse coinages of York', p. 27; Blunt, Stewart and Lyon, *Coinage in Tenth-
     Century England*, p. 105.

81   *Ibid.*, p. 105; R. A. Hall, 'A kingdom too far. York in the early tenth century', in
     Higham and Hill (eds), *Edward the Elder*, pp. 188–99, at 190.

82 Blunt, Stewart and Lyon, *Coinage in Tenth-Century England*, p. 105; Blackburn, 'The coinage of Scandinavian York', pp. 333–5.

83 Dolley, 'The Anglo–Danish and Anglo–Norse coinages of York', p. 27.

84 Blackburn, 'The coinage of Scandinavian York', pp. 334–5.

85 Blunt, Stewart and Lyon, *Coinage in Tenth-Century England*, p. 107.

86 I. Stewart, 'The anonymous Anglo-Viking issue with sword and hammer types and the coinage of Sihtric I', *BNJ*, 52 (1982), 108–16; Blackburn, 'The coinage of Scandinavian York', p. 335.

87 Blunt, Stewart and Lyon, *Coinage in Tenth-Century England*, pp. 219–23; Dolley, 'The Anglo–Danish and Anglo–Norse coinages of York', pp. 28–9; Blackburn, 'The coinage of Scandinavian York', p. 336; see also Rollason, *Northumbria 500–1100*, pp. 226–7.

88 Blackburn, 'Expansion and control', p. 136.

89 Blackburn, 'The coinage of Scandinavian York', p. 338; R. A. Hall, *Viking Age York* (London, 1994), pp. 90–1, is, however, more cautious about interpreting the discovery of this die, the cap of another and three lead strips bearing the imprint of other dies, as evidence that minting occurred on Coppergate.

90 Dolley, 'The Anglo–Danish and Anglo–Norse coinages of York', p. 28.

91 Hall, *Viking Age York*, p. 20; Smyth, *Scandinavian York and Dublin*, II, p. 96.

92 M. Townend, *Language and History in Viking Age England. Linguistic relations between speakers of Old Norse and Old English* (Turnhout, 2002), p. 195. The term CUNUNC also appears on the early coins of Olaf's immediate successors and also on some of the coins of Eric: Blunt, Stewart and Lyon, *Coinage in Tenth-Century England*, p. 227.

93 We do not know for certain that Olaf was ever converted to Christianity. On Olaf's religious persuasions, see L. Abrams, 'The conversions of the Scandinavians of Dublin', *ANS*, 20 (1998), 1–29, at 25–6.

94 Dolley, 'The Anglo–Danish and Anglo–Norse coinages of York', p. 29.

95 S. Keynes, 'The Vikings in England, c.790–1016', in Sawyer (ed.), *The Oxford Illustrated History of the Vikings*, pp. 48–82, at 70; *EHD I*, pp. 548–51.

96 Keynes, 'The Vikings in England', p. 70; D. Whitelock, 'The dealings of the kings of England with Northumbria in the tenth and eleventh centuries', in P. Clemoes (ed.), *The Anglo-Saxons: studies presented to Bruce Dickins* (London, 1959), pp. 70–88, at 71–2; *EHD I*, pp. 219–21.

97 Keynes, 'The Vikings in England', p. 70.

98 *EHD I*, p. 221.

99 *Ibid.*, p. 222. Æthelweard stated, however, that it was Wulfstan and the ealdorman of the Mercians who drove them out: Campbell, *The Chronicle of Æthelweard*, p. 54. See also S. Keynes, 'Wulfstan I', in M. Lapidge, J. Blair, S. Keynes and D. Scragg (eds), *The Blackwell Encyclopaedia of Anglo-Saxon England* (London, 1999), pp. 492–3.

100 *Ibid.*, p. 493; *EHD I*, p. 223.

101 *Ibid.*

102 *Ibid.*, p. 223; Keynes, 'Wulfstan I', p. 493.

103 *EHD I*, p. 223.

104 *Ibid.*, p. 224 and n. 2; Keynes, 'Wulfstan I', p. 293; Whitelock, 'The dealings of the kings of England with Northumbria', p. 73.

105 See also Rollason, *Northumbria 500–1100*, pp. 224–30, where the archbishops of York are posited as the dominant political force in York.

106 J. T. Lang, *Corpus of Anglo-Saxon Stone Sculpture, Vol. 3. York and Eastern Yorkshire* (Oxford, 1991), pp. 58–9, 71–2.

107 *Ibid.*, pp. 28–30, 56–9, 69, 74, 79–80, 85, 96–7, 104.

108 On the range of burials at York Minster, see D. Phillips, 'The Pre-Norman cemetery', in D. Phillips and B. Heywood (eds), *Excavations at York Minster, Volume I* (2 parts) (London, 1995), pp. 75–92.

109 Lang, *Corpus of Anglo-Saxon Stone Sculpture, Vol.3*, pp. 69, 75–6.

110 D. Stocker and P. Everson, 'Five towns funerals: decoding diversity in Danelaw stone sculpture', in Graham-Campbell, Hall, Jesch and Parsons (eds), *Vikings and the Danelaw*, pp. 223–43, at 229–33; D. Stocker, 'Monuments and merchants: irregularities in the distribution of stone sculpture in Lincolnshire and Yorkshire in the tenth century', in Hadley and Richards (eds), *Cultures in Contact*, pp. 179–212, at 193–8.

111 *Ibid.*, p. 196.

112 Rollason, *Northumbria 500–1100*, pp. 229–30.

113 *EHD I*, p. 207.

114 *Ibid*, and n. 10.

115 Rollason, *Sources for York History*, p. 65; Blackburn, 'The coinage of Scandinavian York', p. 329.

116 *EHD I*, p. 208.

117 Dumville, *Wessex and England*, p. 10.

118 *EHD I*, p. 208.

119 P. A. S. Stafford, *Unification and Conquest: a political and social history of England in the tenth and eleventh centuries* (London, 1989), p. 24.

120 *EHD I*, pp. 209–10; Rollason, *Sources for York History*, p. 66.

121 Blackburn, 'The coinage of Scandinavian York', pp. 327–8.

122 *EHD I*, pp. 213–15.

123 On the capture and construction of these *burhs*, see *ibid.*, pp. 210–17.

124 *EHD I*, pp. 209, 546–7; P. H. Sawyer, *Anglo-Saxon Charters, II: Charters of Burton Abbey* (Oxford, 1979), pp. 5–7.

125 F. M. Stenton, *Types of Manorial Structure in the Northern Danelaw*, Oxford Studies in Social and Legal History, 2 (Oxford, 1910), pp. 74–86.

126 *EHD I*, pp. 211–16.

127 *Ibid.*, p. 216.

128 *Ibid.*, p. 217.

129 *Ibid.*

130 Blackburn, 'Expansion and control', pp. 137–8.

131 *EHD I*, p. 217.

132 M. Davidson, 'The (non)submission of the northern kings in 920', in Higham and Hill (eds), *Edward the Elder*, pp. 200–11.

133 South, *Historia de Sancto Cuthberto*, pp. 61–3. The rulers of Bernicia in the early tenth century are referred to as kings in Irish sources: see Davidson, 'The (non)submission of the northern kings', pp. 205–6.

134 *Ibid.*, pp. 208–9, and p. 63 of this book; see, however, S. Driscoll, 'Church archaeology in Glasgow and the Kingdom of Strathclyde', *Innes Review*, 49 (1998), 95–114, at 114.

135 Davidson, 'The (non)submission of the northern kings', pp. 206–9.

136 Blunt, Stewart and Lyon, *Coinage in Tenth-Century England*, pp. 106–7; Blackburn, 'Expansion and control', pp. 128, 132–3.

137 *Ibid.*, p. 138.

138 S. Lyon, 'The coinage of Edward the Elder', in Higham and Hill (eds), *Edward the Elder*, pp. 67–78, at 73–4.

139 Dumville, *Wessex and England*, pp. 151–3.

140 E. O. Blake (ed.), *Liber Eliensis*, Camden 3rd series, 92 (1962), pp. 98–9; C. R. Hart, *The Danelaw* (Hambledon, 1992), pp. 226–7.

141 Dumville, *Wessex and England*, pp. 152–3.

142 *Ibid.*, p. 152.

143 Blake (ed.), *Liber Eliensis*, pp. 98–9; discussed in Innes, 'Danelaw identities', pp. 82–3.

144 *EHD I*, p. 550. Scandinavian names among the witness lists of charters disappear towards the end of Athelstan's reign, which may indicate that they ceased to attend the king's meetings, because they had been replaced by men of English origins or because the scribes had ceased to think it important to include men of such low rank among the witness lists, although it has also been suggested that they may have died fighting for the king against the Scots in 934: Keynes, 'The Vikings in England', pp. 69–70; Hart, *The Danelaw*, pp. 572 (n. 9), 577.

145 *EHD I*, p. 213; Hart, *The Danelaw*, p. 37.

146 G. Fellows-Jensen, 'Scandinavian place-names of the Irish Sea province', in J. Graham-Campbell (ed.), *Viking Treasure From the North-West: the Cuerdale Hoard in its context* (Liverpool, 1992), pp. 31–42.

147 S. Mac Airt and G. Mac Niocaill (eds), *The Annals of Ulster to AD1131*, p. 353; J. H. Radner, *Fragmentary Annals of Ireland* (Dublin, 1978), pp. 00–00; G. Fellows-Jensen, 'Scandinavian settlement in the Isle of Man and North-West England', in C. Fell, P. Foote, J. Graham-Campbell and R. Thomson (eds), *The Viking Age in the Isle of Man. Select papers from the Ninth Viking Congress* (London, 1983), pp. 37–52, at 48–9; P. Cavill, S. Harding and J. Jesch (eds), *Wirral and Its Viking Heritage* (Nottingham, 2000).

148 D. Griffiths, 'The north-west frontier', in Higham and Hill (eds), *Edward the Elder*, pp. 167–87, at 179–81.

149 South, *Historia de Sancto Cuthberto*, p. 61.

150 *EHD I*, pp. 548–51.

151 Rollason, *Northumbria 500–1100*, pp. 249–55; C. Phythian-Adams, *Land of the Cumbrians: a study in provincial origins AD400–1120* (Menston, 1996), pp. 77–87, 110–22.

152 R. N. Bailey and R. Cramp Bailey, *Corpus of Anglo-Saxon Stone Sculpture Vol.2 Cumberland, Westmorland and Lancashire North-of-the-Sands* (Oxford, 1988), pp. 100–3.

153 D. Griffiths, 'Settlement and acculturation in the Irish Sea region', in Hines, Lane and Redknap (eds), *Land, Sea and Home*, pp. 125–38, at 131–8.

154 Rollason, *Northumbria 500–1100*, p. 263.

155 *EHD I*, pp. 219–20.

156 *Ibid.*, pp. 222, 283; on what was meant by 'Cumberland' see Rollason, *Northumbria 500–1100*, p. 266.

157 *Ibid.*, pp. 269–71.

158 Griffiths, 'Settlement and acculturation', p. 126.

159 *EHD I*, p. 218.

160 For example, in 926 his sister Eadhild was married to Hugh, Dux Francorum; in 930 his half-sister Eadgyth married Otto I of Germany, while another half-sister, Ælfgifu, married Konrad the Peaceable of Burgundy, and in 939 his remaining half-sister, Eadgifu, married Louis the Blind of Aquitaine: S. Sharp, 'The West Saxon tradition of dynastic marriage', in Higham and Hill (eds), *Edward the Elder*, pp. 79–88, at 82–6.

161 *EHD I*, pp. 218, 283.

162 *Ibid.*, p. 218; Rollason, *Northumbria 500–1100*, p. 263.

163 *EHD I*, p. 219; Rollason, *Sources for York History*, p. 67.

164 South, *Historia de Sancto Cuthberto*, pp. 65–7; D. W. Rollason, 'St Cuthbert and Wessex: the evidence of Cambridge, Corpus Christi College MS 183', in Bonner, Stancliffe and Rollason (eds), *St Cuthbert, His colt and His Community*, pp. 413–24.

165 J. J. North, *English Hammered Coinage, Volume 1, Early Anglo-Saxon to Henry III, c.600–1272* (London, 1994), pp. 135, 137.

166 On coinage, see C. E. Blunt, 'The coinage of Athelstan, 924–39. A survey', *BNJ*, 42 (1973), pp. 35–160, at 46–51; Athelstan's charters are discussed in H. Loyn, 'Wales and England in the tenth century: the context of the Athelstan charters', *Welsh Hist. Review*, 10 (1980–1), 283–301, at 292–5; the implications of the submissions of the various kings are discussed in I. Williams, *Armes Prydein: the Prophecy of Britain* (Dublin, 1972), pp. 2–3, 6–11, and M. Lapidge, 'Some Latin poems as evidence for the reign of Athelstan', *ASE*, 9 (1981), 61–98, at 98; for a charter with a diverse array of witnesses, see *EHD I*, pp. 548–51.

167 Blackburn, 'The coinage of Scandinavian York', pp. 339–40.

168 Smart, 'Scandinavians, Celts and Germans', pp. 178–9.

169 *EHD I*, pp. 219–20.

170 Hart, *The Danelaw*, pp. 569–84.

171 Blunt, Stewart and Lyon, *Coinage in Tenth-Century England*, pp. 109–10.

172 *EHD I*, pp. 221, 279; Blunt, Stewart and Lyon, *Coinage in Tenth-Century England*, pp. 216–19.

173 The political relationship between these two kings and a King Sihtric, attested by coins from York, is unclear: *ibid.*, pp. 221–3; *EHD I*, pp. 221–2.

174 P. H. Sawyer, 'The charters of Burton Abbey and the unification of England', *North. Hist.*, 10 (1975), 28–39, at 34–9; Sawyer, *Charters of Burton Abbey*, pp. 9–13.

175 Rollason, 'St Cuthbert and Wessex', p. 424.

176 Simpson, 'The King Alfred/St Cuthbert episode'; South, *Historia de Sancto Cuthberto*, pp. 53–9, 90–4.

177 *EHD I*, p. 222; Rollason, *Northumbria 500–1100*, p. 265.

178 *EHD I*, pp. 223–4; Smyth, *Scandinavian York and Dublin*, I, pp. 155–6; P. H. Sawyer, 'The last Scandinavian kings of York', *North. Hist.*, 31 (1995), 39–44, alternatively suggests that Olaf may have ruled from 947 to 950 and Eric from 950 to 952/4.

179 *EHD I*, p. 284; Rollason, *Northumbria 500–1100*, pp. 263–4.

180 *Ibid.*, pp. 266–70.

181 Kershaw, 'The Alfred–Guthrum treaty', p. 44; Wormald, *The Making of English Law*, pp. 438–9.

182 Innes, 'Danelaw identities', p. 73.

183 *EHD I*, pp. 434–7; Wormald, *The Making of English Law*, p. 442.

184 S. Reynolds, 'What do we mean by "Anglo-Saxon" and "Anglo-Saxons"?', *J. Brit. Stud.*, 24 (1985), 395–414, at 411.

185 Whitelock, 'The dealings of the kings of England with Northumbria'.

186 Stenton, *Anglo-Saxon England*, pp. 364–72; Keynes, 'The Vikings in England', p. 72; Wormald, *The Making of English Law*, pp. 126, 132, 317–20; N. Lund, 'King Edgar and the Danelaw', *Mediaeval Scandinavia*, 9 (1976), 181–95.

187 *EHD I*, p. 225.

188 *Ibid.*, p. 559; Keynes, 'The Vikings in England', p. 72.

189 F. Liebermann, *Die Gesetze der Angelsachsen*, 3 vols (Halle, 1903–16), I, pp. 228–33.

190 P. Wormald, 'Æthelred the lawmaker', in D. Hill (ed.), *Ethelred the Unready: papers from the millenary conference*, BAR Brit. Ser., 59 (Oxford, 1978), pp. 47–80; at 61–2.

191 Wulfstan used the term *Dena lagu* in a law-code drafted for Æthelred in 1008 and, probably slightly earlier, in a tract concerned with the rights of the Church in eastern and northern England: Liebermann, *Die Gesetze der Angelsachsen*, I, pp. 128–35, 246–59.

192 *Ibid.*, I, pp. 128–35; D. Whitelock, 'Wulfstan and the so-called Laws of Edward and Guthrum', *EHR*, 56 (1941), 1–21.

193 Innes, 'Danelaw identities', pp. 72–7.

194 Wormald, *The Making of English Law*, p. 132.

195 P. Wormald, 'Viking studies: whence and whither', in R. T. Farrell (ed.), *The Vikings* (Chichester, 1982), pp. 128–53, at 144.

196 Keynes, 'The Vikings in England', p. 67.

197 D. Griffiths, 'The coastal trading ports of the Irish Sea', in J. Graham-Campbell (ed.), *Viking Treasure from the North-West: the Cuerdale Hoard in its context* (Liverpool, 1992), pp. 63–72; *idem*, Griffiths, 'Settlement and acculturation', p. 131.

198 On the political situation in England in the later tenth and earlier eleventh centuries, see Whitelock, 'The dealings of the kings of England with Northumbria'; Stafford, *Unification and Conquest*, pp. 50–68.

199 Griffiths, 'Settlement and acculturation', p. 126.

3

Scandinavian rural settlement

The extent and impact of Scandinavian rural settlement in England have been fiercely debated. Recently, the recovery of new forms of material culture evidence and reconsideration of well-known sources have begun to pave the way to address afresh, and to pose new questions of, aspects of Scandinavian rural settlement. In the following discussion, the estate structures adopted and adapted by the settlers are considered, and evidence for social structure, language change, place-names and personal names are all scrutinised for their capacity to illuminate the context of settlement and the social mechanisms that fostered Anglo–Scandinavian interaction and eventual acculturation. The ways in which Scandinavian rural settlements have previously been identified in northern and eastern England are reviewed, and comparisons with the evidence and debates concerning Scandinavian rural settlements elsewhere in Britain are offered. As we shall see, identification of the influence of incoming groups in the settlement record is difficult, and many of the established criteria are unsatisfactory. Accordingly, it is important to broaden the traditional perspective and consider a wider range of settlement evidence, and to examine the social and tenurial contexts in which rural settlements were both created and restructured, drawing on the results of archaeological excavation and survey, documentary sources, buildings, and settlement layout. Together, this evidence has much to reveal about the impact of the settlers, their relationships with the indigenous populations, and the diverse and changing environments in which both groups lived. Finally, some of the material culture from the region will be discussed, especially jewellery and dress-fittings, as evidence for small-scale day-to-day relationships between the settlers and indigenous peoples of northern and eastern England.

The context of Scandinavian settlement

Why people chose to leave Scandinavia and settle overseas is unclear. Recent interpretations have, as we have seen (see pp. 18–20), focused on socio-political developments within various regions of Scandinavia, driving disaffected lords and rival claimants for authority overseas in search of fortune and land. Yet this does not explain why others followed such lords; presumably some chose to do so in the hope of material gain, while others may have been coerced. That some chose to leave independently of their lords and irrespective of changed political circumstances is not implausible. There is some archaeological evidence for trading contact between Scandinavia and Britain pre-dating the earliest recorded raids, and it is possible that some of the settlers were following a long-standing, if undocumented, tradition. It is indeed, possible that Scandinavians began to settle in England before the settlements noted in the *Anglo-Saxon Chronicle*.[1]

When considering the nature of the settlements, it is important to remember that migrant populations rarely mirror exactly the societies from which they came; the elderly, children and women are likely to be under-represented, especially among settlers who had set out as war-bands.[2] References in the *Anglo-Saxon Chronicle* indicate that the earliest raiders and settlers were sometimes accompanied by wives and children, but there is reason to doubt that women were numerous among the settlers. In 893 the viking fortress at Benfleet (Essex) was captured including 'both goods, and women and also children', and subsequently 'the *wif* ['wife' or 'woman'] and two sons' of the army's leader Hæsten were taken to King Alfred. Since Hæsten had not been in the country long enough to have acquired a wife or concubine and also two children, it is likely that she was from Scandinavia or Frankia, where Hæsten had been raiding over many years.[3] In 895 it was reported that 'the Danes had placed their women in safety in East Anglia'.[4] The impression conveyed by the *Chronicle* that women were occasionally at the heart of viking activity is reinforced by references in Frankish annals to the presence of women and children alongside the male leaders of raiding parties. For example, the *Frankish Royal Annals* record that when the Danish ruler Harald Klak was baptised at Mainz in 826, he was accompanied by 'his wife [*cum uxore*] and a large number of Danes', and the *Annals of St-Bertin* record that in 862 another viking leader, Weland, 'came with his wife and children to Charles [the Bald] and was made a Christian with them'. References to their conversion to Christianity confirm that these women were of Danish origins, rather than local Frankish women who would already have been Christian.[5] Writing in the early tenth century, Regino of Prüm records that in 873 a band of raiders arrived in the deserted city of Angers 'with women and children', suggesting that, as in England, the viking armies were inclined to place their women and children in fortified bases while they continued their raiding in the vicinity.[6] Nonetheless, despite these examples, it is not certain that the armies were accompanied by large numbers of women and children, and there is circumstantial evidence to suggest that among those who settled there were disproportionately more men. Written sources of the tenth to fourteenth century record far fewer females than males with Scandinavian personal names, and a much narrower range of female than male names, which is doubtless a reflection of the smaller number of female settlers introducing fewer female naming models.[7]

Such a gender imbalance must have subsequently encouraged intermarriage with the native population. We have already seen that political negotiation between King Athelstan and Sihtric Caoch of York was sealed by the marriage of the latter to Athelstan's sister, and that Olaf Guthfrithson may have married the daughter of his ally King Constantin of the Scots.[8] After he captured York, Olaf is said by a later source to have married the daughter of one Earl Orm. While Orm has a Scandinavian name, his daughter, Aldgyth, has an English name, and one wonders whether this indicates that she had an English mother.[9] At a later date, Cnut formed a relationship with Ælfgifu, daughter of the former ealdorman of York, and then married Emma, the widow of his predecessor, Æthelred II, and such political marriages may have been common, since the enforced marriage of widows was a source of contemporary complaint. Marriage to the daughters and widows of English landholders was a strategy adopted by some Danish lords in the early eleventh century and later by the Normans, as an effective means of securing their grasp on the lands they had conquered.[10] It would not be surprising, then, if an important dynamic in the settlement and integration of the Scandinavians from the later ninth century, whether as kings, lords or more humble landowners, was the taking of local women as wives or concubines. If so, large numbers of children must have been reared in ethnically and culturally diverse households in the late ninth and early tenth centuries.

We should not assume that the Scandinavian settlers had a common identity, or that they and their descendants were bound together by innate ethnic affiliations. Whatever labels the chroniclers assigned to the raiders and settlers, it is unlikely that even the smaller war-bands were ever composed exclusively of people from the same region, and their ability to acquire followers from the regions where they raided is attested.[11] While it is not improbable that a sense of group solidarity was forged in the face of conflict, the fact that (as we saw in the previous chapter) the political tide turned so often, meant that any feelings of common ethnic identity and military solidarity among the Scandinavian leaders, their followers and other settlers, must frequently have been thrown into confusion, as the distinctions between conqueror and conquered, friend and foe, neighbour and ally were subject to rapid change.[12] We must also remember that many of those we label as Scandinavians or Norse had come to England via the continent or western Britain, and their sense of ethnic and cultural identity may have been modified by these experiences.[13] Moreover, it is reasonable to expect that any commonality of interest among the Scandinavian settlers was also challenged by such factors as social status, age, gender, family connections, profession, and so on. There is no reason to expect a uniform response among the Scandinavian settlers to the circumstances of conquest and settlement, any more than we should expect a uniform indigenous response. The Scandinavian elite seem to have done little to cultivate a sense of ethnic unity with those who followed in their wake, as they quickly formed allegiances with the local elite and adapted themselves to local modes of authority.

Settlement, estate structures and social status in northern and eastern England

There is some evidence to suggest that the Scandinavian settlement was effected through the occupation and exploitation of pre-existing estate structures in northern and eastern England. Many studies have demonstrated that in the period prior to the Scandinavian settlements the rural landscape was organised into extensive multi-vill estates, often called 'multiple estates' by historians and historical geographers. These typically consisted of an estate centre occupied by the king, a member of the secular aristocracy or an ecclesiastical community, and a number of outlying properties, the inhabitants of which owed dues and services to the estate centre, services that were often of a specialised nature with respect to agriculture or animal husbandry.[14] In its account of the various grants made to the community from its foundation in 635 onwards, the *History of Saint Cuthbert* confirms that the basic organisation of settlement in pre-viking Northumbria was the large, multi-vill estate, and it describes such estates being occupied and exploited by the settlers. Following the first recorded battle at Corbridge (914), Ragnall granted to two of his followers large tracts of land held by one of the tenants of the community of St Cuthbert between the rivers Wear and Tees:

> he divided the estates of St Cuthbert, and he gave the one part, towards the south, from the estate which is called Eden as far as Billingham, to a certain powerful warrior of his who was called Scula; and the other part, from Eden as far as the River Wear, to one called Onlafbal

This grant appears to include the lands granted some years earlier by the community to one of its tenants, Alfred.[15] Ragnall adopted the same policy of rewarding supporters after the second recorded battle of Corbridge (918), when he gave substantial estates to Esbrid and Ælstan, the sons of the previous tenant who had died in the battle. One estate extended 'from Chester-le-Street as far as the River Derwent, and from there south to the Wear, and from there as far as the road which is called *Deorestrete* to the south-west', while the other was at Gainford 'with whatever belongs to it' (fig. 6).[16]

This is significant information, and may help us to flesh out the rather less informative accounts provided by the *Anglo-Saxon Chronicle* of earlier Scandinavian settlement. When the *Chronicle* records that in 876 Halfdan and his army 'shared out the land of the Northumbrians, and they proceeded to plough and to support themselves' it seems likely that in most cases Halfdan's leading followers took over such multi-vill estates and supported themselves by the income from such estates, rather than taking up the plough themselves, which may have been left to the humbler warriors and other followers, and doubtless also the pre-existing tenants of these estates. Indeed, Roger of Wendover's thirteenth-century compilation based on earlier annals, describes the events of 876 as follows: 'Halfdan occupied Northumbria and divided it among himself and his thegns and had it cultivated by his army'. Peter Sawyer has argued that this is more likely to be a rendering of an earlier annal than an invention by Roger, and that it indicates that the settlement was an affair organised by the leaders of the army, and was more than a 'free-for-all'.[17] In Æthelweard's late tenth-century version of the *Anglo-Saxon Chronicle*, the army that settled in East Anglia is said to have 'brought all the inhabitants of that land under the yoke of their lordship', which seems to point to a similar turn of events.[18]

The progress of Scandinavian settlement in northern and eastern England is largely undocumented, but circumstantial evidence suggests that the settlers frequently occupied and exploited pre-existing estates. Those regions are characterised in tenth-century charters and the Domesday Book (compiled in 1086) by large multi-vill estates, which had not, as previously

11   Places referred to in the text.

thought, been created by the settlers, as analogous examples have been identified across Britain.[19] Admittedly, there is little documentary evidence to illuminate the earlier history of these estates, but the major estate centres of the tenth and eleventh centuries were commonly important ecclesiastical or royal vills in the ninth century or earlier, which we can reasonably assume to have been at the centres of relatively large territories, and this suggests a degree of organisational continuity through the period of Scandinavian settlement and subsequent West Saxon conquest (the fate of churches at these estate centres is another matter, discussed in chapter 5). Examples include large estates attached to Bakewell, Repton, Wirksworth (Derbys), Southwell (Notts), West Halton (Lincs), Otley, Beverley, Ripon (Yorks), Blythburgh, Bury St Edmunds, Ely (Suff), Reedham (Norf) and Peterborough (Cambs) (see fig. 11).[20] Estates detailed in tenth- and eleventh-century documents frequently coincide with the parishes of the mother churches located at their centres, and this supports the likelihood of continuity of organisation, since such correspondence between estates and parishes has been traced in many regions of England and has typically been assigned origins in the seventh to ninth centuries.[21] In many regions much of the pre-existing estate structure appears, then, to have survived the Scandinavian settlement.[22] However, we must not overstate the case for continuity, as some Domesday estates include properties additional to those listed in tenth-century charters and there are a number of estates with widely scattered properties, interspersed with parts of other estates, that have the appearance of having been put together in the later tenth or eleventh century.[23]

Many estates were doubtless seized by the Scandinavians, but other mechanisms for land-taking are possible. The *Anglo-Saxon Chronicle* records that in 896 some Scandinavian raiders 'who were moneyless got themselves ships and went south across the sea to the Seine', and Peter Sawyer has argued that this implies that they did not have the resources to purchase land in the districts where Scandinavians were already settled.[24] The Cumberland district-name Copeland (ON *kaupaland*, 'bought land') and a similar place-name in County Durham also indicate the purchase of land by the settlers from local lords.[25] It is debatable whether it is really plausible that Scandinavians commonly bought land, but it is certainly apparent that they acquired lands by means other than seizure. For example, some Scandinavians may have been granted land by indigenous lords to make them desist from further raiding, such as Ingimund, the leader of a raiding party expelled from Ireland, who was apparently given land in the vicinity of Chester by Æthelflaed in c.902 (see pp. 61–2), and Guthred, whose elevation to king by the community of St Cuthbert was apparently accompanied by the acquisition of land (see p. 40). The settlement of raiders in remote and frontier regions of kingdoms was also a policy pursued by continental kings, and it is not implausible that it occurred in England.[26]

The processes of settlement and the adoption of pre-existing estates, by whatever means, must have resulted in settlers and indigenous peoples living and working alongside each other from an early date. As Scandinavian leaders took over estates and had them cultivated, they must have relied not only on whatever followers they had, but also on local labour, and perhaps also local estate administrators. Scandinavian lords may also have settled followers on their estates, and even if the latter subsequently lived in separate settlements from local people the mechanisms of the larger estates typical of northern and eastern England are likely to have encouraged rapid interaction, most obviously at the level of rendering dues and services, marketing, and agricultural management. Scandinavian place-names occur among estates that seem to have been continuously in English hands, such as the Gainford estate of the community of St Cuthbert (see p. 42) (fig. 6), suggesting that the incomers sometimes settled on the lands of English lords, especially, perhaps, if that lord owed his position to a Scandinavian leader.[27] Not all of those Scandinavians who settled in England necessarily followed in the wake of a particular lord, and such settlers may have attempted to acquire land of their own volition, whether through seizure or purchase, but it is unlikely that they would have remained beyond the control of a lord, once settled. It is notable that in regions of dense concentrations of Scandinavian place-names, lands were typically outliers of larger estates, leading to inevitable interaction with local people, although it is certainly possible that those lands were held independently by settlers for a period before being incorporated into these larger estates (see p. 88).[28]

Much of northern and eastern England is distinguished from other parts of the country in Domesday Book by significantly greater numbers of 'free' peasants, called *sokemen* and *liberi homines*. Almost half the recorded total of *sokemen* are found in Lincolnshire, where c.11,000 (roughly half of the recorded population of this county) are enumerated, and around 96% of the total number of *liberi homines* are found in the entries for Norfolk and Suffolk.[29] Although there are some differences in their status, Domesday Book and later sources reveal that the two groups share a number of characteristics and privileges, including freedom to alienate their lands without the lord's permission (Domesday Book often records that they were free 'to give and sell it'), and they also owed a range of distinctive dues, including food renders, labour services, the performance of military service, escort duty and carrying service, and were obliged to make suit to the lord's mill and his sheep-fold. These peasants owed their privileged status to their relationship with the king, to their access to public courts, and to the fact that the obligations placed on them did not derive from estate or manorial custom as was the case for the rest of the peasantry, instead being organised through the public institution of the hundred rather than the lord's manor.[30] Ethnic explanations for this stratum of society have long since been abandoned, given the similarity of these peasant freedoms with those found in regions not settled by the Scandinavians, and it is no longer believed that the free peasants were the descendants of the 'rank and file' of the Scandinavian armies as Stenton had suggested.[31] The distinctiveness of the society of much of northern and eastern England may be ascribed instead to the disruption of land-holding and lordship in the wake of the Scandinavian and West Saxon conquests; large numbers of vills with divided lordship; the large and scattered nature of many estates; a vigorous land-market, and the low level of ecclesiastical land-holding, as these are all factors that may have undermined the capacity of lords to burden the upper echelons of the local peasantry with labour services and other obligations that would have undermined their freedoms. Indeed, it is notable that peasant freedoms were less in evidence on the estates of the Benedictine religious houses founded in the later tenth century in the fenlands, and these have recently been described as 'islands of a much more "manorialized" peasantry than was typical of the region as a whole'.[32] Many of the factors accounting for the survival of the free peasants were prompted or encouraged by the Scandinavian conquest and settlement, but the essential and distinctive status of the 'free' peasantry of parts of northern and eastern England was not a Scandinavian innovation.

Local administration

In later Anglo-Saxon England, shires were divided into smaller administrative units known as 'hundreds' in most parts of the country, but in parts of northern and eastern England these units were commonly known as 'wapentakes' (from the Norse *vápnatak*, 'a taking of weapons'). Wapentakes are found in Derbyshire, Nottinghamshire and much of Yorkshire, and there is a single example in Durham at Sedbergh, which is notably in a district with comparatively large numbers of Scandinavian place-names and a cluster of the hogback sculptures which have been

89

described as the 'colonial monuments' of the Scandinavian settlers. In contrast, hundreds were found in East Anglia, most of Durham and eastern Yorkshire.[33] In Cumbria the equivalent administrative district was called a ward, and although it is not recorded before the late thirteenth century, the coincidence of Norman baronies with the wards suggests that they are of much earlier origin.[34] Both hundreds and wapentakes served as communal meeting-places and had courts that sat in judgment on trespasses and disputes over land, and were responsible for monitoring the policing of the area and the muster of its levies.[35] The first mention of a hundred court by name occurs in the mid-tenth century, when an ordinance was issued regulating the functions of the hundred, during the reign of either Edmund or Edgar.[36] However, some of the responsibilities of the hundreds are mentioned earlier in law-codes of Edward the Elder and Athelstan.[37] The wapentake is first recorded as an institution in Edgar's fourth law-code, probably of the 970s. Some studies have suggested that the Scandinavians transformed local administration, while others argue that, irrespective of the Scandinavian impact, the West Saxon conquerors imposed their own administrative system in their newly won territories.[38] More recently, however, it has been suggested that both hundreds and wapentakes were probably based on much earlier administrative arrangements.

It is certainly likely that places of public assembly existed before the mid-tenth century. In the early ninth-century King Cenwulf of Mercia freed land in Middlesex from the burden of *popularia concilia* (public assembly), while the bounds of an estate at Calbourne (Isle of Wight) recorded in a charter of 826 refer to a *gemot beorh* or 'meeting mound'.[39] In the early tenth century a law-code of Edward the Elder referred to the holding of local meetings every four weeks by reeves at which *inter alia* dates were to be assigned for hearing and settling lawsuits, and although the term 'hundred' is not used, the meetings bear some of the hallmarks of the later hundred courts.[40] In a discussion of royal administration in Wessex, Barbara Yorke suggested that the hundredal system first described in the mid-tenth century may have grown out of earlier administrative arrangements whereby estates were grouped together under the supervision of a royal vill to meet fiscal and other royal demands, since many of the hundreds first named in Domesday Book were attached to places that were, or had been, royal vills.[41] In many other regions, hundreds are also often named after royal vills, while others were named after their meeting-places, often in isolated locations and focused on either natural or constructed features, such as barrows, stones, trees, fords and crossroads, while a few include the names of early Anglo-Saxon social groups (for example,

Hurstingstone (Hunts) 'the stone of the people of (-*inga*) the wooded hill'), and both the nomenclature and geography of such meeting-places suggest an ancient origin for the administrative system on which the hundreds were later based.[42]

Sam Turner has recently highlighted the similarity of the names of meeting-places in northern and eastern England with those further south and west, and proposed that the wapentakes of northern England and the hundreds of East Anglia may have had similar origins to the hundreds of 'English' England. For example, the wapentakes of Morleyston (Derbys) and Guthlaxton (Leics) are named after prominent stones; Gartree (Leics), Appletree (Derbys), Avelund (Lincs) and Skyrack (Yorks) are named after trees; while *Walecros* (Derbys) met at a crossroads and Winnibriggs (Lincs) at a river crossing. Among the names of the East Anglian hundreds, some preserve the names of primitive folk-groups (e.g. Clavering, Loddon and Happing); a number indicate that meetings were held at the sites of early earthworks (e.g. Launditch); while others indicate meeting-places located at river crossings (e.g. Mitford, Eynesford and Depwade ('the deep ford')).[43] The Norse element *haugr* ('mound') is found in the names of Haverstoe, Wraggoe and Threo wapentakes in Lincolnshire, and the hundreds of Grimshoe in Norfolk and Thingoe in Suffolk, and this may indicate that Norse-speakers renamed an existing meeting-place, perhaps one originally known by a cognate English name, such as *hlaew* or *beorg*.[44]

Further evidence that a local system of jurisdiction was in place long before the tenth century is provided by the position of judicial execution cemeteries, some of which date back to the seventh or eighth centuries, on the boundaries of hundreds, suggesting that the hundredal boundaries sometimes respected the boundaries of earlier administrative units.[45] Indeed, some of these execution cemeteries continued in use through and after the Scandinavian settlement. For example, radiocarbon dates suggest that an execution cemetery at South Acre (Norf), which lies close to the boundaries of the hundreds of Freebridge Lynn, South Greenhoe and Launditch, was used periodically from at least the seventh to tenth century, as was another execution cemetery at Walkington Wold (Yorks) on the boundary of Welton hundred.[46]

Thus, while detailed information regarding local administration across England is lacking prior to the mid-tenth century, circumstantial evidence suggests that hundreds originated in administrative arrangements of much earlier times, and that the wapentakes and hundreds of northern and eastern England had similar origins. It is not surprising that Scandinavians should have adopted the local administrative systems of the regions in which they settled, as they were apparently used to the concept of public assembly in their homelands. These assemblies were known as a 'thing' (*þing*), and this word occurs in a small number of place-names in England, including Thingwall (found in both Cheshire and Lancashire), and in the names of hundreds in both Suffolk and Norfolk (Thingoe).[47]

However, while there may have been elements of continuity in local administration following both the Scandinavian and West Saxon conquests, evidence for administrative reorganisation can also be found. A number of places with names suggesting that they had once served as meeting-places no longer served this function by the time of the Domesday Book. For example, Barrie Cox has drawn attention to examples in Leicestershire, including Finger Farm (Norse *thing*, 'assembly' and *haugr*, 'mound, hill'), *Thingou* ('assembly mound') and Spellow (*spell, hlaew*, 'speech-mound').[48] Some hundred boundaries in Norfolk dissect groups of parishes with similar names, indicating that they have subdivided earlier territories, and by the time of the Domesday Book several hundreds and wapentakes had been attached to the manors of prominent local lords, often taking the name of the manor.[49] Yet, such changes to administrative organisation were widespread phenomena, and cannot be attributed solely, if at all, to disruption attendant upon Scandinavian settlement. In sum, while it is plausible that the administrative system of northern and eastern England in the later Anglo-Saxon period pre-dated the Scandinavian settlement, we should not overlook evidence for periodic reorganisations of local administration, seemingly resulting from the same range of factors prompting change elsewhere in England.

Language change and the impact of the Scandinavian settlers

A considerable amount of ink has been spilt over the linguistic evidence for the Scandinavian settlement. Although Old English sources contain only around 150 loans from Scandinavian languages, in Middle English sources there are many thousands. The Scandinavian impact also extended to matters of grammar, and was clearly considerable.[50] There is little doubt that the linguistic impact reflects a sizeable contingent of settlers, and that a small-scale elite conquest numbering a few hundreds could not possibly have created such linguistic change, but it is difficult to refine our assessment of the scale or the chronology of the settlement any further, since the relationship between settlement and linguistic change is not predictable.[51] Thus, the following discussion focuses on the linguistic evidence for insight into the nature of the social contacts between settlers and indigenous peoples.

Many studies have commented on the social and diplomatic relations between settlers and indigenous people recorded in documentary sources from the late ninth century onwards, but have rarely stopped to consider the linguistic challenges this must have entailed. In the mid-ninth century, Ealdorman Ælfred and his wife Werburg purchased from the 'heathens' manuscripts including a gospel book, the so-called 'Golden Gospels' (*Codex Aureus*), which the raiders had presumably looted from a monastery; but what, as Matthew Townend has asked, 'were the linguistic means by which Ealdorman Ælfred negotiated with the vikings for the recovery of the gospel-book?'. How did Alfred and Guthrum and their advisers not only negotiate peace in 878 but also manage 'to discuss the rudiments of the Christian faith and to pass almost a fortnight of hospitality together'? The purchase of lands from 'the pagans' prior to the West Saxon campaigns of conquest must have involved contact between speakers of different languages; how was this facilitated?[52] Aside from these, and many other, documented cases of social and diplomatic interaction, there is also the implicit evidence provided by the coinage and other forms of material culture for early interaction between settlers and local people in northern and eastern England. In seeking to clarify the ways in which encounters between English speakers and Norse speakers were conducted Matthew Townend has recently posed the following crucial questions:

> Did the Anglo-Saxons learn to speak Norse or the Scandinavians learn to speak English; or was there something of both? If so, was such bilingualism widespread, or were negotiations conducted via a few specialist interpreters? Or was it the case, as has often been suggested, that speakers of the two languages enjoyed adequate mutual intelligibility for each side to be understood by the other while speaking their own language?[53]

Opinions about the mutual intelligibility of Old English and Old Norse have varied, and range from confident statements ('The Scandinavians and the English could understand one another without much difficulty'), through more cautious assessments ('The two [languages] may even have been mutually intelligible to a limited extent') to more sceptical views ('it is hardly likely that the ninth-century Northumbrians . . . would easily be able to understand Danes and Norwegians').[54] However, until recently, few studies had discussed the matter of Anglo–Norse intelligibility in detail, or offered much supporting evidence for their views.

In a much-needed extended study of Anglo–Norse language conduct, Matthew Townend has recently argued strongly for the 'adequate mutual intelligibility' of speakers of Old English and Old Norse. He demonstrates that dialect intelligibility may be traced, first, through examination of the Scandinavianisation of Old English place-names by Norse speakers, in which 'the substitution of cognate sounds and words suggests that, by and large, Norse speakers recognised and understood the words they heard in the place-names used by their English neighbours'. Although the processes of substituting cognate words has been detailed at length in various studies of place-names in northern and eastern England, it has not previously been made explicit that this implies a significant level of intelligibility.[55] Second, analysis of a number of documentary sources of the ninth to eleventh centuries also illuminates Anglo–Norse linguistic contact. The accounts customarily known as 'The Voyages of Ohthere and Wulfstan', which are incorporated in the late ninth-century Old English translation of Orosius's early fifth-century *Historiarum adversum Paganos Libri Septem* ('Seven Books of History Against the Pagans'), record the journeys of a Scandinavian in England (Ohthere) and an Englishman in Scandinavia (Wulfstan). The evidence of Norse influence on the account of Ohthere's journey recorded at the court of King Alfred suggests to Townend that Ohthere communicated with the court in his native Norse. In the account of both journeys the extent of the substitution of cognate Old English elements in names derived from Old Norse and the phonetic representation of unfamiliar Old Norse names reveal 'both the successful operation of a switching-code where cognates existed and an impressive clarity of hearing where they did not'.[56] The late tenth-century Latin adaptation of the *Anglo-Saxon Chronicle* by Æthelweard contains many glosses on the language of the Scandinavians in England, of which one of the most well-known relates to the death in 871 of Ealdorman Æthelwulf whose body was carried 'to the place called *Northworthig*, but in the Danish language Derby'.[57] This knowledge of the Scandinavian forms for names and the author's ability to reproduce Old Norse names accurately, rather than opting for Anglicised forms, suggests 'a preference for forms derived from contemporary spoken contact rather than inherited book-forms'.[58] Ælfric of Eynsham's late tenth-century homily *De Falsis Diis* ('On False Gods') equates Classical gods with Norse gods: for example, in discussing the days of the week he notes that '[t]hey appointed the sixth day to the shameless goddess called Venus, and Frigg in Danish'. Ælfric renders the names in forms close to the Norse original, rather than by substituting cognate English forms, implying not only a good knowledge of the original forms, but also a homiletic strategy to depict these pagan gods as Norse, and to avoid drawing attention to English pagan traditions in the process.[59]

The third form of evidence for Anglo–Norse intelligibility derives from narrative sources commenting on linguistic contact. The absence of reference to interpreters in any written account of Anglo–Norse contact appears a significant omission when set alongside the plentiful references in Anglo-Saxon texts to interpreters in circumstances of contact between speakers of English and other languages, such as Irish and Latin. This suggests that interpreters were not used for Anglo–Norse communication, and that presumably they were not, therefore, necessary.[60] Although the Scandinavian sagas were written down later than events with which we are interested here, they are thought to contain some more-or-less reliable elements of historical record, and for what it is worth they suggest that individuals from England and Scandinavia could communicate with ease.[61] In the light of this body of evidence for mutual intelligibility, Matthew Townend concludes not only that the Scandinavian raiders and settlers would have been able to communicate in their own language with English speakers, but also that later Anglo-Saxon England was a bilingual society in which both the English and Norse languages were spoken. The concern in the accounts of both Æthelweard and Ælfric to provide alternative Norse names apparently imparts a sense of two vernaculars co-existing in late Anglo-Saxon England, a deduction supported by the existence of English and Norse alternatives among the recorded place-names corpus for northern and eastern England.[62]

This analysis is compelling – not least because it pays close attention to a vital range of issues, too often overlooked or dealt with summarily, that are essential to our understanding of Anglo–Scandinavian social interaction. It also provides a new linguistic perspective on the nature of Scandinavian settlement. That Anglo–Scandinavian social interaction could be conducted relatively easily between some, if not all, of the relevant parties confirms the impression gleaned from documentary and above all archaeological evidence for the speedy mutual influence of settlers and locals on each other in northern and eastern England.

More difficult to ascertain is the longevity of Old Norse as a spoken language, since the available evidence does not easily lend itself to the task. The main sources of evidence scrutinised in discussions of the fate of the Old Norse language are epigraphy, loan-words, runic inscriptions and place-names, but none offers convincing insight. First, the epigraphic evidence: inscriptions were provided for churches in St Mary Castlegate in York, Kirkdale and Aldborough (Yorks) by individuals with Norse names, but were written in Old English, incorporating occasional Norse loan-words, and on the basis of this evidence Eilert Ekwall long ago suggested that the descendants of the settlers had given up their language in some regions of northern England by the early eleventh century.[63] However, since eleventh-century individuals with Norse names need not be of Norse ancestry, their failure to use Norse in their inscriptions may therefore not be significant for discussions of linguistic history. Moreover, if they were not inclined to use Latin, then the public context of these inscriptions may have encouraged the use of the language normally employed in vernacular texts.[64] Thus, the epigraphic evidence does not prove that Norse was *not* spoken in the earlier eleventh century by the descendants of earlier generations of settlers in the districts where these inscriptions were located.[65] Matthew Townend has argued, that given the settlers came from a largely non-literate background into a society with a well-established written script in Old English and Latin using the Roman alphabet, it is, perhaps, not surprising that the incomers should have adopted this when a written script was required. That spoken and written languages need not be the same is demonstrated in the early eleventh century at the court of King Cnut, where Old Norse skaldic poetry was composed and enjoyed, while legislation was promulgated in Old English.[66]

Second, loan-words from Norse can sometimes be dated in broad terms (if only, in many cases, to before or after c.1000) on the basis of, for example, sound changes, and the archaic appearance of many loan-words has sometimes been used to infer that the Norse language may have died out early.[67] However, as David Parsons has commented, while archaic loan-words may reveal something about language forms at the time of the borrowing into English, they cannot help us to understand the subsequent development of Old Norse, and they need not imply that the language had died out at a relatively early date.[68] Third, runic inscriptions on some portable artefacts need not necessarily have been manufactured in England, and therefore may be misleading in discussions of the fate of the Norse language in England. However, a Lincoln comb case, inscribed with the runic inscription 'Thorfastr made a good comb', once thought to have been an import from Scandinavia, may have been manufactured in the town, as archaeological evidence for comb-making has been found nearby.[69] Yet the possibility that Thorfastr worked locally is only partly illuminating, as this comb case is difficult to date: the workmanship has been dated stylistically to the tenth century, but the runic inscription is believed to date to the eleventh century. Runic inscriptions on animal bones from St Albans (Herts) are similarly difficult to date or assign to a historical context.[70] Runic inscriptions on stone sculpture from St Paul's in London and from Old Minster in Winchester (Hants) are thought to have been carved for followers of Cnut in the early eleventh century, and thus cast no light on the survival of the Norse language among the descendants of earlier generations of settlers.[71] A runic inscription on the wall of Carlisle Cathedral – 'Dolfinn carved these runes on this stone' – has been dated to around 1100, but this need not indicate the survival of Norse-speaking communities two centuries after settlement commenced, since, as Raymond Page has observed, there is a strong possibility of renewed Scandinavian influence in the area from the Isle of Man, where the Norse language is known to have survived into the twelfth century.[72]

Fourth, place-name evidence is often adduced in discussions of the survival of Old Norse in England, but the evidence is equivocal. For example, the cluster of place-names in Cumbria formed with a Norman or Continental Germanic personal names and the Old Norse ending -by may, as Eilert Ekwall long ago suggested, indicate that Norse was spoken locally as late as the late eleventh century when William Rufus captured Carlisle.[73] However, there are alternative explanations, including the substitution of personal names for earlier first elements of place-names formed in -by and the possibility that the place-name element -by had passed into local usage.[74] That Norse may have been spoken by some of the community in north-west England in the late eleventh century is not implausible, as the Carlisle graffito and a handful of other runic inscriptions suggest, but as Parsons has commented, whether the Norse spoken in this region was by recent immigrants or the descendants of earlier immigrants is impossible to say on present evidence.[75]

David Parsons has contributed to the debate over the fate of the Norse language with a discussion of place-names formed with a Scandinavian personal name and the Old English element -tun ('village/settlement/estate'). He noted that previous discussions of these names commonly state that the places concerned were renamed by Scandinavian settlers, and some of these names can, indeed, be shown to preserve Norse genitive forms. Given their general distribution in prime agricultural land, these place-names may, it has been argued, represent the earliest phases of Scandinavian settlement, a scenario made especially likely where the place-names incorporate archaic personal names. Yet, as Parsons comments, if this is so, then it is striking that hybrid names formed with -tun are far more common than hybrid names formed with other English habitative elements, and this may indicate that at an early date some of the settlers had adopted the element -tun into their vocabulary and were 'making a choice to conform to English language-patterns'.[76]

Assessing how long the Norse language was spoken in England is complicated by evidence that individuals from Scandinavia and Norse-speakers from other areas of Scandinavian settlement in Britain, continued to arrive in England through the tenth and eleventh centuries, and because consequently the Norse language was reintroduced from several directions long after the initial phases of settlement. Late examples of the existence of the Norse language in England can be cited, such as runic inscriptions from churches in Carlisle, Skelton (Yorks) and Pennington (Lancs), and a skaldic poem by a follower of Earl Waltheof written in the late eleventh century, possibly in northern England. However, the usefulness of such evidence is hampered by its miscellaneous nature, the absence of historical context, and the probability that it derives from relatively recent settlers.[77] How long the Norse language existed in England, and how long it survived among the settlers of descendants, are not the same issues. In sum, conclusive evidence for the longevity of Norse speech among the descendants of the earliest generations of settlers is lacking.

John Hines has presented a rather different analysis from that outlined above of the language(s) spoken by the settlers and their descendants. Hines has argued that Anglo–Scandinavian acculturation was consciously articulated both through the creation of distinctive forms of material culture and the elaborate range of what he terms 'Scandinavian English'.[78] Certainly, as David Parsons has said of this suggestion that the settlers may have given up their language relatively early and perhaps consciously as an aspect of the acculturation process, 'it is not easy to imagine tangible linguistic evidence that would illustrate it', yet the general context of Scandinavian settlement makes this model seem more plausible than the alternative argument for the long-term division of English society among English-speakers and Norse-speakers.[79] Widespread evidence for social, economic and cultural interaction between the settlers and local people, and the Scandinavian adoption and adaptation of many aspects of English culture (from coinage to monumental stone sculpture) suggests rapid assimilation by many, if not most, settlers to indigenous society. In this context, an argument that the linguistic evidence can 'uphold broadly Stentonian perspectives on the reality of the English/Danish distinction in Viking Age England' appears anomalous.[80]

Intermarriage between the settlers and the local population must have played an important part of the acculturation process, and this prompts one to ask what language(s) the offspring of such unions might have spoken. The predominant local language must have played a part in determining the language of mixed marriages, although the probable role of mothers in educating their children may have been as, or more, important.[81] In some circumstances, the shift to speaking English must have occurred within a generation of settlement, especially where the descendants of settlers were born of English mothers. Townend argues that the descendants of the settlers were eventually to shift to speaking English, probably during the eleventh and twelfth centuries following 'the gradual breakdown of a distinctive Scandinavian culture and identity'. Yet, it is arguable, as we saw in the sphere of diplomacy and politics, and as we shall discuss with respect to a wide range of forms of material culture, that a distinctive Scandinavian culture and identity was transformed, if not broken down, rapidly among at least some of the settlers.[82] Finally, we must expect that the complexity of Anglo–Scandinavian contact on a local level is likely to have given rise to a wide range of responses, including on a linguistic level.

Place-names and Scandinavian rural settlement

The significance of the distribution of wholly and partially Scandinavian place-names in England has been extensively debated (fig. 1). Large numbers of such names are found in Leicestershire, Lincolnshire, Nottinghamshire, southern Derbyshire, Yorkshire and Cumbria, although the density of Scandinavian and Scandinavianised place-names is uneven within these regions. In Yorkshire, for example, Scandinavian influence has been detected in 48% of names recorded in Domesday Book in the East Riding and 46% in the North Riding, but only 31% in the West Riding.[83] Smaller scatters of Scandinavian and Scandinavianised place-names are found in some other regions, including County Durham, East Anglia, Cheshire (where they are largely restricted to Wirral), Northamptonshire, Warwickshire and the Lake District.[84] There is no dispute that Scandinavian place-names are largely found in the areas of documented Scandinavian settlement, but 'reading between the dots' of the place-name distribution map has proved a tricky business.[85]

There have been many attempts to use distribution maps of place-names to produce a narrative account of Scandinavian settlement, which have attempted *inter alia* to trace the movements of armies, to assess the scale of the settlement, to indicate zones of landscape colonisation, and to identify the precise locations of Scandinavian settlement at given periods.[86] Kenneth Cameron, for example, attempted to distinguish on the basis of place-name evidence the earliest phases of Scandinavian settlement (represented by place-names formed with a Scandinavian element or personal name and English *-tun* in areas of prime agricultural land), from subsequent settlement by the 'secondary migrants' he posited (represented by place-names formed with the Scandinavian elements *-by* ('farmstead, settlement') and -*thorp* ('secondary/outlying settlement') typically in upland and wolds regions). Taking a different perspective, Peter Sawyer suggested that the absence of Scandinavian place-names in regions known to have been recovered early in the tenth century by English lords suggests that the proliferation of Scandinavian place-names was a later event, probably occurring in the context of estate fragmentation.[87] Such attempts to generate chronologies of Scandinavian colonisation have failed to reach any kind of consensus, and some efforts have been rejected as unsophisticated or refuted by archaeological evidence. It is now widely thought that the distribution of Scandinavian place-names may owe more to the social status of the settlers in various regions, the nature of land-taking and land-holding, and the density of settlement, rather than to chronology.[88]

There are some regions in which Scandinavian occupation is documented, or where it is indicated by the Scandinavian influence on stone sculpture, but where there are few or no Scandinavian place-names. Gillian Fellows-Jensen has commented that the Scandinavian settlers sometimes 'left the English names unchanged', noting, for example, that in north-eastern England although the *History of Saint Cuthbert* records a number of vills passing into Scandinavian lordship, none has a Scandinavian name.[89] However, as Matthew Townend has recently observed, it is very likely that the Scandinavian occupants of this district coined their own names for places, whether giving new names or Scandinavianised versions of existing names, but, crucially, it is unlikely that the author of the *History of Saint Cuthbert* would have recorded those names.[90] Similarly, the low numbers of Scandinavian place-names in the vicinity of each of the Five Boroughs of the east midlands (Nottingham, Derby, Stamford, Lincoln and Leicester) may not only imply that Scandinavian settlement was concentrated in the *burhs*, but that the subsequent West Saxon conquest may have reduced the likelihood of recording whatever Scandinavian place-names were circulating locally.[91] The coinage of names and their preservation are not the same thing. Factors such as the low density of Scandinavian settlement; brevity of Scandinavian overlordship; lack of success of settlers in acquiring or retaining land; and the subsequent estate histories of the regions (including the extent to which large estates remained intact) may have determined whether Scandinavian place-names entered into local currency or were recorded.[92]

It is now also recognised that the Scandinavian place-names first recorded, in most cases, in Domesday Book, were coined over a long period of time, not just during the initial phases of settlement. For example, some of the names formed with a Scandinavian personal name and -*tun* have been shown to be late formations, probably relating to changes in manorial ownership, and it is also possible to distinguish some archaic word, sounds and names from eleventh-century examples.[93] However, in general, tying groups of place-names to particular periods and events rests on historical probability rather than on linguistic grounds.[94] Some places were once thought on the basis of their Scandinavian names to have been newly founded by Scandinavian settlers, but excavation reveals that many were settled long before the later ninth century, although whether they were inhabited continuously is admittedly difficult to demonstrate.[95] Nonetheless, it is now thought that the density of Scandinavian place-names in some upland and wolds regions reflects the intensification, rather than the advent, of settlement in the tenth and eleventh centuries. Disproportionate numbers of new names may have been generated as settlements in such regions were detached from their parent settlements in the river valleys, but it is undeniable that the settlers must have formed a high proportion of the occupants of those districts, especially in regions where purely Scandinavian names, with little or no evidence for hybridisation, occur.[96]

The use of place-name evidence to identify the origins or ethnic identity of settlers is also now regarded as dubious. There have been attempts, for example, to use place-names to infer the chronology and ethnic orientation of Scandinavian settlement in the north-west of England, where Norwegian influence has been detected in some names, where Gaelic influence indicates the presence of settlers who had previously spent time in Ireland or western Scotland, and where Danish influence may indicate settlers who had moved westwards from eastern Northumbria. While the place-names certainly reflect, to some extent, the diverse influences on the region, the identification of the relevant place-name elements has proved controversial and dating is difficult. Accordingly, caution is now urged in the use of place-names to infer the ethnic identity of occupants of particular districts, especially where there appear to be many cross-cutting ethnic and social influences in which identities may have been relatively fluid and subject to rapid change.[97]

Despite the problems of using place-name evidence to contribute to debates about the nature, extent and chronology of Scandinavian settlement, nonetheless some recent papers have indicated the potential for place-name evidence to illuminate the relationships between settlers and the local populations of northern and eastern England. For example, the combination of English and Scandinavian elements to form place-names, the replacement of an English name with a cognate Scandinavian one, and names in which a Norse sound has replaced an English one, all indicate not only the mutual intelligibility of Norse and English, as we have seen, but that some Scandinavian place-names were created in the context of contact between the settlers and members of local society.[98] Interaction between the two groups is also reflected by the presence of both Scandinavian and English place-names within the same estate, although the chronology and nature of the interaction is unclear from the onomastic evidence alone.[99] The fact that place-names formed with the element -by contain a high percentage of personal names as the first elements, probably reflects the influence on the settlers of indigenous naming practices and also attitudes to land, since in Denmark the combination of personal names with -by is much less common, implying that the close association of a person with a particular territory was also comparatively much less common in Denmark than in England. It is, however, difficult to determine how quickly such developments may have occurred.[100]

Matthew Townend has recently drawn attention to evidence for the existence of both English and Scandinavian names for the same place (of which Northworthy/Derby and Streoneshalh/Whitby (Yorks) are the most well-known), and different versions of names showing more-or-less English or Scandinavian influence (e.g. Stainmore (Westmor) Stānmōr/Steinn-mór; Bleasby (Notts) Blisetune/Bleseby). He argues that this reveals that different names for a place might circulate locally, and that the final form might be determined by a combination of the nature of the language spoken locally and the attitudes of scribes. This existence of different names – and different versions of names – for the same place has led Townend to the conclusion that there were in northern and eastern England 'two separate speech communities independently referring to the same place by different names'.[101] However, aside from the problem addressed above of knowing how long the Norse language survived in England and the possibility that various forms of Norse-influenced English may have been spoken among the settlers and their descendants, we should remember that new place-names were routinely coined within England, often in response to transformations of estates and changes in lordship, and these processes may also have given rise to more than one name for the same place, both of which doubtless circulated locally for a time. Thus, the existence of different names for a place is not simply the result of two different linguistic groups coming into contact with each other, but is also a product of normal social and political factors within early medieval society.

In a recent survey, Lesley Abrams and David Parsons have drawn attention to the following characteristics of -by names in an attempt to provide historical context for the names. First, these names are overwhelmingly formed with Old Norse rather than Old English first elements (a ratio of 4:1). Second, around half of the -by names incorporate personal names as first elements. From this they conclude that the majority, although far from all, of these names were created among predominantly Norse-speaking communities, and that large amounts of land had become associated with individuals in regions where such communities were settled. They suggest that the -by names form a largely coherent group, and that they are likely to have been formed early in the period of Scandinavian settlement, perhaps largely in the ninth century, before extensive assimilation between the settlers and the local population had occurred. The names also, they suggest, betoken 'Scandinavian settlers beyond a small military élite', a conclusion supported by the large numbers of Scandinavian field-names and the diverse range of personal names introduced into England by the settlers.[102] The -by names are few in number on estates that appear to have been continuously in the hands of English lords, or else quickly returned to them following West Saxon conquest, and are largely associated with lower-status sites, typically away from the prime agricultural land, and it may be that this possession of poorer-quality land far from the estate centres of the powerful meant that the grasp of the settlers and their descendants on this land was more enduring.[103] Indeed, a recent comparison of the distribution of Scandinavian place-names with the Domesday estate structure in the north midlands and Yorkshire revealed that while Scandinavian place-names are rare among the central manors of large estates (or *sokes*) and those lands over which the lord had closest control (*berewicks*), they are, by contrast, quite common among the lands over which lords had less control (*sokelands*), some of which are widely scattered and appear to have been attached to the estate in the tenth century.[104] Thus, in parts of northern England and the north midlands, Scandinavian place-names appear to be more common in the context of transformations to estate organisation; in areas of less-attractive agricultural land; at a distance from major estate centers; and also, as Abrams and Parsons argue of the names in -by, in areas of dense Scandinavian settlement.

The evidence of place-names is plentiful, but its application to historical questions that it can plausibly hope to illuminate has proved challenging. It seems clear that the place-name distribution map is not a straightforward index of Scandinavian settlement. Factors such as the chronology of settlement, its scale, the nature of pre-existing patterns of landownership, the survival of English landowners, the rapid reacquisition of land from Scandinavian lords by English landowners, the uneven distribution of

Scandinavian settlement, and the nature of interaction with the indigenous population, all contributed to the corpus of Scandinavian place-names. Although the -*by* names may, indeed, be largely early, and formed in the context of largely Norse-speaking communities prior to significant Anglo–Scandinavian acculturation, nonetheless, some -*by* names occur in small clusters among larger estates consisting overwhelmingly of Old English place-names, while others, such as those formed with the Old Norse word for a church (e.g. Kirkby), must have been created within the context of substantial Anglo–Scandinavian contact. It is difficult to generalise about the significance of Scandinavian place-names, and it is only really on a localised basis that we can begin to understand their historical context.

The problems and possibilities of identifying Scandinavian rural settlements in the archaeological record

Traditional approaches

Although the historical record has little to say about Scandinavian rural settlement, and there are difficulties attendant on using place-names to identify the precise locations of Scandinavian settlement, it is, nevertheless, reasonable to assume that many rural settlements in northern and eastern England were partially or wholly occupied by Scandinavian settlers. Whether we can, however, identify such settlements archaeologically is another matter. Discussions of Scandinavian rural settlements have typically focused on a limited selection of excavated sites of the relevant date. These include the upland sites of Simy Folds (Dur), Bryant's Gill (Cumb) and Ribblehead (Yorks). However, a brief review of the evidence from each site exposes how tenuous are claims that they were ever occupied by Scandinavians.

The farmstead at Ribblehead consisted of three buildings set within an enclosed farmyard with an associated field system, and was located at an altitude of 340 m above sea-level (fig. 12). The buildings comprised a long, narrow dwelling, and two other structures interpreted as a bakery and a 'workshop', possibly a smithy. Only a few artefacts were recovered during excavation, including an iron cow-bell, a horse bit, a spearhead, a stone spindle-whorl, and two iron knives. None of these artefacts is closely datable, but three Northumbrian stycas found within a wall date the construction of the site to some time after the late ninth century.[105] Located at 290 m above sea-level, a farmstead comprising a long, narrow structure, associated with wall footings, post-holes and paved areas, has been excavated at Bryant's Gill. Associated artefacts included stone spindle-whorls and over 20 honestones.[106] At Simy Folds three farmsteads have

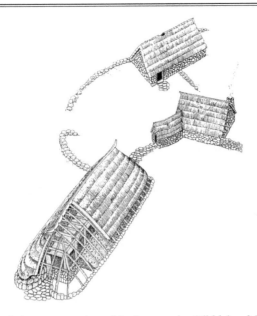

12   An artist's reconstruction of the farmstead at Ribblehead (Yorks). It is thought that the three buildings were a dwelling-place, a bakery or kitchen, and a workshop (possibly a smithy).

been excavated, each comprising a long, narrow structure and other associated buildings arranged around a yard. The few finds include a spindle-whorl, honestone and quernstone, while quantities of iron slag indicate that iron-working occurred nearby.[107] In the interim publication, Alan King expressed uncertainty about whether the farmstead at Ribblehead was '*landnam* Norse viking or typically Northumbrian Anglo-Saxon' and concluded that 'at present it would be unreasonable to answer the question'.[108] The excavators of both Simy Folds and Bryant's Gill were equally circumspect; indeed, charcoal from hearths at Simy Folds has produced calibrated radiocarbon dates of the mid- to late eighth century, and it thus seems too early to have been founded by Scandinavian settlers.[109] Nonetheless, these sites are regularly cited as examples of Scandinavian settlement, despite the fact that there is little about them that can be said to be indicative of Scandinavian influence, let alone settlement.[110] Equally unconvincing is an attempt to identify a Scandinavian origin for a structure excavated at Waltham Abbey (Essex). This has been interpreted as a 'viking hall' of the era of Cnut, based in part on the knowledge that land was held there by Tovi the Dane in the early eleventh century, and in part on the supposedly Scandinavian character of the building. The structure is over

15 m in length, represented by a row of aisle posts, trenches for timber sill beams, and massive corner post-holes at the west gable end, and it has been suggested that the absence of timber wall-posts implies that the hall was turf-walled.[111] However, James Graham-Campbell has disputed this Scandinavian attribution, arguing that the building may be later in date than the era of Tovi, and that anyway a turf-walled building is unlikely to have been the choice of a man of Tovi's standing.[112] It is clear that discussion of the Scandinavian impact on rural settlement needs to expand its focus beyond such sites.

In a recent review of Scandinavian settlement in Britain, Julian Richards has summarised the criteria commonly used by archaeologists to identify Scandinavian rural settlements.[113] These criteria include: distinctive building forms; innovations in construction techniques; evidence for dislocation of settlement; and the presence of distinctive artefact assemblages, demonstrating either clear Scandinavian influence or evidence for innovation in manufacture or design. He has suggested that while in certain circumstances some of these criteria are suggestive of Scandinavian influence, few provide conclusive evidence, and some are misleading. A review of these criteria follows.

Bow-sided buildings are characteristic of some tenth-century Danish settlements, such as Ömgard, Sædding and Vorbasse, and also occur in the so-called Trelleborg-type fortresses of the late tenth century; some excavators have suggested that the presence of such buildings in England is indicative of Scandinavian settlement, in both rural and urban contexts.[114] Examples have been excavated at Buckden (Cambs), St Neots (Cambs), Cheddar (Som), Catholme (Staffs), Chester, Durham, *Hamwic* (Southampton, Hants), Goltho (Lincs), Thetford, North Elmham (Norf), and Sulgrave (Northants).[115] However, the usefulness of the introduction of bow-sided buildings as an indicator of Scandinavian settlement in England is questionable, as the known examples are of widely differing size, form, construction methods and date. Bow-shaped buildings in England are frequently smaller than excavated Danish examples, and do not appear to have contained byres, unlike the bow-shaped buildings at Vorbasse and Sædding. On the other hand, bow-shaped buildings in the Trelleborg-type fortresses do not appear to have had byres either, and this suggests that even if bow-shaped buildings were introduced by Scandinavian settlers, there was more than one prototype from different social contexts and eras. Indeed, the Trelleborg buildings date to the latter part of the tenth century, and their influence on building forms in England, if any, would have been in the era of Cnut rather than among the settlers of earlier generations. We should also note that in Scandinavia dwellings were not invariably bow-shaped, and square and rectangular buildings are also known, meaning that the settlers did not all arrive with a tradition of constructing bow-shaped houses.[116]

Nonetheless, Julian Richards has argued that in some circumstances bow-shaped buildings in England may have been intended as statements of military power, rather than serving as agricultural structures. This is certainly possible, although some such buildings seem to pre-date the period of Scandinavian military ascendancy, such as the example from *Hamwic* which had been destroyed by the ninth century, while at Cheddar it seems unlikely that a building apparently constructed prior to 930 in the West Saxon heartlands could have been a statement of Scandinavian power. There is also a striking lack of evidence for other overt statements of Scandinavian identity accompanying the buildings at any of these sites, of the type that might be expected if the bow-shaped buildings really did represent the imposition of a Scandinavian military identity. Moreover, if bow-shaped buildings were overt statements of Scandinavian identity, it is peculiar that they have not been found in some places where Scandinavian settlement *is* known, in particular York.[117] In sum, while a Scandinavian influence on the construction of bow-shaped buildings in England is possible, it appears to have been inconsistently exerted.

In a useful review of the evidence for Scandinavian influence on rural settlement in northern Britain, Coleen Batey identified a series of what she argued were Scandinavian characteristics common to the archaeology of rural settlements in areas of Scandinavian settlement. These included aspects of settlement layout (e.g. settlement clusters, buildings associated with yards and paved areas, rebuilding on the same site), construction methods (e.g. walls with facing stones and rubble interior, clay bedding for walls, use of flat stones to provide a level surface) and building types (e.g. presence of a kitchen, smithy and storehouses, and wall benches).[118] While she states that 'there are strands of evidence which can support a Scandinavian genesis for these structures', she concludes that the diversity of buildings found and the inevitable archaeological focus on buildings constructed of stone at the expense of timber and turf construction, combine to advise against speaking of 'a typical viking building'. Although Batey is cautious about the possibility of identifying sites of Scandinavian occupation, she remains optimistic that the settlers are archaeologically identifiable as long as they instituted change.[119] However, as Julian Richards has pointed out, the sites she discusses span several hundred years, and some of the features of rural settlement supposedly diagnostic of Scandinavian settlement may also be found at an earlier date.[120] In the

Scottish Isles and Isle of Man, rectangular, and occasionally bow-shaped, buildings have been assigned Scandinavian origins, in contrast to the native circular buildings. There is certainly evidence from some sites, such as Buckquoy (Orkney) and Jarlshof (Shetland), that rectangular buildings superseded circular structures. However, at other sites, such as the Braaid, Isle of Man, there is no evidence to indicate the phasing of different building forms, while at Pool (Sanday), excavation has revealed a rectangular courtyard dating to the sixth century, and a pre-Norse origin has been suggested for a roughly rectangular building at Wag of Fosse (Caithness), suggesting that rectangular construction sometimes preceded Scandinavian influence.[121] Moreover, at Jarlshof, although Scandinavian influence has been inferred from the introduction of rectangular buildings, interpretation of the site is complicated by evidence that local construction techniques were employed in at least one rectangular building.[122] At some sites where Scandinavian occupation has been inferred from the form, construction or layout of buildings, such as Buckquoy, Pool and the Brough of Birsay (Orkney), the range of accompanying material culture includes both indigenous and Scandinavian artefacts, suggesting some level of interaction with the local community.[123] Indeed, the use of local pottery at sites where Scandinavian occupation has been identified, for example at The Udal, North Uist (Hebrides) and Pool, implies dependence on the local community, since the Norse settlers did not arrive with a tradition of pottery production, relying in their homelands on wooden and soapstone vessels.[124] Thus, while many of the sites discussed by Batey may, indeed, have experienced Scandinavian settlement, the available evidence is not conclusive. Once the indigenous population adopted the new building forms, even assuming that the Scandinavians invariably innovated, and given the diverse range of material culture found at many rural settlements, the settlers and the locals become archaeologically indistinguishable. As Batey rightly concludes: 'Sadly, archaeology itself cannot yet always identify the foreigner, especially not if that foreigner is content to continue local traditions'.[125]

Reliance on assemblages of finds from rural settlements to infer Scandinavian occupation is problematic. In aceramic regions, such as the north-west of England, even dating the settlements to within a few hundred years can be very difficult, while excavated rural settlements of the ninth and tenth centuries typically yield few finds, although field-walking and metal-detecting can increase the range of material recovered.[126] Yet even when distinctively Scandinavian artefact types are found, their ability to indicate the arrival of new peoples is limited by the possibility that they arrived at the site through trade. Moreover, as we shall see, some artefacts with Scandinavian form or motifs also betray indigenous influence, and therefore while they may indicate Scandinavian settlement in the vicinity of where the material was found, the settlers had clearly been influenced by local society. The mixture of cultural influences on the finds recovered from rural settlements in northern and eastern England suggests that assigning ethnic labels to settlements is far from straightforward, and in many cases may be positively unhelpful.[127]

Evidence for settlement disruption or dislocation has also sometimes been used to identify Scandinavian occupation, although the deductions drawn are often contradictory. For example, the transition from dispersed to nucleated settlement in parts of Yorkshire has been attributed to the Scandinavian conquest.[128] In contrast, it has been claimed that the Scandinavian settlement retarded the processes of village nucleation in Derbyshire and Nottinghamshire, and instigated the resurgence of a more dispersed settlement pattern.[129] However, it should be remembered that transformations in settlement layout may be attributable to many factors, and they are, indeed, a feature of many diverse medieval settlement contexts both in regions of Scandinavian settlement and elsewhere. The widespread distribution of village nucleation from the ninth century onwards, combined with its absence in some regions of northern and eastern England, suggests that it was a process that occurred independently of Scandinavian settlement.[130]

One final type of evidence from rural settlements sometimes assigned Scandinavian origins, is a method of land division found in parts of northern England. The institution of *solskifte* involves the allocation of strips in the fields in relation to the movement of the sun across the sky. Later medieval evidence for land division according to *solskifte* comes in the form of references to land lying 'opposite the sun', 'next to the shade', 'further from the sun', and so on.[131] *Solskifte* occurs in Scandinavia, and it was once thought that the settlers brought this form of rural organisation with them to England, but more recently it has been suggested that it may have originated in England and been subsequently adopted in Scandinavia.[132] The direction of the spread of the *solskifte* method of organisation is difficult to resolve, and it thus does not offer reliable evidence of Scandinavian settlement in England.

Previous attempts to identify Scandinavian rural settlement have been inconclusive, and sometimes contradictory. The identification of incoming groups in the archaeological record of rural settlements is far from straightforward, and it is necessary to rethink our approach. We also need to address what we hope to learn from the identification of the Scandinavians in the archaeology of rural settlement.

New approaches to Scandinavian rural settlements

Given the difficulty of identifying Scandinavian settlers in the archaeology of rural settlement, Julian Richards has recently suggested that we have not been asking the most appropriate questions of our evidence:

> The question 'Where are the Scandinavian settlements in the Danelaw?' is therefore not a sensible one to ask . . . We cannot claim . . . that the inhabitant of a settlement was Scandinavian. What we *are* able to do is to identify the use of material culture to proclaim a particular identity, and to invent new ones.[133]

In this respect, fieldwork at two rural settlements in Yorkshire, Wharram Percy and Cottam, invites detailed attention. Although it is difficult to say whether any Scandinavian settlers occupied either of these settlements, the Scandinavian influence on expressions of status within these rural settlements can certainly be identified and linked to aspects of settlement transformation in the tenth century.

Excavation at the location of the late medieval South Manor in the village of Wharram Percy, has revealed continuity of occupation of an elite site from the seventh or eighth to tenth centuries. Among the middle Saxon occupation foci identified within the parish of Wharram, this site at the South Manor was the only one still occupied in the later Middle Ages. Given its later medieval manorial status, this continuity of occupation may reflect the early origins of a lordly or 'manorial' focus.[134] In the earliest phases, a post-built hall was associated with a smithy. The site is dated by pottery, an early eighth-century coin, two sword pommels and a seventh- or eighth-century hilt-guard, and the latter finds are indicative of high-status occupation.[135] Although a tenth-century hall has not been identified, it seems likely that it was in the vicinity, since the smithy continued in use on the same site. It is thought that at some point in the tenth century both the manorial boundary bank and the peasant tofts were laid out nearby.[136] The range of tenth-century material culture from the South Manor site includes a decorated sword-hilt similar to an example from Coppergate in York; a belt-slide and strap-end decorated in the so-called Borre style (named after a place in Norway where decorated metalwork was found); and honestones made from Norwegian stone, and this suggests that transformations in the settlement were accompanied by cultural change.[137] This combination of settlement reorganisation and the appearance of new forms of material culture has been interpreted in two ways. One interpretation suggests the presence of a Scandinavian settler, attested by the presence of artefacts brought from Scandinavia, whose high status is suggested by the quality of the strap-end and belt-slide.[138] The other interpretation suggests that the lord may not have been a Scandinavian, but had nonetheless adopted Scandinavian fashions, reflecting the Scandinavian influence in local society.[139] Whatever the background of successive lords, it is apparent that they adopted and transformed a pre-existing high-status settlement site, and that this was undertaken with reference to the Scandinavian influence in local society. If in the tenth century a Scandinavian lord did, indeed, takeover the site, then it suggests that Scandinavian lordship in rural society was predicated upon continuity of settlement foci and of centres of lordship.[140]

At Cottam excavation, survey, metal-detecting and field-walking has revealed a shift in the settlement focus in the late ninth or early tenth century. One site has produced metal artefacts and pottery of eighth-century date, and excavation revealed post-hole buildings and settlement debris of the eighth and ninth century. To the north-east a second site has produced metalwork and pottery of late ninth- and tenth-century date; magnetometer survey has revealed a series of sub-rectangular enclosures; and excavation identified clusters of post-holes and ditches. This later settlement focus has produced examples of Scandinavian metalwork, including eight lead weights, a Borre-style buckle and a brooch decorated in the Jelling style (named after the decorated items found at the tenth-century royal burial site of Jelling). While the takeover and reorganisation of the site by a new Scandinavian lord and his retinue is possible, there is no evidence of violent takeover, and in this respect the site reveals a localised settlement shift, of a type identified at many ninth- and tenth-century occupation sites. Indeed, this second settlement site at Cottam did not last long, and was subsequently abandoned, seemingly later in the tenth century, with settlement probably being relocated to nearby villages at Cottam and Cowlam.[141]

Intriguingly, the later site produced evidence for a gateway structure. Although other ditches at the site were shallow, the gateway was associated with a substantial external ditch with an internal rubble bank, possibly topped by a timber palisade, and massive post-holes to either side of the entrance. The excavator, Julian Richards, has concluded that the gateway could not have been intended as a defensive structure, given the lack of other defensive features around the site, and he interprets it as a status symbol, facing towards the recently abandoned settlement to the south-west and visible to those coming up the valley along the approaching trackway.[142]

Textual evidence provides insight into the significance of a gateway structure as an expression of lordly status. The early eleventh-century compilation on status known as *Geþyncðo* ('concerning wergilds and dignities') describes how a *ceorl* ('peasant proprietor') may aspire to become a person of higher social rank, termed a thegn: 'And if a *ceorl* prospered, that he possessed fully five hides of land of his own, a church and kitchen, a bell[-house], and *burh-geat*, a seat and special office in the king's hall, then he was henceforth entitled to the rights of a thegn'.[143] Ann Williams has commented that the term *burh-geat* refers to the gatehouse of the lord's enclosure, and other eleventh-century sources reveal that a lord's residence was typically enclosed with hedges, fences or ditches.[144] As Richards has observed of the tenth-century site at Cottam, 'the existence of a gatehouse may have had a special significance for contemporary visitors to the site'.[145] This significance must have been related to the expression of a particular type of local lordship, which was perhaps more apparent and more significant to locals than the ethnic identity of the lord and other inhabitants of tenth-century Cottam. The discovery of two small metal copper-alloy bells may also fit into this context of transformations in lordly status. Such bells have been found on a variety of sites in the parts of Britain where Scandinavians settled, including York, Cowlam, Fincham and Cranwich (Norf), Meols (Ches), Lincoln, Goltho, and as metal-detector finds elsewhere in Lincolnshire, Freswick Links (Caithness), and from the Isle of Man.[146] These bells are not imports, as none have been found in Scandinavia. They are typically decorated with ring-and-dot ornament, reminiscent of insular styles of decoration, and may have served as decorative fittings on horse harnesses.[147] If so, they may have emerged in the context of lordly display. It must have been important to maintain status in the turbulent times and rapidly changing political circumstances of the tenth century, and innovative lordly display must have played an important role.

Recent analysis of the evidence from Wharram Percy and Cottam displays sensitivity to the difficulties of identifying ethnic identity in the archaeological record. Moreover, the sites are interpreted not only in the context of the impact on incoming groups, but with reference to other developments in local society. Although the arrival of Scandinavian lords and other settlers was an important factor in the societies of northern and eastern England, it is clear that changes in the structure of lordship, transformations of local patterns of land-holding, and the general reorganisation of settlement were also important, and not confined to regions of Scandinavian influence. Lordly residences, consisting of halls and associated buildings, sometimes including towers and churches, which were often enclosed, appear in the archaeological record of the late ninth and tenth centuries at many rural sites across England, including Goltho (Lincs), Portchester, Faccombe Netherton (Hants), Trowbridge (Wilts), Raunds and Sulgrave (Northants).[148] At Goltho a small number of artefacts of Scandinavian or continental origin were found in early tenth-century contexts, including a gaming piece, four bone pins, seven knife blades and a bridle-bit.[149] While these are insufficient to conclude that the fortified residence of the early tenth century, consisting of a hall, kitchen, garderobes and ancilliary buildings, perhaps including a weaving shed, was constructed for a Scandinavian lord, we can say that this lordly complex replaced a farmstead, implying a restructuring of local society, which found expression in the settlement structure. Whatever the origins of the instigator of these changes, they primarily reveal the actions of someone with pretensions to lordly status, and it was a restructuring that persisted through the tenth and eleventh centuries when modifications to the buildings and defences were made.

It is also worth noting that some settlements were occupied for considerable periods of time and reveal no evidence for any discernible changes attendant on Scandinavian settlement in the vicinity. Excavations at Flixborough (Lincs) reveal that continuity of occupation from at least the eighth to eleventh centuries was coupled with transformations in the form, economy and status of the site both before and after the period of Scandinavian settlement. This was a high-status estate centre and possibly even a monastic complex during its earliest phases, but evidence for ecclesiastical activity ceases after the ninth century, and by the tenth century it had been transformed into a proto-manorial centre. The site subsequently became peripheral to occupation, which appears to have been relocated to the east, near to the church of North Conesby.[150] The excavations at Flixborough reveal a settlement that underwent changes of status, and considerable transformations in building construction and settlement layout, some of which respected earlier building plots, while others did not. The disruptions attendant on the Scandinavian raids and settlement are not revealed in the settlement archaeology of Flixborough; furthermore, no metalwork influenced by Scandinavian styles has been recovered.[151] Thus, the excavated site at Flixborough reveals evidence of continuity coupled with fluidity of organisation, and the latter was seemingly independent of Scandinavian influence. At Catholme (Staffs), just 18 km from Repton (Derbys) where the 'great army' overwintered in 873-4 (see p. 12-15), a group of farmsteads, comprising buildings located within ditched or fenced enclosures, arranged around trackways, was occupied from the sixth to the tenth centuries, and 'appears to have passed through this period [of Scandinavian conquest] without any obvious changes to its layout, architecture or location'.[152] At the middle to later Anglo-Saxon settlement site at Sedgeford (Norf) there is similarly no indication of a hiatus in occupation coincident with the period of Scandinavian rule in East Anglia, although the discovery of a single brooch with an Anglo-Saxon form but decorated in a Scandinavian style indicates that at least one inhabitant of Sedgeford had adopted and adapted the new cultural influences of the Scandinavians (see also pp. 120–7).[153]

The origins of nucleated villages

Many regions of northern and eastern England were characterised in the Middle Ages by nucleated villages, and any discussion of the impact of Scandinavian settlers on the rural landscape must take account of the extensive literature on the thorny problem of the origins of village nucleation. Although it has been attributed by some studies to Scandinavian influence, a brief review of the evidence suggests that in some cases this is unlikely, and in others the determining factor appears to be not so much the ethnic identity of the occupants of a settlement as their social status.

The evidence of excavation and field-walking permits a number of insights into developments in rural settlements in the ninth, tenth and eleventh centuries. In the broader field of rural settlement studies, recourse to ethnic explanations for the regional character of rural settlements has largely been abandoned.[154] Instead, it has been demonstrated that the nature of the local landscape played an important part in shaping the form of rural settlement, and many studies have revealed that regions of prime agricultural land, upland, woodland, marsh and fenland are each typically characterised by distinctive settlement types.[155] In attempting to identify the factors that prompted settlement nucleation, the various settlement zones across the country have been mapped against a whole series of variables, including topography; geology; population density; land use including the distribution of woodland, arable and pasture; the structure of lordship and land-holding; and the development of urban centers. However, it is clear that no single factor accounts for the distribution of nucleated villages.[156] The reasons for village nucleation remain elusive, but are believed to have included the increasing desire to participate in a market economy, the developing demands of the state, reorganisation associated with creation of communal 'open' fields resulting from soil exhaustion, and disputes over access to land.[157] The respective contributions of lords and peasant communities to the layout of rural settlements have also been extensively debated. Several studies have suggested that while the nucleation of settlement may have been instigated by peasant communities, the form that villages eventually took may have been influenced by lords.[158]

There is evidence for considerable rural settlement mobility throughout the Anglo-Saxon period. It is now clear that the nucleated village was a relatively late and anomalous development, and it is now widely accepted that the nucleated villages of the later Middle Ages find their origins in the period c.800–1200. Some studies suggest that village nucleation occurred, at least in some regions, in a very short period of time and constituted a veritable revolution in settlement organisation, while elsewhere the 'village moment' was a more gradual process.[159] Village nucleation must have been accompanied by a range of social and economic transformations. For example, a recent survey of building types has suggested that across England the tenth century witnessed the widespread emergence of increasingly durable buildings, previously limited to high-status sites such as monasteries, and that this was linked to the establishment of villages on permanent sites and the increasingly fixed boundaries and agricultural regimes that accompanied them.[160] Few villages in northern and eastern England have been extensively excavated; nonetheless, limited excavation and field-walking cast light on the emergence of villages. Pottery scatters from around and within many villages in northern and eastern England, including the extensively studied Wharram Percy, suggest that while the seventh- to ninth-century material is often found at various sites around the townships of those villages, later Anglo-Saxon pottery is virtually unknown from anywhere but the site of the medieval village. This suggests that the transition from a dispersed to a nucleated settlement pattern had occurred by the tenth or eleventh century.[161] Similarly, field-walking around the edge of the village at Langar (Leics) has produced large amounts of late Saxon pottery, and this is a pattern common to Leicestershire, where the vast majority of late Saxon settlements that have been identified coincide with later medieval villages.[162] At the same time, increasing numbers of villages are producing pottery pre-dating the ninth century, suggesting that there was a settlement focus present prior to the nucleation of the village. For example, a survey of villages in Launditch hundred in Norfolk revealed that tenth- and eleventh-century occupation was typically on the same sites as eighth- and ninth-century settlement, although it usually extended over a larger area. In such cases, as at an increasing number of sites across the country, nucleation witnessed the aggregation of settlement at one of a series of earlier settlement foci, rather than a de novo plantation.[163]

In parts of north Yorkshire many villages have a regular layout, typically consisting of two rows of evenly spaced properties on either side of a street. It is widely assumed that these villages date to the same period, and many studies suggest that they were seigneurial plantations, founded either in the wake of the Scandinavian conquest or following the devastation caused by William the Conqueror's 'harrying of the north' in 1069–70.[164] While the actions of William's army appear to have been severely destructive, they do not seem to account for the origins of village nucleation, although they may have required the reorganisation of existing villages. Domesday Book records that many vills were 'waste' in 1086, and many of these settlements exhibit a regular layout, suggesting that they had been restructured following the 'harrying'. Yet the correspondence between regular plans and waste vills is not exact, and it has recently been suggested that the economic importance of the vale of York provided an economic imperative to reorganisation that was less in evidence in, for example, the upland regions of neighbouring Nidderdale.[165] This debate relates to a period rather later than that with which this chapter is primarily concerned, but it provides useful parallels. It suggests that the impact of the conquest of regions by new groups is likely to be mediated by a range of factors, including the nature of the local landscape, local economy and the regional structure of lordship and land-holding. Indeed, a study of villages in the vale of Pickering suggested that, whenever they were founded, the manorial structure had an important impact on the layout of villages. Simple, and regular, village plans are commonly associated with vills with a single manorial lord, while some of the more complex village plans are associated with a multiplicity of manorial holdings.[166] This correlation between manorial structure and village morphology has also been noticed in Holderness (east Yorks) and parts of Lincolnshire.[167]

Lords did not show wide-ranging interest in the agricultural regimes of peasants in the better-documented later Middle Ages, and probably did not do so at an earlier date, yet it is not improbable that lords came to have an interest in the activities of the peasants whom they most intensively exploited, and this may have extended to the places where these peasants lived.[168] Rosamond Faith has recently suggested that the core (or 'inland') of a lord's estates commonly took on distinctive forms in the later Anglo-Saxon period, and included both the lord's residence and associated buildings (sometimes dubbed a *curia*) and a complex of regularly arranged tenements, sometimes enclosed within a boundary of some sort.[169] Such estate foci may have acted as magnets for settlement among the remainder of the peasant community.[170] Indeed, excavation at Goltho suggests that the village was a planned addition to a pre-existing seigneurial focus, and similar conclusions have been drawn from the study of Wharram Percy, Firsby (Lincs), Isham (Northants) and County Durham, where many villages comprised a manorial complex and associated tenements occupied by peasant villagers.[171] Village plans also sometimes appear to reflect the nature of lordship. For example, villages on episcopal estates in Durham are typically regular in plan, in contrast to irregular village plans and dispersed hamlets and farmsteads found elsewhere in the region, while the relatively servile tenants of Burton Abbey (Staffs) appear to have occupied a small number of larger and more tightly nucleated villages in the Trent valley of Derbyshire than was typical of this region. In Norfolk the more heavily burdened peasants lived in closely grouped rows in villages, while the freer peasants lived either in villages with more irregular plans or in scattered farmsteads.[172] It has been suggested that the creation of such regular plots for peasants may have been a territorialisation of peasant holdings, representing a transformation of what had hitherto been rights to a share in local resources enjoyed by peasants.[173]

The chronology of the development of the distinctive village layouts discussed above is generally difficult to date closely, and may date to a period beyond the focus of this chapter. Nonetheless, the discussion serves as an important reminder that the form of later medieval villages does not invariably reflect the form of villages at an earlier date, and settlements continued to undergo transformation, sometimes quite radical, after nucleation had occurred. For example, a recent survey of Lincolnshire villages revealed evidence that, at various dates, peasant tofts, manorial enclosures and churchyards were laid out over one another and over former arable land.[174] Meanwhile, fieldwork in Launditch Hundred in Norfolk revealed a complete absence of later Anglo-Saxon occupation around the greens typical of villages in this region, suggesting that they may have been a twelfth-century or later creation.[175] Thus, inferring origins from the later medieval plan of a village is hazardous, and in the absence of archaeological evidence we are unlikely to be able to illuminate either the settlement pattern at the time of the Scandinavian settlements or their subsequent contribution to the rural landscape.

We should remember that the settlers were not only distinguished by their place of origin; both they and their descendants consisted of leaders of various types, peasants, craftspeople and merchants. The Scandinavian impact on rural settlement must have been mediated by the status and interests of the occupants of given settlements. There is little reason to believe that lords of Scandinavian origin, many of whom we know to have continued to hold positions of authority long after the English conquest of parts of northern and eastern England (see p. 60), behaved in a significantly different fashion from indigenous lords. Given that it is no longer thought that the settlers played a significant role in colonising the countryside, but rather entered an extensively settled and cultivated landscape, and given that there is also no good evidence for the imposition by the newcomers of new agricultural practices, methods of exploitation of the peasantry or estate structures, it therefore seems unlikely that the Scandinavian settlers initiated distinctive settlement forms.[176] There seems little reason to doubt that they occupied the same range of villages, hamlets and dispersed farmsteads that were familiar to the local populations of northern and eastern England.

Identifying Scandinavian settlers in the archaeology of rural settlement is clearly difficult, and it is unlikely that, on its own, evidence for distinctive building types, or settlement dislocation and reorganisation will reveal Scandinavian influence. Aside from the moot point of whether early medieval peoples habitually expressed their ethnic identity in their houses and settlements, the impact of ethnic identity on rural settlements must have been mediated by the nature of the landscape, and by social and economic status. We must address the much wider range of evidence for rural settlement in the ninth, tenth and eleventh centuries than the small number of upland sites on which attention has traditionally focused, and also consider the broader context of rural settlement development, of which the arrival of Scandinavian settlers was but one element. In certain contexts, for example, extensively investigated settlements such as Wharram Percy and Cottam, it is possible to relate changes in the settlement layout and associated material culture to broader developments, and while the sites of Scandinavian settlement continue to prove elusive, the impact of the settlers on local expressions of status is much more readily identifiable.

Social interaction and personal names

The settlers and indigenous populations had a mutual influence on personal naming practices, and Domesday Book provides many examples of families whose members had a mixture of Scandinavian and English names.[177] The settlers may simply have started a new fashion in personal names. However, successive Scandinavian conquests and the survival of Scandinavian lords in positions of authority even after the West Saxon conquest of northern and eastern England may have encouraged people to align themselves and their children with their new overlords through a variety of means, including their choice of personal name.[178] In this context it is a nice question whether the reign of Guthrum in East Anglia in the late ninth century saw the name Guthrum adopted among local families, or whether his baptismal name Æthelstan proved more popular.

Many of the 'Scandinavian' personal names found in northern and eastern England are rather different from personal names recorded in Scandinavia, and it seems that in England new names were created out of the individual elements of compound names. For example, a much greater variety of compound names formed with -*brandr*, -*grímr*, -*hildr*, -*steinn* and -*ulfr* are found in England than in Scandinavia. The circumstances of settlement, and perhaps also the dissemination of these names among indigenous peoples, appear to have given rise to new naming practices.[179] Another development in personal naming practices that arose from the Scandinavian settlements, concerns the names of moneyers attested on coins of the later ninth and tenth centuries, many of which were Frankish. They are most numerous in areas of Scandinavian settlement, but are also found among the moneyers in the West Saxon heartlands. It may be that a group of Carolingian moneyers came to England following the Scandinavian conquest, but rather than indicating an ongoing influx of Carolingian moneyers, the continuing use of such names might be because such names came to be regarded as appropriate to someone of this profession. Indeed, some of the coins from East Anglia present Old Norse or Old English names in a Continental guise.[180]

It is notable that names of Scandinavian origin were often written in texts, on coins and on sculpture in the Roman alphabet to conform with either Old English or Latin spelling. For example, the Domesday tenant of Flixton (Suff) was called *Osketellus*: an Anglicised and Latinised version of the Scandinavian name *Ásketil*.[181] The majority of the coins minted in England for Scandinavian lords contained Latin inscriptions, while, as we have seen, runic inscriptions in any medium are comparatively rare. This presentation of names reflects scribal conformity, and the context in which documents, sculptures and coins were produced. Nonetheless, it must have played an important part in presenting successive Scandinavian rulers in the guise of Christian, English rulers. One wonders how long personal names of Scandinavian origin would have continued to be recognised as such, both by local society and also by subsequent generations of Scandinavian settlers and conquerors, especially once they had been adopted by prominent individuals within English society. The contemporary perception of personal names and their bearers is unlikely to have been limited to matters of etymology, and must have been determined by matters such as pronunciation and spelling, at least for the literate. We might note here the Anglicised -*cytel* (ON -*kætil*) in the names of Bishop Oscytel

(d. 971) and Ulfcytel (who died fighting Danish raiders in 1016) recorded in the *Anglo-Saxon Chronicle*.[182] Moreover, the associations that a name carried (genealogical, historical, legendary, familiar and so on) must also have affected perceptions of it.[183] Some personal names of Scandinavian origin may quickly have come to be regarded primarily as elite names, as they were borne by individuals in positions of authority.[184] Choices of personal names were not determined solely by genealogy, or by ethnic origins, and social and 'class' factors must also have been relevant.

Social interaction and material expressions of identity

The contribution of artefact studies to discussions of the Scandinavian settlement has traditionally been limited largely to stone sculpture. This evidence is hugely informative for studying the elite members of society, but is of limited value in understanding the response of the majority of the settlers to their new surroundings, or the reactions of the majority of local people to their new neighbours. In the light of this, recently recovered and reported finds of Scandinavian and Anglo–Scandinavian metalwork from northern and eastern England promise to make a significant, and potentially revolutionary, contribution to our understanding of the Scandinavian settlements. Although much of the relevant material is, as yet, unpublished, recent papers by Kevin Leahy, Caroline Richardson, Gabor Thomas and the late Sue Margeson have revealed that considerable amounts of metalwork have been recovered from, in particular, Norfolk, Suffolk, Lincolnshire and eastern Yorkshire.[185] The material consists of jewellery and dress-fittings (including brooches, buckles and strap-ends), Thor's hammers, horse-fittings (including mounts for harnesses and stirrups, and bridle cheek-pieces), weights and ingots. While some finds were imported from Scandinavia, many more artefacts were manufactured in England and combine English and Scandinavian styles and forms. Most of this newly discovered material has been recovered by metal-detectorists, and the distribution pattern must, to some extent, reveal both the amounts of land under the plough in those counties, which facilitates metal-detecting, and also the excellent contacts between the relevant museum curators and the metal-detecting fraternity.[186] Although the nature of recovery means that the finds generally lack any context, it does mean that they are a more widespread category of artefact than those found during excavation of settlements and cemeteries, and accordingly they derive from a much broader range of sites.

Preliminary analyses have tended towards comparing the distribution of the metalwork with a series of variables. For example, high densities of

Scandinavian and Anglo–Scandinavian metalwork have apparently been found in some regions with large numbers of Scandinavian place-names, such as the Yorkshire Wolds, the Lincolnshire Wolds and Kesteven to the south-east of Lincoln.[187] In Lincolnshire, the metalwork has been said to correlate well with the density of Domesday *sokemen*, suggested to be the descendants of the 'great army' that settled in the late ninth century, with *sokemen*, metalwork and Scandinavian place-names all, in contrast, rare in the immediate vicinity of Lincoln.[188] In Norfolk, however, no such correlation has been noted between Scandinavian place-names and Scandinavian and Anglo–Scandinavian metalwork.[189] The widespread distribution of the metalwork, the poor-quality execution of many pieces and the base metals in which much was produced have encouraged more than one commentator to conclude that the metalwork reflects the low status of the settlers and the widespread nature of the settlement. Moreover, in some studies, the metalwork has been used to bolster the case for a large-scale peasant settlement.[190]

In seeking the most appropriate interpretative framework, it is important to address three fundamental issues. First, the material needs to be considered in the context of similar finds from across England, and elsewhere in Britain. Second, we need to examine the relative Scandinavian and English influences on the form and design of the metalwork. Third, it is important to consider what, if any, aspects of social identity such small and relatively personal items of material culture might have conveyed.

Gabor Thomas has recently drawn attention to the widespread reduction in the production and circulation of dress-accessories and jewellery made of precious metals across the country in the tenth century. At the same time there was a general increase in the use of base-metals to produce more humble examples of the silver dress-accessories common at an earlier date. In other words, one of the characteristics of the metalwork discovered in eastern England is not, in fact, limited to that region. The general increase in base-metal artefacts may be accounted for by a variety of economic factors, while elite status and wealth may increasingly have been expressed less through personal adornment than through property-ownership, investment in estate centres, church-building and, in northern and eastern England, the commissioning of stone sculpture. Yet, whatever factors encouraged the increased production and use of base-metal dress-fittings and jewellery, as Thomas concludes, we have to be wary of a simple equation of such artefacts with low-status Scandinavian immigrants.[191] Nonetheless, the widespread distribution of these finds does imply that they belonged to a broad cross-section of society.

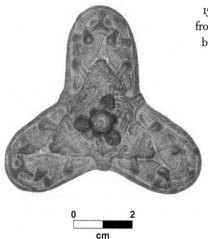

13 Scandinavian trefoil brooch from Stallingborough (Lincs). This brooch features 'gripping beasts' typical of the Borre style.

0   2

cm

Examples of Scandinavian metalwork recovered from eastern England include trefoil brooches (fig. 13), small quadrangular openwork brooches (fig. 14) and convex disc-brooches (fig. 15).[192] However, the Scandinavian metalwork is outweighed by metalwork that combines Scandinavian and English forms and styles (fig. 18). For example, a number of disc-brooches have been recovered that combine a typically English form with Scandinavian-style decoration (figs 16 and 22). English and Scandinavian disc-brooches are easily distinguished, as the former have a flat profile and two attachment lugs located in alignment with the perimeter of the brooch, while the latter are convex and the two attachment lugs are usually accom-panied by an attachment for a pendant.[193] Anglo-Saxon style flat disc-brooches recovered during excavation in York are decorated with backward-looking animals in the Jelling style (fig. 22), and a series of flat disc-brooches from East Anglia are decorated with an interlace pattern springing from a lozenge, with a central sunken circle, which appears to derive from, although is not identical to, the Borre style.[194] The distribu-tion of the latter suggests that they were manufactured in Norwich, perhaps in Norfolk, where a particularly fine example was found during excavation in the castle bailey (fig. 16).[195]

The decoration of disc-brooches of typically English form with Scandinavian motifs, does not, however, simply represent the transfer of Scandinavian motifs from Scandinavian-style disc-brooches, as many of the Scandinavian decorative motifs are found in Scandinavia not on disc-brooches but on other forms of jewellery, such as pendants. Furthermore,

14   Scandinavian quadrangular brooch from Elsham (Lincs). Such small openwork brooches are a typically Scandinavian form, with zoomorphic terminals.

0   1

cm

much of the metalwork found in eastern England that combines both Scandinavian form and style is different from prototypes found in Scandinavia. For example, among the trefoil brooches found in Norfolk, only two, from Taverham and Colton, have the very fine decoration typical of examples from Scandinavia, and it is consequently thought that many other examples were made locally.[196] Several disc-brooches from eastern England, including a published example from South Ferriby (Lincs), have a typically Scandinavian convex profile and are decorated with Jelling-style backward-looking animals, but rather than being imported Scandinavian artefacts, it is likely that they were produced in England, since convex disc-brooches decorated with this motif are virtually unknown in Scandinavia. The motif is, however, common in Scandinavia on pendants, and the disc-brooches from England appear, therefore, to represent the transfer of a Scandinavian motif from one type of artefact to another.[197] Thus, many artefacts found in England that are labelled as 'Scandinavian', on detailed investigation turn out to be Scandinavian with a difference.

Strap-ends are another dress-accessory common to both England and Scandinavia, which were associated with such dress-fittings as girdles, baldrics, garters and spur-straps, and decorated the item as well as preventing it from fraying (figs 17 and 21). Gabor Thomas has recently surveyed this class of artefact and has revealed the wide range of cultural influences present among strap-ends from eastern England. A small number of strap-ends can be widely paralleled in Scandinavia, including a tongue-shaped strap-end decorated with a Borre-style ring-knot design from Great Walsingham (Norf) (fig. 17).[198] More common are examples combining Scandinavian and Anglo-Saxon or Irish features. Examples include a strap-end from St Mary Bishophill Senior in York, combining

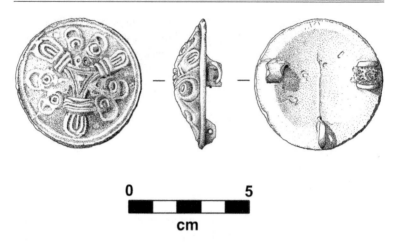

0   5
cm

15   Scandinavian convex disc-brooch from Heckingham (Norf). Convex
disc-brooches were common in Scandinavia. This example features three
cat-like animals. On the reverse are two lugs and a loop for a pendant, which
is a typical feature of Scandinavian brooches.

Borre-style decoration with an indigenous ring-and-dot design on its
underside (fig. 21), and a second from the city, from Coppergate, on which
Borre-style interlace has been modified into a form similar to the triquetra
motif of Irish metalwork.[199] Indeed, a number of strap-ends displaying
Irish influence have been found in eastern England, and many are believed
to have been made in England, rather than being imports, as there are
subtle differences in manufacture.[200] A group of tongue-shaped strap-ends
decorated with cat-like animal masks represent another example of the
transfer of a decorative motif from one artefact to another, because although
this motif is familiar from Scandinavian metalwork, it is commonly found
not on strap-ends but on convex disc-brooches.[201] In the north-west of
England a range of metalwork incorporating Irish and Scandinavian
designs has been recovered, prompting consideration of the likelihood that
the cultural milieu in which the inhabitants of this region – whatever their
origins – operated, was focused around the North Sea zone. Indeed, similarities in this region in elite material culture, including stone sculpture and
mound burials, point in the same direction.[202]

The dress-accessories displaying Scandinavian influence recovered
recently from eastern England do not provide a simple index of the locations or scale of Scandinavian settlement, but do have much to reveal about
the ways in which individuals and groups actively used material culture

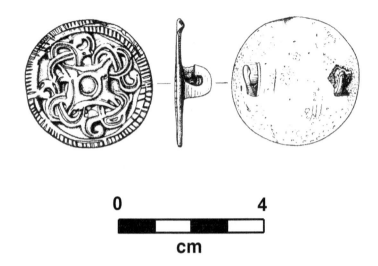

0   4

cm

16   Anglo–Scandinavian flat disc-brooch from Norwich (Norf). The disc-brooch has a typically Anglo-Saxon flat profile, but is decorated in the so-called Borre style. Several have been found in Norfolk, prompting speculation that they were manufactured in the area, perhaps at Norwich, where this particularly fine example was found during excavations in the castle bailey.

in the processes of cultural assimilation. The dress-fittings recovered from eastern England reflect a mixture of cultural influences, and those purchasing and wearing such dress-fittings were offered a choice that extended to items of Anglo-Saxon, Scandinavian, Irish and Carolingian origin and influence, and it appears that metalworkers adopted and adapted a diversity of forms and styles. The transfer of Scandinavian motifs from one artefact to another has been identified, and thus even artefacts of Scandinavian form bearing Scandinavian decoration sometimes display differences from metalwork found in Scandinavia, and these are presumed to have been produced in England. While pendants, oval-brooches and equal-arm brooches were common in Scandinavia, few such items of certain Scandinavian manufacture have been found in England. There is some debate about whether these typically Scandinavian forms of jewellery were becoming less fashionable in Scandinavia during the tenth century, with the increasing adoption of western European dress-accessories.[203] Certainly, this may partly account for the rarity of such artefacts in England, but the similarity between other forms of dress-accessory, especially

17 Scandinavian strap-end from Walsingham (Norf). This strap-end is
decorated in the Borre style, and features a so-called 'ring-chain' motif,
consisting of an interlacing motif and raised lozenges.

disc-brooches and strap-ends, in both England and Scandinavia may have
encouraged their production for a wide market in England and also rendered them especially likely media for cultural exchange and integration.
There appears to have been rapid cultural integration at the level of dress-
fittings and jewellery, and this implies that there was also rapid cultural
integration in the realm of costume, particularly for women, given the rarity
of oval brooches, which were typical of Scandinavian strap-dresses but
which could not easily have been adopted into Anglo-Saxon costume.[204]
These dress-accessories must have reflected a relatively personal statement, and are quite unlike the stone sculptures of northern and eastern
England, which were statements of lordly status and regional affiliations,
and which both recorded and doubtless contributed to the acculturation
process through the common juxtaposition of Scandinavian and indigenous motifs (see pp. 215–19). That certain types of typically Scandinavian
dress-fittings were abandoned soon after settlement, may also, as Thomas
suggests, indicate an avoidance of obviously 'foreign' accessories.[205]
Meanwhile, the combination of Anglo-Saxon and Scandinavian forms and
motifs (fig. 16) suggests that settlers and local people were exercising
mutual influence on aspects of personal adornment. It seems unlikely that
these fittings expressed a distinction between those of Scandinavian and
those of local origins, implying that in this medium, at least, cultural and
ethnic differences were not articulated.

126

18   Anglo–Scandinavian trefoil brooch
       from Cranwell (Lincs). This trefoil
       mount is an Anglo-Saxon copy of a
       Scandinavian object.

0   2
cm

That much artistic experimentation was conducted on female dress accessories, in particular disc-brooches as they were familiar to both Anglo-Saxon and Scandinavian society, may reflect the fact that Scandinavian acculturation was achieved within the context of intermarriage.[206] It is also a trait common to many early medieval contexts that experimentation in aspects of personal adornment was more common for women. For example, in the seventh century, previous regional differences in burial displays across Anglo-Saxon England gave way to a more uniform type of display drawing on the Roman heritage, which was most clearly expressed in female graves through pendants, necklaces, dress-fittings and chatelaines.[207] It is also primarily in female graves that we find a reflection of the growing influence of Christianity on Anglo-Saxon society, in the form of cross-shaped pendants in the seventh century, and a similar pattern has been noted in the cemeteries excavated at Birka (Sweden), dating to the period when Christianity was first becoming influential in Scandinavian society.[208] This is not to suggest, however, that men were immune to Scandinavian tastes, and a letter from an unknown author written later in the tenth century complains to a certain brother Edward about the deplorable practice of dressing 'in Danish fashion with bared necks and blinded eyes'.[209]

Hoards of coins and other metalwork have traditionally been studied as an index of the disruption attendant on the Scandinavian raids and settlement. It has, for example, been noted that hoards of coins not subsequently recovered are particularly frequent during the 860s and 870s when the great army was active in England.[210] Typically 'viking' hoards, containing hacksilver and ingots, as well as or instead of coins, have been found in a number of places, including Croydon (Surrey, deposited c.872), Cuerdale

(Lancs, c.905), Harkirke (Lancs, c.910), Goldsborough (Yorks, c.920) and Bossall (Yorks, c.927).[211] The Cuerdale hoard consisted of c.7,500 coins, including Scandinavian issues from York and East Anglia, Anglo-Saxon, Frankish, Italian, Arabic and Byzantine coins, four imitations of continental coins struck in Hedeby (Germany), hacksilver and ingots. It was found on what must have been the major trade route between York and Dublin, and it has been suggested that it may have been an army 'paychest', perhaps brought together during the circumstances of Scandinavian expulsion from Dublin in 902.[212] As we saw in the previous chapter, the political dimension of coins, many recovered from hoards, has also been extensively explored. However, hoards can also illuminate the nature of economic transactions conducted by the settlers. The discovery of many hoards throughout the country, containing Arabic and Frankish coins, jewellery, ingots and hacksilver, is also a reminder that at least some Scandinavians did not immediately adapt to the new monetary system adopted in East Anglia and in York, and continued to engage in their traditional barter economy. The longevity of this practice is open to debate, but, for at least a generation after settlement commenced, a dual economy existed among the Scandinavian newcomers, indicating that the monetary economy promoted by Scandinavian rulers in East Anglia and York was not universally adopted.[213] A hoard from Thurcaston (Leics), deposited in the mid-920s, included coins from York and Lincoln, Arabic dirhems, and coins of Edward the Elder, suggesting that at least some members of this community persisted with a barter economy after the *burh* at Leicester, just five miles away, was captured by Æthelflaed in 918.[214] This evidence is an important reminder of the diverse strategies adopted by the Scandinavians, and that the modes of behaviour of their overlords were not invariably adopted by the remainder of the settlers.

Ethnic solidarity in the later tenth century?

Evidence has often been sought to support the presumption that Danish raiders of the late tenth and early eleventh centuries received support from the regions where Scandinavians had settled in earlier generations. However, while the strategies of these raiders may have been encouraged by memories of earlier Scandinavian settlement in northern and eastern England, to take one example, the choice of Gainsborough (Lincs) as the starting point for Swein Forkbeard's attempts to conquer England in 1013 was probably determined by its distance from the heartlands of the English kings and the disaffection of northern nobles from King Æthelred, rather than the expectation of being able to draw upon latent feelings of ethnic allegiance. The support he received in northern England and the north Midlands was regional rather than discernibly 'Danish', and political calculation, rather than expectation of ethnic loyalties, probably lay behind his decision to desist from doing great damage until he had crossed Watling Street. We should also note that the citizens of 'English' Oxford and Winchester and those in the vicinity of Bath also quickly submitted to Swein.[215] Attempts to argue that the political and military events of the later tenth and early eleventh centuries reflect innate 'ethnic' differences between Danes (the descendants of earlier settlers) and English north of Watling Street, depend upon assumption and circular argument – the evidence we have does not prove it, and often suggests that ethnic affiliation was not relevant at all during this period of conflict.[216] This is not, however, to deny that regional disputes and affiliations, political manoeuvring, military conquest, and disputes over land may have periodically revived memories of the diverse ancestry of inhabitants of parts of England, creating or reviving ethnic differences, rather than vice versa.[217] In the early twelfth century, 'Florence' of Worcester blamed the failure of the English army to oppose the Danish fleet that arrived in the Humber in 993 on the Danish ancestry of three of the generals, but rather than proving that ethnic sympathies with the Danish raiders ran deep, it as plausibly suggests that in times of conflict any discernible difference about enemies and traitors might be seized upon and framed in ethnic terms.[218]

The law-codes referring to 'Danes', discussed in chapter 2, had a political and social dimension that renders them, at best, indirect indicators of ethnic identities in the regions that experienced Scandinavian settlement. Of themselves, they throw little light on interpersonal relations in northern and eastern England, or on the ways in which individuals of diverse backgrounds experienced the law. Only rare surviving accounts of local legal disputes, such as that concerning land in Bluntisham (Hunts), can reveal the ways in which law was put into practice. In the case of the Bluntisham dispute, which concerns land granted to a family's ancestor following submission to Edward the Elder (see p. 60), there is no suggestion of legal separatism, at least among this family of Danish descent, and the matter was resolved in a forum common to all the local inhabitants. Nonetheless, as Matthew Innes has recently observed, this dispute suggests a family apparently maintaining a Danish ethnic identity in order to lay claim to land – notably on the basis that the ancestor had submitted to the English king decades earlier. Thus, while Danish ancestry may not have been a factor determining everyday behaviour, in certain circumstances this ethnic identity could become 'live'.[219]

In the light of these debates, it is notable that eleventh-century artefacts of Scandinavian type, decorated in the so-called Urnes and Ringerike styles, are rare in the northern and eastern midlands and in the north of England, and such finds appear to have been largely limited to East Anglia and southern England and the heartland of Cnut's kingdom.[220] A similar pattern emerges from the study of stone sculpture, with the later Scandinavian influences, again, almost exclusively found in southern England and East Anglia.[221] This suggests that the cultural influences of Cnut's followers were largely on a regional scale, and that this subsequent conquest did not have the effect of renewing a sense of Scandinavian solidarity among the inhabitants of those regions settled by earlier generations of Scandinavians.

Conclusions

The scale of the Scandinavian settlements has been extensively debated (see pp. 2–6), and while none of the evidence discussed in this chapter can resolve the debate conclusively, it seems most unlikely that the settlement could have been limited to that of an elite conquest by a few hundred warriors. However, this does not mean that the settlement was a folk migration, and perhaps a few thousand settlers may account for the Scandinavian influence discernible in so many aspects of the society and culture of northern and eastern England. A more profitable line of enquiry than continuing attempts to quantify the settlement is offered by evidence for the ways in which the settlers and local populations reacted to each other. Violent and disruptive as the settlements were, a remarkably consistent picture of adoption and adaptation emerges from a variety of evidence. Written sources suggest, for example, that some of the Scandinavian settlers took over existing administrative organisation and estate structures. Many of the characteristic social and economic features of northern and eastern England find their origins long before the Scandinavian settlements, although this is not to suggest that they were not modified by the settlers, or as a result of the disruption they caused. This should not be surprising, since in the turbulent circumstances of the later ninth and tenth centuries it would not only have been desirable, but often entirely necessary, to make use of existing institutions if the conquerors were to secure their authority and make a living. We have already seen, in the chapter 2, that the leaders of the Scandinavians occupied existing centres of power, adopted practices and styles of leadership that were familiar to the local population and drew on the support of the local elite. Moreover, from the evidence discussed in the present chapter, it appears that their leading followers also adopted and adapted native institutions.

Recent linguistic analysis suggests that Anglo–Scandinavian interaction is likely to have been facilitated by the mutual intelligibility of Old English and Old Norse, but whether this led to the swift emergence of 'Scandinavian English', or saw the settlers rapidly switch to speaking English rather than continuing to speak in their native language, remains a debatable point. Most other lines of enquiry point to rapid assimilation, but we must allow for the possibility that alongside the adoption of many aspects of English society, culture and rural organisation, there remained for a time aspects of undiluted Scandinavian culture and Norse-speaking communities. Given recent work on place-names, it seems possible that in some regions there was very dense Scandinavian settlement, and a period of little or no assimilation during which purely Scandinavian place-names were coined, before Anglo–Scandinavian acculturation commenced. Intriguingly, however, these appear to be the very regions producing huge quantities of metalwork in which Anglo-Saxon and Scandinavian influences were combined. Either the latter evidence post-dates the formation of the place-names, or they are contemporary, suggesting that for a time the settlers preserved aspects of their culture while simultaneously modifying others.

It remains difficult to identify the places where Scandinavians settled. Place-names indicate regions of dense settlement, but absence of surviving Scandinavian place-names does not indicate an absence of any settlement, although it suggests that the settlers were in a minority in those regions. In a few cases archaeological evidence reveals the impact of the settlers on expressions of lordly status, but on the whole the settlers and the local populations are indistinguishable in the archaeological record for rural settlement. Rather than continuing to argue that this is a lacuna in our evidence, we have to begin to address the probability that the settlers and the local populations of northern and eastern England occupied a similar range of settlement types and buildings, and that both this and subsequent change were as much influenced by environment and social and economic factors as by a sense of ethnic distinctiveness. For this reason, the recent discovery of large numbers of dress-accessories in eastern England offers an important perspective on Anglo–Scandinavian interaction and integration. Perhaps the most striking insight to emerge from the range of evidence explored in this chapter is that the inhabitants of northern and eastern England appear to have behaved in a manner determined more by their social status than by their ethnic identity; ethnic differences doubtless persisted in various aspects of life, but expressing this on a day-to-day basis seems to have been rare. In sum, it appears that the practicalities of everyday life dictated that social status and its underpinnings were more pressing concerns than ethnicity; the dynamics of social interaction between the settlers and the local population were complicated by social standing and existing regional cultures; and that in seeking a pure, undiluted Scandinavian imprint in the archaeological record, we will therefore rarely succeed.

Notes

1. B. Myrhe, 'The beginning of the Viking Age – some current archaeological problems', in A. Faulkes and R. Perkins (eds), *Viking Revaluations* (London, 1993), pp. 182–216; for comparable situations see C. D. Morris, 'Comments on the early settlement of Iceland', *Norwegian Arch. Review*, 24 (1991), 18–20; L. Abrams and D. N. Parsons, 'Place-names and the history of Scandinavian settlement in England', in J. Hines, A. Lane and M. Redknap (eds), *Land, Sea and Home* (London, 2004), pp. 379–431, at 415–21.
2. See, for example, D. W. Anthony, 'Migration in archaeology: the baby and the bath-water', *American Anthropology*, 92 (1990), 895–914.
3. J. Jesch, *Women in the Viking Age* (Woodbridge, 1991), p. 97.
4. *EHD I*, p. 205.
5. J. L. Nelson (ed.), *The Annals of St-Bertin* (Manchester, 1991), p. 99; Jesch, *Women in the Viking Age*, p. 104.
6. *Ibid.*, pp. 104–5.
7. C. Clark, 'Clark's first three laws of Applied Anthroponymics', *Nomina*, 3 (1979), 13–19, at 17–18.
8. *EHD I*, p. 218.
9. *Ibid.*, p. 283.
10. P. A. Stafford, *Unification and Conquest: a political and social history of England in the tenth and eleventh centuries* (London, 1989), pp. 24, 31–40; A. Williams, ' "Cockles among the wheat": Danes and English in the western midlands in the first half of the eleventh century', *Midland History*, hereafter: *Mid. Hist.*, 11 (1986), 1–22, at 14; *idem, The English and the Norman Conquest* (Woodbridge, 1995), pp. 199–202.
11. N. Lund, 'Allies of God or Man? The Viking expansion in a European context', *Viator*, 19 (1989), 45–59, at 52–6.
12. Stafford, *Unification and Conquest*, pp. 27–34.
13. See, for example, D. Griffiths, 'Settlement and acculturation in the Irish Sea region', in Hines, Lane and Redknap (eds), *Land, Sea and Home*, pp. 125–38.
14. See, for example, G. R. J. Jones, 'Multiple estates and early settlement', in P. H. Sawyer (ed.), *English Medieval Settlement* (London, 1979), pp. 9–34; *idem*, 'Early territorial organization in Northern England and its bearing on the Scandinavian settlement', in A. Small (ed.), *The Fourth Viking Congress* (Edinburgh, 1965), pp. 67–84; G. W. S. Barrow, *The Kingdom of the Scots: government, church and society from the eleventh to the thirteenth century* (London, 1973),

pp. 10–60; J. Blair, *Early Medieval Surrey: land-holding, church and settlement* (Stroud, 1991), pp. 12–34; D. M. Hadley, 'Multiple estates and the origins of the manorial structure of the northern Danelaw', *Journal of Historical Geography*, hereafter: *JHG*, 22 (1) (1996), 3–15.

15 T. J. South, *Historia de Sancto Cuthberto. A history of Saint Cuthbert and a record of his patrimony* (Cambridge, 2002), pp. 61, 104–6. The grant to Alfred was as follows: 'Then Bishop Cuthheard . . . granted him these estates: Easington, Monk Hesleden, Thorpe, Horden, Eden, the two Shottons, South Eden, Hulam, Hutton, *Twinlingtun*, Billingham with its members, Sheraton'.

16 *Ibid.*, pp. 63, 106–7.

17 *EHD I*, p. 283; P. H. Sawyer, *Kings and Vikings: Scandinavia and Europe AD 700–1100* (London, 1982), pp. 104–5; *idem, Anglo-Saxon Lincolnshire* (Lincoln, 1998), p. 98.

18 A. Campbell (ed.), *The Chronicle of Æthelweard* (Edinburgh, 1962), p. 43.

19 See note 14 above.

20 Hadley, 'Multiple estates'; D. M. Hadley, *The Northern Danelaw: its social structure, c.800–1100* (London, 2000), pp. 118–40; P. Warner, 'Pre-Conquest territorial and administrative organisation in East Suffolk', in D. Hooke (ed.), *Anglo-Saxon Settlements* (Oxford, 1985), pp. 9–34; S. Keynes, 'Ely Abbey, 672–1109', in P. Meadows and N. Ramsey (eds), *A History of Ely Cathedral* (Woodbridge, 2003), pp. 3–58, at 15–18; T. Williamson, *The Origins of Norfolk* (Manchester, 1993), pp. 144–5; D. Whitelock, 'The pre-viking church in East Anglia', *ASE*, 1 (1972), 1–22.

21 Hadley, *The Northern Danelaw*, pp. 131–8; S. R. Bassett, 'In search of the origins of Anglo-Saxon kingdoms', in S. R. Bassett (ed.), *The Origins of Anglo-Saxon Kingdoms* (Leicester, 1989), pp. 3–27, at 17–20.

22 Jones, 'Early territorial organization'; W. E. Kapelle, *The Norman Conquest of the North. The Region and Its Transformation, 1000–1135* (London, 1979), pp. 62–85.

23 Hadley, *The Northern Danelaw*, pp. 140–55.

24 *EHD I*, p. 205; Sawyer, *Anglo-Saxon Lincolnshire*, p. 97.

25 A. Armstrong, A. Mawer, F. M. Stenton and B. Dickins, *The Place-Names of Cumberland*, 3 vols (Cambridge, 1950–2), II, p. 2; V. Watts, 'Scandinavian settlement-names in County Durham', *Nomina*, 12 (1988–9), 17–63, at 28, 40; see also M. Townend, *Language and History in Viking Age England. Linguistic relations between speakers of Old Norse and Old English* (Turnhout, 2002), p. 5.

26 N. Higham, 'Viking Age settlement in the north-western countryside: lifting the veil?', in Hines, Lane and Redknap (eds), *Land, Sea and Home*, pp. 297–311, at 303; South, *Historia de Sancto Cuthberto*, pp. 59, 95.

27 C. D. Morris, 'Aspects of Scandinavian settlement in northern England: a review', *North. Hist.*, 20 (1984), 1–22, at 7.

28 Hadley, *The Northern Danelaw*, pp. 153–4.

29 H. Loyn, *Anglo-Saxon England and the Norman Conquest* (2nd edn, London, 1991), pp. 357–62.

30 F. M. Stenton, *Types of Manorial Structure in the Northern Danelaw* (Oxford, 1910), pp. 35–7; B. Dodwell, 'The free peasantry of East Anglia in Domesday',

Norfolk Arch., 27 (1947), 145–57; R. H. C. Davis, *A Kalendar of abbot Samson of Bury St Edmunds and Related Documents*, Camden 3rd ser., 84 (1954); E. King, 'The Peterborough *"descriptio militum"* ', *EHR*, 84 (1969), 84–101; Loyn, *Anglo-Saxon England*, pp. 357–62; R. Faith, *The English Peasantry and the Growth of Lordship* (Leicester, 1997), pp. 114–25; Hadley, *The Northern Danelaw*, pp. 180–9.

31   F. M. Stenton, 'The Danes in England', *Proceedings of the British Academy*, 13 (1927), 1–46, at 17–18.

32   The relevant debates are summarised in Faith, *The English Peasantry*, pp. 114–25, and p. 83 for the quotation; and Hadley, *The Northern Danelaw*, pp. 189–96.

33   F. M. Stenton, *Anglo-Saxon England* (3rd edn, Oxford, 1971), pp. 298–300; H. Loyn, 'The hundred in England in the tenth and eleventh centuries', in H. Hearder and H. Loyn (eds), *British Government and Administration. Studies presented to S. B. Chrimes* (Cardiff, 1974), pp. 1–15; Williamson, *The Origins of Norfolk*, pp. 126–33; Morris, 'Aspects of Scandinavian settlement', 8; R. Cramp, *Corpus of Anglo-Saxon Stone Sculpture, Vol. 1. County Durham and Northumberland*, Part One (Oxford, 1984), p. 29; J. Lang, 'The hogback: a Viking colonial monument', *ASSAH*, 3 (1984), 85–176.

34   A. Winchester, *Landscape and Society in Medieval Cumbria* (Edinburgh, 1987), pp. 13–16.

35   Stenton, *Anglo-Saxon England*. pp. 298–300; D. Roffe, *The Lincolnshire Domesday* (London, 1992), p. 32.

36   *EHD I*, pp. 429–30; P. Wormald, *The Making of English Law: King Alfred to the twelfth century* (Oxford, 1999), pp. 378–9.

37   Loyn, 'The hundred in England', pp. 3–7.

38   Roffe, *The Lincolnshire Domesday*, pp. 40–1.

39   S 106, 274; Stenton, *Anglo-Saxon England*, p. 298; A. Reynolds, *Later Anglo-Saxon England: life and landscape* (Stroud, 1999), pp. 76–7.

40   Stenton, *Anglo-Saxon England*, pp. 298–9.

41   B. Yorke, *Wessex in the Early Middle Ages* (London, 1985), pp. 124–5.

42   A. Meaney, 'Pagan sanctuaries, place-names and hundred meeting-places', *ASSAH*, 8 (1995), 29–42, at 35–7; S. Turner, 'Aspects of the development of public assembly in the Danelaw', *Assemblage*, 5 (2000) available at www.shef.ac.uk/assem/, last accessed 24 December 2005.

43   Williamson, *The Origins of Norfolk*, pp. 128–9.

44   Turner, 'Aspects of the development of public assembly'; Meaney, 'Pagan sanctuaries, place names', p. 36.

45   Reynolds, *Later Anglo-Saxon England*, pp. 108–9.

46   A. Reynolds, 'The definition and ideology of Anglo-Saxon execution sites and cemeteries', in G. De Boe and F. Verhaege (eds), *Death and Burial in Medieval Europe: Papers of the Medieval Europe 1997 Conference* (Brugge, 1997), pp. 34–41, at 36–7; Turner, 'Aspects of the development of public assembly', 9.

47   G. Fellows-Jensen, 'Tingwall, Dingwall and Thingwall', in *Twenty-Eight Papers Presented to Hans Bekker-Nielsen on the Occasion of His Sixtieth Birthday* (Odense, 1993), pp. 53–67, at 58.

48 B. Cox, 'Leicestershire moot-sites: the place-name evidence', *Leicestershire Archaeological and Historical Society Transactions* hereafter: *LAHST*, 47 (1971–72), 14–21, at 19; Turner, 'Aspects of the development of public assembly', 9; Fellows-Jensen, 'Tingwall', p. 57.

49 Williamson, *The Origins of Norfolk*, pp. 126–8.

50 J. Geipel, *The Viking Legacy. The Scandinavian influence on the English and Gaelic languages* (Newton abbot, 1971), p. 70; B. Hansen, 'The historical implications of the Scandinavian element in English: a theoretical valuation', *Nowele*, 4 (1984), 53–95; D. Kastovsky, 'Semantics and vocabulary', in R. M. Hogg (ed.), *The Cambridge History of the English Language*, vol. 1 (Cambridge, 1992), pp. 290–408, at 320, 332–6.

51 M. Barnes, 'Norse in the British Isles', in Faulkes and Perkins (eds), *Viking Revaluations*, pp. 65–84, at 81.

52 Townend, *Language and History in Viking Age England*, pp. 4–9.

53 *Ibid.*, p. 3. In this study 'the term "Old Norse" is used to designate the language spoken by Scandinavians in the Viking Age: it does not mean "Norwegian"'.

54 O. Jespersen, *Growth and Structure of the English Language* (9th edn, Oxford, 1956), p. 75; G. Fellows-Jensen 'The Vikings in England: a review', *ASE*, 4 (1975), 181–206, at 201–2; R. M. Hogg, 'Introduction', in Hogg (ed.), *The Cambridge History of the English Language*, pp. 1–25, at 7; see also Townend, *Language and History in Viking Age England*, pp. 9–10.

55 *Ibid.*, pp. 43–87, at p. 67 for the quotation.

56 J. M. Bateley, *The Old English Orosius*, EETS supplementary series, 6 (London, 1980); Townend, *Language and History in Viking Age England*, pp. 90–109.

57 Campbell, *The Chronicle of Æthelweard*, p. 37; Townend, *Language and History in Viking Age England*, pp. 117–18.

58 *Ibid.*, p. 127.

59 J. C. Pope, *Homilies of Ælfric: a supplementary collection*, 2 vols, Early English Text Society, hereafter: EETS (Oxford, 1967–68), II, pp. 683–6; Townend, *Language and History in Viking Age England*, pp. 128–38, 143.

60 *Ibid.*, pp. 161–71.

61 *Ibid.*, pp. 145–61.

62 *Ibid.*, pp. 138, 187.

63 E. Ekwall, 'How long did the Scandinavian language survive in England?', in N. Bøgholm, A. Brusendorff and C. Bodelsen (eds), *A Grammatical Miscellany Offered to Otto Jespersen on His Seventieth Birthday* (London and Copenhagen, 1930), pp. 17–30, at 20–1.

64 R. I. Page, 'How long did the Scandinavian language survive in England? The epigraphical evidence', in P. Clemoes and K. Hughes (eds), *England Before the Conquest: studies in primary sources presented to Dorothy Whitelock* (Cambridge, 1971), pp. 165–81, at 181.

65 D. Parsons, 'How long did the Scandinavian language survive in England? Again', in J. Graham-Campbell, R. A. Hall, J. Jesch and D. Parsons (eds), *Vikings and the Danelaw: Select papers from the proceedings of the Thirteenth Viking Congress* (Oxford, 2001), pp. 299–312, at 300.

66 Townend, *Language and History in Viking Age England*, pp. 192–3.

67 Ekwall, 'How long did the Scandinavian language survive in England?', p. 21.

68 Parsons, 'How long did the Scandinavian language survive in England? Again', p. 301.

69 K. Holman, *Scandinavian Runic Inscriptions in the British Isles: their historical context* (Trondheim, 1996), pp. 48–50; Parsons, 'How long did the Scandinavian language survive in England? Again', p. 305.

70 Holman, *Scandinavian Runic Inscriptions*, pp. 43–5; Parsons, 'How long did the Scandinavian language survive in England? Again', p. 307.

71 Holman, *Scandinavian Runic Inscriptions*, pp. 41–3; Parsons, 'How long did the Scandinavian language survive in England? Again', pp. 303, 307.

72 Page, 'How long did the Scandinavian language survive in England? The epigraphical evidence', pp. 172–3; R. I. Page, *Runes and Runic Inscriptions: collected essays on Anglo-Saxon and Viking runes* (Woodbridge, 1995), p. 196.

73 Ekwall, 'How long did the Scandinavian language survive in England?', p. 29.

74 G. Fellows-Jensen, *Scandinavian Settlement Names in the North-West* (Copenhagen, 1985), pp. 22–4; J. Insley, 'Toponymy and settlement in the North-West: a review of Gillian Fellows-Jensen, *Scandinavian Settlement Names in the North-West*', *Nomina*, 10 (1986), 169–76, at 172; B. K. Roberts, 'Late -*bý;* names in the Eden Valley, Cumberland', *Nomina*, 13 (1989–90), 25–40, on pp. 34–5.

75 Parsons, 'How long did the Scandinavian language survive in England? Again', p. 305.

76 *Ibid.*, p. 308. He does, however, express the caveat that these names require further investigation, and it is possible that 'the distinctively Norse genitives that have been identified in some examples will not stand up to scrutiny'.

77 Townend, *Language and History in Viking Age England*, pp. 192–4.

78 J. Hines, 'Scandinavian English: a creole in context', in P. S. Ureland and G. Broderick (eds), *Language Contact in the British Isles* (Tübingen, 1991), pp. 403–27, at 417–18.

79 Parsons, 'How long did the Scandinavian language survive in England? Again', p. 308.

80 Townend, *Language and History in Viking Age England*, p. 3.

81 Textual evidence has little to say about domestic arrangements among wider society, but among the elite, at least, mothers had a historically attested role in educating their children: P. A. Stafford, *Queens, Concubines and Dowagers. The king's wife in the early Middle Ages* (London, 1983), pp. 112–13.

82 Townend, *Language and History in Viking Age England*, pp. 201–4.

83 J. D. Richards, *Viking Age England* (2nd edn, Stroud, 2000), p. 45.

84 See the map in *ibid.*, p. 44.

85 S. Keynes, 'The vikings in England, c.790–1016', in P. H. Sawyer (ed.) *The Oxford Illustrated History of the Vikings* (Oxford, 1997), pp. 48–82, at 64.

86 The literature is vast, but examples include Stenton, 'The Danes in England'; *idem, Anglo-Saxon England*, p. 521; K. Cameron, *Scandinavian Settlement in the Territory of the Five Boroughs: the place-name evidence* (Nottingham, 1965);

idem, 'Scandinavian settlement in the territory of the Five Boroughs: the place-name evidence, part II, place-names in thorp', *Mediaeval Scandinavia*, III (1970), 35–49; *idem*, 'Scandinavian settlement in the territory of the Five Boroughs: the place-name evidence, part III. the Grimston-hybrids', in Clemoes and Hughes (eds), *England before the Conquest*, pp. 147–63; P. H. Sawyer, *The Age of the Vikings* (2nd edn, 1971), pp. 154–67; N. Lund, 'The settlers: where do we get them from – and do we need them?', in H. Bekker-Nielsen, P. Foote and O. Olsen (eds), *Proceedings of the Eighth Viking Congress* (Odense, 1981), pp. 147–71; G. Fellows-Jensen, 'Of Danes – and thanes – and Domesday Book', in I. Wood and N. Lund (eds), *People and Places in Northern Europe, 500–1600* (Woodbridge, 1991), pp. 107–21; *idem*, 'Scandinavian settlement in Yorkshire – through the rear-view mirror', in B. Crawford (ed.), *Scandinavian Settlement in Northern Britain* (Leicester, 1995), pp. 170–86; the relevant literature has recently been reviewed in Abrams and Parsons, 'Place-names', pp. 379–92.

87 Cameron, *Scandinavian Settlement*; *idem*, 'Place-names in thorp'; *idem*, 'The Grimston-hybrids'; P. H. Sawyer, 'Conquest and colonisation: Scandinavians in the Danelaw and in Normandy', in Bekker-Nielsen, Foote and Olsen (eds), *Proceedings of the Eighth Viking Congress*, pp. 123–31, at 129; *idem*, *Kings and Vikings*, p. 103.

88 Sawyer, *Medieval English Settlement*, p. 5; *idem*, *The Age of the Vikings* (2nd edn, London, 1971), pp. 154–67; H. Fox, 'The people of the wolds in English settlement history', in M. Aston, D. Austin and C. C. Dyer (eds), *The Rural Settlements of Medieval England* (London, 1989), pp. 85–96, at 92; P. Wormald, 'Viking studies: whence and whither?', in R. T. Farrell (ed.), *The Vikings* (Chichester, 1982), pp. 128–53, 135–6; Hadley, *The Northern Danelaw*, pp. 330–1; Abrams and Parsons, 'Place-names', pp. 404–5, 414–15.

89 G. Fellows-Jensen, 'Danish place-names and personal names in England: the influence of Cnut?', in A. Rumble (ed.), *The Reign of Cnut, King of England, Denmark and Norway* (London, 1994), pp. 125–40, at 132.

90 Townend, *Language and History in Viking Age England*, p. 188.

91 G. Fellows-Jensen, 'Scandinavian settlement in the Danelaw in the light of the place-names of Denmark', in Bekker-Nielsen, Foote and Olsen (eds), *Proceedings of the Eighth Viking Congress*, pp. 133–45, at 141; Sawyer, *Anglo-Saxon Lincolnshire*, p. 102; Abrams and Parsons, 'Place-names', p. 412.

92 G. Fellows-Jensen, *Scandinavian Settlement Names in Yorkshire* (Copenhagen, 1972), p. 118; K. Cameron, 'Early field-names in an English-named Lincolnshire village' in F. Sandgren (ed.), *Otium et Negotium* (Stockholm, 1973), pp. 38–43, at 41; Lund, 'The settlers', pp. 156–67; G. Fellows-Jensen, 'Place-names and the Scandinavian settlement in the North Riding of Yorkshire', *North. Hist.*, 14 (1978), 19–46, at 38; Morris, 'Aspects of Scandinavian Settlement', pp. 10–11.

93 G. Fellows-Jensen, 'Danish place-names and personal names'; *idem*, 'In the steps of the Vikings', in Graham-Campbell, Hall, Jesch and Parsons (eds), *Vikings and the Danelaw*, pp. 279–88, at 285–6; Parsons, 'Scandinavian language', pp. 301–2.

94 Fellows-Jensen, 'Of Danes – and thanes'; *idem*, 'Scandinavian settlement in Yorkshire'.

95 P. H. Sawyer, 'Medieval English settlement: new interpretations', in Sawyer (ed.), *English Medieval Settlement*, pp. 1–8, at 2; Richards, *Viking Age England*, p. 47.

96 Fox, 'The people of the wolds'; Wormald, 'Viking studies', pp. 135–6.

97 G. Fellows-Jensen, 'Scandinavian place-names of the Irish Sea province', in J. Graham-Campbell (ed.), *Viking Treasure from the North-West: the Cuerdale Hoard in its context* (Liverpool, 1992), pp. 31–42; Higham, 'Viking Age settlement', pp. 299–303.

98 Townend, *Language and History in Viking Age England*, pp. 43–68, esp. 52–7.

99 Sawyer, *Kings and Vikings*, pp. 102–3; Hadley, *The Northern Danelaw*, p. 331.

100 K. Hald, *Vore Stednavne* (Copenhagen, 1965), 109–13; G. Fellows-Jensen, *Scandinavian Settlement Names in the East Midlands* (Copenhagen, 1978), pp. 15–17, 27–8; Abrams and Parsons, 'Place-names', pp. 404–11.

101 M. Townend, 'Viking Age England as a bilingual society', in D.M. Hadley and J.D. Richards (eds), *Cultures in Contact: Scandinavian Settlement in England in the ninth and tenth centuries* (Turnhout, 2000), pp. 89–105, at 98.

102 Abrams and Parsons, 'Place-names', pp. 394–403; on field-names see, for example, K. Cameron, 'The Scandinavian element in minor names and field-names in north-east Lincolnshire', *Nomina*, 19 (1996), 5–27.

103 Abrams and Parsons, 'Place-names', pp. 412–13.

104 Sawyer, *Kings and Vikings*, p. 106; Hadley, *The Northern Danelaw*, pp. 139–40.

105 A. King, 'Gauber high pasture, Ribblehead – an interim report', in R. A. Hall (ed.), *Viking Age York and the North,* CBA Research Rep., 27 (London, 1978), pp. 21–5.

106 S. Dickinson, 'Bryant's Gill, Kentmere: another "viking-period" Ribblehead?', in J. R. Baldwin and I. D. Whyte (eds), *The Scandinavians in Cumbria* (Edinburgh, 1985), pp. 83–8.

107 D. Coggins, K. J. Fairless and C. E. Batey, 'Simy Folds: an early medieval settlement in Upper Teesdale, Co. Durham', *Medieval Archaeology*, hereafter: *Med. Arch.*, 27 (1983), 1–26.

108 King, 'Gauber high pasture, Ribblehead', p. 25.

109 Coggins, Fairless and Batey, 'Simy Folds', 22–3. See now A. King, 'Post-Roman upland architecture in the Craven dales and the dating evidence', in Hines, Lane and Redknap (eds), *Land, Sea and Home*, pp. 335–44; D. Coggins, 'Simy Folds: twenty years on', in *ibid.*, pp. 326–34.

110 B. J. N. Edwards, *Vikings in North West England* (Lancaster, 1998), p. 5; F. Philpott, *A Silver Saga: Viking treasure from the North West* (Liverpool, 1990), p. 56; Morris, 'Aspects of Scandinavian settlement', 15; C. Batey, 'Aspects of rural settlement in Northern Britain', in D. Hooke and S. Burnell (eds), *Landscape and Settlement in Britain AD 400–1066* (Exeter, 1995), pp. 69–94, at 90. This literature is reviewed in J. D. Richards, 'Identifying Anglo–Scandinavian settlements', in Hadley and Richards (eds), *Cultures in Contact*, pp. 295–309, at 298–9.

111 P. J. Huggins, 'The excavation of an 11th-century Viking hall and 14th-century rooms at Waltham Abbey, Essex, 1969-71', *Med. Arch.*, 20 (1976), 75–133.

112 J. Graham-Campbell, 'British Antiquity 1976–77: Western British, Irish and later

Anglo-Saxon', *Archaeological Journal*, hereafter: *Arch. J.*, 134 (1977), 418–35, at 427; see also Richards, 'Anglo–Scandinavian settlements', pp. 300–1.

113 Richards, 'Anglo–Scandinavian settlements', pp. 299–302.

114 L. C. Nielsen, 'Ömgard: a settlement from the late iron age and the viking period in west Jutland', *Acta Archaeologica*, 50 (1980), 173–209; I. Stoumann, 'Sædding: a Viking Age village near Esbjerg', *Acta Archaeologica*, 50 (1980), 95–118; S. Hvass, 'Viking Age villages in Denmark – new investigations', *Acta Visbyensia*, 7 (1983), 211–28; P. Nørlund, *Trelleborg* (Copenhagen, 1968); H. Schmidt, 'The Trelleborg house reconsidered', *Med. Arch.*, 17 (1973), 52–77. On English examples, see P. Rahtz, 'Buildings and rural settlement', in D. M. Wilson (ed.), *The Archaeology of Anglo-Saxon England* (Cambridge, 1976), pp. 49–99, at 88.

115 C. F. Tebbutt, 'An eleventh-century "boat-shaped" building at Buckden, Huntingdonshire', *Proceedings of the Cambridge Antiquarian Society, PCAS*, 55 (1962), 13–15; P. Addyman, 'Late Saxon settlements in the St Neots area: III. The village or township at St Neots', *PCAS*, 64 (1972), 45–99; P. Rahtz, *The Saxon and Medieval Palaces at Cheddar*, BAR Brit. Ser., 65 (Oxford, 1979); S. Losco-Bradley and H. M. Wheeler, 'Anglo-Saxon settlement in the Trent Valley: some aspects', in M. Faull (ed.), *Studies in Late Anglo-Saxon Settlement* (Oxford, 1984), pp. 101–14, at 103–11; D. J. P. Mason, *Excavations at Chester: 26–42 Lower Bridge Street 1974–6: the Dark Age and Saxon periods* (Chester, 1985); M. Carver, 'Three Saxo-Norman tenements in Durham city', *Med. Arch.*, 23 (1979), 1–80; P. Holdsworth, 'Saxon Southampton: a new review', *Med. Arch.*, 20 (1976), 26–61, at 35–60; G. Beresford, *Goltho: the development of an early medieval manor c.850–1150* (London, 1987), pp. 38–47; B. K. Davison, 'The late Saxon town of Thetford: an interim report on the 1964–6 excavations', *Med. Arch.*, 11 (1967), 189–207; P. Wade-Martins, *Excavations in North Elmham Park 1967–72*, East Anglian Archaeology hereafter: EAA, 9, 2 vols (Gressenhall, 1980), I, pp. 137–9; B. K. Davison, 'Excavations at Sulgrave, Northamptonshire, 1968', *Arch. J.*, 125 (1968), 305–7.

116 Richards, 'Identifying Anglo–Scandinavian settlements', pp. 301–2; Batey, 'Aspects of rural settlement', p. 89.

117 Richards, 'Identifying Anglo–Scandinavian settlements', pp. 301–2.

118 Batey, 'Aspects of rural settlement'.

119 *Ibid.*, pp. 90–1.

120 Richards, 'Identifying Anglo–Scandinavian settlements', pp. 299–300.

121 J. Graham-Campbell and C. Batey, *Vikings in Scotland: an archaeological survey* (Edinburgh, 1998), pp. 171–3; M. Cubbon, 'The archaeology of the Vikings in the Isle of Man', in C. Fell, P. Foote, J. Graham-Campbell and R. Thomson (eds), *The Viking Age in the Isle of Man. Select Papers from the Ninth Viking Congress* (London, 1983), pp. 13–26, at 18–19; Batey, 'Aspects of rural settlement', p. 90.

122 Graham-Campbell and Batey, *Vikings in Scotland*, p. 157.

123 *Ibid.*, pp. 163, 173; A. Ritchie, *Viking Scotland* (London, 1993), pp. 56–7.

124 Graham-Campbell and Batey, *Vikings in Scotland*, pp. 173–4.

125 Batey, 'Aspects of rural settlement', p. 91. See also, J. H. Barrett, 'Beyond war or peace: the study of culture contact in Viking-age Scotland', in Hines, Lane and Redknap (eds), *Land, Sea and Home*, pp. 207–18.

126 See, for example, Higham, 'Viking Age settlement', pp. 308–10.
127 Richards, 'Identifying Anglo–Scandinavian settlements', p. 302.
128 J. Hurst, 'The Wharram research project: results to 1983', *Med. Arch.*, 28 (1984), 77–111, at 82; M. Beresford and J. Hurst, *Wharram Percy: deserted medieval village* (London, 1990), p. 84.
129 T. Unwin, 'Towards a model of Anglo–Scandinavian rural settlement in England', in Hooke (ed.), *Anglo-Saxon Settlements*, pp. 77–98, at 97.
130 C. Lewis, P. Mitchell-Fox and C. C. Dyer, *Village, Hamlet and Field* (Manchester, 1995), pp. 94–8; Yorke, *Wessex in the Early Middle Ages*, p. 269; J. D. Richards, 'The Anglo-Saxon and Anglo–Scandinavian evidence', in P. Stamper and R. Croft (eds), *Wharram: a study of settlement in the Yorkshire Wolds VIII: the South Manor*, York University Archaeological Publications, 10 (York, 2000), pp. 195–200.
131 S. Göransson, 'Regular open-field pattern in England and Scandinavian *solskifte*', *Geografikser Annaler*, 43 (1961), 80–104.
132 M. L. Faull and S. Moorhouse, *West Yorkshire: an archaeological survey to AD 1500*, 4 vols (Wakefield, 1981), II, pp. 197–8.
133 Richards, 'Identifying Anglo–Scandinavian settlements', pp. 302–3.
134 Richards, 'The Anglo-Saxon and Anglo–Scandinavian evidence'; *idem*, 'Finding the Vikings: the search for Anglo–Scandinavian rural settlement in the northern Danelaw', in Graham-Campbell, Hall, Jesch and Parsons (eds), *Vikings and the Danelaw*, pp. 269–77, at 274.
135 Richards, 'The Anglo-Saxon and Anglo–Scandinavian evidence', p. 198.
136 Richards, 'Finding the Vikings', p. 274.
137 A. Goodall and C. Paterson, 'Non-ferrous metal objects', in Stamper and Croft (eds), *Wharram: a study of settlement in the Yorkshire Wolds*, pp. 126–32; I. Goodall and E. Clark, 'Iron objects', in *ibid.*, pp. 132–47, at 139; E. Clark and G. Gaunt, 'Stone objects', in *ibid.*, pp. 101–17, at 104–9.
138 Goodall and Paterson, 'Non-ferrous metal objects', pp. 128–31.
139 Richards, *Viking Age England*, p. 52.
140 Richards, 'Finding the Vikings', p. 276.
141 J. D Richards, 'Cottam an Anglian and Anglo–Scandinavian settlement in the Yorkshire Wolds', *Arch. J.*, 156 (1999), 1–110, on p. 98.
142 Richards, 'Cottam', *idem*, 'Identifying Anglo–Scandinavian settlements', pp. 303–5.
143 *EHD I*, p. 468.
144 A. Williams, 'A bell-house and a burh-geat: lordly residences in England before the Norman Conquest', in C. Harper-Bill and R. Harvey (eds), *Medieval Knighthood IV: papers from the fifth Strawberry Hill Conference 1990* (Woodbridge, 1992), pp. 221–40.
145 Richards, 'Identifying Anglo–Scandinavian settlements', p. 305.
146 C. Batey, 'A Viking Age bell from Freswick Links, Caithness', *Med. Arch.*, 31 (1988), 213–16; Richards, 'Identifying Anglo–Scandinavian settlements', pp. 305–6.
147 Richards, 'Identifying Anglo–Scandinavian settlements', p. 305.
148 A useful summary appears in Reynolds, *Later Anglo-Saxon England*, pp. 123–35.

149 I. Goodall, 'Objects of iron', in Beresford, *Goltho*, pp. 181, 184; A. MacGregor, 'Objects of bone and antler', in *ibid.*, pp. 188, 192.

150 C. Loveluck, 'Wealth, waste and conspicuous consumption: Flixborough and its importance for middle and late Saxon rural settlement', in H. Hamerow and A. MacGregor (eds), *Image and Power in the Archaeology of Early Medieval Britain: essays in honour of Rosemary Cramp* (Oxford, 2001), pp. 79–130.

151 *Ibid.*, pp. 119–20.

152 H. Hamerow, 'Catholme: the development and context of the settlement', in S. Losco-Bradley and G. Kinsley, *Catholme. An Anglo-Saxon Settlement on the Trent Gravels in Staffordshire* (London, 2002), pp. 123–9, at 128 for the quotation.

153 S. Cabot, G. Davies and R. Hoggett, 'Sedgeford: excavations of a rural settlement in Norfolk', in Hines, Lane and Redknap (eds), *Land, Sea and Home*, pp. 313–23, at 321–2.

154 Lewis, Mitchell-Fox and Dyer, *Village, Hamlet and Field*, pp. 1–37.

155 A. Everitt, 'River and wold: reflections on the historical origin of regions and pays', *JHG*, 3 (1977), 1–19; Fox, 'The people of the wolds'.

156 Lewis, Mitchell-Fox and Dyer, *Village, Hamlet and Field*, pp. 158–223; B. K. Roberts and S. Wrathmell, *Region and Place. A study of English rural settlement* (London, 2002).

157 Lewis, Mitchell-Fox and Dyer, *Village, Hamlet and Field*, pp. 227–42; R. Jones and M. Page, 'Characterising rural settlement and landscape: Whittlewood Forest in the Middle Ages', *Med. Arch.*, 47 (2003), 53–83.

158 C. C. Dyer, 'Power and conflict in the medieval village', in D. Hooke (ed.), *Medieval Villages* (Oxford, 1985), pp. 31–43; P. D. A. Harvey, 'Initiative and authority in settlement change', in Aston, Austin and Dyer (eds), *The Rural Settlements of Medieval England*, pp. 31–43; Faith, *The English Peasantry*, p. 235; C. C. Dyer, *Making a Living in the Middle Ages. The People of Britain 850–1520* (London and New York, 2002), pp. 21–2.

159 Jones and Page, 'Characterising rural settlement and landscape', 57–8.

160 M. Gardiner, 'Timber buildings without earth-fast footings in Viking-Age Britain', in Hines, Lane and Redknap (eds), *Land, Sea and Home*, pp. 345–58, at 357.

161 Hurst, 'Wharram research project', 82; Richards, 'The Anglo-Saxon and Anglo–Scandinavian evidence', p. 98; D. Hall and P. Martin, 'Brixworth, Northamptonshire – an intensive field survey', *JBAA*, 132 (1979), 1–6.

162 Lewis, Mitchell-Fox and Dyer, *Village, Hamlet and Field*, p. 95.

163 P. Wade-Martins, *Village Sites in Launditch Hundred*, EAA, 10 (Gressenhall, 1980), pp. 84–6.

164 J. Sheppard, 'Metrological analysis of regular village plans in Yorkshire', *Agricultural History Review*, hereafter: *AgHR*, 22 (1974), 118–35; P. Allerston, 'English village development: findings from the Pickering district of north Yorkshire', *Institute of British Geographers Transactions*, hereafter: *IBGT*, 51 (1970), 95–109, at 100, 105–6.

165 D. M. Palliser, 'Domesday Book and the "harrying of the North"', *North. Hist.*, 29 (1993), 1–23; R. Muir, 'The villages of Nidderdale', *Landscape History*, hereafter: *Land. Hist.*, 20 (1998), 65–82.

166 Allerston, 'English village development'.

167 M. Harvey, 'Irregular villages in Holderness, Yorkshire: some thoughts on their origin', *Yorkshire Archaeological Journal*, hereafter: *YAJ*, 54 (1982), 63–71; P. Everson, C. C. Taylor and C. Dunn (eds) *Change and Continuity. Rural settlement in north-west Lincolnshire* (London, 1991), pp. 16–28.

168 Dyer, 'Power and conflict', pp. 27–8.

169 Faith, *The English Peasantry*, pp. 79, 163–77.

170 Everson, Taylor and Dunn (eds), *Change and Continuity*, pp. 32–3, 41–3.

171 *Ibid.*, p. 17; Richards, 'The Anglo-Saxon and Anglo-Scandinavian evidence', p. 198; Lewis, Mitchell-Fox and Dyer, *Village, Hamlet and Field*, pp. 6–7, 124; L. H. Campey, 'Medieval village plans in County Durham: an analysis of reconstructed plans based on medieval documentary sources', *North. Hist.*, 25 (1989), 60–87.

172 B. K. Roberts, *The Making of the English Village: a study in historical geography* (Harlow, 1987), pp. 178–81; Faith, *The English Peasantry*, pp. 242–4.

173 P. D. A. Harvey, 'Introduction', in P. D. A. Harvey (ed.), *The Peasant Land Market in Medieval England* (Oxford, 1984), pp. 1–19, at 12–14; Faith, *The English Peasantry*, p. 235.

174 Everson, Taylor and Dunn, *Continuity and Change*, pp. 13–14, 31–3.

175 Wade-Martins, *Village Sites in Launditch Hundred*, pp. 82–6.

176 Dyer, *Making a Living in the Middle Ages*, pp. 47–8.

177 F. M. Stenton, *Documents Illustrative of the Social and Economic History of the Danelaw* (Oxford, 1920), pp. cxiv–xv; O. Von Feilitzen, *The Pre-Conquest Personal Names of Domesday Book* (Uppsala, 1937), pp. 18–26; E. Ekwall, 'The proportion of Scandinavian settlers in the Danelaw', *Saga-Book of the Viking Society*, 12 (1937–45), 19–34; R. H. C. Davis, 'East Anglia and the Danelaw', *TRHS*, 5th ser., 5 (1955), 23–39, at 29; D. Whitelock, 'Scandinavian personal names in the *Liber Vitae* of Thorney Abbey', *Saga-Book of the Viking Society*, 12 (1937–45), 127–53; G. Fellows-Jensen, *Scandinavian Personal Names in Lincolnshire and Yorkshire* (Copenhagen, 1968).

178 C. Clark, 'Personal-name studies: bringing them to a wider audience', *Nomina*, 15 (1991), 21–34; Williams, *The English and the Norman Conquest*, pp. 206–7.

179 G. Fellows-Jensen, 'From Scandinavia to the British Isles and back again. Linguistic give-and-take in the viking period', in B. Ambrosiani and H. Clarke (eds), *Developments Around the Baltic and North Sea in the Viking Age* (Stockholm, 1994), pp. 253–68, at 259.

180 O. Von Feilitzen and C. E. Blunt, 'Personal names on the coinage of Edgar', in Clemoes and Hughes (eds), *England Before the Conquest*, pp. 183–214; V. Smart, 'The moneyers of St Edmund', *Hikuin*, 11 (1985), 83–90; *idem*, 'Scandinavians, Celts and Germans in Anglo-Saxon England: the evidence of moneyers' names', in M. A. S. Blackburn (ed.), *Anglo-Saxon Monetary History* (Leicester, 1986), pp. 171–84, at 174–7.

181 Fellows-Jensen, 'Danish place-names and personal names', pp. 134–5.

182 *Ibid.*, p. 135.

183 Clark, 'Personal-name studies', 26.

184 J. Insley, 'Regional variation in Scandinavian personal nomenclature in England', *Nomina*, 3 (1979), 52–60, at 54; Smart, 'Scandinavians, Celts and Germans', pp. 179–80.

185 S. Margeson, 'Viking settlement in Norfolk: a study of new evidence', in S. Margeson, B. Ayres and S. Heywood (eds), *A Festival of Norfolk Archaeology* (Hunstanton, 1996), pp. 47–57; *idem*, *The Vikings in Norfolk* (Norwich, 1997); G. Thomas, 'Anglo–Scandinavian metalwork from the Danelaw: exploring social and cultural interaction', in Hadley and Richards (eds), *Cultures in Contact*, pp. 237–55; K. Leahy and C. Paterson, 'New light on the viking presence in Lincolnshire: the artefactual evidence', in Graham-Campbell, Hall, Jesch and Parsons (eds), *Vikings and the Danelaw*, pp. 181–202.

186 Thomas, 'Anglo–Scandinavian metalwork', pp. 238–9.

187 *Ibid.*, p. 239; Leahy and Paterson, 'New light on the viking presence', p. 189.

188 *Ibid.*, pp. 183–91.

189 Margeson, 'Viking settlement in Norfolk', p. 48.

190 *Ibid.*; Leahy and Paterson, 'New light on the viking presence', p. 189.

191 Thomas, 'Anglo–Scandinavian metalwork', pp. 239–40.

192 Margeson, 'Viking settlement in Norfolk', pp. 50–5; Thomas, 'Anglo–Scandinavian metalwork', pp. 241–2; Leahy and Paterson, 'New light on the viking presence', pp. 192–5.

193 Margeson, *The Vikings in Norfolk*, pp. 20–3; Thomas, 'Anglo–Scandinavian metalwork', p. 242; Leahy and Paterson, 'New light on the viking presence', pp. 195–6.

194 R. A. Hall, 'Markets of the Danelaw', in E. Roesdahl (ed.), *The Vikings in England* (London, 1981), pp. 95–140, at 121; Leahy and Paterson, 'New light on the viking presence', p. 196.

195 Margeson, *The Vikings in Norfolk*, p. 23.

196 *Ibid.*, pp. 18–19.

197 Leahy and Paterson, 'New light on the viking presence', pp. 195–6.

198 Thomas, 'Anglo–Scandinavian metalwork', pp. 243–4.

199 *Ibid.*, pp. 244, 246, and fig. 18.

200 Thomas, 'Anglo–Scandinavian metalwork', p. 249; Leahy and Paterson, 'New light on the viking presence', p. 193.

201 Thomas, 'Anglo–Scandinavian metalwork', p. 244.

202 Griffiths, 'Settlement and acculturation'.

203 Leahy and Paterson, 'New light on the viking presence', pp. 193–5.

204 Thomas, 'Anglo–Scandinavian metalwork', p. 252; G. Speed and P. Walton, 'A burial of a viking woman at Adwick-le-Street, South Yorkshire', *Med. Arch.*, 48 (2004), 51–90, at 86.

205 Margeson, *The Vikings in Norfolk*, pp. 15–18; Leahy and Richardson, 'New light on the Viking presence', p. 193; Thomas, 'Anglo–Scandinavian metalwork', p. 252.

206 Disc-brooches are widely regarded as female dress-accessories on the grounds that they are rarely found in male graves: J. Graham-Campbell, *Viking Artefacts: a select catalogue* (London, 1980), no. 80. Note, however, that disc-brooches are

thought to have been sometimes worn by men: see G. Owen-Crocker, *Dress in Anglo-Saxon England* (Manchester, 1986), pp. 133–4, 151–2. I am grateful to Gabor Thomas for discussion of this matter.

207 H. Geake, 'Invisible kingdoms: the use of grave goods in seventh-century England', in T. Dickinson and D. Griffiths (eds), *The Making of Kingdoms* (Oxford, 1999), pp. 203–15, at 205–11.

208 J. Blair, *Anglo-Saxon Oxfordshire* (Stroud, 1994), pp. 70–1; Jesch, *Women in the Viking Age*, pp. 22–3.

209 *EHD I*, pp. 895–6.

210 J. Graham-Campbell, 'The Cuerdale hoard: comparisons and context', in Graham-Campbell (ed.), *Viking Treasure*, pp. 107–15, at 107.

211 *Ibid.*, pp. 110–13; M. A. S. Blackburn and H. Pagan, 'A revised checklist of hoards from the British Isles c.500–1100', in Blackburn (ed.), *Anglo-Saxon Monetary History*, pp. 291–313, at 294–5.

212 Graham-Campbell, 'The Cuerdale hoard', pp. 113–14; M. M. Archibald, 'Dating Cuerdale: the evidence of the coins', in Graham-Campbell (ed.), *Viking Treasure*, pp. 15–21, at 16–18.

213 M. A. S. Blackburn, 'Expansion and control: aspects of Anglo–Scandinavian minting south of the Humber', in Graham-Campbell, Hall, Jesch and Parsons (eds), *Vikings and the Danelaw*, pp. 125–42, at 134–5.

214 *Ibid.*, p. 137.

215 *EHD I*, pp. 245–6.

216 S. Reynolds, 'What do we mean by "Anglo-Saxon" and "Anglo-Saxons"?', *J. Brit. Stud.*, 24 (1985), 395–414, at 410–11.

217 For general discussion of these issues in the early medieval context, see P. Geary, 'Ethnic identity as a situational construct in the early Middle Ages', *Mitteilungen der Anthropologischen Gesellschaft in Wien*, 113 (1983), 15–26, esp. pp. 25–6; M. Innes, 'Danelaw identities: ethnicity, regionalism and political allegiance', in Hadley and Richards (eds), *Cultures in Contact*, pp. 65–88, at 83–5.

218 R. Darlington and P. McGurk, *The Chronicle of John of Worcester*, vol. 2 (Oxford 1995), p. 443; Reynolds, 'What do we mean by "Anglo-Saxon" and "Anglo-Saxons"?', 410–11.

219 Innes, 'Danelaw identities', p. 82.

220 D. Williams, *Late Saxon Stirrup-strap Mounts: a classification and catalogue*, CBA Research Rep., 111 (York, 1997), p. 8; Gabor Thomas, pers. comm.

221 R. N. Bailey, *England's Earliest Sculptors* (Toronto, 1997), pp. 95–104.

4

Scandinavians in the urban environment

The tenth century witnessed the expansion of urban life across most of later Anglo-Saxon England, but the Scandinavian conquest and settlement appear to have been followed by a particularly intensive phase of urban growth in parts of northern and eastern England. Examination of the status of tenth-century urban centres prior to the Scandinavian settlement suggests that they were largely existing centres of regional importance, although there are few indications that any of these sites were already urban. There is little doubt that the period of Scandinavian conquest was important in the urbanisation of society in northern and eastern England, although, as we shall see, the Scandinavian imprint is not particularly easy to identify. The West Saxon conquest was also important to the processes of urban development, while some of the urban characteristics of the towns of northern and eastern England appear to have emerged only in the later tenth century. In order to evaluate the Scandinavian impact, and in an attempt to distinguish between the direct and indirect effects of the Scandinavian settlements, the evidence from a selection of urban settlements will be examined in this chapter. As we shall see, little of the Scandinavian contribution to urbanisation can be described as being characteristically Scandinavian. Rather, a diverse range of influences from within English society and further afield can be discerned.

The origins of Anglo-Saxon urban settlements

Urban origins in England have been extensively debated, but defining a town has proved tricky. Historians have traditionally tended to prefer legalistic and institutional definitions, which are not entirely appropriate in an early medieval context. In the face of this, and given growing archaeological evidence from urban contexts, in a paper on Anglo-Saxon towns written in 1976 Martin Biddle famously produced a list of criteria for defining urban status, a list that included: defences, a planned street system, a mint, a market, a role as a central place, legal autonomy, a relatively large and dense population, a diversified economic base, social differentiation, religious complexity, a judicial centre and plots and houses of 'urban' type.[1] However, as Christopher Scull has observed, although this definition permits an archaeological contribution to the debate about urban origins, it still leans towards criteria linked to legal institutions and morphology, some of which are difficult to identify in an early medieval context, because they are rarely documented; are not archaeologically visible; or they depend on extensive archaeological investigation, which is rarely possible in urban centres that continue to be occupied. Other criteria potentially identify settlements as towns even though they are clearly non-urban, such as religious communities, where marketing and manufacturing often occurred, or hundred and wapentake centres, few of which were in urban settings, but which possessed judicial functions.[2] Nonetheless, as Biddle argued, evidence that a particular site has three or four of the criteria that he outlined is sufficient to consider it urban. More recently, attention has become focused on economic definitions of urban status, which are more archaeologically visible than legal and institutional characteristics, with some archaeologists defining urban status as 'any settlement with a densely populated and permanently occupied site and a specialised non-agrarian economy'.[3] Currently, the consensus is that truly urban places, with evidence for dense occupation, defences, industrial production and a diversity of commercial activity, emerged in the late ninth and earlier tenth centuries in most parts of the country.[4]

However, at an earlier date, there were clearly centres with some urban functions. Trading centres, often dubbed *wics* or emporia, of the later seventh and eighth centuries have been more-or-less extensively excavated at Ipswich (Suff), *Hamwic* (Southampton, Hants), York and London, and evidence for relatively dense occupation, planned streets, boundaries, imported goods and craft production has been recovered, especially at *Hamwic* and London.[5] These riverine and coastal trading places were part of long-distance trading networks, along with similar sites on the continent, and are thought to have operated under royal control. However, in none of these places was there a direct path to later towns; during the ninth century the *wics* declined and trading activity was commonly relocated. Hence, although some aspects of urban life can be detected in the archaeological record at an earlier date, the urbanisation evident in Domesday

Book owes its origins largely to developments occurring in the later ninth century. The West Saxons, the Mercians and the Scandinavian conquerors have all been variously identified as the initiators of urban growth, in particular following their foundation of defensive sites, many of which eventually developed into towns. There is evidence for the establishment of such defended places in Mercia from perhaps as early as the late eighth century, at Hereford, Tamworth (Staffs) and Winchcombe (Glos), while, by the later ninth century, planned settlements were being established in Wessex, some of which were within former Roman towns, such as Winchester (Hants), while others were founded within new defences, such as Lyng (Som).[6] More recently, the discussion of urban origins has also focused on high-status secular sites and ecclesiastical centres, which acted as foci for administrative, economic and manufacturing activities – leading to a more organic urban development.[7]

York

York has been far more extensively excavated than any of the other towns in the regions of Scandinavian settlement, and much has been revealed about the layout, economy, manufacturing activities, houses and lifestyles of its inhabitants (fig. 19). Before the Scandinavian conquest, York was known as *Eoforwic*, and the final -*wic* element was common among the names of pre-viking trading centres, such as *Hamwic, Lundenwic* (London), *Gipeswic* (Ipswich) and Quentovic (France).[8] However, York appears to have been less densely occupied than contemporary trading settlements at Southampton, London and Canterbury, and no traces of the densely built-up streetscape of the tenth-century town existed this early in York.[9]

The kings of Northumbria had a base in York, although there is no archaeological evidence for where it was located. They minted coins there, although, as we have seen (see p. 45), during the ninth century the coinage became increasingly debased and had apparently ceased to be issued before the Scandinavian conquest in 867.[10] Documentary evidence reveals that the Archbishop had his cathedral in York, which was built by King Edwin following his conversion in 627.[11] This church has not been identified archaeologically, but beneath the later Minster a cemetery of at least ninth-century origins has been excavated, from which much earlier grave-markers have been recovered in reused contexts. This seems likely to have been the cathedral cemetery, where a number of royal and episcopal burials are recorded in the seventh century.[12] Several other churches are known from documentary and archaeological evidence. A church

19   Plan of York.

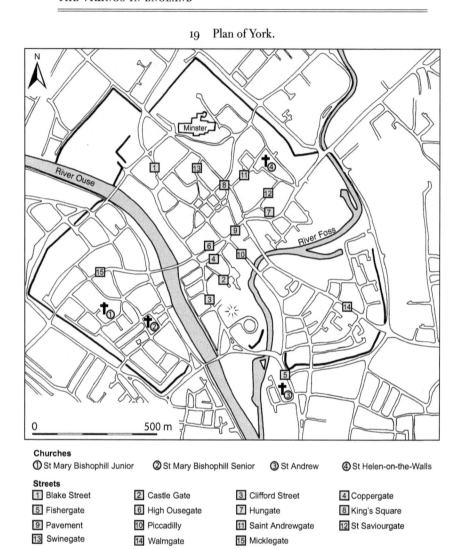

Churches

① St Mary Bishophill Junior   ② St Mary Bishophill Senior   ③ St Andrew   ④ St Helen-on-the-Walls

Streets

1 Blake Street	2 Castle Gate	3 Clifford Street	4 Coppergate
5 Fishergate	6 High Ousegate	7 Hungate	8 King's Square
9 Pavement	10 Piccadilly	11 Saint Andrewgate	12 St Saviourgate
13 Swinegate	14 Walmgate	15 Micklegate	

dedicated to the Holy Wisdom was built in c.780, and although its location is uncertain, it has been suggested that it may have been at the site of the church of Holy Trinity.[13] St Mary Bishophill Junior was another early religious foundation, indicated by the survival of an eighth- or early ninth-century inscription.[14] A chapel of the mother of Christ (possibly either St Mary Bishophill Junior or St Mary Bishophill Senior) and a cell of St Stephen are both mentioned by Alcuin in c.800, while Folcard's

148

eleventh-century *Life of John of Beverley* states that there was a church of St Michael the Archangel in York in the early eighth century – possibly the church later known as St Michael le Belfrey.[15] In the vicinity of the church of All Saints Pavement, a helmet with an eighth-century religious inscription was found, which is difficult to translate, but on one reading may make reference to the dedication of an individual called Oshere to a church of All Saints. Further evidence for the early origins of this church is provided by sculptural fragments of eighth-century date found nearby on Coppergate, and by the fact that All Saints appears to have been the mother church of St Mary Castlegate.[16] There was possibly also a hospital in York by c.800, since Alcuin wrote to Archbishop Eanbald urging him to found one and because an early Latin inscription on a stone shaft has been found in the vicinity of St Peter's (later St Leonard's) hospital.[17] Thus, there were probably at least six or seven other churches besides the cathedral in pre-viking York, revealing that it was a major centre of ecclesiastical life.

York was clearly a centre of manufacture and trade in the eighth and ninth centuries. Excavations south-east of the Roman fortress at Fishergate investigated two plots of land in which three 'hall'-type buildings dating to c.700 to 850 were identified, and where evidence for the working of iron, copper-alloy, bone, antler, fur, leather, skin, textiles and, possibly, glass was recovered. However, in the light of the small numbers of finds it is difficult to gauge the scale of manufacturing activity.[18] Nonetheless, imported items from the Rhineland, Northern France and the Low Countries recovered from Fishergate indicate a wide range of continental contacts. Documentary sources also refer to foreign traders, including Frisian merchants, in York in the late eighth century. As Alcuin observed, 'this beautiful, healthy place of noble setting was destined to attract many settlers by its richness. To York from divers peoples and kingdoms all over the world they come in hope of gain, seeking wealth from the rich land, a home, a fortune, and hearth-stone for themselves'.[19] The use of coinage appears to have been widespread in York in the eighth and ninth centuries, to judge from the large numbers of single finds of coins recovered from around the city, and a number of hoards of this date consist of hundreds, and in a couple of cases thousands, of coins, suggesting that coinage was an accepted medium of exchange and implying that 'an incipient market economy was beginning to develop'.[20]

Craft-working at the Fishergate site appears to have ceased in the later ninth century, and these activities may have been relocated to the Coppergate district (fig. 20), where excavations have recovered evidence for blacksmithing, textile-making, and the working of copper-alloy, antler, bone

20   Excavations at Coppergate in York. This photograph was taken during
excavation of four tenements dating to the early tenth century.
Scale is two metres

and amber. This craft-working seems to have been on a similar scale to the
earlier activity at Fishergate, and the Coppergate excavations suggest that in
the later ninth century the subdivision of plots characteristic of the tenth-
century town had not yet occurred.[21] However, from the last decade of the
ninth century there is evidence that trade and manufacturing in York began
to flourish. One sign of this is the issuing of a regal coinage of large volume
in c.895 (see pp. 45–6), which must have been intended to encourage trade
and to facilitate taxation – a development influenced by the Scandinavian
kings, the Archbishop and doubtless also by continental moneyers. A little
later the Coppergate site was reorganised into tenements and, together with
the reintroduction of coinage, this may, as Richard Hall has argued, 'mark a
new and deliberate fiscal policy to create an urban economic infrastructure
which would raise revenue for York's rulers'.[22] The tenth century witnessed
a massive increase in craft production, which has been identified archaeologically at various sites in York through both finished products and manufacturing debris. For example, evidence for iron-working has been identified
during excavation at Coppergate, where huge quantities of slag and smelting
waste were recovered; at Feasegate, where an iron smelting hearth was
located; and near the Minster, where remains of a forge were also found.
A lead tank containing iron-working tools was found at St Saviourgate, and
this may indicate the location of a smithy in the vicinity.[23] Evidence for non-
ferrous metalworking occurs in the form of large amounts of copper-

alloy sheet offcuts found at High Ousegate; a brooch mould and a crucible fragment found at Blake Street; and Stamford-ware crucibles for metalworking from a number of sites. At Coppergate, evidence has been recovered for the working of copper alloy, lead, pewter and tin.[24] Woodworking tools and the waste from the lathe-turning of cups and bowls have been found at Coppergate ('street of the makers of wooden vessels') and Piccadilly, and the quantity of material has led to the deduction that this part of the town was a centre of specialist lathe-turning activity from the ninth to eleventh centuries.[25] Large quantities of leather offcuts and artefacts were recovered during excavations at Coppergate; manufacturing debris and shoes, sheaths and scabbards were found at Micklegate; while offcuts indicative of cobbling have been found at Hungate, Feasegate, Pavement, King's Square and St Andrewgate.[26] The debris from bone- and antler-working, indicating the making of combs, pins and skates, has been found at a number of locations in the city, including Coppergate, Castlegate, Ousegate, Clifford Street and near the Minster, and it appears to have been a fairly ubiquitous industry.[27] There is a small amount of evidence for amber working and possibly also jet working and the working and recycling of glass, while textile manufacture appears to have been a widespread activity, probably largely conducted within the household.[28]

The picture that emerges from excavation is of a multiplicity of crafts, which at Coppergate at least were conducted within and across the various tenements. It is not, however, easy to tell whether different crafts were practised concurrently or sequentially within the same tenement, and it is rarely possible to date closely the inception and longevity of a particular craft. The extent to which various crafts were practiced on a permanent or seasonal basis is also unclear, although those crafts requiring a hearth or a forge are more likely to have been practised on a permanent basis than those crafts, such as antler-working, for which the supply of raw materials was seasonal. Neither is it apparent whether the craftworkers lived on the tenements at Coppergate, or simply rented working space. Cooperation between craftworkers is likely. For example, tinned iron objects from the vicinity of the smithies in Coppergate tenements C and D suggest that a non-ferrous metalworker either tinned the items or at least supplied the materials.[29]

The wide range of finds recovered during excavation permits insights into the Scandinavian impact on York. A range of raw materials and finished articles clearly made their way to York from Scandinavia, either as personal possessions or as a result of trade, including honestones worked from phyllite and ragstone schist, walrus ivory, amber, a fragment of a coin (*penning*) from Hedeby, clubmoss (probably used for textile dyeing), and

21 A copper-alloy strap-end from York, decorated with Borre-style ring chain ornament. The form and the decoration are paralleled in Scandinavia, but the fact that the reverse is decorated with a ring-and-dot motif indicates that it was produced in an Anglo–Scandinavian context. It is thought likely that it was manufactured in York itself, where another strap-end, this time of Anglo-Saxon form, was decorated with Borre-style ring-knot.

possibly also vessels of steatite and talc schist, although these may have come from Shetland (Scotland). A number of items from places other than Scandinavia were doubtless brought to York by Scandinavian settlers and traders, including Arabic and Carolingian coins; Byzantine silks; lava quernstones from the Mayen region of Germany; pottery from the Rhineland; Frisian textiles; and dress-accessories from Ireland, Scotland and north-west Europe, while the adoption of 'Celtic' sculptural forms was probably also due to Scandinavian influence.[30] Scandinavian influence has also been identified on a wide range of artefacts manufactured in York, including jewellery (figs 21 and 22), store sculpture (fig. 10), and products made of antler. Yet we should not overemphasise these finds, as purely Scandinavian artefacts seem to be few in number. Even where Scandinavian influence can be identified, it is often not a direct copy of artistic forms from Scandinavia, or is found on artefacts that are different from Scandinavian forms, such as Anglo-Saxon and Carolingian style strap-ends decorated in the Borre style (fig. 21), and Anglo-Saxon style disc-brooches decorated in the Jelling style (fig. 22). English influence can often be detected in supposedly Scandinavian motifs, alongside influences from other parts of Britain where Scandinavians settled. Indeed, many artefacts once confidently assigned to one or other of the well-known Scandinavian artistic traditions (Borre, Jelling, Mammen, Ringerike, Urnes) have subsequently been reinterpreted as betraying English influence. For example, a clay mould for producing a Scandinavian-style tri-lobed dress accessory, probably a brooch, was once thought to be decorated with Borre-style motifs, but more recently the decorative scheme has been identified as typical of the English Winchester style. Indeed, it is

22   Anglo–Scandinavian flat disc-brooch from York. This brooch was manufactured in lead, and has a typically Anglo-Saxon flat profile, but was decorated in what has been described as an 'artistically second-rate example of Jellinge decoration'.

now apparent that, following the Scandinavian conquest, York remained open to artistic influences from southern England, arguably remaining more up to date with this artistic tradition than with that in Scandinavia.[31] In addressing this range of material, Richard Hall suggests that the political climate in York, characterised by factional disputes, not only between those of Scandinavian descent and locals, may have meant that the display of items of clear Scandinavian or English associations may not have been wise, and that in this context it is perhaps not surprising that there emerged a hybrid culture, reflecting 'an innate affinity with ambiguity' among the craftworkers and inhabitants of York.[32]

Excavations have also revealed much about the layout of York following the Scandinavian conquest. Four extensively excavated tenements in Coppergate, which were of equal width and defined by wattle fences, were laid out c.890–930 (fig. 20). While the location of the street at Coppergate was not identified, the tenements appear to have been aligned upon the present course of Pavement, implying that it was laid out in the early tenth century, as doubtless were the other streets in the vicinity, which are arranged in a grid-like fashion. The Coppergate tenements were established on the site of earlier and larger plots of land where a modest array of earlier craft-working has been identified, and the regularity and longevity of the narrow tenements – combined with an increased level of craft-working – has prompted the suggestion that they were created as a result of a deliberate act of town-planning.[33] In the area of the former *colonia* there is also archaeological evidence for the laying out of properties in the tenth century, and although the range of activities that took place here is unclear, excavations on the river frontage noted the presence of a number of wattlework hurdles, which implies that the beaching area was periodically stabilised in the Anglo–Scandinavian era. Furthermore, a variety of tenth-century occupational features, including wattlework and stake alignments running at right angles to the street, have been excavated along

Walmgate, and many of the medieval streets in the former fortress were also laid out during the Anglo–Scandinavian period.[34]

While analysis of the street layout provides persuasive evidence for town-planning during the period of Scandinavian control and cultural influence, whether the Scandinavians themselves were instrumental in this development, rather than other powerful figures in York, is another matter. There is nothing distinctively Scandinavian about these developments of the York townscape, which can be paralleled in the same period at, for example, Winchester.[35] Neither were commercial and industrial activities initiated by the Scandinavians, as the Fishergate excavations reveal, and even their relocation in the mid-ninth century can be paralleled in other towns at this time, including London.[36] Furthermore, there is nothing distinctively Scandinavian about the buildings excavated at Coppergate, the earliest of which were of post-and-wattle construction, replaced around 975 with cellared, two-storey plank-built structures.[37] Sunken-floored buildings are almost exclusively an urban phenomenon in the tenth century, and appear to belong to a wider north-west European tradition, doubtless intended to make the most of the available space within the confines of urban communities.[38] Consequently, David Rollason has suggested that these various developments in the urban profile of York were more likely to have been prompted by the Archbishop of York and the Northumbrian aristocracy than the Scandinavian kings, whose reigns were typically short and often turbulent.[39] In the absence of excavated evidence for elite sites in ninth- and tenth-century York, such as a royal palace, it is indeed difficult to know how the Scandinavian rulers of York constructed and expressed their identity and style of rule, and, therefore, to evaluate the likelihood that they were responsible for the development of York's urban profile. Only the coinage minted in York illuminates the nature of Scandinavian kingship, and it suggests that these rulers generally chose to adapt and modify an indigenous component of royal authority. Thus, it is not inherently implausible that they should have concerned themselves with commerce and industrial activities within the city, but, if so, all the evidence suggests that they were adopting an indigenous practice, probably supported by local lords, rather than innovating. Finally, while there is certainly evidence for Scandinavian influence on York – the city was not isolated from southern England and the continent, or absorbed into a purely Scandinavian milieu, and this seems to be true among the consumers of both elite products, such as stone sculpture, and more humble items, such as base-metal dress accessories.[40]

The *burhs* of the north and east midlands

The *Anglo-Saxon Chronicle* implies that in the early tenth century local administration in the north and east midlands was based on a networks of *burhs*: fortified centres that in most cases developed into towns of various sizes in the tenth century (see pp. 54-6). In comparison with York there has been very little archaeological investigation of mid to later Anglo-Saxon contexts in the *burhs*; nonetheless it is possible to identify the emergence and growth of a number of specifically urban characteristics in the archaeological record, including craft-working and manufacture, the minting of coins, the provision of defences and planned street systems, and the presence of religious complexity, while the limited written record illuminates the role of the *burhs* as administrative centres.

The early history of the burhs

Prior to the Scandinavian conquest it is apparent that both Derby and Leicester were major ecclesiastical centres. Æthelweard's late tenth-century version of the *Anglo-Saxon Chronicle* records that after Ealdorman Æthelwulf was killed while fighting the Danes at Reading (Berks) in 871, his body was taken from Reading into Mercia 'to the place called *Northworthig*, but in the Danish language, Derby'.[41] This account enables us to identify the resting-place of St Ealhmund (or Alkmund), which is recorded as '*Northworthy*' in an Old English list of saints' resting-places, in the portion of the document believed to contain information pertaining to the late ninth century.[42] According to a twelfth-century source, Ealhmund, the son of King Alhred of Northumbria, was murdered on the orders of another Northumbrian king, Eardwulf. It has been suggested that his cult may have been promoted for political reasons by Eardwulf's rival, King Cenwulf of Mercia, implying that Derby possessed a major Mercian church.[43] Irrespective of this speculation, there was certainly an important church in Derby by the ninth century. Excavation of the church of St Alkmund revealed fragments of ninth-century stone sculptures and an impressive sarcophagus, which is viewed as appropriate for either a saint or an ealdorman (fig. 23).[44] It is possible that the church of All Saints also had pre-viking origins. Both St Alkmund's and All Saints were collegiate churches at the time of Domesday Book, and All Saints was also a medieval Royal Free Chapel, both of which are typically signs of churches of early foundation. That All Saints was the principal church in Derby is suggested by the fact that the later medieval parishes of Derby appear to have been carved out of that of All Saints, and in the medieval period St Alkmund's

23 Ninth-century sarcophagus from Derby. Excavation has revealed little of the nature of pre-viking Derby; however, this sarcophagus, which dates to the early ninth century, provides evidence for the existence of an important church prior to the Scandinavian settlement.

was subordinate to All Saints.[45] A bishopric was located in the former Roman fort at Leicester by 737, and may have been founded in the 680s when the see of Lichfield was divided.[46] The site of the bishopric is conjectural, although the church of St Nicholas is a candidate. Its earliest fabric is late Saxon, but it appears to perpetuate the site of an earlier church. It is located adjacent to surviving Roman fabric known as the Jewry wall, which had separated the exercise hall from the main baths, and it has been suggested that the wall survived because it had been incorporated into an early church. Excavation revealed two walls of a stone construction extending between the Jewry wall and St Nicholas, which pre-date the standing fabric of the latter, and which may perhaps have been the remains of an earlier church. Twelfth-century documentary evidence indicates that the church of St Nicholas was then dedicated to St Augustine, and that it was associated with a chapelry to its east dedicated to St Columba. If the tradition is reliable, then this arrangement, associated with the respective founding fathers of Roman and Celtic Christianity, implies that the church of St Nicholas was an early and important foundation.[47]

In contrast to their ecclesiastical status, little is known of pre-viking secular activity in either Derby or Leicester. Derby may have been an estate centre of some sort, since analysis of the parish boundaries of its five medieval churches indicates that they served a substantial area around the town. Studies in many parts of the country have revealed that such arrangements typically reflect, at least in part, the estate attached to the settlement in which the churches were founded, dating back perhaps as early as the eighth or ninth century.[48] Unfortunately, limited excavation in Derby provides no further insight into its middle Saxon status, but the name *Northworthy* has prompted speculation that the site was of regional importance, perhaps, given the similarity with the name of the Mercian capital at Tamworth, it may have been a northern Mercian capital.[49] The parish boundaries of the churches in Leicester are not as helpful, and evidence for secular occupation of any type in Leicester is limited to early/middle Saxon pottery in the north-east of the town and early/middle Saxon sunken-featured buildings to the south of the town.[50]

The former Roman town of Lincoln may have been the seat of the bishops of Lindsey in the pre-viking period, but this is not confirmed by either textual or archaeological evidence, and there are other plausible candidates (fig. 26).[51] There were certainly cemeteries, and perhaps also a church, in Lincoln before the mid-ninth century. During excavations at the church of St Paul-in-the-Bail, over 200 burials dating to between the late fourth and the ninth century were uncovered, and some of these were associated with an apsidal building constructed with earth-fast plank walls, possibly a church. A stone-lined grave was excavated just inside the east end of this building, but was not stratigraphically related to it and may be later. The body had been removed from this grave, in which a seventh-century hanging-bowl was found behind one of the stones with which it was lined. This building was sealed with a layer of soil through which later burials were subsequently cut. Several of these clearly pre-dated a single-celled stone church, which may date to the ninth or tenth century.[52] It is possible, then, that there was a continuous focus of burial, perhaps with an associated church, from the sub-Roman period onwards.[53] Bede records that in the early seventh century Bishop Paulinus founded a church in Lincoln, but it is conjectural whether this church was at St Paul-in-the-Bail, not least because Bede states that the church was built of stone, and the radiocarbon dates of skeletons laid across the line of the timber building suggest that it was constructed earlier than the seventh century.[54] Excavations at Saltergate revealed five burials cut into the rubble from a collapsed Roman building and sealed by a tenth-century occupation layer. At a later date, two parish churches, St Peter-at-Arches and St Peter-at-Pleas, were located nearby and occupied the same churchyard, and they have been identified as a possible early religious foundation, with which the Saltergate burials may have been associated.[55] Our knowledge of the community buried at the St Paul-in-the-Bail and Saltergate sites is, however, limited. The status of Lincoln within the territory of Lindsey, which constituted a kingdom by the seventh century, if one constrained by more powerful neighbours and over-kings, is unknown.[56] The first convert of Paulinus in Lincoln was the *praefectus* Blæcca, who was probably of royal stock or a royal official, but this does not prove that Lincoln was the main administrative centre of Lindsey, and the fluidity of seventh- to ninth-century royal centres has been noted elsewhere.[57] Seventh- to ninth-century pottery has been found at a number of sites to the north of the River Witham, with the majority coming from outside the Roman west gate, but the lack of stratified contexts or associated features makes interpretation of the material difficult. A number of ninth-century artefacts were recovered during excavation at St Paul-in-the-Bail, including a silver strap-end, two silver buckles and four mid-ninth-century coins, but they were not in a stratified context, and it is not clear whether they were stray finds or a disturbed single deposit, perhaps a hoard.[58] In the light of this, a recent survey of the archaeological record for Lincoln concluded that until the mid-ninth century it had a small non-urban population in and around the crumbling ruins of the Roman city of *Lindum Colonia*.[59]

Little is known about Nottingham before the tenth century. There is no good evidence that any of the medieval parish churches of Nottingham were early foundations.[60] Excavation has revealed a series of middle Saxon ditches in the east of the town, in the vicinity of Woolpack Lane and Fishergate, and this is where the majority of the middle Saxon pottery from Nottingham has been recovered (fig. 24). The ditches are thought to have formed part of an enclosure, but its function is unknown; since the site is overlooked by higher ground to the west, it may not have been primarily defensive.[61] Whatever function it served, it is notable that the church of St Mary is located outside the enclosure, and may, thus, post-date it.[62] In 868, Nottingham was occupied by a viking army, and the combined efforts of a West Saxon and Mercian army failed to breach its defences, but while this suggests that Nottingham was defended at that time, its defences remain elusive in the archaeological record.[63]

During excavations at Stamford castle an earlier double-ditched enclosure with internal palisade was found (fig. 25). The upper part of the fill of the inner ditch included a late ninth-century coin, while the outer ditch preceded a pottery kiln dated archaeomagnetically to the second half of the ninth century.[64] Although only short sections of the ditches were uncovered, projection of their curving alignment suggests that they may have enclosed the location where St Peter's church once stood. This church appears to have been the mother church of Stamford, possessing the largest parish in the town, incorporating much suburban land, although there is

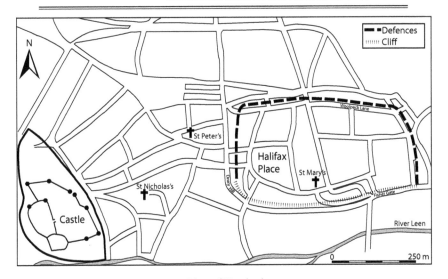

24   Plan of Nottingham.

no documentary or archaeological evidence for its origins.[65] If this circumstantial evidence is, nonetheless, reliable, it suggests that the church of St Peter's existed when the double-ditched enclosure was constructed, and, thus, before the Scandinavian occupation. It is unknown whether the enclosure surrounded a purely ecclesiastical complex focused on St Peter's church, or whether the church was associated with a secular estate centre – a precursor to queen Edith's estate in the town – with which the church was associated in Domesday Book.[66] What is believed to be an early routeway from the south, crosses the River Welland via a causeway across the meadows and heads towards the St Peter's nucleus, which may reflect its primacy in the development of Stamford.[67]

In the *Anglo-Saxon Chronicle* entry for 1015 there is a reference to 'the chief thegns of the seven boroughs', and it has been assumed that this must refer to the 'five boroughs' of Derby, Nottingham, Leicester, Stamford and Lincoln referred to in the *Chronicle* entry for 942, and to two other *burhs* in the vicinity.[68] One plausible candidate is Torksey (Lincs), since the evidence for its tenth-century development is similar to that from the 'five boroughs' (see p. 167), and the importance of which may have rested on its location close to the Foss Dyke, a canal linking Lincoln with the Trent.[69] Coins found in and near to Torksey indicate that it was already a place of some importance in the eighth and ninth centuries with continental links. The existence of an early trading centre has been posited, and

159

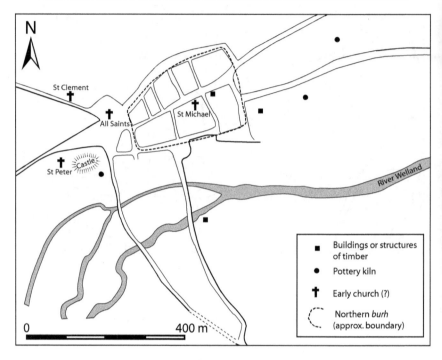

25   Plan of Stamford.

it is thought that this may account for the overwintering of a raiding army
at Torksey in 872/3.[70]

Excavations in Northampton have revealed an important centre dating
to the eighth to ninth century, although there has been a divergence of
opinion over the nature of the site. The archaeological evidence for a series
of monumental halls associated with other timber structures, and gullys,
has been interpreted by John Williams as a royal palace complex. A timber
hall of the late seventh or eighth century with two smaller annexes, one at
either end, was superseded by a stone hall of the eighth or early ninth
century to which two compartments were subsequently added at the west
end. Attention has been drawn to the similarities between this second hall
and the halls of contemporary Frankish palaces.[71] However, John Blair has
recently argued that the halls may have been part of the domestic range
associated with an early church, and has suggested that the churches of St
Peter and St Gregory, which were located to either side of the halls, were
part of a linear west–east arrangement typical of early minster sites.
Although St Gregory's was demolished in 1840, it was associated with

burials that were radiocarbon dated to the seventh to ninth centuries. St Peter's was a medieval mother church which housed the relics of a saint, and it contains Anglo-Saxon fabric, while the footings of a building found to the east of the chancel may have been an earlier phase of the church. Associated, if unstratified, finds of probably ecclesiastical associations include a stylus and a shrine mount.[72] Two concentric roads appear to define a boundary feature curving around the site, although it is not certain that this was contemporary with the pre-viking complex.[73]

Excavations adjacent to the castle in Bedford revealed a number of middle Saxon structures, and concentrations of middle Saxon pottery have been found in several places within the town, but the nature of the activity that these represented is impossible to state on present evidence.[74] There is a later medieval tradition that King Offa of Mercia was buried at Bedford in 796. If reliable, and since it is implausible that a king would be buried in any other setting, this would indicate that Bedford was the location of an eighth-century religious community.[75] Indeed, evidence for an early church is indicated by an Old English list of saints' resting-places, which records an otherwise unknown St Aethelbert at Bedford.[76] Jeremy Haslam has suggested that Bedford may have been established as a Mercian *burh* by Offa, perhaps as part of a defensive network to protect against the viking raiders. This argument rests on the rectilinear plan of Bedford north of the Ouse, which Haslam suggests is more indicative of West Saxon or Mercian *burh*-building, and to which he assigns pre-viking Mercian origins on the grounds that the northern *burh* was already in existence when Edward the Elder captured it in 915.[77] It is, however, impossible to validate this on present evidence. Haslam has made a similar case for Cambridge, but there is little documentary or archaeological evidence to support its origins as an important centre, let alone a *burh* of Offa, in the eighth century.[78]

There is little evidence of the nature of ninth-century activity in most of the other *burhs* subsequently occupied by Scandinavians. At Colchester (Essex), for example, while there is a wide range of material of fifth- to seventh-century date, including burials, there is a general dearth of eighth- and ninth-century evidence. Several churches certainly have Anglo-Saxon origins, but the claims that any of these churches dates to as early as the ninth century are tenuous.[79] There is little to suggest that Huntingdon, which the *Chronicle* states was abandoned by the Scandinavians in 917 in favour of Tempsford, was an important centre in the pre-viking period, or, indeed, Godmanchester on the opposite banks of the River Great Ouse, where some have suggested that the Scandinavians were in fact based.[80] Although it did not come under Scandinavian control, Chester was certainly occupied by Scandinavians from the early tenth century. Little, however, is known of the former Roman fortress. Excavations at Lower Bridge Street suggest an agricultural level of activity and that the site was abandoned some time during the ninth century, and the *Anglo-Saxon Chronicle* refers to Chester as 'a deserted city in Wirral'.[81] It is, however, possible that two of Chester's churches were of early origins: St John's, which briefly became the seat of the bishopric of Lichfield in 1075 but was clearly of importance prior to this, and St Werburgh's, which later tradition alleges to have been re-founded by Æthelflaed, who transferred the relics of St Werburgh from Hanbury (Staffs). These two churches had extensive medieval parishes and dominated burial provision in Chester, and as such appear to be minster churches of considerable antiquity.[82]

The documentary and archaeological evidence for the *burhs* of the north and east midlands suggests that many were already important religious, administrative or estate centres prior to the Scandinavian conquest, and this implies aspects of continuity in local and regional organisation, as these places were subsequently adopted as the centres of Scandinavian organisation. We should note, however, that some of the *burhs*, such as Colchester, have as yet produced very little evidence for having served as important places in the pre-viking period, although in this instance the survival of the Roman walls may have been a factor in the Scandinavian occupation.[83] There is little evidence for trade or manufacture prior to the late ninth century at most of the *burhs*, and although the limited scale of excavation may partly account for this, it should be noted that excavations at Lincoln, which have been comparatively extensive, have also produced few signs of urban life prior to the later ninth century.

The burhs *during the period of Scandinavian control*

Most of the *burhs* of the midlands were captured by Edward the Elder or Æthelflaed during the second decade of the tenth century, and only Lincoln may have remained under Scandinavian control for longer (see pp. 54–9). Thus, most were under Scandinavian control for a maximum of around thirty-five years. It should, however, be remembered that it is only during the period of the West Saxon offensive that most are first recorded as centres of Scandinavian occupation, and it is possible that the burghal system was of comparatively recent origin by the second decade of the tenth century, and that Scandinavian occupation was very short-lived. When King Edmund captured the north midlands in 942, the *Anglo-Saxon Chronicle* notes that he took the 'five boroughs' of Leicester,

Lincoln, Nottingham, Stamford and Derby, but whether this grouping had long had any significance is debatable.[84] Nonetheless, as we shall see, there is archaeological evidence to suggest that at least some of the *burhs* were certainly occupied by Scandinavians in the later ninth century.

Excavation reveals that there was considerable expansion of occupation in Lincoln in the late ninth and tenth centuries (fig 26), during the period of Scandinavian control. Two sites in the lower city have produced evidence for occupation in the late ninth century, at Silver Street and at Flaxengate, where a rubbish pit containing pottery of this date was excavated. While the remains reveal little of the nature of the occupation at this early date, it is notable that shortly afterwards buildings were constructed that faced on to Flaxengate, Silver Street and nearby at Danesgate, and since none of these streets has a Roman predecessor, this indicates that considerable development of the townscape was under way in the late ninth and early tenth centuries in Lincoln.[85] By the early tenth century the number of occupied streets had expanded, and included the suburb of Wigford to the south of the river.[86] There is no evidence for the modification of the Roman walls, which in places stood to a considerable height, and the likelihood is that they continued to offer defence. At the same time, however, the Roman road pattern appears to have exerted little influence over the street pattern of the late ninth and tenth centuries, and while some Roman buildings remained partially standing, others were demolished.[87]

By the late ninth century an urban profile begins to emerge in the archaeological evidence from Lincoln. Pottery may have been produced in the vicinity of Flaxengate from the late ninth century, given that during excavations in this area large quantities of pottery of this date, known as Lincoln Gritty-ware, were found.[88] Pottery kilns have been excavated at Silver Street, and while these date to the mid-tenth century, the presence of earlier pottery on the site suggests that they were constructed for an established industry in the vicinity, which may have begun in the mid- to later ninth century. These kilns have been described as 'effective instruments of mass production', and the pottery produced at Silver Street (known as Lincoln Kiln-type shelly ware) has been found in huge quantities all over Lincoln and further afield. One of these kilns (kiln 200) is the largest yet known in medieval Britain or Europe. It is not clear, however, whether the potters were specialists or whether they were also engaged in other crafts.[89] The excavations were limited in scale but suggested that this district witnessed a number of craft activities, including the working of both ferrous and non-ferrous metals.

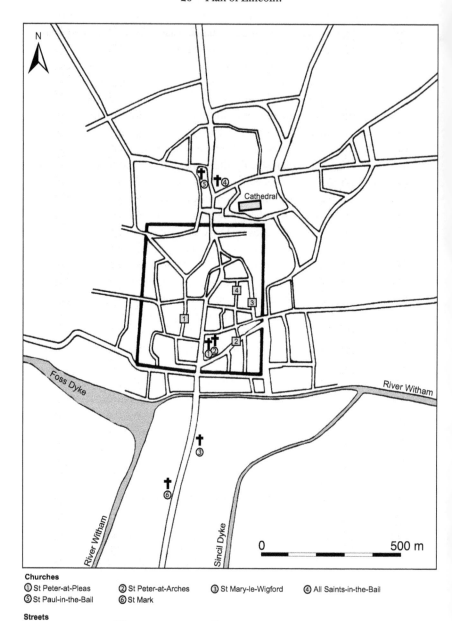

Churches
① St Peter-at-Pleas   ② St Peter-at-Arches   ③ St Mary-le-Wigford   ④ All Saints-in-the-Bail
⑤ St Paul-in-the-Bail   ⑥ St Mark

Streets
1 Hungate   2 Silver Street   3 Danesgate   4 Flaxengate

Attempts have been made to identify urban development in Lincoln from the ceramic sequences, although this is difficult, as the ceramics of the period included both earlier types and newer types that carried on into the eleventh century, and therefore unstratified finds are impossible to date closely. Nonetheless, in some stratified contexts study of the principal wares present has permitted the assigning of assemblages to particular periods, and Alan Vince has suggested that, for example, the frequency of Lincoln Late Saxon Shelly ware on both sides of the River Witham suggests that land was reclaimed at the waterfront when this fabric was at its peak of popularity in the mid-tenth century.[90]

Coins were minted at Lincoln in the 920s. The St Martin's pennies were modelled on those minted at York in the name of St Peter, and doubtless indicate political links between the two places, as do those coins minted for King Sihtric Caoch (921–7) that show close affinities with the sword St Peter's coins.[91] Excavations on Flaxengate revealed that workshops were constructed there in the mid- to late tenth century, replacing earlier domestic occupation, but it was apparent that various craft activities were being conducted in the vicinity from the late ninth century, including glass- and metalworking, while a range of ceramics from France, the Low Countries, the Rhineland, China and Syria, along with ivory, mica schist and soapstone, indicate extensive trading contacts.[92]

When Edward the Elder captured Stamford in 918 the *Chronicle* records that the people 'who belonged to' the northern *burh* submitted to him.[93] This *burh* was constructed during the period of Scandinavian control and is thought to have been located to the east of St Peter's church (fig. 25). This deduction is partly based on analysis of the layout of this part of the medieval town, which suggests a planned development. Excavation in the area where a defensive structure had been predicted revealed a system of upright and horizontal timbers, possibly a defensive structure, while two timber buildings with a dividing fence were excavated facing on to High Street, implying a planned layout. In both cases the excavated structures date to the late ninth or early tenth century.[94] This site may already have been an industrial area, as excavation revealed that at the eastern end of this *burh* the High Street was laid out over an iron-working surface.[95]

Scandinavian activity in Stamford can also be detected in the presence of coins. A hoard from the castle site, dated at c.890, consisted of coins from Lincoln, Leicester, and York; copies of Alfred's coinage struck in eastern England; and at least one Carolingian coin.[96] Many of the coins from this hoard had been nicked or 'pecked', which was a distinctively Scandinavian technique of testing the silver content of coins with a sharp knife.[97] Some of the St Edmund pennies were struck in the north-east midlands, and it is possible that this was at Stamford.[98] The Scandinavian impact on Stamford has been most firmly identified in the pottery industry that began in the late ninth century, although it is possible that it began a little before the Scandinavian occupation of Stamford. Sherds of Stamford ware from the kiln at the castle site were found underneath what are believed to have been the eastern defences of the northern *burh*, revealing that the defences post-dated the instigation of the pottery industry.[99] The pottery produced in the kilns excavated at the castle site is different from earlier pottery produced locally, which was handmade.[100] Stamford ware was wheel-made, and red-painted decoration and glaze are occasionally found on the earliest pottery, and continental influence is likely. While red-painted decoration and glaze are characteristics of pottery produced in several continental regions, similarities of style, technique and vessel types consistently point to an influence from northern France. Accordingly, it has been suggested that the Stamford pottery industry was prompted by continental potters who arrived in the wake of the Scandinavian army that occupied Stamford. These potters may have been captives of the army, or followers who were keen to take advantage of the raiders' conquest of parts of England, although the evidence for continental influence on both pottery production and the minting of coins may indicate that the settlers had good contacts on the continent, which facilitated the recruitment of craftworkers.[101] If the Scandinavian occupation of Stamford was the catalyst to the pottery industry, it is salutary to note that Scandinavian influence is identifiable in material culture of non-Scandinavian type.

Evidence from the period of Scandinavian control in other *burhs* is much more elusive. When Derby was captured by Æthelflaed in 917, four of the town's thegns are said to have been killed 'within the gates', implying a defended centre at that time if not earlier.[102] It has, however, been suggested that the former Roman fort on the opposite bank on the River Derwent, at Little Chester, may have been the defended centre in the early tenth century. Excavations within the fort produced a small number of tenth-century artefacts from unstratified contexts, a cess-pit containing St Neots and Stamford ware, and five unaccompanied burials, which are likely to be mid- to late Anglo-Saxon in date. A rubble platform added to the south-east corner of the fort sealed layers including tenth-century pottery, and an associated ditch contained pottery of similar date, implying some level of activity if not occupation at the fort in the Anglo–Scandinavian period.[103] The accounts of William Stukeley in the early eighteenth century reveal that parts of the Roman walls were still standing, and it is plausible that the site was still defensible eight centuries earlier.[104] At Nottingham, sections of a second, larger circuit of ditches have been excavated at Drury Hill, where it cut an earlier sunken-featured structure, and Woolpack Lane, and this dates to some time after the mid-ninth century (fig. 24). It is not clear whether this was the defensive site occupied by the Scandinavians in 868, or whether it was created during their period of control or even later. Excavations and analysis of the street layout suggest that there was an enclosed area of around 13.75 hectares. Although buildings of late ninth- or early tenth-century date have been excavated at Woolpack Lane, Drury Hill, Halifax Place and Fishergate, there is no evidence to characterise the activities which may have taken place in these buildings, although the large size of some of the buildings has suggested that they were important elite structures.[105] Two burials containing swords have been identified as viking graves, yet one of the swords may date to the tenth or eleventh century and thus post-date the period of Scandinavian control.[106]

There is very little evidence from the period of Scandinavian control at Leicester. The location of the *burh* has not been demonstrated archaeologically, and sites both within and outside the later medieval town have been suggested on the basis of circumstantial evidence. It is plausible to suppose that the Roman circuit may have been reused, but suggestions that the axial roads on either side of High Street were laid out as part of the *burh*, or that the curving back lanes were part of a defensive circuit within the Roman walls, are archaeologically unsubstantiated.[107] There are few finds of any type from this period, and the handful of pottery sherds, a collection of Anglo–Scandinavian bonework, a bronze pendant and ring-headed pins, lack archaeological context.[108] However, a halfpenny minted at Leicester in the late ninth century, which was found in a hoard at Stamford, reveals that coins were being struck during the period of Scandinavian control, but the anonymous nature of this coin offers little insight into the rulers of Leicester (fig. 27).[109]

Large numbers of ninth-century Northumbrian *stycas* from Torksey, a putative *burh* (see p. 159), probably derive from the period of occupation by the Scandinavian army, as do fragments of Islamic dirhems, hacksilver, hackgold, ingots and Scandinavian-style copper-alloy weights.[110] It is not clear whether Torksey was defended, and we know nothing of its layout in the ninth and tenth centuries. Nonetheless, we do know that it developed as a centre of pottery production – from the excavation of tenth-century kilns producing wheel-made wares. Torksey ware found at Lincoln indicates that manufacture must have begun in the late ninth century during the period of Scandinavian control of the district (fig. 28).[111]

27   Coin minted in Leicester in the late ninth century. This halfpenny was from a hoard found at Stamford (Lincs). The coin contains only the name of the mint and the moneyer.

At Northampton the large stone hall, which was part of either a royal palace or a minster complex, had been abandoned by the end of the ninth century. This is indicated by the fact that robber trenches of the walls are filled with late Anglo-Saxon pottery, much of which dates to the late ninth or early tenth centuries, and radiocarbon dates from silt in the gully to the south of the hall indicate that it had silted up by the late ninth century. Timber buildings and metalworking debris to the south-west indicate industrial activity, which probably post-dates the period of the stone hall. Evidence for pottery production, including a kiln, has also been identified, and shown to have been influenced by Stamford-ware, but it is not certain that this belongs to the period of Scandinavian control.[112] Scandinavian influence in the archaeological record is slight, but includes honestones from Norway. Several timber-built structures have been excavated in the vicinity of St Peter's church, and although they are difficult to date, the association of some of them with St Edmund coins suggests that they belong to the period of Scandinavian control.[113] Many of the other *burhs* have produced little or no evidence for the period of Scandinavian control, but it is difficult to be sure of the significance of this lacuna, given the limited possibilities for urban excavation and the broad date-ranges offered by many of the most visible archaeological remains.

28   Torksey-type ware storage vessel from Coppergate in York. Such wheel-thrown wares began to be produced in the later ninth century, and this example may have been produced in the vicinity of York.

Evidence for the period of Scandinavian control of the *burhs* of the north and east midlands is, as we have seen, limited. Artefacts of Scandinavian manufacture are scarce, and rarely from stratified contexts, and problems are posed by both the limited scale of excavations in most of the *burhs* and by the difficulties of dating many of the significant developments in the *burhs* specifically to the period of Scandinavian control. Nonetheless, there is some indication that the *burhs* were transformed by the settlers. The pottery industries of Lincoln, Stamford and Torksey took off during the period of Scandinavian control, and the *burhs* witnessed the production of pottery completely different from that produced in the north and east midlands at an earlier date. Although the evidence is tentative, it is possible that the pottery industry in some of the *burhs* began to be transformed before the Scandinavian settlement, and therefore it should not be assumed that the settlers were responsible for its inception, although the industry was certainly apparently fostered during their period of control. Many of the *burhs* have evidence for other forms of craft activity and for trade, and the products were often widely distributed.[114] The minting of coins also occurred during the period of Scandinavian control, certainly at Lincoln and Leicester, possibly at Stamford, and also at Derby during the brief re-establishment of Scandinavian rule south of the Humber under Olaf Guthfrithson (see p. 50). The new political regime prompted a revitalisation of the coinage and pottery production, drawing on continental craftworkers who appear to have been brought to eastern England in the wake of Scandinavian conquest.

The burhs *following West Saxon conquest*

From the second quarter of the tenth century onwards, the *burhs* of the north and east midlands all developed a range of urban characteristics, although it is rarely possible to date them closely. For example, the defences of many of the *burhs* were repaired or extended following the West Saxon conquest. There is evidence for recutting of the ditches of the enclosure at Nottingham, and although there is no material evidence to date this closely, it may be attributable to the capture of the *burh* in 918 by Edward the Elder, who ordered it to be repaired and manned with both Danes and English.[115] In 920 a second *burh* was built on the opposite bank of the Trent, along with a bridge over the river. The location of this *burh* has not been securely identified, and both West Bridgeford (the site of the medieval bridge) and Wilford have been suggested.[116] In 918 the *Anglo-Saxon Chronicle* records that King Edward came to Stamford and ordered a new *burh* to be built to the south of the river.[117] Its location has not been identified archaeologically, but is suggested by the diversion of a road from the earlier routeway heading for the St Peter's complex (see p. 159) (fig. 25). This presumed new routeway of the early tenth century crossed the Welland at the site of the medieval bridge. Parts of a twelfth-century predecessor to the modern bridge survive, and this may have been the location of a bridge built by Edward to link the two *burhs*, in an arrangement similar to that constructed later at Nottingham.[118] The rectilinear street layout to the south of the Welland suggests the site of the *burh*, and it is estimated that it was a rectilinear enclosure of 3.75 hectares. A north–south ditch excavated at the rear of properties on High Street St Martin's may have been part of the defences.[119]

The *Anglo-Saxon Chronicle* records that Chester was re-founded as a *burh* by Æthelflaed in 907, and, although the course of the defences in the tenth century is uncertain, much of the Roman circuit remained in use, and Æthelflaed is believed to have created defences running from both the north-west and south-east corners of the fortress to meet the River Dee. Excavations at Foregate Street, just to the north of the east gate, revealed securely dated Roman and medieval ditches, and an intermediate-period ditch, which may have been part of the late Anglo-Saxon defences.[120] The *Anglo-Saxon Chronicle* records that in 915 Edward the Elder spent four weeks at Bedford 'and before he went away he ordered the *burh* on the south side of the river to be built'. Edward's intention must have been to create a fortified bridgehead to protect against attack along the river. The location of this *burh* is suggested by the U-shaped plan of the medieval King's ditch to the south of the River Ouse, although its Anglo-Saxon origins could not be confirmed by excavation.[121] Newark (Notts) was not certainly a tenth-century *burh*, but it has been suggested that it may have been one of the 'seven boroughs' mentioned by the *Chronicle* in 1015 (see p. 159), and it does have certain characteristics in common with known *burhs*. The position of Newark on the River Trent near to the convergence of three Roman roads, placed it in a strategically important location, but the date of the 'new work' that gave the settlement its name is unknown, since the pre-Conquest defences identified during excavation cannot be closely dated.[122] Given that the defences are on the southern banks of the River Trent, it has been suggested that the *burh* must be a West Saxon, rather than Scandinavian, foundation intended to protect against attack from the north.[123] Edward the Elder repaired the *burh* at Huntingdon, but there is no conclusive evidence for its location, or to determine in what way the Scandinavian *burh* may have been modified, while the suggestion that the Roman site across the river at Godmanchester may have formed part of the

Edwardian defensive structure, in an arrangement similar to that found at Stamford, Nottingham and Bedford, remains conjectural.[124] Edward captured in Cambridge in 917, and it has been suggested that the medieval King's Ditch, on the south side of the River Cam from the Roman town, may mark a defensive structure created by Edward, thus resulting in another of the double *burhs*, but the evidence for this is circumstantial.[125]

Most of the *burhs* have evidence for the presence of manufacturing activities during the tenth century, in particular, pottery production. Lincoln continued to be a major centre for pottery production through the later tenth century and on into the eleventh century.[126] The pottery industry at Stamford continued to thrive after the *burh* was captured by Edward the Elder in 918, and the variety of tenth-century pottery fabrics infers multiple production centres, although only one, at Wharf Road, has been extensively excavated.[127] Stamford ware was traded widely around eastern England, and has also been found at sites much further afield.[128] Although the continental influence was crucial to the beginnings of the Stamford pottery industry, it is clear that the Stamford potters soon developed new styles and forms, presumably responding to demand. Red-painted decoration had seemingly gone out of use by the mid-tenth century, but glaze continued to be used, and experimentation in glazing has been identified.[129] Evidence for pottery production has been found at various sites around the town and, unlike in other towns such as Norwich and Ipswich, the pottery industry was not concentrated in a particular zone. This may be an indication of greater space and freedom to expand the industry in places like Stamford and Thetford (Norf), where a lack of zoning has also been identified.[130]

The pottery known as Chester Ware appeared around the beginning of the second quarter of the tenth century, and has been found both within Chester and further afield in western Merica, Dublin and even Trondheim (Norway). Wherever this pottery was produced – and it is, admittedly, not certain that it was in Chester – it seems that Chester played a part in its distribution.[131] Tenth-century kilns have been excavated in Torksey, and their products were widely distributed throughout eastern England.[132] Among other *burhs*, evidence for pottery production has also been found, although little is known of the nature or longevity of the industry or of the wares produced. For example, a late Anglo-Saxon pottery kiln was observed during a watching brief in Newark in 1994, and in Leicester the stoke-pit of a pottery kiln has been excavated at Southgate, the southernmost extension of High Street, and this appears to date to earlier than the mid-tenth century. Excavation at Halifax Place in Nottingham has revealed evidence for tenth-century pottery production, in the form of pottery wasters and kiln material, but it is not thought that this ware was of regional significance, as it has not been found outside the town.[133]

Debris indicative of iron-working has been encountered on a number of sites within and outside the northern *burh* at Stamford, while two sites on High Street have yielded evidence of the roasting and smelting of iron-ore. These activities can only be broadly dated to the tenth to early eleventh century.[134] Given the virtual absence of finished products from these sites, it appears that Stamford witnessed the mass-production of wrought iron, rather than the manufacture of metal items, and this is thought likely to have been of regional significance.[135] In Lincoln, various crafts have been identified in the tenth century, including the working of glass, copper, silver, bone and antler, jet, slate, amber and Norwegian schist. It is, however, difficult to assign these various activities to precise chronological brackets.[136] The large amounts of Stamford ware found in Derby may indicate the involvement of the town in the commercial exploitation of the lead deposits of the Peak District, since considerable quantities of lead would have been required to produce the glaze typical of Stamford ware.[137]

Coins were minted in many of the *burhs* from the reign of Athelstan (924-39). The output of the mint at Derby during Athelstan's reign suggests that it was one of the major mints in the country. Coins were briefly minted for Olaf Guthfrithson, after he took control in York (939-41), indicating the reality of his authority south of the Humber. The continuity of minting, and the ability of moneyers to adapt themselves to changed political circumstances, is reflected in those coins struck for Olaf that appear to have made use of dies intended for the obverse of coins for Athelstan.[138] Proximity to Peak District lead deposits may account for the prominence of Derby in minting by the mid-tenth century, perhaps giving rise to a supply of silver through the cupellation process, by which lead is separated out from precious metals.[139] There was possibly a mint in Chester during the reign of Edward the Elder, but more secure is the fact that during the reign of Athelstan the mint at Chester was one of the most prolific in the country, and it continued to have an enormous output until the 970s. Many Chester coins are found in hoards in Ireland, and it is likely that this and the commercial pre-eminence of Chester rest on its position as the major trading centre and port on the English side of the Irish Sea.[140] Coins were minted in Nottingham from the time of Athelstan, although it was apparently the least prolific of the mints of the Five Boroughs.[141] Stamford was also the location of a mint from at least the mid-tenth century, and possibly earlier. A number of the moneyers who minted St Edmund coins in the north-east midlands went on to mint coins for Edward the Elder, Athelstan and Olaf Cuarán, and it has been suggested that this mint was at Stamford.[142] Following the reform of the coinage by Edgar in c.973, the mint at Stamford had a huge output, making it among the ten most prolific mints in the country.[143] If this minting activity does reflect the prosperity of Stamford, it has been argued that this wealth cannot be accounted for by the pottery and iron-working industries alone, possibly indicating that the export of wool and cloth, which was certainly important to the economy of the later medieval town, may have begun in the tenth century.[144] The mint at Lincoln was also prolific in the later tenth century, and by the early eleventh century was producing around 10% of the total coinage of England.[145] Coins were also minted in Leicester in the tenth century, but it did not become a major mint until the last quarter of the century.[146] By the middle of the tenth century, coins were also being minted in the *burhs* of Bedford, Northampton and Huntingdon, and by the late tenth century in Colchester.[147] Newark and Torksey, each a candidate as one of the 'seven boroughs', were both minting coins by the end of the tenth century.[148]

Most of the *burhs* had numerous churches, according to Domesday Book, and excavation and the presence of stone sculpture reveal that many of these were founded during the tenth century. Domesday Book records that there were thirty-five churches in Lincoln, and tenth-century sculptures have been identified at the churches of St Mark, St Mary le Wigford, St Paul-in-the-Bail, and the predecessor of the cathedral, St Mary, while burials and/or churches of this date have been excavated at St Mark's, St Paul-in-the-Bail, St Mary and All-Saints-in-the-Bail.[149] Although it seems unlikely that the upper city was unoccupied from the mid-ninth to late tenth century, little evidence of occupation from this period has been found, despite extensive excavations, and it is possible that it was a largely ecclesiastical enclave at this time.[150] Domesday Book records five churches in Derby, six in Leicester and four in Stamford.[151] Domesday Book names only the church of St Peter's in Colchester, but excavation indicates there were at least four churches at this time.[152] The proliferation of churches in urban centres in the tenth and eleventh centuries is characteristic of the towns of eastern England, as is the association of these churches with burial grounds. This contrasts with the towns of southern and western England, in which there were generally far fewer churches, where a single mother church typically dominated ecclesiastical provision, and where lesser parish churches were frequently denied burial rites.[153] Various factors may account for this contrast, including the detrimental effects of the Scandinavian raids and settlement on the senior churches of the *burhs*, and their resulting inability to control the proliferation of new churches from the tenth century or to limit their acquisition of burial rites. It is striking that Chester, which did not fall under Scandinavian control, has a pattern of ecclesiastical provision more typical of the south-west, with two religious communities dominating burial provision.[154] The proliferation of stone sculptures in some tenth-century churches in Lincoln, such as St Mark and St Mary le Wigford, has recently been interpreted as an indication that they were located in districts with an unusual elite population, presumably a mercantile group, and that these monuments may have been produced as a result of the social competition engendered by the arrival of significant numbers of newcomers to the towns concerned.[155]

Most of the urban characteristics of the *burhs* can only be identified in the period following the West Saxon conquest, although close dating of urban defences, pottery manufacture and other industrial activity, and churches and their cemeteries, is often not possible. Nonetheless, despite the difficulties of establishing a precise chronology for urban growth, it is apparent that not only was there significant continuity of local administration following the West Saxon conquest, but the circumstances of the Scandinavian conquest appear to have paved the way for the urban expansion of the tenth century. Following West Saxon conquest, the *burhs* subsequently continued – or began – to mint coins and produce pottery. Many of the *burhs* were centres of production of regional significance by the mid-tenth century. Pottery from Lincoln, Stamford and Torksey was widely distributed, and the presence of Chester Ware in Ireland, especially Dublin, along with coins minted in Chester, indicates the importance to the prosperity of Chester of the links forged by Scandinavians between northern England and Ireland in the tenth century.[156]

East Anglia

Burhs do not appear to have been founded in East Anglia, but urban expansion during the late ninth and tenth centuries has also been identified at several sites in the region, including Thetford (Norf), Norwich and Ipswich. According to the *Anglo-Saxon Chronicle*, Thetford was occupied by a viking army during the winter of 870–1, and in Æthelweard's late tenth-century version of the *Chronicle*, it is recorded that they 'laid out a camp in the winter season at Thetford', although this has not been identified archaeologically.[157] Little is known of Thetford before the late ninth century, and consequently it is difficult to assess the nature of the settlement the Scandinavians occupied; presently the only evidence for middle Saxon occupation in the vicinity comes from outside of the later Anglo-Saxon settlement, with only stray finds from within the town.[158] The defences on the south side of the rivers Little Ouse and Thet enclose an area of dense tenth- to twelfth-century occupation, and extensive excavations have been made possible by the subsequent contraction of occupation in this area of the town. The circuit encloses an area of some 60 hectares, and, since it is thought to be too big to have constituted a fortified camp, it has been suggested that it was probably built to enclose an existing settlement, and, as such, probably dates to the mid- to later tenth century. These southern defences had gone out of use by the end of the tenth century, and excavation has revealed sections that were covered by eleventh-century industrial activity. The northern defensive circuit is smaller and forms a semi-circle focused on a river-crossing. This is thought to have had military origins, although again there is insufficient archaeo-logical evidence – either from the line of the defences or for the nature of later Anglo-Saxon occupation – to decide whether it was constructed by the Scandinavians, by Edward the Elder following the submission of East Anglia in 917 or even later. Excavation suggests that this part of the town was not densely occupied.[159] One possible clue to the relationship between the two defensive enclosures is provided by ecclesiastical organi-sation. The church of St Mary, in the southern part of the town, was the mother church of Thetford, and four of the other churches in the town, including St Peter's in the northern defensive circuit, are said in Domesday Book to have been subsidiary to it. The pre-eminence of St Mary's church implies that the earliest settlement focus was in the southern part of the town, and that the northern defensive circuit and settlement was a later addition. Nonetheless, it is notable that the parish of St Peter's extends beyond the northern defences, and this suggests that these defences and the associated street layout and settlement succeeded an earlier settlement focus to the north of the rivers.[160]

Several pottery kilns have been excavated in Thetford to the south of the river, and these appear to date to the later tenth and eleventh centuries, although it is thought that the pottery industry began in the later ninth century.[161] Although there was more than one pottery kiln at a site excav-ated by Brian Davison in 1967, leading him to suggest that this was an industrial quarter, not all of the pottery workers were grouped together, and other kilns have subsequently been excavated elsewhere in the town.[162] Evidence for other manufacturing activities has also been excavated, in the form of artefacts and manufacturing debris. For example, the discovery of a number of crucibles reveals that silversmithing and copper-alloy working took place in Thetford, and sawn antler tines and horn cores demonstrate the occurrence of bone- and antlerworking.[163] Large quantities of iron slag were encountered during the excavations of the 1940s and 1950s, along with various metalworking tools, although no hearths or furnaces were identified, and scattered evidence for textile production, cord making, leatherworking and tanning have also been identified.[164] More recent excavation to the south of the river in Mill Lane has revealed evidence for iron-smelting and silver-refining, possibly associated with minting, a proposition rendered more likely by the recent recovery of an iron coin-die.[165] It is, however, difficult to date or quantify the scale of industrial activity in Thetford, although the distribution of finds suggests that 'most areas were given over to diverse small-scale activities'.[166] In common with the *burhs* of the midlands, by the last quarter of the tenth century Thetford had acquired a mint, and it was also characterised by a multiplicity of churches, with Domesday Book recording twelve and a half.[167] Although it is generally thought that the Scandinavian occupation was the catalyst for urban expansion in Thetford, there is little that can be confidently assigned to Scandinavian influence; the few exceptions include metalwork, such as a Carolingian-style lead-plate brooch and a similar brooch decorated in the Borre style.[168]

Eighth- and ninth-century occupation has been identified at several sites in Norwich, including the districts of *Westwick, Needham* and *Northwic* to the south of the River Wensum, where large quantities of middle Saxon pottery have been found, and on the north side of the river in the area of Fishergate, which has produced both domestic and imported pottery, coins and metalwork, including a caterpillar brooch and a pin. The Fishergate settlement may have been focused on a crossing over the river at the site of the later Fye bridge, where a timber-piled causeway has been excavated, although unfortunately not dated. These clusters of middle Saxon material indicate that urban growth was preceded by a number of rural settlements, but they are not thought to have exerted any strong influence on the town plan. The settlement on the north bank was enclosed by a ditch of tenth-century date, but there is disagreement about which part of the century it originated in, while attempts to identify Anglo-Saxon defences around the districts to the south of the river have not been successful.[169] Excavation suggests that occupation to the south of the river developed gradually during the late tenth and eleventh centuries, and that it was not, as once thought, an early tenth-century *burh*. Concentrations of tenth-century pottery have been found at *Northwic, Westwick* and just to the east of

Westwick around Pottergate, where kiln sites dating from the later part of the century have been excavated. Little tenth-century material has been recovered from north of the river, although this is largely attributable to the limited possibilities for excavation.[170] Evidence that can be attributed to the period of Scandinavian control is limited, and consists of a gold ingot from the area of the medieval French borough, and Anglo-Saxon-style disc brooches with Borre-style decoration (from the castle bailey excavation and elsewhere in the town) which suggest that Norwich may have been a centre of production of these dress-accessories (fig. 16). There is also metalwork influenced by later tenth- and eleventh-century Scandinavian styles, including horse harnesses and strap-ends; a capital from the cathedral in the Scandinavian Urnes style (named after the carvings on a wooden church at Urnes, Norway); and stone carving in the Mammen style (named after a decorated axe found at Mammen in Denmark) now in the castle museum.[171] As with most of the towns discussed in this chapter, coins were minted at Norwich, probably from the early tenth century, and, by the end of the tenth century, Norwich was one of the most prolific mints in the country.[172] There were at least 23 churches in Norwich by 1066, and there may have been many more, since excavation has recovered a number of abandoned churches and cemeteries of later Anglo-Saxon date, such as those found during excavation of the castle baileys.[173]

The earliest occupation in Ipswich dates to the early seventh century. Its distinctive pottery began to be produced on a large scale in the early eighth century, and was distributed widely around eastern England, especially the coastal districts. Imported continental pottery, vessel glass, honestones and quernstones reflect the involvement of the site in long-distance trade networks in the eighth and ninth centuries, and it is thought that coins were minted at or near Ipswich in the early eighth century (the so-called Anglian Series R sceattas). There is also evidence for metal-, bone-, horn- and leatherworking and textile production. A cemetery immediately to the north of the earliest phase of settlement remained in use from the early seventh century until the late eighth century, and the settlement appears to have been ringed with a burial zone. In the earlier ninth century, however, there was considerable expansion of the settlement, and, to the north of the earlier focus, streets were laid out on to which buildings fronted. Excavations at the Butter Market revealed that metalled streets superseded the abandoned cemetery. In the late ninth or early tenth century, occupation at both Butter Market and Foundation Street became less dense, and the now fewer buildings were set back from the street. It is not clear whether pottery production continued in Ipswich without a break, but continuity of activity is suggested by the fact that tenth-century pottery was produced in the same area as earlier pottery. This pottery was akin to that produced at Thetford, and kilns for its manufacture have been excavated in Ipswich.[174] A Scandinavian imprint on Ipswich is difficult to identify, and a defensive circuit has not been convincingly demonstrated.[175] As in many towns of eastern England, a mint was (re-)established at Ipswich by the end of the tenth century, and there were numerous churches, probably more than the twelve recorded by Domesday Book.[176]

Pottery

The study of pottery has long made an important contribution to discussions of urban development, but recently the study of pottery has been used to discuss social issues. For example, Leigh Symonds has examined the distribution of pottery produced in Lincolnshire, and suggested that it has much to reveal about regional identities. Wares from Lincoln and Torksey are found across Lindsey, while Stamford wares – although widely distributed across England – within Lincolnshire are largely found south of the River Witham, in the districts of Kesteven and Holland. Symonds argues that this pattern indicates the distinctive territorial identities of Lindsey and 'Stamfordshire', observing that the different pottery traditions in these two regions are mirrored by the different sculptural traditions of Lindsey and south Lincolnshire. She concludes that regional identities were expressed not only by the elite but also by wider society, through their trading contacts and consumption of regionally distinctive patterns of pottery.[177]

It has long been recognised that the Scandinavian settlement prompted a transformation in pottery production in eastern England, and that it had become primarily, if not exclusively, an urban industry in these regions.[178] These developments have been extensively studied, yet the personnel involved in pottery production have received little attention, beyond the recognition of the presence of continental potters. With the urbanisation and increased industrialisation of pottery production from the late ninth century in eastern England, and the closer association of pottery production with other manufacturing activities, it is likely that the processes involved in the procurement of raw materials, manufacture and decoration of pottery were transformed from a household activity to a workshop mode of production.[179] While there is little direct evidence for the implications of such developments, ethnographic parallels, of the type drawn on by prehistorians, emphasise the likelihood that women, and also children, were heavily involved in pottery production in household contexts, but that their involvement decreased with the increasingly industrialised nature of production.[180] It is certain that there were changes in the personnel involved in pottery production from the late ninth century onwards, and, although it is impossible to prove, it is plausible that these transformations affected women disproportionately.[181]

The impact of the Scandinavian conquerors on pottery production was far greater than that of continental traders in earlier centuries, whose imported wares had no discernible impact on local methods of production.[182] In part this must have been because the Scandinavians came as conquerors and in greater numbers, and because of disruption to existing manufacturing processes and trade networks. Nonetheless, since there is no necessary link between conquest and the adoption of new forms of material culture, the consumers of this pottery must have been willing to adopt it. Both the settlers, who generally had no extensive tradition of pottery use, and the local population, with a tradition of handmade pottery, were faced with a new product. The consumption of food is a basic requirement, yet the vessels used in preparing, serving and eating food seem rarely to have been merely functional items; thus, the occupants of eastern England were also faced with a new cultural medium. The adoption of these new fabrics; the absence of evidence for enclaves of cultural conservatism; and the paucity of evidence for the importation of steatite vessels that would have been more familiar to some of the settlers, suggests that there was a widespread process of acculturation among the communities of eastern England. It was within the household that this process of acculturation was achieved, in the processes of cooking and serving food, in contexts that were at once both private, family spaces and also the public face of the family. As Paul Blinkhorn has observed, 'Placing a vessel which transmitted social information at the visual focus of a room would have meant that its message could not have been missed by anyone present'.[183] Again, one cannot but infer that women in Anglo–Scandinavian England played at least as important a part as the pottery manufacturers in dictating this social phenomenon.

Conclusions

A recent review of the archaeological evidence for the development of York concluded that the Anglo–Scandinavian period was fundamental to the development of York, but that it is difficult to refine the chronology of many developments within the broad period from the later ninth to the mid-eleventh century, and that therefore 'the overall picture of urban growth remains somewhat unfocused'.[184] Such a conclusion is even more applicable to the other urban places of northern and eastern England, which have experienced far less excavation. Nonetheless, it is possible to draw a number of tentative conclusions concerning the nature of the places occupied by Scandinavian armies that subsequently became urban, the Scandinavian contribution to that urbanism, and the subsequent fate of those places.

That the Scandinavian conquerors should seek out defended, or at least defensible, sites and pre-existing centres of authority and economic activity from which to take control of northern and eastern England is understandable enough. However, it is not clear that they occupied only the most important administrative, royal, economic or ecclesiastical centres in a district, or that those sites that emerged as the major towns of northern and eastern England had been the pre-eminent centres in their district at an earlier date. Other important early centres are known in the vicinity of many of the places that developed into tenth-century towns.[185] For example, although *wics* may have been major centres for trade in the pre-viking period, other possible centres where resources were collected and redistributed have been identified in the archaeological record, many through the activities of metal-detectorists. Such centres, often dubbed 'productive sites', are typified by concentrations of seventh- to ninth-century coins and metalwork. Examples include Flixborough, Melton Ross (Lincs), Coddenham (Suff), Bawsey, Burnham, Congham, Rudham and Wormegay (Norf).[186] While doubt has been expressed about the historical significance of such sites – with at least one archaeologist believing that they may only appear anomalous because of the methods of artefact recovery – nonetheless the context of such 'productive' sites (many of which are associated with early religious communities or royal centres) suggests that they do represent a real historical phenomenon.[187] By the tenth and eleventh centuries, many of these sites were major estate centres, sometimes with markets, and there were important churches at some of them, while others were major endowments of other churches. Along with the recovery of unusual quantities of tenth- and eleventh-century metalwork from some of these sites, this suggests aspects of institutional continuity, although it is important not to overlook the fact that some of the early 'productive' sites, such as Barham and Coddenham, were not prominent places at a later date.[188] In the north-west a number of early trading centres have also been identified, and these appear to have been part of a trading network focused on the Irish Sea area, including Luce Sands near Galloway (Scot), Whithorn (Scot), Nendrum (Northern Ireland), Dundrum (Irish Republic), Ronaldsway (Isle of Man) and Meols (Ches), in what have been dubbed 'politically-neutral market-places'. In this region, in contrast to East Anglia, there appears to have been a transformation of trading activity in the tenth century, which became increasingly controlled by the secular elite, in major centres such as Chester and Dublin, and most of these earlier centres ceased to be involved in exchange of imported goods. At Meols, however, trade appears to have resumed in the later tenth century, and it has been suggested by David Griffiths that it served the Wirral peninsula – perhaps finding its origins in the Scandinavian settlement of the early tenth century in this district, and in contrast with the West Saxon burghal foundation at Chester.[189] In sum, there was a range of trading centres in pre-viking England, and, following the Scandinavian settlements, some of these early trading places declined in importance and trade was transferred to the *burhs* or other major towns, but others seem to have retained their local prominence, often seemingly because of association with religious communities.

The majority of the *burhs* occupied by Scandinavians, however briefly, acquired urban status during the late ninth or, more commonly, the tenth century. Although close dating is only possible in a few cases, the archaeological evidence suggests that this period witnessed considerable investment in the trading and manufacturing structure, and also in the built environment of urban places in eastern England and the north midlands, as well as in York. In evaluating the Scandinavian contribution, we should note that rapid urban development of the later ninth and tenth centuries was not restricted to the areas of Scandinavian settlement, although the fastest growth of such urban places appears to have occurred in those regions. That most of the urban centres in the regions of Scandinavian conquest are located inland, on navigable rivers, perhaps implies that international trade was of less significance than trade with regional hinterlands. There is no reason to suppose that these places were occupied solely by Scandinavians and the continental moneyers and potters who followed in their wake. The range of material culture, especially from York, suggests that the economic and political climate of the period witnessed a rapid emergence of a hybrid artistic culture, and although it is possible that a Scandinavian cultural milieu survived in some towns, in most of the material expressions of identity an undiluted Scandinavian influence is rare. The indigenous populations clearly contributed to urban developments, and the disruptions attendant on the Scandinavian raids and conquest may have played a part in weakening patterns of rural organisation and tenurial control, rendering many rural dwellers more able or more willing to leave the estates they occupied and move into the new manufacturing and trading centres.[190] Indeed, urban expansion was not limited to the *burhs* and the major towns of East Anglia, and there are other centres with evidence for trade, manufacture, minting and local and regional importance, such as Louth, Horncastle, Caistor (Lincs) and Sudbury (Suff), some of which appear to have been ecclesiastical, royal or trading centres prior to the late ninth century.[191]

Few signs of truly urban places can be found prior to the Scandinavian settlements, although many of the component parts of urbanism can be identified in the pre-viking period, including trading and manufacturing places and defended administrative centres. Many of the characteristic features of urban centres in northern and eastern England are difficult to date securely to the period of Scandinavian control, and many appear to have developed in the mid- to later tenth century. Even where it is possible to assign developments to the period of Scandinavian control, there is little that can be characterised as being specifically Scandinavian. It has been observed that the Scandinavians do not seem to have prompted urban development in regions which did not otherwise have the necessary prerequisites, including Scotland and the Isle of Man, and even in Ireland the urban imprint appears to have been prompted by the English example.[192] Thus, it appears that urban growth in northern and eastern England was the result of a combination of factors, including the circumstances of the Scandinavian settlements, such as disruptions to the political and administrative system, the desire of Scandinavian rulers to takeover existing centres of power and to rule in a fashion that owed much to the pre-existing style of lordship; the attendant arrival of continental craftworkers; the capacity of the indigenous elite to work with their new overlords; and the policy of the West Saxon kings to continue to promote the status of the emerging urban centres of the regions of Scandinavian conquest.

Notes

1 M. Biddle, 'Towns', in D. M. Wilson (ed.), *The Archaeology of Anglo-Saxon England* (London, 1976), pp. 99–150, at 100.

2 C. Scull, 'Urban centres in pre-viking England?', in J. Hines (ed.), *The Anglo-Saxons from the Migration Period to the Eighth Century* (Woodbridge, 1997), pp. 269–98, at 271.

3 *Ibid.*; B. Ambrosiani, 'The prehistory of towns in Sweden', in R. Hodges and B. Hobley (eds), *The Rebirth of Towns in the West AD 700–1050*, CBA Research Rep., 68 (London, 1988), pp. 63–8.

4 See, for example, J. D. Richards, *Viking Age England* (2nd edn, Stroud, 2000), pp. 59–78; D. Griffiths, 'Exchange, trade and urbanisation', in W. Davies (ed.), *From the Vikings to the Normans* (Oxford, 2003), pp. 73–104, at 83.

5 P. Holdsworth, *Excavations at Melbourne Street, Southampton*, CBA Research Rep., 33 (London, 1980); P. Andrews (ed.), *The Coins and Pottery from Hamwic* (Southampton, 1988); M. Brisbane, 'Hamwic (Saxon Southampton): an 8th-century port and production centre', in Hodges and Hobley (eds), *The Rebirth of Towns*, pp. 101–8; A. Morton, *Excavations at Hamwic: Volume 1*, CBA Research Rep., 84 (London, 1992); K. Wade, 'Ipswich', in Hodges and Hobley (eds), *The Rebirth of Towns*, pp. 93–100; idem, 'The urbanisation of East Anglia: the Ipswich perspective', in J. Gardiner (ed.), *Flatlands and Wetlands: current themes in East Anglian archaeology*, EAA, 50 (Gressenhall, 1993), pp. 142–51; A. Vince, 'The Aldwych: mid-Saxon London discovered?', *Curr. Arch.*, 8 (1984), 310–12; R. Cowie and R. Whytehead, 'Lundenwic: the archaeological evidence for Middle Saxon London', *Antiquity*, 241 (1989), 706–18; R. Kemp, *Anglian Settlement at 46–54 Fishergate*, The Archaeology of York, 7 (1) (York, 1996); Scull, 'Urban centres', pp. 275–80.

6 P. Rahtz, 'The archaeology of West Mercian towns', in A. Dornier (ed.), *Mercian Studies* (Leicester, 1977), pp. 107–29; D. Hill and A. Rumble (eds), *The Defence of Wessex: the Burghal Hidage and Anglo-Saxon fortifications* (Manchester, 1996); a brief overview of relevant debates and evidence appears in Richards, *Viking Age England*, pp. 59–78.

7 J. Blair, 'Minster churches in the landscape', in D. Hooke (ed.), *Anglo-Saxon Settlements* (Oxford, 1988), pp. 35–58; J. H. Williams, 'From "palace" to "town": Northampton and urban origins', *ASE*, 13 (1984), 113–36; Scull, 'Urban centres', p. 274.

8 G. Fellows-Jensen, 'The origin and development of the name York', in D. W. Rollason (ed.), *Sources for York History to AD 1100*, The Archaeology of York, 1 (York, 1998), pp. 226–37, at 230.

9 Scull, 'Urban centres', p. 280.

10 M. A. S. Blackburn, 'The coinage of Scandinavian York', in R. A. Hall (ed.), *Aspects of Anglo-Scandinavian York*, The Archaeology of York, 8 (York, 2004), pp. 325–49, at 325.

11 Rollason (ed.), *Sources for York History*, pp. 132–5, and pp. 136–45 on subsequent restoration and endowments.

12 D. Phillips and B. Heywood (eds), *Excavations at York Minster, Volume 1: from Roman fortress to Norman cathedral* (London, 1995), pp. 75–92; Rollason, *Sources for York History*, pp. 146–8 on documented burials.

13 *Ibid.*, pp. 155–7.

14 *Ibid.*, p. 157.

15 *Ibid.*, pp. 158–60.

16 *Ibid.*, pp. 160–1, 176–7.

17 *Ibid.*, pp. 161–2.

18 J. Naylor, 'York and its region in the eighth and ninth centuries AD: an archaeological study', *Oxford Journal of Archaeology*, hereafter: *Oxford J.*

of Arch., 20 (1) (2001), 79–105; R. A. Hall, 'The topography of Anglo-Scandinavian York', in Hall (ed.), *Aspects of Anglo–Scandinavian York*, pp. 488–497, at 489–90.

19 *Ibid.*, p. 490; Rollason, *Sources for York History*, pp. 129–32.

20 Hall, 'The topography of Anglo–Scandinavian York', pp. 489–90.

21 R. A. Hall, 'Afterword', in Hall (ed.), *Aspects of Anglo–Scandinavian York*, pp. 498–502, at 498–9.

22 *Ibid.*, p. 499.

23 A. Mainman and N. Rogers, 'Craft and economy in Anglo–Scandinavian York', in Hall (ed.), *Aspects of Anglo–Scandinavian York*, pp. 459–87, at 464–7.

24 J. Bayley, *Anglo–Scandinavian Non-Ferrous Metalworking from 16–22 Coppergate*, The Archaeology of York, 17 (7) (York, 1992); Mainman and Rogers, 'Craft and economy in Anglo–Scandinavian York', pp. 467–8.

25 C. A. Morris, *Craft, Industry and Everyday Life: wood and woodworking in Anglo–Scandinavian and Medieval York*, The Archaeology of York, 17 (13) (York, 2000); Mainman and Rogers, 'Craft and economy in Anglo–Scandinavian York', p. 469.

26 G. Mould, I. Carlisle and E. Cameron, *Craft, Industry and Everyday Life: leather and leatherworking in Anglo–Scandinavian and Medieval York*, The Archaeology of York, 17 (13) (York, 2003); Mainman and Rogers, 'Craft and economy in Anglo–Scandinavian York', p. 469.

27 A. MacGregor, A. Mainman and N. Rogers, *Craft, Industry and Everyday Life: bone, antler, ivory and horn from Anglo–Scandinavian and Medieval York*, The Archaeology of York, 17 (12) (York, 1999); Mainman and Rogers, 'Craft and economy in Anglo–Scandinavian York', pp. 469–72.

28 *Ibid.*, pp. 472–4.

29 *Ibid.*, pp. 476–82.

30 Hall, *Viking Age York*, pp. 83–7; *idem*, 'Anglo–Scandinavian attitudes: archaeological ambiguities in late ninth- to mid-eleventh-century York', in D. M. Hadley and J. D. Richards (eds), *Cultures in Contact: Scandinavian settlement in England in the ninth and tenth centuries* (Turnhout, 2000), pp. 295–324, at 315–17.

31 Hall, *Viking Age York*, p. 110; *idem*, 'Anglo–Scandinavian attitudes', pp. 318–19; C. Paterson, 'The Viking Age trefoil mount from Jarlshof: a reappraisal in the light of two new discoveries', *Proceedings of the Society of Antiquaries of Scotland*, hereafter: *PSAS*, 127 (1997), 649–57, on p. 655; D. Tweddle, 'Art in pre-Conquest York', in Hall (ed.), *Aspects of Anglo–Scandinavian York*, pp. 446–58, at 451–8.

32 Hall, 'Anglo–Scandinavian attitudes', pp. 319–20.

33 *Ibid.*, pp. 314–15; D. W. Rollason, *Northumbria 500–1100. Creation and destruction of a kingdom* (Cambridge, 2003), p. 221.

34 Hall, 'The topography of Anglo–Scandinavian York', pp. 493–5.

35 *Ibid.*, pp. 314–15; Richards, *Viking Age England*, pp. 62–7; Rollason, *Northumbria 500–1100*, p. 223.

36 *Ibid.*, p. 224.

37 Hall, *Viking Age York*, pp. 55–69.

38 Richards, *Viking Age England*, p. 85.

39 Rollason, *Northumbria 500–1100*, pp. 223–4, 230.

40 Tweddle, 'Art in pre-Conquest York', p. 458.

41 A. Campbell (ed.), *The Chronicle of Æthelweard* (Edinburgh, 1962), p. 37.

42 D. W. Rollason, 'List of saints' resting-places in Anglo-Saxon England', *ASE*, 7 (1978), 61–94, at 69.

43 *EHD I*, p. 276; D. W. Rollason, *Saints and Relics in Anglo-Saxon England* (Oxford, 1989), p. 122; *idem*, 'The cults of murdered royal saints in Anglo-Saxon England', *ASE*, 11 (1983), 1–22, at 4–5; see also A. T. Thacker, 'Kings, saints and monasteries in pre-viking Mercia', *Mid. Hist.*, 9 (1984), 1–25, at 15–16.

44 C. A. Ralegh Radford, 'The church of St Alkmund, Derby', *Derbyshire Archaeological Journal*, hereafter: *DAJ*, 96 (1976), 26–61; M. Biddle, 'Archaeology, architecture and the cult of saints in Anglo-Saxon England', in L. Butler and R. K. Morris (eds), *The Anglo-Saxon Church*, CBA Research Rep., 60 (London, 1986), pp. 1–31, at 16.

45 D. M. Hadley, *The Northern Danelaw: its social structure, c.800–1100* (London, 2000), p. 273.

46 R. N. Bailey, *The Early Christian Church in Leicester and its Region* (Leicester, 1980), p. 10.

47 P. Courtney, 'Saxon and medieval Leicester: the making of an urban landscape', *TLAHS*, 73 (1998), 110–45, at 129–32.

48 *Ibid.*, pp. 136–8.

49 R. A. Hall, 'The Five Boroughs of the Danelaw: a review of present knowledge', *ASE*, 18 (1989), 149–206, at 155.

50 Courtney, 'Saxon and medieval Leicester', 110–13.

51 R. Gem, 'The Episcopal churches of Lindsey in the early ninth century', in A. Vince (ed.), *Pre-Viking Lindsey* (Lincoln, 1993), pp. 123–7; D. Stocker, 'The early church in Lincolnshire', in *ibid.*, pp. 101–22, at 115–19.

52 A. Vince, 'Lincoln in the early medieval era, between the 5th and 9th centuries', in D. Stocker (ed.), *The City by the Pool. Assessing the archaeology of the city of Lincoln* (Oxford, 2003), pp. 141–56, at 147–51.

53 Hall, 'The Five Boroughs', 174.

54 Vince, 'Lincoln in the early medieval era', pp. 145, 149–51.

55 *Ibid.*, pp. 154–6.

56 S. Foot, 'The kingdom of Lindsey', in Vince (ed.), *Pre-Viking Lindsey*, pp. 128–40.

57 Vince, 'Lincoln in the early medieval era', p. 145.

58 *Ibid.*, p. 147; A. Vince, 'Lincoln in the Viking Age', in J. Graham-Campbell, R. A. Hall, J. Jesch and D. Parsons (eds), *Vikings and the Danelaw. Select papers from proceedings of the Thirteenth Viking Congress* (Oxford, 2001), pp. 157–80, at 159–60.

59 *Ibid.*, p. 157.

60 A. Rogers, 'Parish boundaries and urban history', *JBAA*, 3rd ser., 35 (1972), 46–64, at 55.

61 Hall, 'The Five Boroughs', 189.

62 Rogers, 'Parish boundaries and urban history', 51–6.

63 *EHD I*, p. 192; S. Keynes and M. Lapidge, *Alfred the Great. Asser's* Life of King Alfred *and other contemporary sources* (Harmondsworth, 1983), p. 241.

64 C. Mahany, 'Excavations at Stamford castle 1971–1976', *Château Gaillard*, viii (1976), 223–45, at 232–3; K. Kilmurry, *The Pottery Industry of Stamford, Lincs*, BAR Brit. Ser., 84 (Oxford, 1980), p. 32.

65 Rogers, 'Parish boundaries and urban history', 56–62; C. Mahany and D. Roffe, 'Stamford: the development of an Anglo–Scandinavian borough', *ANS*, 5 (1985), 197–219, at 203–4.

66 *Ibid.*, 200–3.

67 *Ibid.*, 206.

68 *EHD I*, p. 247.

69 There is, however, debate about the origins of the Dyke. It may have been Roman, but whether it was still navigable in the later Anglo-Saxon period is questionable. Nonetheless, Domesday Book notes Torksey as an important link in the water-borne trade between York and Lincoln, suggesting that it was navigable in the mid-eleventh century: P. H. Sawyer, *Anglo-Saxon Lincolnshire* (Lincoln, 1998), p. 197.

70 *Ibid.*, p. 260.

71 Williams, 'From "palace" to "town"', 118–31; J. H. Williams, M. Shaw and V. Denham, *Middle Saxon Palaces at Northampton* (Northampton, 1985), pp. 31–6.

72 J. Blair, 'Palaces or minsters? Northampton and Cheddar reconsidered', *ASE*, 25 (1996), 97–121, at 101–8.

73 *Ibid.*, 98–9.

74 D. Baker, E. Baker, J. Hassall and A. Simco, 'Excavations in Bedford', *Bedford Archaeological Journal*, hereafter: *BAJ*, 13 (1979), 20–6, 151–9, 240–1, 294.

75 J. Campbell (ed.), *The Anglo-Saxons* (London, 1982), pp. 87, 110.

76 Rollason, 'List of saints' resting-places', 64, 90.

77 J. Haslam, 'The origin and plan of Bedford', *BAJ*, 16 (1983), 29–36, at 30–4.

78 J. Haslam, 'The development and topography of Saxon Cambridge', *Proceedings of the Cambridge Archaeological Society*, hereafter: *PCAS*, 72 (1982), 13–29, at 13–18.

79 P. Crummy, *Aspects of Anglo-Saxon and Norman Colchester*, CBA Research Rep., 39 (London, 1981), pp. 1–24, 40–67; W. Rodwell, *Historic Churches: a wasting asset*, CBA Research Rep., 19 (London, 1977), pp. 31–6.

80 P. Spoerry, 'The topography of Anglo-Saxon Huntingdon: a survey of the archaeological and historical evidence', *PCAS*, 84 (2000), 35–47.

81 D. J. P. Mason, *Excavations at Chester, 26–42 Lower Bridge Street 1974–6, the Dark Age and Saxon periods* (Chester, 1985), pp. 2–6.

82 A. T. Thacker, 'Chester and Gloucester: early ecclesiastical organization in two Mercian burhs', *North. Hist.*, 18 (1982), 199–211, at 199–206.

83 Crummy, *Aspects of Anglo-Saxon and Norman Colchester*, pp. 70–3.

84 *EHD I*, p. 221.

85 A. Vince, 'The new town: Lincoln in the high medieval era (c.900 to c.1350)', in Stocker (ed.), *The City by the Pool*, pp. 159–296, at 192.

86 *Ibid.*, pp. 192–4.

87 Hall, 'The Five Boroughs', 177–80.

88 Vince, 'Lincoln in the Viking Age', p. 171.

89 P. Miles, J. Young and J. Wacher, *A Late Saxon Kiln Site at Silver Street, Lincoln*, The Archaeology of Lincoln, 12 (3) (London, 1989), pp. 185–94, 198–204, 234.

90 Vince, 'Lincoln in the high medieval era', p. 194.

91 C. E. Blunt, B. H. I. H. Stewart and C. S. S. Lyon, *Coinage in Tenth-Century England. From Edward the Elder to Edgar's reform* (Oxford, 1989), pp. 106–7.

92 D. Perring, *Early Medieval Occupation at Flaxengate, Lincoln*, The Archaeology of Lincoln, 9 (1) (London, 1981), pp. 41–5.

93 *EHD I*, p. 216.

94 C. Mahany, A. Burchard and G. Simpson, *Excavations in Stamford Lincolnshire 1963–1969* (London, 1982), p. 10; Mahany and Roffe, 'Stamford', 209–11.

95 Kilmurry, *The Pottery Industry of Stamford*, p. 145. However, Hall points out that the residues need not be *in situ*, and may have been brought in from elsewhere as road make-up: Hall, 'The Five Boroughs', 198.

96 M. A. S. Blackburn, 'Expansion and control: aspects of Anglo–Scandinavian minting south of the Humber', in Graham-Campbell, Hall, Jesch and Parsons (eds), *Vikings and the Danelaw*, pp. 125–42, at 130–1.

97 *Ibid.*, p. 135.

98 Blunt, Stewart and Lyon, *Coinage in Tenth-Century England*, pp. 100–2; Blackburn, 'Expansion and control', pp. 132–3

99 Mahany and Roffe, 'Stamford', 209.

100 Kilmurry, *The Pottery Industry of Stamford*, pp. 176–7.

101 *Ibid.*, pp. 176–95; Mahany and Roffe, 'Stamford', 199.

102 *EHD I*, p. 214.

103 R. Birss and H. Wheeler, 'Introduction', *DAJ*, 105 (1985), 7–14, at 11; C. Clews, 'Human remains, Little Chester', *JDANHS*, 49 (1927), 376–7.

104 Hall, 'The Five Boroughs', 160.

105 C. S. B. Young, *Discovering Rescue Archaeology in Nottingham* (Nottingham, n.d.); Hall, 'The Five Boroughs', 192; D. Roffe, 'The Anglo-Saxon town and the Norman Conquest', in J. Beckett (ed.), *A Centenary History of Nottingham* (Manchester, 1997), pp. 24–42, at 32.

106 Hall, 'The Five Boroughs', 193; J. Graham-Campbell, 'Pagan Scandinavian burials in the central and southern Danelaw', in Graham-Campbell, Hall, Jesch and Parsons (eds), *Vikings and the Danelaw*, pp. 105–23, at 106.

107 Various analyses of the development of the town plan of Leicester are discussed in Courtney, 'Saxon and medieval Leicester', 115–19.

108 *Ibid.*, 115.

109 Blackburn, 'Expansion and control', pp. 130–1, and pl. 7.8 and table 7.1.

110 M. A. S. Blackburn, 'Coin finds and coin circulation in Lindsey, c.600–900', in Vince (ed.), *Pre-Viking Lindsey*, pp. 80–90, at 82; R. A. Hall, 'Anglo–Scandinavian urban development in the east midlands', in Graham-Campbell, Hall, Jesch and Parsons, *Vikings and the Danelaw*, pp. 143–55, p. 150.

111 M. W. Barley, 'The medieval borough of Torksey: excavations 1963–8', *Antiq. J.*, 61 (1981), 264–91; C. Palmer-Brown, 'Torksey: Castle Farm', *Lincolnshire History and Archaeology*, hereafter: *LHA*, 30 (1995), 49–50.

112 Williams, 'From "palace" to "town"', 132; Paul Blinkhorn, pers. comm.

113 Williams, 'From "palace" to "town"', 131–2.

114 Hinton, *Archaeology, Economy and Society*, pp. 82–5.

115 Hall, 'The Five Boroughs', pp. 189–91.

116 *EHD I*, p. 217; J. Haslam, 'The second *burh* of Nottingham', *Land. Hist.*, 9 (1987), 45–52.

117 *EHD I*, p. 216.

118 Mahany and Roffe, 'Stamford', 204.

119 Hall, 'The Five Boroughs', 197–8.

120 *EHD I*, p. 209; S. Ward, 'Edward the Elder and the re-establishment of Chester', in D. Hill and N. Higham (eds), *Edward the Elder 899–924* (Manchester, 2001), pp. 160–6, at 162–4.

121 J. Hassall and D. Baker, 'Bedford: aspects of town origins and development', *BAJ*, 9 (1974), 75–94, at 79–80; Baker, Baker, Hassall and Simco, 'Excavations in Bedford', 67, 97–102, 112–15, 119–20, 127–30, 296.

122 Hall, 'Anglo–Scandinavian urban development', p. 151; A. G. Kinsley, 'Excavations of the Saxo-Norman town defences at Slaughter House Lane, Newark-on-Trent, Nottinghamshire', *Transactions of the Thoroton Society*, hereafter: *TTS*, 97 (1993), 14–63.

123 Sawyer, *Anglo-Saxon Lincolnshire*, p. 123.

124 Spoerry, 'The topography of Anglo-Saxon Huntingdon', 40–2.

125 Haslam, The development and topography of Saxon Cambridge', 20–3

126 Vince, 'The new town: Lincoln in the high medieval era', pp. 194–6, 276–81.

127 Kilmurry, *The Pottery Industry of Stamford*, pp. 42–6, 148.

128 *Ibid.*, pp. 155–75.

129 *Ibid.*, pp. 133–4, 142.

130 *Ibid.*, p. 151.

131 Ward, 'Edward the Elder and the re-establishment of Chester', p. 161.

132 Barley, 'The medieval borough of Torksey'.

133 Hall, 'Anglo–Scandinavian urban development', p. 151; M. Hebditch, 'A Saxo-Norman pottery kiln discovered in Southgate Street, Leicester', *TLAHS*, 43 (1986), 4–9; A. V. Nailor, 'A preliminary note on a late Saxon Ware from Nottingham', *Medieval Ceramics*, 8 (1984), 59–64.

134 Mahany, Burchard and Simpson, *Excavations in Stamford*, pp. 23–4, 106–7; Hall, 'The Five Boroughs', 200.

135 Hall, 'Anglo–Scandinavian urban development', p. 149.

136 Perring, *Early Medieval Occupation at Flaxengate*, pp. 41–5.

137 D. Hinton, *Archaeology, Economy and Society. England from the fifth to the fifteenth century* (London, 1990), p. 84.

138 C. E. Blunt, 'The coinage of Athelstan, King of England 924–39. A survey', *BNJ*, 42 (1974), pp. 35–60, at 49–50, 57; Blunt, Stewart and Lyon, *Coinage in Tenth-Century England*, pp. 216–19, 268.

139 Hall, 'The Five Boroughs', 162.

140 D. M. Metcalf, 'The monetary history of England in the tenth century viewed in the perspective of the eleventh century', in M. A. S. Blackburn (ed.), *Anglo-Saxon Monetary History* (Leicester, 1986), pp. 133–57, at 143–4.

141 Blunt, 'The coinage of Athelstan, King of England 924–39', 95–6; Metcalf, 'Continuity and change', 76–7.

142 Blunt, Stewart and Lyon, *Coinage in Tenth-Century England*, pp. 101–2, 219.

143 Hall, 'Anglo-Scandinavian urban development', p. 149.

144 P. H. Sawyer, 'The wealth of England in the eleventh century', *TRHS*, 5th series, 15 (1965), 145–64, at 161–4; *idem, Anglo-Saxon Lincolnshire*, pp. 181–2, 195–6; Hall, 'Anglo-Scandinavian urban development', p. 149.

145 D. M. Metcalf, 'Continuity and change in English monetary history c.973–1086', *BNJ*, 51 (1981), 52–89, at 74–7.

146 A coin bearing the mint name of Leicester was found in a hoard deposited at Stamford c.890: Blackburn, 'Aspects of Anglo-Scandinavian minting', pp. 130–1; Hall, 'Anglo-Scandinavian urban development', p. 148.

147 D. Hill, *An Atlas of Anglo-Saxon England* (London, 1981), pp. 130–2.

148 *Ibid.*, pp. 126–32; Sawyer, *Anglo-Saxon Lincolnshire*, pp. 125, 186.

149 *Domesday Book*, hereafter: *DB*, i, 336a–c; P. Everson and D. Stocker, *Corpus of Anglo-Saxon Stone Sculpture, Vol. 5. Lincolnshire* (Oxford, 1999), pp. 198–221; B. J. J. Gilmour and D. Stocker, *St Mark's Church and Cemetery*, The Archaeology of Lincoln, 13 (1) (London, 1986), pp. 15–17; Vince, 'Lincoln in the early medieval era', pp. 147–51; *idem*, 'The new town: Lincoln in the high medieval era', p. 198.

150 Vince, 'Lincoln in the Viking Age', p. 161.

151 *DB* i, 280b, 336d, 000.

152 Rodwell, *Historic Churches*, pp. 31–6.

153 J. Barrow, 'Urban cemetery location in the high Middle Ages', in S. R. Bassett (ed.), *Death in Towns. Urban responses to the dying and the dead, 100–1600* (Leicester, 1992), pp. 78–100.

154 Thacker, 'Chester and Gloucester', 198–206.

155 D. Stocker, 'Monuments and merchants: irregularities in the distribution of stone sculpture in Lincolnshire and Yorkshire in the tenth century', in D. M. Hadley and J. D. Richards (eds), *Cultures in Contact: Scandinavian settlement in England in the ninth and tenth centuries* (Turnhout, 2000), pp. 179–212, at 186–91, 200–6.

156 Ward, 'Edward the Elder and the re-establishment of Chester', p. 161; D. Griffiths, ' The coastal trading ports of the Irish Sea', in J. Graham-Campbell (ed.), *Viking Treasure from the North-West: the Cuerdale Hoard in its context* (Liverpool, 1992), pp. 63–72, at 65, 68.

157 *EHD I*, p. 192; Campbell (ed.), *The Chronicle of Æthelweard*, p. 37.

158 C. Dallas, *Excavations in Thetford by B. K. Davison between 1964 and 1970*, EAA, 62 (Gressenhall, 1993), pp. 2–14; P. Andrews and K. Penn, *Excavations in Thetford, North of the River, 1989–90*, EAA, 87 (1999), pp. 38–46, 91.

159 Dallas, *Excavations in Thetford*, pp. 76–9, 218–19; A. Rogerson and C. Dallas, *Excavations in Thetford, 1948–59 and 1973–80*, EAA, 22 (Gressenhall, 1984), p. 197; Andrews and Penn, *Excavations in Thetford, North of the River*, pp. 1–4, 9–11, 91.

160 Dallas, *Excavations in Thetford*, pp. 208–15; Rogerson and Dallas, *Excavations in Thetford*, p. 198.

161 Dallas, *Excavations in Thetford*, pp. 58–75.

162 B. K. Davison, 'The late Saxon town of Thetford', *Med. Arch.*, 11 (1967), 189–208; Kilmurry, *The Pottery Industry of Stamford*, p. 151.

163 Rogerson and Dallas, *Excavations in Thetford*, pp. 198–9.

164 *Ibid.*, p. 199.

165 H. Wallis, *Excavations at Mill Lane, Thetford, 1995*, EAA, 108 (Gressenhall, 2004), pp. 45–7, 117.

166 Rogerson and Dallas, *Excavations in Thetford*, p. 198.

167 Blunt, Stewart and Lyon, *Coinage in Tenth-Century England*, p. 255; Dallas, *Excavations in Thetford*, p. 195.

168 Wallis, *Excavations at Mill Lane*, pp. 38–9, 115.

169 A. Carter, 'The Anglo-Saxon origins of Norwich: the problems and approaches', *ASE*, 7 (1978), 175–204, at 196–9; M. Atkin and A. Carter, 'General introduction', in M. Atkin, A. Carter and D. Evans (eds), *Excavations in Norwich 1971–78, II*, EAA, 26 (Gressenhall, 1985), pp. 1–6; M. Atkin, 'The Anglo-Saxon urban landscape in East Anglia', *Land. Hist.*, 7 (1985), 27–40, at 32–5; B. Ayers, 'How Norwich began', *Curr. Arch.*, 170 (2000), 48–51, at 49–50.

170 Carter, 'The Anglo-Saxon origins of Norwich', 200–1.

171 S. Margeson, *The Vikings in Norfolk* (Norwich, 1997), pp. 23–5, 33–9.

172 *Ibid.*, 201–2; Blackburn, 'Expansion and control', p. 138; S. Lyon, 'The coinage of Edward the Elder', in Higham and Hill (eds), *Edward the Elder*, pp. 67–78, at 73–4.

173 E. Shepherd, 'Norwich Castle', *Curr. Arch.*, 170 (2000), 52–9, at 54.

174 Wade, 'Ipswich'; Scull, 'Urban centres', pp. 277–8; Hinton, *Archaeology, Economy and Society*, p. 82.

175 C. R. Hart, *The Danelaw* (Hambledon, 1992), p. 44.

176 R. H. M. Dolley, *Anglo-Saxon Coins: studies presented to F. M. Stenton* (London, 1962), pp. 153–4; *DB*, ii, 290a–b.

177 L. Symonds, 'Territories in transition: the construction of boundaries in Anglo-Scandinavian Lincolnshire', in D. Griffiths, A. Reynolds and S. Semple (eds), *Boundaries in Early Medieval Britain* (Oxford, 2003), pp. 28–37, at 30–3.

178 Kilmurry, *The Pottery Industry of Stamford*; A. McCarthy, and C. Brooks, *Medieval Pottery in Britain AD 900–1600* (Leicester, 1998), pp. 60–8.

179 Rogerson and Dallas, *Excavations in Thetford*, pp. 197–9; Hall, 'Anglo-Scandinavian urban development', p. 149; Miles, Young, and Wacher, *A Late Saxon Kiln Site at Silver Street*, pp. 185–94, 198–204, 234; Mainman and Rogers, 'Craft and economy in Anglo-Scandinavian York'.

180 R. Wright, 'Women's labour and pottery production in prehistory', in J. Gero and M. Conkey (eds), *Engendering Archaeology: women and prehistory* (Oxford, 1991), pp. 194–223.

181 McCarthy and Brooks, *Medieval Pottery*, pp. 60–8.

182 P. Blinkhorn, 'Habitus, social identity and Anglo-Saxon pottery', in C. Cumberpatch and P. Blinkhorn (eds), *Not So Much a Pot, More a Way of Life* (Oxford, 1997), pp. 113–24, at 120–1.

183 *Ibid.*, p. 123.

184   Hall, 'The topography of Anglo–Scandinavian York', p. 497.
185   In particular, see the comments of Williams, 'From "palace" to "town"', 130–1.
186   K. Ulmschneider, 'Settlement, economy and the "productive" site: Anglo-Saxon Lincolnshire AD 650–780', *Med. Arch.*, 44 (2000), 53–79; see also the various contributions to T. Pestell and K. Ulmschneider (eds), *Markets in Early Medieval Europe. Trading and 'productive' sites, 650–850* (Macclesfield, 2003).
187   For a sceptical view, see J. D. Richards, 'What's so special about "productive sites"?', in D. Griffiths and T. M. Dickinson (eds), *The Making of Kingdoms* (Oxford, 1999), pp. 71–80.
188   Sawyer, *Anglo-Saxon Lincolnshire*, pp. 171–8; Ulmschneider, 'Settlement, economy and the "productive" site', 72–7; J. Newman, 'Exceptional finds, exceptional sites? Barham and Coddenham, Suffolk', in Pestell and Ulmschneider (eds), *Markets in Early Medieval Europe*, pp. 97–109; A. Rogerson, 'Six middle Anglo-Saxon sites in west Norfolk', in *ibid.*, pp. 110–21; T. Pestell, 'The afterlife of "productive" sites in East Anglia', in *ibid.*, pp. 122–37.
189   Griffiths, 'The coastal trading ports', pp. 65–70.
190   Richards, *Viking Age England*, p. 78.
191   Sawyer, *Anglo-Saxon Lincolnshire*, pp. 154, 186, 193; Hill, *An Atlas of Anglo-Saxon England*, pp. 130–2; Stocker, 'The early church in Lincolnshire', pp. 114, 117.
192   Richards, *Viking Age England*, pp. 77–8.

5

Churches and the Scandinavians:
chaos, conversion and change

For twelfth-century chroniclers, it was the viking raiders' attacks on churches that marked them out as 'a most vile' people, and there have been many papers detailing the havoc wreaked on Anglo-Saxon ecclesiastical life by the invaders.[1] Certainly, the impact of the viking raiders was never less than terrifying and was sometimes devastating, and the indirect effects of Scandinavian raiding and settlement on ecclesiastical prosperity must also have been substantial. Yet, as we shall see, there is also evidence, if sometimes circumstantial, that some churches survived – albeit in an altered state. This chapter begins with an overview of the ways in which the relevant documentary and archaeological evidence has been interpreted to support the cases for both disruption and discontinuity of ecclesiastical organisation on the one hand, and survival and continuity on the other. The documentary and archaeological evidence from a small number of churches is then examined in detail. As we shall see, the evidence is rarely conclusive and, while it is not difficult to accept that churches suffered during the ninth and tenth centuries, in order to argue that our patchy evidence may also betoken aspects of ecclesiastical continuity it is necessary to consider the broader circumstances in which ecclesiastical life may have survived. It is also important to set the impact of the Scandinavians in context and to explore factors that had a detrimental effect on the Anglo-Saxon Church both before and after the period of Scandinavian raids and settlements.

The fate of churches during the Scandinavian raids and settlement: outline of the debate

Traditionally, studies of the Anglo-Saxon Church have placed considerable emphasis on the destructive aspects of the Scandinavian raids and settlement. Sir Frank Stenton, for example, summed up the situation as follows: 'The Danish invasions of the ninth century shattered the organisation of the English Church'.[2] In keeping with this view, the scholarly literature contains numerous examples of religious houses that were supposedly destroyed or forced out of existence in northern and eastern England by Scandinavian atrocities. For example, in an appendix to their volume on *Medieval Religious Houses*, David Knowles and Neville Hadcock cite the demise of religious communities at Whitby (Yorks, which they state was destroyed c.867), Beverley (Yorks, c.867), Barking (Essex, 870), Crowland (Lincs, c.870), Ely (Cambs, 870), Jarrow (Dur, c.867), Lindisfarne (Northumb, 875), Carlisle (Cumb, c.875), Hackness (Yorks, c.870), Thorney (Cambs, c.870), and Peterborough (Cambs, 870).[3] This list has been used on more than one occasion as a guide to the fate of ecclesiastical life in ninth-century England, yet much of it rests on evidence of a most doubtful nature, and is heavily reliant on antiquarian speculation.[4] The dates given for the demise of various communities are consistently in the 860s and 870s, but since there is little reliable evidence for the destruction of any church at this time, and it is admittedly not in the nature of contemporary sources to comment on the disappearance of a religious house, the chronology of destruction seems to rest on the assumption that it is linked to the activities of the viking 'great army'.[5] Only in the case of Peterborough is there comment in the *Anglo-Saxon Chronicle* about its destruction at the hands of a viking army: 'In this same time [870] they came to *Medeshamstede* [Peterborough], burnt and destroyed it, killed the abbot and the monks and all they found there, and brought it to pass that it became nought that had been very mighty'. However, this entry only appears in the E manuscript, copied out at Peterborough in the early twelfth century.[6] While it is not inconceivable that such a statement was based on a reliable tradition, it remains the case that this is an interpolation entered over two centuries after the event, and if it is an accurate portrayal, one wonders how seventh-century documents arrived in the archive of the later Anglo-Saxon monastery.[7]

Undoubtedly influential on some of the secondary literature are the twelfth-century and later sources providing lurid details of the destruction of churches by viking armies. For example, the twelfth-century history of Ely

(*Liber Eliensis*) describes the burning of the church and its contents, and the massacre of the community, by a viking army led by Inguar and Hubba:

> Indeed, when the mob of evil ones reaches the monastery of the virgins which Æthelthryth the glorious virgin and bride of Christ had built, alas, it invades, pollutes the holy things, tramples and tears. The sword of the madmen is stretched out over the milk-white consecrated necks[8]

Roger of Wendover's thirteenth-century *Flores Historiarum* ('Flowers of the Histories') recounts how the nuns of Coldingham (Berwicks) cut off their noses so that viking raiders would kill them rather than compromise their virtue.[9] The late date of such sources does not, of itself, negate their usefulness, not least because their authors often had access to earlier documents now lost, but tellingly they often contain conflicting accounts about the fate of particular churches or else are contradicted by other sources, both historical and archaeological, as we shall see. This is not to suggest that churches were not destroyed or otherwise driven out of existence by the Scandinavian raiders, but it is important to establish that the evidence on which some discussions are based is either unreliable or non-existent.

Following the excavation of a small number of ecclesiastical sites in northern and eastern England, archaeologists have contributed to the debate about the Scandinavian impact by highlighting sites that were apparently abandoned or destroyed between the late eighth and tenth centuries. However, it is in the nature of archaeological evidence that close dating of destruction or abandonment is rarely possible, and accounting for it is more difficult still. To take an example, at Burrow Hill, Butley (Suff), a site occupied between the seventh and ninth centuries has been interpreted as a religious community, in part because of the high proportion of small finds for a middle Saxon site, and in part because of the preponderance of males in the cemetery of c.200 burials, and the eventual abandonment of this site has been attributed to Scandinavian raiders: 'If Burrow Hill was a monastery, then, . . . it would have been an obvious target for the Danes and, once destroyed, must have vanished from the record'.[10] While the supposition may not be untrue, it is important to recognise that there is no specific evidence for either the date of abandonment, or its cause. Such casual remarks about Scandinavian destructiveness have been made in many other reports on excavations of ecclesiastical sites. Other excavators are more measured in their interpretations, but those who draw on their work have not always minded the caveats. For example, Rosemary Cramp identified evidence for burning, in the form of charred wood and ash, melted lead and glass and burnt baluster shafts, during her excavations at Monkwearmouth (Dur), but cautiously noted that it was uncertain 'whether this burning was the result of a 9th-century viking sack or of later Scottish raids', and was able to identify slim evidence for continuing activity at Monkwearmouth into the tenth century (see p. 201). Yet, the same report was cited by another author as demonstrating that the site was abandoned from the beginning of the viking attacks until the eleventh century.[11] It should also be noted that excavation has revealed many abandoned churches that went out of use both long before and after the period of viking raids and settlement, suggesting that the vikings were just one, albeit brutal, development in early medieval society to which churches were vulnerable.[12]

Recently there has been increasing emphasis by historians on continuity of ecclesiastical organisation following the Scandinavian raids and settlement. One feature of the ecclesiastical history of northern and eastern England that has occasioned recent comment is the consistency with which the major pre-viking churches are the mother churches of later centuries. There is a group of churches in northern and eastern England that exhibit a series of variables, which suggest the relative antiquity and stability of those churches as a broad but distinct class. These variables include pre-viking documentary references, stone sculpture, saints' cults, royal and episcopal patronage, and evidence for distinctive topography and complex planning. At a later date there is typically evidence for superior status, in the form of residual staffs of clergy and landed property, in Domesday Book, royal or episcopal ownership in the eleventh century, and medieval mother-church rights over large parishes.[13] Furthermore, archaeological evidence, in particular for burial, and the presence of tenth-century stone sculpture, offers supporting evidence to the case for continuity of some form of ecclesiastical life at many sites. Thus, it has been argued that, destructive and disruptive as the Scandinavian raiding and settlement may have been, some religious communities did survive, retaining aspects of their pastoral roles and their resources.[14] However, it should be recognised that in few cases is the evidence more than circumstantial, and it is less the evidence from individual churches than the weight of the overall pattern that supports the case for continuity.[15] Moreover, even if we accept that the evidence supports the case for continuity of ecclesiastical activity at a given site, it is clear that this was accompanied by considerable changes in the fortunes of the relevant religious communities.

When examining the fate of churches in the wake of Scandinavian raids and settlement, generalisations are not easy. That churches suffered terrible depredations garners ready assent, but the historical sources proffer few reliable examples. That some churches survived is not unlikely, but proving this is – in all but a few cases – impossible. There are four ways forward. The first is to examine in detail the textual, archaeological and sculptural evidence from a small number of religious communities. As we shall see, some of those churches that according to post-Conquest accounts were destroyed in the 860s and 870s, at which religious life was supposedly not re-founded until late in the tenth or the eleventh century, were clearly in existence earlier in the tenth century. Second, we need to assess the case for continuity based on the consistency with which eleventh-century and later superior churches coincide with the locations of early religious communities. Can we place this circumstantial evidence beyond reasonable doubt? If we are to do so, it is essential to consider the contexts in which ecclesiastical life may have continued to exist, if not thrive, through the ninth and tenth centuries. Third, we need to set the Scandinavian impact in perspective. We cannot produce a balanced account by attributing to the Scandinavians all the misfortunes that befell the later Anglo-Saxon Church. Finally, we need to address the issue of how quickly and by what means the pagan Scandinavians were converted to Christianity, as this must surely have been a key factor in ecclesiastical fortunes.

Churches in northern and eastern England: continuity and change

It is useful to begin with the small number of churches that render any specific evidence for their fate, status and activities in the later ninth and earlier tenth centuries. The experiences of the religious community at Lindisfarne offer a salutary reminder of contemporary perceptions of the impact of viking raids. The D and E manuscripts of the *Anglo-Saxon Chronicle*, with their northerly perspective, describe the raid on the island in 793 as follows:

> In this year dire portents appeared over Northumbria and sorely frightened the people. They consisted of immense whirlwinds and flashes of lightning, and fiery dragons were seen flying in the air. A great famine immediately followed those signs, and a little after that in the same year, on 8 June, the ravages of heathen men miserably destroyed God's church on Lindisfarne, with plunder and slaughter.[16]

The severity of the attack and evidence for the contemporary appreciation of the threat posed by this event is demonstrated in the letters of Alcuin, a monk trained in Northumbria, who subsequently joined the Carolingian court. In a letter to King Ethelred of Northumbria, Alcuin wrote:

> Lo, it is nearly 350 years that we and our fathers have inhabited this most lovely land, and never before has such terror appeared in Britain as we

have now suffered from a pagan race, nor was it thought that such an inroad from the sea could be made. Behold, the church of St Cuthbert spattered with the blood of the priests of God, despoiled of all its ornaments; a place more venerable than all in Britain is given as prey to pagan peoples. And where first, after the departure of St Paulinus from York [in 634], the Christian religion in our race took its rise, there misery and calamity have begun. Who does not fear this? Who does not lament this as if his country were captured?[17]

That Alcuin was writing some distance from the events does not mean that he was not well informed about events at Lindisfarne, and the content of his many letters referring to these events must have contributed to the sense of fear within the Northumbrian Church.[18] A famous sculpture from Lindisfarne, reproduced in many books on the vikings, portrays a row of armed men, of which three are brandishing swords and two are wielding axes (fig. 29). It appears to depict a raid of armed men, and it has been suggested that it represents the events of 793.[19]

29   Sculpture at Lindisfarne (Northumb).

Yet, despite this, religious life continued on Lindisfarne into the ninth century. The community remained on the island until the time of Bishop Ecgred (830–45) when it departed with the body of the saint for Norham (Northumb). The *History of St Cuthbert* adds that at this time the church built on Lindisfarne by Bishop Aidan in the seventh century was removed and rebuilt at Norham.[20] The body of the saint must have been returned to Lindisfarne some time later, as we are told that it was with the community when it departed from Lindisfarne again c.875.[21] As we have seen (see pp. 38–9), it has been suggested that the wanderings of the community from c.875 before they settled at Chester-le-Street (Dur) in c.883 may actually have been a series of strategic moves intended to secure control over landed possessions, rather than the pitiful progress recounted in later sources.[22] Whatever difficulties it experienced, and in spite of the move from Lindisfarne, there is little doubt that the community of St Cuthbert retained a corporate identity, which revolved around the saint.[23] Excavation has revealed that the island continued to be occupied through the ninth century. A farmstead at Green Shiel has produced evidence for a group of buildings linked by enclosing walls and yards, and while there is no explicit connection with the religious community, the large numbers of cattle bones have given rise to the suggestion that the farmstead supplied the community with vellum from which manuscripts were produced.[24] A firmer indication of the continuing vitality of ecclesiastical life through the ninth century lies in the stone sculptures of this date from Lindisfarne. The aforementioned dramatic sculpture is dated stylistically, and according to the details of the sword pommels, to the later ninth century, and could, it must be admitted, as easily depict a raid by the Scots as the events of 793 – or, perhaps more likely, it represents a Doomsday scene. Moreover, it may even post-date the departure of some of the community with the body of the saint in c.875.[25]

The community on Lindisfarne was re-founded on monastic lines at the end of the eleventh century by the monks of Durham.[26] However, there is evidence to suggest that some form of ecclesiastical life continued on Lindisfarne through the tenth century. John Blair has highlighted the west–east alignment of ritual structures on Lindisfarne, including the medieval parish church of St Mary, the priory church, a well and two cross-bases, and has suggested that this may represent an alignment established at a much earlier date than the post-Conquest refoundation of Lindisfarne.[27] There is evidence to suggest that the priory church was built on the site of St Cuthbert's church: the twelfth-century Durham monk Reginald refers to this foundation as St Cuthbert's church and notes that it contained a tomb of St Cuthbert, which probably, as Blair suggests, refers to one of the cenotaphs marking Cuthbert's various resting-places.[28] The fabric in the east wall of the nave of St Mary's church, revealed during the stripping of plaster, is earlier in date than the mid-twelfth century when the church is first recorded, and the dimensions of the nave appear to be consistent with those of much earlier churches.[29] Rosemary Cramp has tentatively suggested that at least one of the aforementioned cross-bases may date to the eighth or ninth centuries.[30] Finally, the stone-lined well was located within the nave of the priory church and must pre-date it, and it appears to have been within an earlier church, of which sections of wall were found during excavation.[31] Clearly the case is circumstantial, but Blair concludes that 'the Durham monks who recolonised Lindisfarne found a good deal more than ruined walls and memories of ancient sanctity'.[32] Although it cannot prove continuous occupation, the archaeological and sculptural evidence from Lindisfarne does demonstrate that the documentary tradition is partial and defective.

The twelfth-century *Liber Eliensis* gives the impression, as we have seen, that the religious community at Ely, founded in 672 by Æthelthryth, daughter of King Anna of the East Angles, met a terrible fate at the hands of viking raiders. This view is supported by the fact that no early documentation from the community survives, suggesting disruption to the community, if not its complete destruction. Nonetheless, it is clear that a religious community of some sort existed at Ely before the monastic refoundation in c.970 by Bishop Æthelwold of Winchester (963–84). One source of information is the *Libellus Æthelwoldi episcopi* ('Book of Bishop Æthelwold'), which was compiled in the early twelfth century, but is based on tenth-century vernacular texts, which reveal that grants were made to the shrine of St Æthelthryth at least fifteen years before the refoundation.[33] An account of the miracles of St Æthelthryth (*Liber miraculorum beate virginis*) written in the late tenth century, and incorporated in the *Liber Eliensis*, describes events that took place at Ely during the reign of King Eadred (946–55), at which time the author, one Ælfhelm, had been a priest there. At that time the archpriest at Ely had decided, unwisely as it turned out, to open the tomb of St Æthelthryth to ascertain what it contained. This was in spite of the warning against such a course of action given by one of the priests who, over a number of years, had apparently gained first-hand knowledge of the miraculous powers of the saint. Fairly predictably, those involved in opening the tomb either died or went mad soon afterwards. Only Ælfhelm survived, and he appears to have remained at Ely, probably becoming a monk following the refoundation. This tale reveals that, in the mid-tenth century, Ely housed priests and clerics, and indicates that there had been a community at Ely for some time previously. This account also briefly recalls events after the viking attacks, when one of the raiders dared to make a hole in the tomb of the saint and met a suitably terrible fate, and it alleges that eight of the clerics who had been driven from Ely by the raiders subsequently returned. One of these had told a younger man of these events, and the latter was the priest who had challenged the archpriest's folly several decades later.[34] Although this account was written decades after the event and survives in an even later manuscript, it reveals a tradition at Ely that there was continuous ecclesiastical presence on the Isle from the 860s onwards.

It is hardly likely that this community possessed the resources of an earlier era; as has been said, it apparently did not contain the archive (see p. 199), and the nuns of earlier times seemingly no longer existed. Whether the nuns disappeared as a result of viking incursions or other factors is a moot point. Sarah Foot has recently discussed the factors that witnessed a decline in the numbers of nunneries in England during the ninth century, including the impact of Carolingian reform, which sought to restrict the spread of mixed communities of nuns and monks in which most nuns were found; the decline in the numbers of grants of land made to women's religious communities evident from the late eighth century; and the changed priorities of royal families, who seem to have become less inclined than in earlier centuries to use nunneries as repositories for royal lands.[35] Yet the cult of St Æthelthryth remained important and well renowned, and the chronicler working in Wessex c.890 notably included information on the saint at the relevant points in the *Anglo-Saxon Chronicle*. If ever efforts were to be made to preserve the site of a religious community during difficult times then it was likely to be at Ely, whose saint was well known from Bede's *Ecclesiastical History*.[36] As many as eight tenth- or eleventh-century sculptures survive from Ely, but in advance of modern research on these sculptures it is not possible to state confidently that any pre-date the refoundation of the community.[37]

Another oft-cited example of continuity relates to the church at Horningsea (Cambs). A passage in the *Libellus Æthelwoldi* states that at the time of the Scandinavian conquest there was a monastery at Horningsea under a priest called Coenwald and that 'later the people of the place who gathered together from paganism in the grace of baptism gave this minster five hides at Horningsea and two in Eye'. Coenwald's successor was said to have been a follower of King Athelstan, suggesting that Coenwald remained in the post for many years. This evidence indicates, as Dorothy

Whitelock put it, that there was thought to have been little, if any, breach of continuity at this church.[38]

Excavations at Monkwearmouth uncovered information on not only the church but also the associated domestic ranges and burial grounds, and they also suggested that the site was not entirely abandoned in the ninth and tenth centuries.[39] At Monkwearmouth, burial appears to have continued into the later Anglo-Saxon period. One phase of burial was later than the demolition of some of the monastic buildings. Some of these burials overlie earlier burials, while some were located among the monastic buildings. A number of these later Anglo-Saxon burials were full of broken plaster and glass, probably from the adjacent large building (Building B), which appears to have stood in a ruinous condition until it was demolished in the later eleventh century. Other burials seem to post-date the clearance of some of the Anglo-Saxon buildings, but are earlier than the post-Conquest refoundation.[40] The lower part of a tenth-century grave-marker and a fragment of another carved stone of similar date have been found at the church, providing evidence of some form of ecclesiastical presence.[41] Other evidence for late Anglo-Saxon occupation of the site includes a wall that possibly supported a timber superstructure (Wall 2) and a stone structure (Structure C) built against the west wall of Building B, while traces of timber buildings may also belong to this period. The top of the church tower appears to have been added in c.1000.[42] This hardly demonstrates continuity of ecclesiastical occupation, and still less does it demonstrate institutional continuity, especially given the evidence that by the early tenth century the community of St Cuthbert had acquired some of its lands (see p. 39). However, its continuing use for burial does suggest that the site was not completely abandoned after the religious community had disappeared.

Extensive excavations of the now-defunct church of St Alkmund in Derby revealed the foundations and short stretches of masonry of a church of ninth-century or earlier date, along with fragments of several stone crosses and an elaborate ninth-century sarcophagus (fig. 23). The church appears to have undergone some rebuilding and restructuring during the tenth century. At this time, fragments of ninth-century sculpture were built into parts of the wall of an eastern annexe. The south porticus, or side chapel, was abandoned and the area subsequently used for burial. C. A. Ralegh Radford hypothesised that the reconstruction of the church must have followed 'a period of neglect', perhaps even 'a more or less complete destruction of the fabric'. He then pointed to the most conveniently available perpetrators and concluded that 'historically, the period of neglect or destruction can be equated with the period of Danish rule and the foundation of Derby as one of the Five Boroughs'.[43] There is, however, no specific evidence for destruction or neglect, and periods of rebuilding and the reorganisation of ecclesiastical space need not be limited to the period of Scandinavian raids and settlement. Several burials were excavated around the church, and four included a lining of charcoal, a rite common among high-status churches during the tenth century.[44] A fragment of a cross-shaft displaying Scandinavian influences was found in the church during rebuilding of the medieval fabric in 1844, along with part of a hogback sculpture and a section of another tenth-century cross-shaft.[45] The sarcophagus seems to have remained on display in the church until it was buried beneath the floor of the nave when it was rebuilt in the twelfth century, with the lid positioned flush with the floor so that it continued to be visible. Perhaps the sarcophagus had continued to be the focus of local veneration of St Alkmund, even after his remains had been removed to Shrewsbury (Shrops), possibly by Æthelflaed.[46] At any rate it is striking that such a ready supply of building rubble should have survived successive rebuilding campaigns.[47] According to Domesday Book, the church remained one of the most important in Derby, housing a community of clerics.[48]

Twelfth-century authors alleged that the religious community at Beverley (Yorks) was destroyed by the vikings, and that it was re-founded as a secular college by King Athelstan in the 930s. Doubt has been cast on this account of events, largely because it emerged late and is not referred to in various grants and confirmations of the mid- to late eleventh century.[49] Nonetheless, excavations to the south of the present Minster indicated a break in occupation from c.851 to 930, and the report concluded that 'there seems no reason to doubt the tradition that the occupation of the first monastery on the site ended with the onset of viking incursions'.[50] Yet, aside from the unreliability of the historical tradition, the archaeological evidence for this deduction is not convincing. A small coin hoard of c.851 may have been prompted by the uncertainties of the time, but quite why the community should have been abandoned 'in the first year that the viking army overwintered in England', which occurred on the Isle of Thanet (Kent), is not immediately apparent. Interpretation of some of the supposed ninth-century artefacts (such as a Scandinavian-style comb and a bone pin) is complicated because they were not found in ninth-century contexts, and it is, in any case, hard to see what connection these particular artefacts might have had with military activity. It is, thus, difficult to agree that the archaeological record lends support to the twelfth-century claim of viking destruction.[51] Nevertheless, there certainly appears to have been a break in occupation on the site of the excavation (which seems to have covered part of the probable monastic precinct) and while that is not evidence that the religious community as a whole was abandoned or destroyed, this gap perhaps corresponds with that from other ecclesiastical sites which have evidence for the reduction of the intensity and extent of occupation in the ninth or tenth century.[52] Ecclesiastical activity certainly continued through the tenth century, as burials of this date have recently been excavated, and, by the eleventh century, Beverley was a collegiate church with a large estate and numerous privileges, the centre of the cult of Bishop John, and its parish included several chapels.[53]

There was a religious community at Ripon (Yorks) from at least the middle of the seventh century, which housed the relics of saints Wilfrid, Egbert and Wihtberht.[54] Several sites in the vicinity of St Peter's church have produced evidence for cemeteries or churches of the Anglo-Saxon period, and in this respect the religious community at Ripon was like many other early ecclesiastical communities, in being comprised of several foci.[55] The fate of Ripon following the Scandinavian settlement is poorly documented, but there is evidence to suggest that ecclesiastical life of some sort continued there. Most striking in this respect is the reference in the *Anglo-Saxon Chronicle* to King Eadred's campaign northwards in 948, which resulted in the burning of the church at Ripon. It was almost certainly at this point that the relics of St Wilfrid and the Ripon copy of Eddius's *Life of St Wilfrid* were removed to Canterbury.[56] Given the political context of this move, it may, as David Rollason has observed, have been a raid to acquire the relics of 'a particularly self-assertive and independent-minded Northumbrian bishop', and the event was followed by the production of a metrical version of the *Life of St Wilfrid* at Canterbury by Frithegod, thus anchoring the saint more firmly to his new resting-place. Notably, this text justified the removal of Wilfrid's remains on the grounds that the shrine at Ripon was decayed and 'thorn-covered', yet some level of ecclesiastical life at Ripon is indicated by sculptures bearing Scandinavian-style motifs, including a scene from the Sigurd legend, and continuing use of at least some of the burial grounds.[57] Oswald, Archbishop of York (971–92), introduced monks into the religious community at Ripon, although there was a subsequent change to the community, since by the time of Domesday Book there was apparently no trace of monastic life, and the church was served by an unrecorded number of canons.[58] In the later Middle Ages the church of St Peter's at Ripon was an important mother church, serving a large parish.[59]

It is apparent that the great army had a dramatic impact on the religious community at Repton (Derbys) (see pp. 12–15). In addition to the digging of a large ditch adjacent to the church, the mass burial and burials accompanied by weaponry, the excavators have suggested there is also evidence that the church was almost completely demolished in the late ninth century. A change in fabric, between the brown Bunter sandstone used in the lower courses of much of the church and the green Keuper sandstone used in the upper courses, has been interpreted as marking the level from which the destroyed church was rebuilt in the early tenth century. Some of the earliest burials to the north of the church were cut into a layer of debris including burnt Bunter sandstone, charcoal and debris, and two graves lay below a stone setting that incorporated fragments of a cross-shaft. Fragments of a massive eighth-century cross were recovered from a pit to the east of the church, and the excavators surmised 'Who else but the Danish army would have so thoroughly broken such a massive and prominent monument'.[60] If this interpretation is correct then it betokens a terrible fate for the possessions, if not the very lives, of the religious community, although the reuse of Anglo-Saxon stone sculptures for a variety of purposes was not restricted to the period of Scandinavian settlement, and the general context leaves open to debate whether the destruction of the monastery would have been likely (see p. 15). Moreover, burial soon resumed to the east and south of the church; continued to the north where members of the great army appear to have been buried; and a new burial ground was established to the west of the church, over and around the mound covering the former mausoleum – although it is difficult to determine how quickly this occurred. Whatever the burial beneath the mound had signalled, it was not subsequently shunned for burial, and several of these later burials appear to have been of high-status individuals, as they contain fragments of gold embroidery (see p. 243).[61] Other indications of religious life in the tenth century include a hogback sculpture, and the apparent survival of the relics of St Wystan (the murdered grandson of King Wiglaf of Mercia), which were eventually removed to Evesham Abbey (Worcs) in the reign of Cnut.[62] By the time of the Domesday Book, the church was served by two priests, elsewhere taken as a residual sign of a former religious community, and in the later Middle Ages Repton was a mother church serving a large parish with at least eight chapels.[63]

Large numbers of fragments of pre-viking cross-shafts and sarcophagi have been found at Bakewell (Derbys), which may have been an early centre of sculptural production.[64] The fabric of the church contains some Anglo-Saxon work, and its layout has been identified as being of typical Anglo-Saxon aisleless form, although the date of the structure is uncertain.[65] In 949 King Eadred granted an unspecified amount of land at

Bakewell to Uhtred, for the endowment of a religious community. It is not stated that this was a new foundation, and given that Uhtred had possessed a large estate in the vicinity – probably including Bakewell – since the first decade of the century, it is not implausible that a church of regional import-ance should have been revived quickly.[66] The presence of tenth-century sculpture offers supporting evidence that at that date Bakewell was still an important church and centre of sculpture production.[67] By the eleventh century the church at Bakewell possessed its own land, assessed as three carucates, and a number of peasant tenants, and although this is not a very impressive mark of status, it does distinguish Bakewell as a church of some note in this region, and in the later medieval period the church of Bakewell served an enormous parish with many chapelries.[68]

According to Roger of Wendover, in the late ninth century the nuns of Whitby took refuge from the viking threat at the religious community at Tynemouth (Northumb) where they were subsequently massacred.[69] Excavations at Whitby in the 1920s and 1950s have proved notoriously difficult to interpret, due to poor recording and the lack of correspondence between some of the written comments and illustrations produced at the time, and it is, therefore, difficult to assess the validity of the late written tradition.[70] Stone moulds of a type known in Viking Age silver hoards for casting ingots have been interpreted as evidence that the raiders melted down the treasures of the religious community, and a T-shaped groove may have been intended to cast Thor's hammers.[71] Yet, at least two cross-shafts of the late ninth- to mid-tenth century survive at Whitby, indicating that some form of religious or burial activity occurred on the Whitby headland at that time. Moreover, in the eleventh century there were said to be some forty ruined structures, interpreted as oratories, and it seems implausible that they could have survived in this state for two centuries; it is perhaps significant that the site was known in the eleventh century as *Prestebi*, 'priests' farm', and one wonders whether this indicates some more recent ecclesiastical community.[72] There were two eleventh-century churches at Whitby, dedicated to St Peter and St Mary respectively, and the latter served an extensive parish with seven chapelries.[73] St Peter's was believed to be associated with the former monastery, but it is possible that the church dedicated to St Mary also had early origins. Certainly Bede's description of the early monastic complex suggests that it was sufficiently large to have taken in the site of St Mary's church, and it would not be unusual for an early religious community to have had more than one church, and pairs of early churches dedicated to St Peter and St Mary respectively are documented elsewhere.[74]

Ecclesiastical continuity through the period of Scandinavian conquest and settlement has been inferred at many other sites, on the basis of tenth-century or later evidence for the superior status of churches known to have been important churches at a much earlier date. Yet, while there is a large body of evidence of this nature, it must be admitted that the evidence from particular sites is often patchy and separated by decades if not centuries. A few examples suffice to make this point. An important church at Wirksworth (Derbys) may be inferred on the basis of an impressive sculpture dating to between the seventh and ninth centuries, on which the Virgin features prominently, and which, combined with the possession of land at Wirksworth in 835 by an Abbess Cynewaru suggests that it may have housed a community of nuns.[75] Although there was nothing remarkable about the church at Wirksworth according to the Domesday Book, it was one of a small number of major churches granted to the Dean of the newly founded Lincoln cathedral in 1093, and in the later Middle Ages it was a wealthy church with a substantial parish.[76] Eighth- or ninth-century sculptural evidence suggests that Otley (Yorks) was also an important pre-viking church, possibly belonging to the archbishops of York, since Symeon of Durham informs us that in c.867 Archbishop Wulfhere fled from viking raiding at York to Addingham, which in the later tenth century, at least, was a member of the Otley estate.[77] Tenth-century sculpture survives at Otley, and also at various members of the Archbishop's Otley estate including Addingham, Ilkley and Weston, and in the later Middle Ages, the parish of Otley was substantial, and included many of the places which are listed in accounts of the lands of the archbishops of York from the late tenth and eleventh centuries.[78]

There are numerous sites of early religious communities with tenth-century stone sculpture, including Auckland, Sockburn (Dur), Addingham, Urswick (Cumb), Hovingham and Stonegrave (Yorks), and often this is the only indication of ecclesiastical activity at the site after the commencement of Scandinavian raids and settlement. In fact, in some cases it is the only evidence for an ecclesiastical presence since the comparatively well-documented seventh or eighth century.[79] Tenth-century burials have been excavated near churches of earlier origin at, for example, Crayke, Addingham, Pontefract, Ripon, Kirkdale (Yorks), Cherry Hinton (Cambs), St Peter's Heysham (Lancs), at the Minster in York, and St Paul-in-the-Bail in Lincoln.[80] However, it is in the nature of burial evidence that precise dates can rarely be offered for particular burial phases, let alone individual burials. Thus, while the funerary evidence is suggestive of continuous use of burial grounds, it is impossible to prove this, and it must be admitted that any brief hiatus in burial at a particular cemetery would be difficult to identify. Even if burial was continuous, this does not, of course, prove that a church community survived, although it may indicate 'a continued perception of holiness and status'.[81]

Although they have not yielded any tenth-century evidence for superior status, there is also a small group of pre-viking churches that were mother churches, sometimes with communities of clergy, and serving large parishes in the eleventh century and later. Examples include Southwell, Flawford (Notts), Conisborough (Yorks), Caistor (Lincs), Aldborough, Wharram Percy (Yorks), Breedon-on-the-Hill (Leics), Oundle, Brixworth, Brigstock and Geddington (Northants).[82] Finally, in this survey of evidence implying continuity, it is notable that the cults of a diverse array of saints of local and national importance housed in many of the churches of northern and eastern England survived at least until they were spirited away by the West Saxons in the early to mid-tenth century (see pp. 210–1). If the relics had survived the events of the later ninth century, then so too, perhaps, did some form of religious presence to protect them. We have already seen that the shrine of St Æthelthryth was apparently protected by a small group of clerics at Ely until the community was re-founded in c.970, and it may not have been an isolated example.

Evaluating the circumstantial evidence for ecclesiastical fortunes: indications of disruption and change

Is it plausible to argue that the circumstantial evidence cited above and the smaller number of more detailed case-studies really does indicate elements of ecclesiastical continuity through the periods of Scandinavian raiding and settlement? The enthusiasm with which a case for continuity is sometimes made must be tempered by recognition of the firm evidence for the devastation wreaked on the Church by the raiders. Several bishoprics disappeared for good in the ninth century, while others were vacant for decades. The last known Bishop of Hexham died in c.821, and the bishopric at Leicester ceased to exist with the death of Ceolred between 869 and 888. The bishopric of Dommoc in East Anglia disappeared from the historical record some time after 870, and the last ninth-century Bishop of the other East Anglian see, Hunberht, died in 869. The bishopric of Lindsey was vacant from some time in the 860s until 953. The bishopric of Whithorn (Dumfries) disappears from view in the 830s and was not re-founded until c.1129, and the bishopric of London was not historically attested between c.867 and 897.[83] In assessing the significance of this, one can do no better than to repeat the view of Patrick Wormald that bishoprics 'were among the most durable institutions of medieval Europe; they were not lightly abandoned, even for a time, and were very resistant to change, even by ecclesiastical authority'.[84] Gaps in episcopal lists represent a major dislocation in Anglo-Saxon society, although the disappearance of Hexham appears too early to be attributable to the viking raiders.[85]

Only a handful of genuine pre-viking charters, or what appear to be authentic copies, survive from northern and eastern England.[86] This, and the scarcity of books and other manuscripts from the monastic libraries of the region, must be attributable to the raiders, whether through destruction or theft. The inhabitants of religious communities were not always assiduous in preserving their libraries, but, as Patrick Wormald has commented, while clerics may occasionally leave manuscripts on shelves to be devoured by rodents they 'are most unlikely to have stuffed them into the monastic boiler'.[87] There was a notable decline in standards of literacy in the ninth century, and although factors such as the increasing secularisation of monasteries probably played a part in this decline, the viking raiders were doubtless the most significant factor. Analysis of charters produced at Christ Church, Canterbury (Kent) reveals that while the charters of the early ninth century are characterised by excellent calligraphic skills and perfectly adequate Latin, by the 850s and 860s a significant decline in standards was evident, in terms of the script used, spelling and the increasing infiltration of vernacular words into Latin phrases. The output of one scribe whose work can be traced from 855 to 873 is of demonstrably poorer quality than that of earlier scribes, and it has been suggested by Nicholas Brooks that after the attack on Canterbury in 851 the community was forced to recruit far less well-trained scribes. The final error-strewn charter produced by this scribe is full of interlineations, repetitions and omissions and it implies that the scribe now had failing eyesight; as Brooks says, the employment of this man as the sole scribe of the community 'is a vivid testimony to the decline in the quality of instruction there and to the crisis of literacy'.[88] The decline in basic standards of literacy was, indeed, a source for contemporary concern, and was lamented by King Alfred in a famous passage from the preface to his translation of Pope Gregory's *Pastoral Care*:

So completely had learning decayed in England that there were very few men on this side of the Humber who could apprehend their services in English or even translate a letter from Latin into English, and I think that there were not many beyond the Humber . . . Before everything was ravaged and burnt, the churches throughout all England stood filled with treasures and books, and likewise there was a great multitude of the servants of God. And they had very little benefit from those books, for they could not understand anything in them, for they were not in their own language[89]

Ecclesiastical land-holdings were undoubtedly diminished during the later ninth to mid-tenth centuries. The account in the *History of Saint Cuthbert* of the appropriation of church lands by Scandinavian settlers is a rare comment on what may have been a more widespread phenomenon. However, it is not until the production of Domesday Book that we are furnished with an overview of ecclesiastical land-holdings in the period after the Scandinavian conquests. In many cases this provides the first insight into ecclesiastical resources since the seventh, eighth or ninth century, but in others it is the first reliable indication of ecclesiastical possessions, and it is therefore impossible to measure the scale of ecclesiastical losses in the wake of the Scandinavian raids and settlement. We should also note that during the ninth century ecclesiastical fortunes were affected by the actions of indigenous lords. For example, the *History of Saint Cuthbert* alleged that the Northumbrian kings, Osbert and Ælla, had taken land from the community of St Cuthbert in the late ninth century, and it is possible that the circumstances of civil war and the contemporary monetary collapse encouraged Northumbrian kings to recoup their losses at the expense of religious communities.[90] Elsewhere, the ninth century saw kings, bishops and aristocrats struggle for control over churches, sometimes taking their lands in the process, while some late eighth- and ninth-century commentators, including Alcuin and Asser, clearly believed that there had been a decline in Christian standards and practices prompted by avarice and lax moral standards.[91] Nonetheless, it is reasonable to assume both that religious communities in northern and eastern England were more or less as well endowed in their early history as those of western Mercia and Wessex, and that the contrasting amounts of ecclesiastical lands in those regions in the eleventh century reflect different levels of loss following the onset of Scandinavian raids and settlement. In Wessex and western Mercia, between a fifth and a third of land in each county was held by ecclesiastical institutions, according to Domesday Book, but the corresponding figures in those parts of northern England covered by the survey (i.e. excluding Durham and the far north-west) and in the east midlands west of the fens, was consistently less than 10%.[92]

Robin Fleming has argued that land was taken from the Church by secular lords as part of their defence against the invaders. Unfortunately, the evidence on which this case was made included later and probably fraudulent claims by religious houses of the post-Conquest period to the lands of their pre-viking predecessors. Nonetheless, there are a few reliable charters from Wessex that reveal Alfred and Edward the Elder and other secular lords exchanging lands with religious communities and, although in some cases the motivating factor may have been the administrative convenience of the church concerned, in others the prompt may have been a desire to consolidate the lord's landed possessions, in order to endow fortifications (such as that at Chisbury (Wilts)), or to acquire control over major harbours (such as Plympton (Devon) and Portchester (Hants)).[93] That ecclesiastical lands came into secular hands in many parts of northern and eastern England is certain, although the precise mechanisms by which the lands of a deserted religious community were redistributed is obscure, as is the capacity of weakened religious communities to retain their possessions. In sum, although the chronology by which ecclesiastical lands were lost is largely unclear, it was certainly not limited to the late ninth and early tenth century, and neither was it limited to direct Scandinavian intervention.[94]

There is no doubt that contemporaries feared for the fate of the Christian Church in the ninth century. Charters of this date often note that a grant of land is made for 'as long as the Christian faith should last in Britain'.[95] Such fear may have lain behind the decision to translate Orosius' *Historiarum adversum Paganos Libri Septem* ('The Seven Books of History Against the Pagans'), which records the miseries created by pagans and was written to dissuade Christians from abandoning their faith in the face of pagan attacks on the late Roman world. While the circumstances of late ninth-century England were different, the text would have had resonance in the wake of the viking raids.[96]

The acquisition of relics from churches in northern England and the north midlands, and their transfer to churches in Wessex and western Mercia, represents an attack on their prosperity, and would have been unlikely if the religious communities in which they were housed were still thriving. The relics of St Oswald were taken from Bardney (Lincs) into Mercia in 909, and Alfred's daughter Æthelflaed may have been behind the transfer of the relics of St Ealhmund from Derby to Shrewsbury.[97] According to William of Malmesbury, writing in the twelfth century, Glastonbury acquired the relics of many northern saints, including those of Hild of Whitby, Ceolfrith of Monkwearmouth–Jarrow and Aidan of Lindisfarne, and this may have occurred in the wake of West Saxon campaigns in the North.[98] In addition, one wonders what happened to the relics undoubtedly associated with the remains of shrines discovered at, for example, Wirksworth, South Kyme (Lincs) and Hovingham (Yorks).[99] There may have been pious motives behind these translations, but there was clearly also political capital to be gained from the acquisition of relics, and the establishment of *burhs* in western Mercia and the (re)foundation of churches in them doubtless were factors.[100] Saints' relics were extremely important in early medieval society, where they provided a focal point for pilgrimage and patronage, conferred prestige, and were central to local pastoral work and important to regional traditions and identities.[101] Their loss from the religious communities with which they were intimately linked must have been devastating.

The almost complete failure to re-establish the regular life in northern and eastern England, outside of the Fens, also affected the fates of early religious communities. This must have been dictated by a range of factors, including the distance of these regions from the heartlands of religious reform in the later tenth century, and perhaps also the lack of royal lands in those districts and the likelihood that much former ecclesiastical land had fallen into lay hands, discouraging the revival of monasteries.[102]

Although, as we have seen, some commentators have noted the remarkable consistency with which important pre-viking churches emerge as the major churches of a later date, we should note that not all churches of pre-viking origin were mother churches in the later Middle Ages. In Lincolnshire, in particular, there were few churches of superior status by the eleventh century, and those that did exist rarely served large parishes or had communities of clergy. In this region, the disruption of the period of Scandinavian control seems certain, although it should be noted that a factor in the demise of any surviving mother churches must have been the foundation of comparatively large numbers of local, estate churches during the course of the tenth century, in a region characterised by a highly fragmented estate structure.[103]

Absence of evidence is rarely a reliable indicator, but it should be noted that there are no tenth-century sculptures at many churches with early sculptures, including Hartlepool, Staindrop (Dur), Hackness, Gilling East (Yorks), Caistor and Edenham (Lincs).[104] Richard Bailey has commented on the distinction in the north-west between churches with early sculptures that also have tenth-century examples and those that do not. In the valley of Kentmere, for example, there are no later sculptures, either in the churches known to be of early origins, such as Kendal and Heversham (Cumb), or in any of the other churches of the area. The turbulent times in this region are indicated by the *History of St Cuthbert*, which reveals that Tilred, abbot of Heversham, travelled eastwards during the reign of King Edward, and entered Norham (Northumb) as abbot.[105] Bailey suggests that this account, when combined with the absence of tenth-century sculpture and the 'exceptionally dense Gaelic-Norse place-names in the area (including the possible pagan name of Hoff) . . . reflects a more serious social upheaval in this district than occurred elsewhere'.[106] In sum, the circumstantial evidence for continuity must be set firmly alongside evidence for disruption, which appears in some contexts to have been substantial.

Evaluating the circumstantial evidence for ecclesiastical fortunes: the case for survival

Dorothy Whitelock long ago made a case that in eastern England 'Christianity made an early appeal to many of the invaders'.[107] The evidence she cited included: the St Edmund coinage; the absence of both pagan burials and place-names indicative of pagan practices; the account of the early career of Archbishop Oda of Canterbury who was of Danish descent and a native of eastern England; the reference in the *Libellus Æthelwoldi* to the survival of a religious community at Horningsea (see p. 200), and written evidence for the existence of several religious communities prior to the period of monastic reform in the late tenth century. Of this evidence, the absence of supposedly pagan burials is of little value, since burial practices are notoriously unreliable indicators of religious affiliation, and, in any case, burials of Scandinavian type, accompanied by grave goods or with evidence for cremation, are rare anywhere in England in the late ninth and early tenth centuries (see chapter 6). The paucity of Scandinavian place-names incorporating Old Norse deities is intriguing, but such place-names are comparatively rare anywhere in England.[108] It is, however, worth noting that among the growing amount of ninth- and tenth-century metalwork recovered from East Anglia, little of it has overtly pagan connotations. Rare exceptions are miniature Thor's hammers from Surlingham, South Lopham (Norf) and Sibton (Suff), and a mount apparently depicting a horseman with a Valkyrie, from Bylaugh (Norf).[109] The significance of the St Edmund coinage (fig. 5), and the coins minted in the baptismal name of Guthrum (fig. 4), have already been discussed (see p. 00), and they are a sure sign of the official promotion of Christianity and of the importance of the Church in the secular administration in East Anglia.[110]

Whitelock also drew attention to the Danish parentage of Oda, who became Bishop of Ramsbury (Wilts) some time after c.909, and in 941 was promoted to be Archbishop of Canterbury. According to the *Life* of his nephew St Oswald, although Oda's father, said to have been a member of the army of *Hinwar* and *Huba*, 'was not deeply zealous to serve Christ' this did not apparently prevent Oda from expressing his early piety. He entered the household of a 'certain venerable thegn, faithfully believing in God, called Æthelhelm', who took him on pilgrimage to Rome.[111] Unfortunately, we do not know where he was fostered, but his origins in eastern England are suggested by the history of his family and their known land-holdings.[112] Whitelock also identified in a variety of sources a number of small religious communities in the mid-tenth century. For example, the will of Theodred, Bishop of London, which was drawn up between 941 and 953, mentions religious communities at Hoxne, Mendham and Bury St Edmunds (Suff). The will refers to Theodred's *biscopriche* of Hoxne, and it appears that he was also Bishop of Suffolk, if not of the whole of East Anglia.[113] The community at Stoke-by-Nayland (Suff) was endowed by various members of the family of Ealdorman Ælfgar from the mid-tenth century onwards, and communities at Mersea (Essex), Bury St Edmunds and Hadleigh (Suff) were also patronised by this family.[114] There is a later tradition that a small community of clergy protected the relics of the martyred King Edmund from the early tenth century at *Bedericesworth* (later Bury St Edmunds), although when the relics were taken there, and how early the community emerged, are difficult to determine. It is alleged that Stoke-by-Nayland was the site of a religious community from the seventh century, and there was certainly a community of secular clergy when it was re-founded as a Benedictine house in 1020.[115] An abbot of Bedford is first mentioned in 971, and late tradition claims that when the fenland Abbey of Crowland (Lincs) was re-founded as a Benedictine house in the mid-tenth century, there was already a community of clergy in residence.[116] The *Anglo-Saxon Chronicle* reports that in 952 an abbot of an unnamed place was murdered in Thetford (Norf), although it is not certain that he was from a local religious community.[117] Archbishop Wulfstan of York died and was buried at Oundle (Northants) in 957, and, given his status, it is likely that this was the location of a religious community.[118] Whitelock made the point that in all of these cases there was no suggestion that the communities were newly founded.

Dorothy Whitelock concluded that from the mid-tenth century, when documentary sources become more abundant, no impression is given that eastern England was behind the rest of the country 'in piety and zeal for the Church'.[119] It is certainly possible that some of these churches could have been founded or re-founded after the appointment in c.932 of Athelstan Half-King to administer East Anglia, which brought to prominence what Whitelock describes as 'a religious-minded man', who late in life became a monk at Glastonbury.[120] Yet, the context in which some, although not necessarily all, churches could have survived is provided by the conversion of

Guthrum (the reliance of this king and his unknown successors on the Church is attested in the coinage that they issued), and the fact that West Saxon authority was gained in 917 and – unlike in the north midlands and northern England – was not subsequently lost. The rise to prominence within ecclesiastical circles of men from – or with sizeable land-holdings in – eastern England seems to have played an important part in encouraging donations to churches in this region right through the tenth century, and may also have encouraged the reorganisation of locally based episcopal provision. Julia Barrow has recently addressed the issue of the popularity of such communities of secular clergy with the local elite, whose bequests for the provision of post-obit prayers may have assisted the communities to retain sufficient lands to support small communities of clergy. She also notes the requirement to provide prayers for the king, which was first demanded by King Athelstan and reinforced at a later date by Æthelred, who applied the burden not only to the clergy but also to the laity, and which may have prompted some members of the lay elite to hire clerics to perform prayers on their behalf.[121]

A significant feature of the group of pre-viking churches that are the later mother churches of northern and eastern England, is that most are located at the centre of large estates, of the type with a central manor and numerous dependent *berewicks* and *sokelands*. There is commonly a close correspondence between the dependent properties (especially the *berewicks*, whose inhabitants were more closely bound to the estate centre) and the parishes of the respective churches. It is rare for parishes to extend beyond the limits of given eleventh-century estates. This pattern suggests that the churches most likely to retain mother-church functions were those located at the centres of substantial estates, typically those held by major landholders – often royal or episcopal. In the absence of reliable pre-viking estate histories for most of northern and eastern England, it remains speculative, but not inherently implausible, that these large estates find their origins at a much earlier date, and that the larger parishes based on them reflect the early areas of pastoral responsibility for many churches. We should not, however, push this evidence too far, and it remains likely that estates and areas of pastoral provision were modified at various points in the pre-Conquest era.[122]

Sculptural evidence and the fate of churches

Tenth-century stone sculpture is found in at least three times as many places as sculptures of the eighth and ninth centuries, and there is around five times the quantity – indicating that this tradition flourished after the Scandinavian settlements.[123] This body of material is extremely important to our understanding of ecclesiastical provision, in many cases revealing the existence of churches long before they are first historically attested, and the iconography of the sculpture also casts important light on the acculturation of the settlers and their conversion to Christianity. The influence of the Scandinavians on this medium is especially striking, since the production of stone sculpture was scarcely known in Scandinavia at this time. In light of this, it is unfortunate that the sculpture is rarely closely datable. Dating methods are necessarily subjective, since inscriptions revealing the occasion when a carving was completed are rare, and the stratigraphic context in which a sculpture was discovered, whether archaeological or within the fabric of a church, does not usually help to narrow down the possible date-range for its production. Thus, normally we are reliant upon similarity of design with that of illuminated manuscripts or other closely datable artefacts. The presence of Scandinavian influence on iconography or design suggests a date after the later ninth century, although conversely the absence of Scandinavian influence does not mean that sculpture is necessarily of pre-viking date.[124] Neither the place-names of the sites where sculpture is found, nor the 'quality' of a piece of sculpture are reliable guides to a sculpture's antiquity.[125] Given these difficulties, most specialists date sculptures no more closely than to fifty-year periods. Nonetheless, despite the difficulties of establishing absolute chronologies, the study of stone sculptures has much to reveal about Anglo–Scandinavian interaction.

It was once thought that some aspects of tenth-century stone sculptures were 'pagan', with attention focusing on scenes derived from Norse mythology and images thought to be incompatible with the Church, such as hunting scenes or armed warriors. There are depictions of Thor and Odin and images of Ragnarök, the end of the Norse gods, on sculpture at Gosforth (Cumb) (fig. 31), and Ragnarök is also represented on a sculpture from Skipwith (Yorks). Heimdallr and Fenris the wolf are apparently depicted at Ovingham (Dur); a scene possibly from the Norse legend of Hildr and the Everlasting battle is shown on a grave-cover at Lowther (Cumb); while hunt scenes appear on sculptures at Neston (Ches), Heysham (Lancs) and Staveley (Yorks).[126] However, emphasis on the pagan qualities of sculptures has recently been modified, and the body of stone sculpture from northern England is now widely regarded as belonging to a Christian milieu. Indeed, the work of the same sculptor has been identified on both monuments incorporating supposedly pagan images and also on crosses.[127] Richard Bailey has argued that scenes derived from Norse mythology, as well as other secular scenes, could be interpreted as Christian teaching and art 'being presented in Scandinavian terms', in which parallels were drawn between, on the one hand, Christian themes and, on the other, Scandinavian mythology and pagan beliefs.[128] For example, a second sculptor added Scandinavian-influenced images to a late ninth-century cross-shaft at Nunburnholme (Yorks), and one panel seems to draw a parallel between depictions of the Scandinavian legend of Sigurd (who killed a dragon and after tasting its blood learned of the treacherous plans of his stepfather, Reginn) and eucharistic images (fig. 30). A frontally depicted human figure holding a semi-circular vessel was cut back by the second sculptor in order to make room for two figures facing each other, one of which appears to have a monstrous head while the other holds one hand towards his mouth and in the other holds a ring, and this has been interpreted as a depiction of the roasting of the dragon's heart from the Sigurd legend. Both images involve enlightenment through consumption – of the dragon's blood and the Host respectively. The second sculptor modified a pre-existing sculpture, also adding a seated figure grasping a sword on another panel, but at the same time maintaining much of the existing overtly Christian ethos of the sculpture by carving a Virgin and Child scene on yet another panel.[129] Sigurd appears on several sculptures from northern England, and in addition to providing a suitably heroic association for a secular patron, his dragon-slaying may also have had resonance with the Christian struggle with serpents, such as the Archangel Michael's defeat of the Dragon in the Book of Revelation.[130]

Parallels may also have been intended between images of St John with his eagle and Wayland the flying smith, on a cross-shaft from Leeds (Yorks) (fig. 33).[131] Christian parallels were drawn in the depiction of Ragnarök at Gosforth (fig. 31). For example, the Crucifixion of Christ appears on the same face (d) as an image interpreted as Víðarr avenging the death of Odin; beasts attacking the Norse gods are mirrored by a serpent beneath the Crucifixion; and it is notable that there are four horsemen within the Ragnarök narrative, a number whose apocalyptic significance would have been recognisable to Christian viewers. Overall, a link seems to be made between the end of both the Norse and the Christian worlds.[132] On another stone from Gosforth, Thor is depicted struggling with the World-Serpent, and above it is a stag, legs entangled in the coil of a serpent, which is a conventional image of the struggle of Christ and individual Christians with the Devil.[133] Other images may have had resonance for both Christian and pagan viewers. For example, the snakes on a cross-shaft at Masham (Yorks)

30   Sculpture at Nunburnholme (Yorks). The work of more than one sculptor can be detected on this sculpture. On this panel, the lower part of a carving of a priest holding a chalice has been cut away by a depiction of two figures interpreted as Reginn and Sigurd consuming the dragon's heart (J. T. Lang, *Corpus of Anglo-Saxon Stone Sculpture, Vol. 3. York and Eastern Yorkshire* (Oxford, 1991), pp. 189–93).

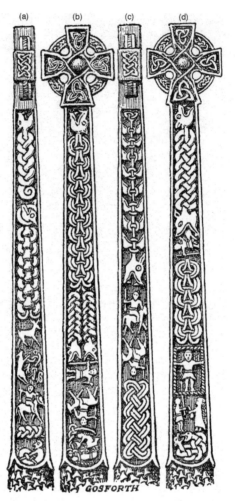

31 Sculpture at Gosforth (Cumb). There has been considerable debate about the significance of the various images on this sculpture. Richard Bailey has recently identified a series of pagan and Christian scenes on the cross, suggesting that, with the exception of the Crucifixion scene (d), all of the other scenes (a)–(c) are associated with Ragnarök, the tale of the overthrow of the Norse gods. These include a depiction of Viðarr avenging the death of his father, Odin, by breaking the jaw of the wolf (above the Crucifixion scene); the watchman of the gods, Heimdallr, holding back two beasts with his staff and horn, which he will blow to awaken the gods (b); and below him the bound God Loki, whose escape will herald Ragnarök (R. N. Bailey, *England's Earliest Sculptors* (Toronto, 1997), pp. 86–90).

32 Sculpture at Kirklevington (Yorks). There
has been debate about whether this figure is a
secular portrait of the deceased for whom the
sculpture was commissioned, or whether it is a
representation of Odin with his attendant
ravens (J. T. Lang, *Corpus of Anglo-Saxon Stone
Sculpture, Vol. 6. Northern Yorkshire* (Oxford,
2001)). Height of sculpture is 80 cm.

may have been understood as either the serpent at the end of the world
from Scandinavian mythology, or the dragons and leviathans of Isaiah, Job,
the Psalms and Revelation, or both. The figure with two birds perched on
his shoulder at Kirklevington (Yorks) may have been understood either as
Odin and his attendant ravens, or as a Christian symbol of resurrection
(fig. 32). Such images may have been deliberately intended to have multiple meanings, perhaps with didactic aims, including assisting the conversion and acculturation processes.[134]

Warrior figures and mounted horsemen are an innovation of tenth-
century sculptures and occur at, for example, Astonfield (Staffs), Neston
(Ches), Brailsford, Norbury (Derbys), Lowther (Cumb), Hart, Gainford,
Chester-le-Street and Sockburn (Dur), Middleton, Old Malton, Weston,
Brompton, Staveley, Holme-upon-Spalding Moor and, as we have seen,
Nunburnholme (Yorks) (figs 30 and 33). The aforementioned sculpture
from Kirklevington (fig. 32) may also have been intended as a warrior
figure.[135] Secular figures are rare at an earlier date, with notable exceptions
being the royal figure on a cross at Repton, and a portrait of a man in secular
clothing accompanied by falconry equipment on a cross at Bewcastle
(Cumb). Although the figural inhabitants of vine-scrolls (ornamentation in
the form of a vine plant) on earlier sculptures at, for example, Hexham,
Jarrow and Auckland included hunters and archers, which 'could have
been interpreted allegorically and may reflect their Classical models. They
are certainly to be viewed as distinct from the armed men in apparently

(a)

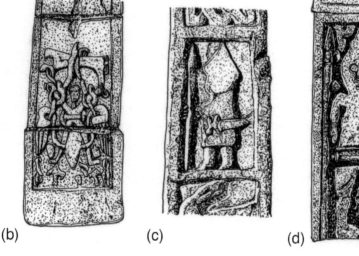

(b)   (c)   (d)

33   Sculptures with warrior and heroic images. A selection of tenth-century
      sculptures from northern England. (a) Sculpture depicting mounted
    warriors, found in Sockburn (Durham) (length 63.5 cm). (b) Sculpture
depicting the flight scene from the heroic story of Wayland the Smith, found
  in Leeds (Yorkshire) (height of section shown is 82.5 cm). (c) An armed
   warrior on a sculpture from Sockburn (Durham) (height 48 cm). (d) An
   armed warrior on a sculpture from Middleton (Yorkshire) (height 56 cm).

contemporary dress that appear in the post-viking period'.[136] There seems little doubt, then, that the armed figures of the tenth century represent both an increased secular influence in the commissioning of sculptures, and also the expansion of the artistic medium beyond the confines of religious communities. They doubtless played a role in lordly display, depicting as they do some of the main attributes of tenth-century lordship (see chapter 6), but they also imply something of the ways in which the Church responded to the circumstances of the Scandinavian conquest. These images seem to represent yet another chapter in the history of the absorption of the aristocratic ethos of society by the Anglo-Saxon Church. The debate about the significance of the armed figures on tenth-century stone sculpture is reminiscent of the debate over the poem *Beowulf*, which scholars long found hard to classify because of its mixture of pagan rites, secular subject matter and biblical citations. Patrick Wormald famously responded to these debates by arguing that the 'aristocratic environment of early English Christianity', makes the creation and the enjoyment of the poem understandable, even within a monastic environment. Equally, it is arguable that there is little, if anything, about the sculpture that can be regarded as un-Christian, assuming that we take an appropriately broad view of what was acceptable within a Christian context. We should, perhaps, add that although we may understand the appeal of *Beowulf* by reminding ourselves of the aristocratic ethos of early Christianity, at the same time there was clearly a strain of contemporary ecclesiastical thought that did not find such poems acceptable.[137] Thus, the sculpture with its incorporation of scenes from heroic mythology and warrior figures implies that the Church was doing what it was well equipped to do, and adapting itself to new circumstances, even if it is likely that some of its members would have disapproved of the methods.

The influence of the patron on sculptures must have been significant. For example, at Gosforth, although the work of two sculptors has been identified from studies of cutting techniques, all of the sculptures reveal a similar interest in Scandinavian mythology, which infers the preferences of a patron.[138] In general, however, it is difficult to identify the type of patron of a particular sculpture. Secular images need not imply that a sculpture was created for a secular lord and displayed at his estate church rather than at a religious community, as the example from Chester-le-Street demonstrates.[139] Nonetheless, contrasts between sculptures on a local basis may occasionally reveal differences in patronage. In Ryedale (Yorks), for example, animal ornamentation and figural carving (including warriors and huntsmen) are prominent on sculptures at Middleton (fig. 33),

Kirkbymoorside and Sinnington, and these new styles reflect an increased secular influence on sculptural production, and may also indicate secular influence over churches, at least some of which may have been newly founded in the tenth century. Yet, in the middle of this region of distinctive new styles of sculpture, Jim Lang has observed that the church at Stonegrave possesses sculpture that owes much more to earlier sculptural traditions, making few concessions to the new styles. Its sculptures were seemingly created by a workshop producing sculptures only for this church, unlike other churches in the district, which were supplied from workshops distributing their products widely.[140] The sculpture may perhaps be an indication of continuity of patronage, and perhaps also of the survival of a religious community at this site. The patrons of newly founded local churches may have been more receptive to new social and cultural trends when they commissioned sculpture, than were some of the older-established churches, which, if they survived, may have tried to maintain past traditions, as well as to respond to new developments.

Peculiar to the tenth century are the so-called hogback monuments, of which over 100 examples survive, and which may have been grave-markers. The hogbacks were clearly intended to resemble houses, and many have roofs – at least one even has a door, and they frequently appear like bow-sided halls (fig. 34).[141] Many have beasts holding on to the gable ends of the roofs, often with their mouths, and these animals appear to be muzzled bears. David Stocker has suggested that the house was intended to represent the lord and/or his family, and that the bear was a symbol of conversion from paganism to Christianity. Although the bear had some negative symbolic qualities (e.g. sloth and lust), it was also thought to give its cubs life by holding them between its paws and licking them, thus making it a suitable symbol of conversion.[142] Although this interpretation

34   Hogback sculptures at Brompton (Yorks). Hogbacks are typically house-shaped sculptures, and many have bear-like animals gripping the ends. Each of the sculptures is approximately 1.30 m in length.

is speculative, it is certainly the case that many of the hogbacks carry Christian symbols. There is vine-scroll on three Cumbrian hogbacks, a Crucifixion scene appears on one gable end of a hogback at Gosforth; crosses are found on both gable ends of a hogback from Lowther; and some of the supposedly pagan scenes, such as serpents, could just as easily have had a Christian context.[143]

Detailed analysis of sculptural motifs suggests that the Scandinavian influence on sculptures did not overwhelm the indigenous style, but rather that there was a native and Christian tradition that continued into the tenth century. Vine-scrolls continue to appear on tenth-century sculptures, as do angels and evangelists, while priests appear on sculptures at Neston, Winwick (Ches) and Brompton (Yorks), and Christ is depicted on sculptures at York, Leeds, Thornton Steward (Yorks) and Thornton-le-Moors (Ches). More unusual Christian images include the death of Isaiah (at Winwick), and the Sacrifice of Isaac and the Fall of Adam and Eve (both on a cross-shaft at Dacre, both of which Richard Bailey thinks may have been inspired by paintings in the church).[144] Many of the zoomorphic designs often thought to reveal Scandinavian influence were clearly informed by, if not directly derived from, earlier English forms.[145] Images and decoration derived from Scandinavia can be found merged with and accompanying decorative schemes that have their parallels at a much earlier date. For example, a tenth-century sculpture at York Minster has an animal in the Jelling style on one face, and on another face there is a portrait head with a dished halo of a type familiar from such sculptures as an eighth-century cross-shaft at Otley. Also, although the figurative narrative on the Gosforth cross is clearly of Scandinavian origin, the essential form of the monument is Anglo-Saxon.[146] Accordingly, Bailey has urged us to think in terms of a 'fusion' of styles rather than the 'overwhelming of one by the other'.[147]

Modern analysis of the sculptures of northern England has identified links between the decorative schemes of sculptures in different locations. For example, sculptures at Sherburn in eastern Yorkshire reveal similarities with examples from Leeds, Lastingham and Bedale some distance away.[148] Some sculptures were transported many miles to the churches where they were eventually displayed. For example, the sculpture at Nunburnholme on which more than one hand has been detected, may have started life in York, where there are similarities with sculptures from Newgate, Coppergate and Clifford Street.[149] Such evidence suggests that although ecclesiastical networks had clearly been disrupted during the later ninth century, some survived, while new networks emerged in the tenth century.

Conversion and Christianisation

Ironically, despite the recognition that the Scandinavians did great damage to the fortunes of the English Church, most commentators tend to suggest that conversion of the settlers occurred relatively rapidly. Representative is the view of Sir David Wilson that 'prolonged contact . . . made the acceptance of a Christian God easy'.[150] Until recently, little detailed attention has been paid to this issue. Some of the obstacles to identifying the speed with which the Scandinavian settlers were converted have been alluded to already. For example, stone sculptures revealing the Scandinavian influence and sometimes drawing parallels between the Scandinavian and Christian belief systems are almost impossible to date narrowly, while burial practices are an unreliable indicator of religious belief, and are equally as difficult to date closely. The written record is scarcely more helpful. The Scandinavian conquerors and settlers are identified as pagans (*hæþene*) by the *Anglo-Saxon Chronicle* and by Asser in his *Life of King Alfred*, where the battles of the later ninth century are depicted as being between *Christiani* and *pagani*. Moreover, charters issued by King Athelstan, referring to the purchase of land in the east midlands and the Peak District in the early tenth century, describe the settlers as *pagani*, and the term also appears occasionally in charters of the mid-tenth century, to refer to some of the inhabitants of northern England. Yet, although it is certain that the majority of the settlers were initially pagan, it is quite another matter to suppose that the longevity of their attachment to paganism can be traced through the continuing use of a term with pejorative overtones for individuals who were frequently enemies.[151] Evidence for the longevity of pagan practices among the settlers is inconclusive. Place-names very occasionally incorporate pagan elements, but are difficult to date closely or set in a historical context.[152] Conversely, the absence of archaeological evidence for pagan cult places may be significant, but only if we could be sure that we would recognise such a site if it were encountered. When, where and by what mechanisms Scandinavians were converted is scarcely documented. The conversions of a number of Scandinavian rulers are noted by the *Anglo-Saxon Chronicle* and Asser, and the latter also refers to a recent convert among the members of Alfred's foundation at Athelney (Som), but other prominent Scandinavians, such as Olaf Guthfrithson, appear to have remained pagan.[153] The employment of Christian iconography on coins implies the importance of at least some churchmen to various Scandinavian rulers, but does not demonstrate that they converted, and still less does it reveal the more general extent of conversion among the Scandinavian settlers.

In seeking to take the debate forwards, Lesley Abrams has recently addressed the processes of Scandinavian conversion in England, and has argued for the importance of distinguishing between conversion and Christianisation. The former was the official recognition of Christianity, signalled above all by baptism, while the latter was a more protracted process by which the teachings of the Christian religion were taken fully on board and filtered through to both the ways in which individuals and communities conducted themselves and to individual personal belief. The conversion of Scandinavian leaders is documented in a few instances, and it would not be unusual in an early medieval context for this to be followed by widespread political conversion among their followers. As Abrams says, religious affiliation in the early Middle Ages was not entirely a matter of personal belief, but also an element of group identity, and the conversion of early medieval peoples was often achieved by the conversion of their leaders.[154] In such a context, whatever the personal beliefs and practices of their followers, such political conversions provide a context in which churches may have been protected and ecclesiastics allowed to go about their business. Indeed, prominent individuals appear to have continued to be buried near to churches, and stone sculptures in or near churches became important aspects of lordly display in many regions. Although the speed with which the process occurred remains elusive, churches became important to the status of local lords, and the survival and foundation of churches becomes readily understandable in such circumstances.[155]

It is easy to imagine that contexts such as trade, intermarriage with local Christians and other forms of social contact promoted the gradual Christianisation of the Scandinavian way of life. Yet, as Abrams observes, '"passive acceptance" . . . or simply admiring your Christian neighbours and believing new things surely could not have been enough'. Institutional structures would have been required to support a Christian way of life, and this required bishops, priests and church buildings.[156] Evangelisation was regarded as the work of bishops, and the loss of most of the locally based bishoprics of northern and eastern England – either temporarily or permanently – must have had a profound impact on the capacity of church-men to evangelise among and convert the settlers. It is natural enough for a historian to doubt that Lindsey, for example, had episcopal support in the early tenth century, yet the archaeological evidence, in particular sculpture and coinage, indicates important links between York and Lincoln at this time, and renders it plausible that the Archbishop was in some way respon-sible for Lindsey, although the extent of his influence south of the Humber remains unquantifiable. The evidence for the fate of individual churches in northern and eastern England has already been discussed, and it is certain that eventually there was a pastoral framework in place to begin the processes of conversion and Christianisation in the tenth century, but how quickly and how extensively it was able to begin this work is a moot point. Moreover, even if churches and their communities survived, the clergy would have needed to have been replenished eventually. Where were new priests trained – in regions of Scandinavian control, or in West Saxon territories? Or, given the links between the house of Wessex and the continent in the early tenth century, did continental clergy play a part in the conversion of the settlers?[157] Such matters are thoroughly obscure, but there is little doubt that clergy were eventually recruited and trained. The Anglo-Saxon Church did not preserve an account of how the conversion was effected; but it certainly occurred, and it must have been an immense undertaking for the Church.[158] As David Dumville has commented, while scholarly attention necessarily focuses on the military achievements of Edward the Elder, Æthelflaed, Athelstan and his brothers, there is some evidence that the ecclesiastical reforms begun earlier by Alfred did not lapse until the reign of Edgar, and that Alfred's children and grandchildren promoted monasteries and the reintroduction of ecclesiastical life into the localities.[159]

Conversion to Christianity necessitated a change in behaviour among the settlers, including both prohibition of certain practices and performance of various obligations, attendance at church and payment of ecclesiastical dues. Abrams has discussed analogies from modern ethnographic studies of the conversion of non-Christians, and has suggested that pagans and Christians may have had very different notions of what constituted religion, and that, therefore, conversion did not simply entail substituting one set of beliefs for another. Thus, early medieval accounts of Scandinavian converts engaging in what is perceived by ecclesiastical commentators as non-Christian behaviour, may, in fact, indicate that the converts saw no contradiction in continuing with various traditional practices. While such actions were prone to condemnation, nonetheless, Pope John X, on hearing of various lapses among the converted Scandinavians, expressed pleasure that they had at least 'turned towards the faith'.[160] Ninth- and tenth-century ecclesiastics must have been confronted with a wide range of behaviour in the name of Christianity.

Conclusions

If we incline towards the view that elements of the pre-viking ecclesiastical network survived the Scandinavian settlements, then we must also acknowledge that, in much of northern and eastern England, the tenth-century churches were a poor and pathetic remnant of what had gone before. Churches proliferated in many parts of eastern England during the tenth century, and while this indicates a remarkable enthusiasm among the laity for churches, we should not overlook the fact that this occurred several generations after the Scandinavian settlements began, or that it was a development made possible by the dismantling of the ecclesiastical network and resources of an earlier date. There is no doubt that the Church suffered greatly during the period of Scandinavian raiding and settlement, and the disappearance or relocation of bishoprics and the loss of almost the entire contents of the libraries of religious communities is testament to this. Neither, however, is there any doubt that churches and ecclesiastics succeeded in converting the settlers in northern and eastern England, although they must have adopted innovative and sometimes controversial methods.

The quality and chronology of the circumstantial evidence for ecclesiastical survival and continuity have been outlined in the foregoing discussion, but how much credence can we give to this circumstantial evidence? Ultimately, this depends on identifying a set of circumstances in which churches could have survived. Foremost among these must have been the political ambitions of successive Scandinavian rulers. Some of these were clearly prepared to utilise the Church and Christian iconography in their quest to establish themselves. Evidence for this comes in the form of the conversion of Guthrum and some of his leading men; the coinage of Guthrum/Athelstan and of Siefrid and Cnut; the St Edmund, St Peter and St Martin coinage; the behaviour of successive rulers in York; and Guthred's involvement with the community of St Cuthbert. The quantity of the sculpture from northern England and its iconography suggest that no matter how weakened the individual churches had become, they were still able to respond to the new circumstances in an innovative fashion. While it may have been severely interrupted in some places, the art of sculpting never completely died out, as is indicated by the continuing use of earlier designs and methods of sculpting using templates. Links between churches are evidenced by similarities in sculptural design, and this implies some vibrancy in the ecclesiastical network in the tenth century. In the long term – and perhaps against the odds – Christianity became an important medium for integration, as the sculpture, above all, testifies. The decades from the late ninth to mid-tenth century were dark days for the Anglo-Saxon Church – yet evidence for a remarkable resilience emerges.

Notes

1 R. Page, 'A Most Vile People': early English historians on the Vikings (London, 1986).

2 F. M. Stenton, Anglo-Saxon England (3rd edn, Oxford, 1971), p. 433.

3 D. Knowles and N. Hadcock, Medieval Religious Houses, England and Wales (London, 1953), pp. 467–87.

4 The limitations of this appendix and the information that it provides are highlighted in S. Foot, Veiled Women, Vol. I: the disappearance of nuns from Anglo-Saxon England (Aldershot, 2000), pp. 79–80, where attention is drawn to researchers who have made uncritical use of this source.

5 Ibid., p. 80. On the problems of sources, compare R. Fleming, 'Monastic lands and England's defence in the Viking Age', EHR, 100 (1985), 247–65 and D. Dumville, Wessex and England from Alfred to Edgar (Woodbridge, 1992), pp. 33–6.

6 EHD I, p. 192, n. 6.

7 An observation made in Dumville, Wessex and England, p. 35, n. 29; see also F. M. Stenton, Preparatory to 'Anglo-Saxon England' (Oxford, 1970), pp. 179–92.

8 E. O. Blake (ed.), Liber Eliensis, Camden 3rd series, 92 (1962), p. 55; translated in J. Barrow, 'Survival and mutation: ecclesiastical institutions in the Danelaw in the ninth and tenth centuries', in D. M. Hadley and J. D. Richards (eds), Cultures in Contact: Scandinavian settlement in England in the ninth and tenth centuries (Turnhout, 2000), pp. 155–76, at 155.

9 J. A. Giles (ed.), Roger of Wendover's Flowers of History, 2 vols (London, 1892), I, p. 192.

10 V. Fenwick, 'Insula de Burgh: excavations at Burrow Hill, Butley, Suffolk, 1978–81', ASSAH, 3 (1984), 35–54, at 41.

11 R. Cramp, 'Excavations at the Saxon monastic sites of Wearmouth and Jarrow, co. Durham: an interim report', Med. Arch., 13 (1969), 21–66, at 24–5; Fleming, 'Monastic lands and England's defence', 248.

12 R. K. Morris, 'The church in the countryside: two lines of inquiry', in D. Hooke (ed.), Medieval Villages (Oxford, 1985), pp. 47–60.

13 J. Blair, 'Ecclesiastical organisation and pastoral care in Anglo-Saxon England', EME, 4 (2) (1996), 193–212, at 199.

14 For discussion of relevant examples see R. K. Morris, Churches in the Landscape (London, 1989), pp. 133–8; C. R. Hart, The Danelaw (London, 1992), pp. 30–3; D. M. Hadley, The Northern Danelaw: its social structure, c.800–1100 (London, 2000), pp. 220–57; S. Keynes, 'Ely Abbey 672–1109', in P. Meadows and N. Ramsey (eds), A History of Ely Cathedral (Woodbridge, 2003), pp. 3–58, at 15–18; see also, pp. 00–00.

15 Blair, 'Ecclesiastical organisation', p. 199; Hadley, The Northern Danelaw, pp. 279–80.

16 EHD I, p. 181.

17 Ibid., p. 843.

18 Alcuin's letters are discussed in D. A. Bullough, 'What has Ingeld to do with Lindisfarne', *ASE*, 22 (1993), 95–115.

19 R. Cramp, *Corpus of Anglo-Saxon Stone Sculpture, Vol: 1: County Durham and Northumberland* (Oxford, 1984), pp. 206–7.

20 T. J. South, *Historia de Sancto Cuthberto: a history of Saint Cuthbert and a record of his patrimony* (Cambridge, 2002), pp. 49, 84–5; John Blair has suggested that the church may have been the wooden church built by Bishop Finan (651–61) and that the author may have been confused: J. Blair, 'The early churches at Lindisfarne', *Archaeologia Aeliana*, 5th ser., xix (1991), 47–53, at 47.

21 South, *Historia de Sancto Cuthberto*, pp. 59, 96–101.

22 D. W. Rollason, 'The wanderings of St Cuthbert', in D. W. Rollason (ed.), *Cuthbert, Saint and Patron* (Durham, 1987), pp. 45–59, at 46–50.

23 E. Cambridge, 'Why did the community of St Cuthbert settle at Chester-le-Street?', in G. Bonner, C. Stancliffe and D. W. Rollason (eds), *St Cuthbert, His Cult and His Community to AD1200* (Woodbridge, 1989), pp. 367–86; Foot, *Veiled Women*, p. 76, on the role of the cults of saints in the retention of communal religious identity despite the insecurity of the site.

24 D. M. O'Sullivan and R. Young, *Lindisfarne. Holy island* (London, 1995), pp. 77–88; J. D. Richards, *Viking Age England* (2nd edn, Stroud, 2000), p. 57.

25 Cramp, *Corpus of Anglo-Saxon Stone Sculpture*, pp. 194–7, 201–2, 206–8.

26 A. J. Piper, 'The first generations of Durham monks and the cult of St Cuthbert', in Bonner, Stancliffe and Rollason (eds), *St Cuthbert*, pp. 437–46, at 444–5.

27 Blair, 'The early churches at Lindisfarne'.

28 *Ibid.*, 48.

29 *Ibid.*, 49.

30 Cramp, *Corpus of Anglo-Saxon Stone Sculpture*, pp. 201–2.

31 Blair, 'The early churches at Lindisfarne', 49–51; C. R. Peers, 'The inscribed and sculptured stones of Lindisfarne', *Archaeologia*, 74 (1925), 255–70, at 257.

32 Blair, 'The early churches at Lindisfarne', 51; Cramp, *Corpus of Anglo-Saxon Stone Sculpture*, pp. 194–208.

33 The *Libellus* was incorporated in the *Liber Eliensis*: Blake (ed.), *Liber Eliensis*, pp. 93–4, 97–8. This discussion of the evidence from Ely is based on Keynes, 'Ely Abbey', pp. 15–18.

34 Blake (ed.), *Liber Eliensis*, pp. 57–61; Keynes, 'Ely Abbey', pp. 15–17.

35 Foot, *Veiled Women*, pp. 62–70.

36 *EHD I*, pp. 166–7; Keynes, 'Ely Abbey', p. 15.

37 David Stocker and Paul Everson, pers. comm.

38 D. Whitelock, 'The conversion of the eastern Danelaw', *Saga-Book of the Viking Society for Northern Research*, 12 (1937–45), 159–76, at 169.

39 Cramp, 'Excavations at the Saxon monastic sites of Wearmouth and Jarrow', 29–42.

40 *Ibid.*, 33–4, 37.

41 Cramp, *Corpus of Anglo-Saxon Stone Sculpture*, pp. 123, 132.

42 Cramp, 'Excavations at the Saxon monastic sites of Wearmouth and Jarrow', 26, 38–9.

43 C. A. Ralegh Radford, 'The church of Saint Alkmund, Derby', *DAJ*, 96 (1976), 20–61, at 34.

44 *Ibid.*, 33–4; on the phenomenon of charcoal burials, see B. Kjølbye-Biddle, 'The disposal of the Winchester dead over 2000 years', in S. R. Bassett (ed.), *Death in Towns. Urban responses to the dying and the dead, 100–1600* (Leicester, 1992), pp. 210–47, at 231.

45 Ralegh Radford, 'The church of Saint Alkmund', pp. 44–55.

46 *Ibid.*, 45; A. Thacker, 'Kings, saints and monasteries in pre-viking Mercia', *Mid. Hist.*, 9 (1984), 1–25, at 15–16.

47 Ralegh Radford, 'The church of Saint Alkmund', pp. 37, 45–6, 55–7.

48 *Ibid.*, 57–8; Hadley, *The Northern Danelaw*, p. 228.

49 R. K. Morris and E. Cambridge, 'Beverley Minster before the early thirteenth century', in C. Wilson (ed.), *Medieval Art and Architecture in the East Riding of Yorkshire*, British Archaeological Association Conference Transactions, 9 (London, 1989), pp. 9–32, at 9–10.

50 P. Armstrong, D. Tomlinson and D. H. Evans, *Excavations at Lurk Lane, Beverley, 1979–82* (Sheffield, 1991), pp. 14, 243.

51 See the review of this excavation report by Richard Hall in *YAJ*, 65 (1993), 182–3.

52 R. Cramp, 'Monastic Sites', in D. M. Wilson (ed.), *The Archaeology of Anglo-Saxon England* (Oxford, 1976), pp. 201–52, at 223–41; J. Blair, 'Palaces or minsters? – Northampton and Cheddar reconsidered', *ASE*, 25 (1996), 97–121.

53 M. Johnson, 'Beverley Minster', *Yorkshire Archaeology Today*, 6 (2004), 12; S. Allen, 'A coffin from Beverley Minster', *ibid.*, 13; D. M. Palliser, 'The "minster hypothesis": a case study', *EME*, 5 (2), (1996), 207–14, at pp. 210–1; Hadley, *The Northern Danelaw*, p. 241.

54 R. A. Hall and M. Whyman, 'Settlement and monasticism at Ripon, North Yorkshire, from the 7th to 11th centuries A.D.', *Med. Arch.*, 40 (1996), 62–150; D. W. Rollason, 'Lists of saints' resting-places in Anglo-Saxon England', *ASE*, 7 (1978), 61–94, at 62–3, 89.

55 Hall and Whyman, 'Settlement and monasticism at Ripon', 136–44; on comparable examples, see J. Blair, 'Anglo-Saxon minsters: a topographical review', in J. Blair and R. Sharpe (eds), *Pastoral Care Before the Parish* (Leicester, 1992), pp. 226–66; E. Cambridge and A. Williams, 'Hexham Abbey: a review of recent work and its implications', *Archaeologia Aeliana*, 5th ser., 23 (1995), 51–138, at 74–6; D. Stocker, 'The early church in Lincolnshire: a study of the sites and their significance', in A. Vince (ed.), *Pre-Viking Lindsey* (Lincoln, 1993), pp. 101–22.

56 *EHD I*, p. 223; N. P. Brooks, *The Early History of the Church of Canterbury: Christ Church from 597 to 1066* (Leicester, 1984), pp. 227–8, 230.

57 Brooks, *The Early History of the Church of Canterbury*, p. 53; D. W. Rollason, 'Relic-cults as an instrument of royal policy c.900–c.1050', *ASE*, 15 (1987), 91–103, at 95–6; on the *Breviloquium Vitae Wilfridi*, see M. Lapidge, 'A Frankish scholar in tenth-century England: Frithegod of Canterbury/Fredegaud of Brioude', *ASE*, 17 (1988), 46–65. On the sculptures, see W. G. Collingwood, 'Anglian and Anglo-Danish sculpture in the West Riding of Yorkshire', *YAJ*, 23 (1915), 129–299,

at 233–5; and R. N. Bailey, *Viking Age Sculpture in northern England* (London, 1980), pp. 120–1. Burials are discussed in Hall and Whyman, 'Settlement and monasticism at Ripon'.

58   J. Raine (ed.), *Vita Oswaldi, Historians of the Church of York and Its Archbishops*, 3 vols (London, 1879–94), I, p. 462; *DB*, i, 303d.

59   Hadley, *The Northern Danelaw*, p. 236.

60   M. Biddle and B. Kjølbye-Biddle, 'Repton and the "great heathen army", 873–4', in J. Graham-Campbell, R. A. Hall, J. Jesch and D. Parsons (eds), *Vikings and the Danelaw: select papers from the proceedings of the Thirteenth Viking Congress* (Oxford, 2001), pp. 45–96, at 54 (pl. 4.4), 60, 66–7.

61   *Ibid.*, pp. 66, 85–6.

62   *Ibid.*, p. 55; D. W. Rollason, 'The cults of murdered royal saints in Anglo-Saxon England', *ASE* ,11 (1983), 1–22, at 5–9.

63   *DB*, i, 272d; Hadley, *The Northern Danelaw*, pp. 225–6.

64   Routh, 'A corpus of pre-Conquest carved stones of Derbyshire', 6–19; R. Cramp, 'Schools of Mercian sculpture', in A. Dornier (ed.), *Mercian Studies* (Leicester, 1977), pp. 191–233, at 218–25.

65   J. Taylor and H. M. Taylor, *Anglo-Saxon Architecture*, 3 vols (London, 1965–78), I, p. 36.

66   S 548; P. H. Sawyer, *Anglo-Saxon Charters II: Charters of Burton Abbey* (London, 1979), pp. 5–7, 14–15; *idem*, 'The charters of Burton Abbey and the unification of England', *North. Hist.*, 10 (1975), 28–39.

67   Routh, 'A corpus of pre-Conquest carved stones of Derbyshire', pp. 8–19.

68   *DB*, i, 272d; Hadley, *The Northern Danelaw*, p. 230.

69   Giles, *Roger of Wendover's Flowers of History*, I, p. 319.

70   Cramp, 'Monastic sites' in Wilson (ed.) *The Archaeology of Anglo-Saxon England*, pp. 223–9; P. Rahtz, 'Anglo-Saxon and later Whitby', in L. R. Hoey (ed.), *Yorkshire Monasticism. Archaeology, Art and Architecture from the 7th to 16th Centuries A.D.*, British Archaeological Association Conference Transactions, 15 (London, 1995), pp. 1–11.

71   D. M. Wilson, 'The vikings' relationship with Christianity in northern England', *JBAA*, 3rd ser., 30 (1967), 37–46, on p. 37; J. Graham-Campbell, 'Pagans and Christians', *Hist. Today*, 36 (1986), 24–8, on p. 24.

72   J. T. Lang, *Corpus of Anglo-Saxon Stone Sculpture, Vol. 6. Northern Yorkshire* (Oxford, 2001), pp. 251–3; Cramp, 'Monastic sites' in Wilson (ed.) *The Archaeology of Anglo-Saxon England*, p. 223.

73   Hadley, *The Northern Danelaw*, p. 247.

74   For example, at Wearmouth, Lichfield (Staffs) and Canterbury: Blair, 'Anglo-Saxon minsters', pp. 246–58.

75   T. E. Routh, 'A corpus of pre-Conquest carved stones of Derbyshire', *DAJ*, 71 (1937), 1–46, at 44–6; R. W. P. Cockerton, 'The Wirksworth slab', *DAJ*, 82 (1962), 1–20; S 1624; R. Gilchrist, *Gender and Material Culture. The archaeology of religious women* (London, 1994), pp. 31–2.

76   Hadley, *The Northern Danelaw*, p. 229.

77   I. N. Wood, 'Anglo-Saxon Otley', *North. Hist.*, 23 (1987), 20–38, at 23; R. Cramp,

'The position of the Otley crosses in English sculpture of the eighth to ninth centuries', *Kolloquium über spätantike und frühmittelalterliche Skulptur*, 2 (1970), 55–63; *EHD I*, p. 565.

78 Bailey, *Viking Age Sculpture*, pp. 162, 170, 189–90, 195; Hadley, *The Northern Danelaw*, pp. 238–9.

79 Other examples include the churches at Billingham, Greatham and Hart (Dur); Bywell, Hexham, Norham, Tynemouth and Jarrow (Northumb); Beckermet St Bridget, Brigham, Carlisle, Dacre, Isel, Kirkby Stephen, Lowther, Penrith and Workington (Cumb); Collingham, Dewsbury, Easby, Gilling West, Hunmanby, Kirby Misperton, Kirkbymoorside, Kirkdale, Lastingham, Leeds, Northallerton, York Minster, St Mary Bishophill Junior in York, Croft on Tees, Gilling West, Hauxwell, Ingleby Arncliffe, Kirby Hill, Lythe, Mascham, Melsonby, Northallerton, North Otterington, Wensley (Yorks); Balsham and Cherry Hinton (Cambs); as well as Lindisfarne, Monkwearmouth, Repton, Ripon, Whitby, and St Alkmund in Derby and Bakewell: see Cramp, *Durham and Northumberland*, *passim*; R. N. Bailey and R. Cramp, *Corpus of Anglo-Saxon Stone Sculpture, Vol. 2: Cumberland, Westmorland and Lancashire North-of-the-Sands* (Oxford, 1988), *passim*; J. T. Lang, *Corpus of Anglo-Saxon Stone Sculpture, Vol. 3: York and Eastern Yorkshire* (Oxford, 1991), *passim*; *idem*, *Corpus of Anglo-Saxon Stone Sculpture: Northern Yorkshire, passim*. Examples have been limited to the regions for which volumes of the British Academy Corpus of Anglo-Saxon Stone Sculpture have been published, but tenth-century sculptures from the locations of earlier churches are also known from the east midlands and East Anglia.

80 K. Adams, 'Monastery and village at Crayke, North Yorkshire', *YAJ*, 62 (1990), 29–50; M. Adams, 'Excavation of a pre-Conquest cemetery at Addingham, West Yorkshire', *Med. Arch.*, 40 (1996), 151–91; T. Wilmott, 'Pontefract', *Curr. Arch.*, 106 (1987), 340–4; Hall and Whyman, 'Settlement and monasticism at Ripon'; P. Rahtz, and L. Watts, 'Kirkdale Anglo-Saxon minster', *Curr. Arch.*, 155 (1998), 419–22; S. Lucy and A. Reynolds, 'Burial in early medieval England and Wales: past, present and future', in S. Lucy and A. Reynolds (eds), *Burial in Early Medieval England and Wales* (London, 2002), pp. 1–23, at 17–18; T. W. Potter and R. D. Andrews, 'Excavation and survey at St Patrick's chapel and St Peter's church, Heysham, Lancashire', *Antiq. J.*, 74 (1994), 55–134, at 73–91; D. Phillips and B. Heywood (eds), *Excavations at York Minster, Volume I* (2 parts) (London, 1995), pp. 75–92; A. Vince, 'Lincoln in the early medieval era, between the 5th and 9th centuries', in D. Stocker (ed.), *The City by the Pool. Assessing the Archaeology of the City of Lincoln* (Oxford, 2003), pp. 141–56, at 147–51.

81 J. Blair, *The Church in Anglo-Saxon Society* (Oxford, 2005), p. 297. This study appeared as the present volume was going to press; similar conclusions about the evidence for ecclesiastical continuity are reached at pp. 291–323.

82 Hadley, *The Northern Danelaw*, pp. 231–3, 253–5, 256–7; D. Parsons, 'Before the parish: the church in Anglo-Saxon Leicestershire', in G. Bourne (ed.), *Anglo-Saxon Landscapes in the East Midlands* (Leicester, 1996), pp. 11–35, at 15–16, 24–5, 31; Hart, *The Danelaw*, pp. 32–3.

83 Stenton, *Anglo-Saxon England*, pp. 433–8; M. A. O'Donovan, 'An interim revi-

sion of Episcopal dates for the province of Canterbury, 850–950', *ASE*, 1 (1972), 23–44 and *ASE*, 2 (1973), 91–113.

84   P. Wormald, 'Viking studies: whence and whither', in R. Farrell (ed.), *The Vikings* (Chichester, 1982), pp. 128–53, at 138.

85   D. W. Rollason, *Northumbria 500–1100. Creation and destruction of a kingdom* (Cambridge, 2003), p. 247.

86   N. P. Brooks, ' England in the ninth century: the crucible of defeat', *TRHS* 5th ser., 29 (1979) 1–20, at 13.

87   Wormald, 'Viking studies: whence and whither', p. 139.

88   Brooks, 'The crucible of defeat', 15–16.

89   S. Keynes and M. Lapidge (eds), *Alfred the Great. Asser's* Life of King Alfred *and other contemporary sources* (Harmondsworth, 1983), p. 125.

90   South (ed.), *The Historia de Sancto Cuthberto*, pp. 51, 85; J. Campbell (ed.), *The Anglo-Saxons* (London, 1982), p. 135.

91   Brooks, *The Early History of the Church of Canterbury*, pp. 184–6, 201–6; Campbell (ed.), *The Anglo-Saxons*, p. 139; *EHD I*, pp. 843, 845; Keynes and Lapidge (eds), *Alfred the Great*, p. 103.

92   The fenland communities, which received substantial endowments in the late tenth century, had much greater landed possessions at the time of Domesday Book than was typical of eastern England: Fleming, 'Monastic lands and England's defence', 249.

93   Fleming's paper is reviewed in Dumville, *Wessex and England*, pp. 29–54, and the exchange of lands in Wessex is addressed at pp. 44–6.

94   Dumville, *Wessex and England*, pp. 32–3; J. Blair, 'Introduction: from minster to parish church', in J. Blair (ed.), *Minsters and Parish Churches. The local church in transition 950–1200* (Oxford, 1988), pp. 1–20, at 3.

95   Brooks, 'The crucible of defeat', 13.

96   J. M. Bateley, *The Old English Orosius*, EETS supplementary series, 6 (London, 1980); Brooks, 'The crucible of defeat', 13–14.

97   *EHD I*, p. 210; Thacker, 'Kings, saints and monasteries', 18.

98   Rollason, 'Relic-cults as an instrument of royal policy', p. 95.

99   Cockerton, 'The Wirksworth slab'; D. Stocker and P. Everson, *Corpus of Anglo-Saxon Stone Sculpture, Vol. 5. Lincolnshire* (Oxford, 1999), pp. 248–51; Lang, *Corpus of Anglo-Saxon Stone Sculpture: York and Eastern Yorkshire*, pp. 146–8.

100   Rollason, 'Relic-cults as an instrument of royal policy', p. 95.

101   A. Thacker, 'Monks, preaching and pastoral care in early Anglo-Saxon England', in Blair and Sharpe (eds), *Pastoral Care Before the Parish*, pp. 137–70, at 166–9; Rollason, 'Relic-cults as an instrument of royal policy', pp. 91–5.

102   Dumville, *Wessex and England*, pp. 161–2.

103   Everson and Stocker, *Corpus of Anglo-Saxon Stone Sculpture: Lincolnshire*, pp. 74–9; Hadley, *The Northern Danelaw*, pp. 287–9.

104   Other examples include Escomb and Hurworth (Durham); Edlingham and Rothbury (Northumb); Heversham and Kendal (Cumbria); Filey, Leven, Patrington, Crayke, Barningham, Cundall, Danby Wiske, Easby, Kirby Knowle, Leake, Marrick, West Tanfield and West Witton (Yorks); and Redbourne and

South Kyme (Lincs): see Cramp, *Corpus of Anglo-Saxon Stone Sculpture: Durham and Northumberland*, *passim*; Bailey and Cramp, *Corpus of Anglo-Saxon Stone Sculpture: Cumberland, Westmorland and Lancashire*, *passim*; Lang, *Corpus of Anglo-Saxon Stone Sculpture: York and Eastern Yorkshire*, *passim*; *idem*, *Corpus of Anglo-Saxon Stone Sculpture: Northern Yorkshire*, *passim*; Everson and Stocker, *Corpus of Anglo-Saxon Stone Sculpture: Lincolnshire*, *passim*.

105 South, *Historia de Sancto Cuthberto*, p. 61.

106 Bailey, *Corpus of Anglo-Saxon Stone Sculpture: Cumberland, Westmorland and Lancashire*, p. 27. It should be noted, however, that Heversham was the mother church of a large parish at a later date: Blair, *The Church in Anglo-Saxon Society*, p. 310.

107 D. Whitelock, 'The conversion of the eastern Danelaw', *Saga-Book of the Viking Society for Northern Research*, 12 (1937–45), 159–76, at 175.

108 M. Gelling, *Signposts to the Past* (London, 1978), pp. 154–61.

109 S. Margeson, *The Vikings in Norfolk* (Norwich, 1997), pp. 12, 14.

110 M. A. S. Blackburn, 'Expansion and control: aspects of Anglo–Scandinavian minting south of the Humber', in J. Graham-Campbell, R.A. Hall, J. Jesch and D. Parsons (eds), *Vikings and the Danelaw: select papers from the proceedings of the Thirteenth Viking Congress* (Oxford, 2001), pp. 125–42, at 135–6.

111 J. Raine (ed.), *Historians of the Church of York and its Archbishops*, 3 vols (London, 1879–94), I, pp. 404–6; Whitelock, 'The conversion of the eastern Danelaw', 171–2.

112 Barrow, 'Survival and mutation: ecclesiastical institutions in the Danelaw', pp. 162–3.

113 D. Whitelock (ed.), *Anglo-Saxon Wills* (Cambridge, 1930), pp. 2–5; *idem*, 'The conversion of the eastern Danelaw', 171.

114 Whitelock, *Anglo-Saxon Wills*, pp. 6–9, 38–43.

115 Hart, *The Danelaw*, pp. 57–9; S. Ridyard, *The Royal Saints of Anglo-Saxon England* (Cambridge, 1988), pp. 211–33.

116 *EHD I*, p. 227; M. Chibnall (ed.), *The Ecclesiastical History of Orderic Vitalis*, 6 vols (Oxford, 1968–80), I, p. 46; II, pp. xxvi–xxvii, 338–50. It should be noted that the traditions about the refoundation of Crowland are fraught with errors and forgeries.

117 *EHD I*, p. 223; Whitelock, 'The conversion of the eastern Danelaw', 173, n. 4.

118 *Ibid.*, 173; *EHD I*, p. 224.

119 Whitelock, 'The conversion of the eastern Danelaw', 176.

120 *Ibid.*, 172.

121 Barrow, 'Ecclesiastical institutions in the Danelaw', p. 166.

122 Hadley, *The Northern Danelaw*, pp. 140–55.

123 R. N. Bailey, *England's Earliest Sculptors* (Toronto, 1997), pp. 77–94, at 79.

124 Bailey, *Viking Age Sculpture*, pp. 45–75.

125 *Ibid.*, p. 53.

126 Bailey, *England's Earliest Sculptors*, pp. 86–94.

127 Bailey and Cramp, *Corpus of Anglo-Saxon Stone Sculpture: Cumberland, Westmorland and Lancashire*, p. 30.

128 Bailey, *England's Earliest Sculptors*, p. 93.

129 Lang, *Corpus of Anglo-Saxon Stone Sculpture: York and Eastern Yorkshire*, pp. 189–93; *idem*, 'Sigurd and Weland in pre-Conquest carving from northern England', *YAJ*, 48 (1976), 83–94. The deduction that the two facing figures represent a scene from the Sigurd legend is, in part, influenced by the form of the more common occurrences of this legend on the sculptures produced at this time in the Isle of Man.

130 Bailey, *England's Earliest Sculptors*, p. 93.

131 Lang, 'Sigurd and Weland', 90–1.

132 Bailey, *England's Earliest Sculptors*, pp. 86–9.

133 *Ibid.*, p. 90.

134 Lang, 'Sigurd and Weland', 91–2; Bailey, *England's Earliest Sculptors*, p. 91.

135 *Ibid.*, pp. 84–5.

136 Cramp, *Corpus of Anglo-Saxon Stone Sculpture: County Durham and Northumberland*, p. 20, for the quotation; on Repton and Bewcastle, see Bailey, *England's Earliest Sculptors*, pp. 67–8.

137 P. Wormald, 'Bede, "Beowulf" and the conversion of the Anglo-Saxon aristocracy', in R. T. Farrell (ed.), *Bede and Anglo-Saxon England*, BAR Brit. Ser., 46 (Oxford, 1978), pp. 32–95, at 57 for the quotation.

138 Bailey, *England's Earliest Sculptors*, pp. 108–9.

139 Cramp, *Corpus of Anglo-Saxon Stone Sculpture: County Durham and Northumberland*, pp. 53–4.

140 M. Firby and J. T. Lang, 'The pre-Conquest sculpture at Stonegrave', *YAJ*, 53 (1981), 17–29; Lang, *Corpus of Anglo-Saxon Stone Sculpture: York and Eastern Yorkshire*, pp. 40–2, 154–8, 175–8, 181–9, 207–13, 215–20.

141 J. T. Lang, 'The hogback: a viking colonial monument', *ASSAH*, 3 (1983), 85–176.

142 D. Stocker, 'Monuments and merchants: irregularities in the distribution of stone sculpture in Lincolnshire and Yorkshire in tenth century', in Hadley and Richards (eds), *Culture in Contact*, pp. 179–212, pp. 198–9.

143 Bailey and Cramp, *Corpus of Anglo-Saxon Stone Sculpture: Cumberland, Westmorland and Lancashire*, pp. 30, 106–8, 131.

144 Bailey, *England's Earliest Sculptors*, pp. 80–1; Bailey and Cramp, *Corpus of Anglo-Saxon Stone Sculpture: Cumberland, Westmorland and Lancashire*, p. 92.

145 Lang, *Corpus of Anglo-Saxon Stone Sculpture: York and Eastern Yorkshire*, pp. 33–6.

146 J. T. Lang, 'The distinctiveness of viking colonial art', in P. Szarmarch (ed.), *Sources of Anglo-Saxon Culture* (Michigan, 1986), pp. 243–60, on p. 244.

147 Bailey, *Viking Age Sculpture*, pp. 83–4.

148 Lang, *Corpus of Anglo-Saxon Stone Sculpture: York and Eastern Yorkshire*, pp. 27, 202–3.

149 *Ibid.*, pp. 38–9.

150 Wilson, 'The vikings' relationship with Christianity', 37; see also A. Binns, *The Viking Century in East Yorkshire* (Beverley, 1963), p. 44; W. S. Angus, 'Christianity as a political force in Northumbria in the Danish and Norse periods', in A. Small (ed.), *Proceedings of the Fourth Viking Congress* (Edinburgh, 1965), pp. 142–64, at 159; Graham-Campbell, 'Pagans and Christians', 28.

151 W. H. Stevenson and D. Whitelock (eds), *Asser's Life of King Alfred* (Oxford,

1959); translated in Keynes and Lapidge (eds), *Alfred the Great*, pp. 67–110, where, it should be noted, the term *pagani* is translated as 'vikings'. See also the discussion in L. Abrams, 'The conversion of the Danelaw', in Graham-Campbell, Hall, Jesch and Parsons (eds), *Vikings and the Danelaw*, pp. 31–44, at 32; *EHD I*, pp. 546–7; Sawyer (ed.), *Anglo-Saxon Charters II*, pp. 5–7; S 520, 544, 548–50, 569, 572.

152 Gelling, *Signposts*, pp. 154–61.

153 *EHD I*, pp. 196, 203; Keynes and Lapidge (eds), *Alfred the Great*, pp. 85, 103, 272; L. Abrams, 'The conversion of the Scandinavians of Dublin', *ANS*, 20 (1998), 1–29, at 25–6.

154 L. Abrams, 'Conversion and assimilation', in Hadley and Richards (eds), *Cultures in Contact*, pp. 135–53, at 137–8; see also *idem*, 'The conversion of the Danelaw'.

155 Barrow, 'Survival and mutation: ecclesiastical institutions in the Danelaw'.

156 Abrams, 'Conversion and assimilation', p. 139.

157 Dumville, *Wessex and England*, pp. 147, 154–62.

158 D. Whitelock, 'Some Anglo-Saxon bishops of London', *History, Law and Literature in 10th–11th Century England*, II (1981), 3–34, at 17.

159 Dumville, *Wessex and England*, pp. 185–205.

160 Abrams, 'Conversion and assimilation', pp. 143–7.

6

Burial practices: ethnicity, gender and social status

According to archaeologist Julian Richards, 'It is one of the most remarkable aspects of Viking Age England that despite several centuries of settlement there are very few viking graves' (fig. 35).[1] In contrast with the period of Germanic settlements in the fifth and sixth centuries, which has produced thousands of graves indicative of Germanic influence, Scandinavian burials have been identified on the basis of evidence for cremation and inhumation with grave goods, at only about thirty sites in England.[2] However, some of the burials among this relatively small corpus are not very different from burials that pre-date the period of Scandinavian influence, while comparable examples can be found in regions that do not appear to have experienced Scandinavian settlement in the ninth and tenth century. We need to place the supposedly Scandinavian burials in context, and explore the full range of burial practices found in northern and eastern England during the ninth and tenth centuries. Moreover, we need to explore the display of funerary sculptures, which were elaborate and highly visible aspects of funerary display. It is also important to examine burial practices in the Scandinavian homelands. Only then will we be able to determine whether the burials of Scandinavian settlers can, as has been argued, be distinguished from the burials of the indigenous populations on the basis of differences in either burial rites or location. Is the difficult task of identifying Scandinavian burials simply the result of a lacuna in the archaeological record? Or does it reveal something important about the ways in which the settlers used burial strategies to integrate into the regions where they settled?

35   Map of Scandinavian burials.

The evidence for viking burial in England: the traditional picture

Evidence for cremation provides the firmest indication of Scandinavian burial. The only cremation cemetery thus far excavated is at Heath Wood, Ingleby (Derbys). The cemetery comprises fifty-nine barrows, of which around one-third have been excavated (fig. 36). Some of the barrows covered the site of a funeral pyre, upon which calcinated human bones remained (fig. 37). Earlier suggestions that some of the mounds served as commemorative cenotaphs to individuals buried elsewhere, have been rejected, as recent excavations have indicated that, by focusing on the centres of mounds, older excavations may simply have missed the cremated remains. Cremated animal bone has also been recovered from the pyres, and has been shown to include the remains of cattle, sheep, pig, horse and dog. A number of metal items, some of Scandinavian type, have been found inside the barrows, including: two broken swords (possibly the result of ritual 'killing' of the swords); a hilt guard and hilt grip; a small knife; iron clamps that were possibly from a shield-rim; buckles; silver wire embroidery; a ring-headed pin; and various fragments of unidentified ferrous and non-ferrous metal artefacts. Some of the mounds were thrown up over the site of funeral pyres, while in other cases the burned remains were brought from elsewhere.[3] Other examples of cremation rite include Hesket-in-the-Forest (Cumb), where a layer of charcoal, bones and ashes was found under a cairn, accompanied by weapons that had been deliberately damaged, including a sword, spears, and shield, an axehead, a pair of spurs, a horse-bit, a bone comb and case, a sickle (not illustrated) and a whetstone (fig. 38). No body was, however, recovered.[4] A sand mound at Claughton Hall (Lancs) contained a pair of gilt copper-alloy oval brooches placed back-to-back to form a container for a tooth and beads; a Carolingian silver mount reused as a brooch; and various iron objects, including a sword, spear, axe and hammer. A cremation urn was also found, but the additional presence of Bronze Age artefacts complicates matters, and it is not clear whether the mound contained a Scandinavian cremation, or an inhumation in a mound previously used for cremation.[5] During gravel-digging at Inskip (Lancs) a Norse-style sword, a dagger and a pottery vessel were recovered, and it is possible that this was another cremation burial.[6] There is no doubt that cremation burials dating to the later ninth or tenth century must be those of Scandinavians, but only at Heath Wood has a cremation cemetery certainly been found, while two of the remaining three examples of Scandinavian cremation burials commonly mentioned in discussions of Scandinavian funerary practices are tentative.

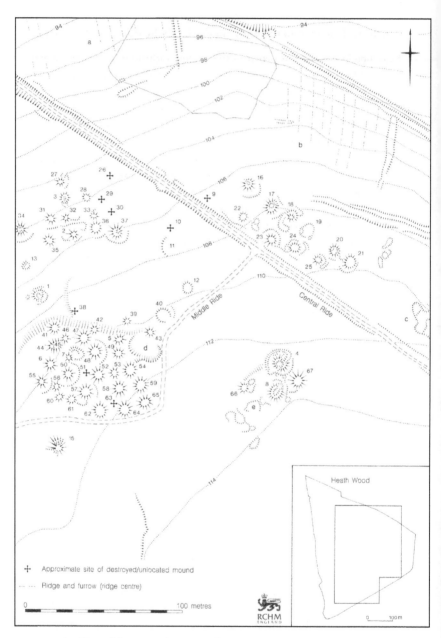

36   Plan of the cremation mounds at Heath Wood, Ingleby (Derbys).

37   Mound 50 at Heath Wood, Ingleby (Derbys) during excavation. This
mound was found to contain the cremated remains of an adult female and a
juvenile, and among the associated artefacts were a fragment of a decorated
mount from a sword hilt, and iron clamps interpreted as being from a shield-
rim (J. D. Richards, 'Excavations at the viking barrow cemetery at Heath
Wood, Ingleby, Derbyshire', *Antiq. J.*, 84 (2004), 23–116, at 57–61, 68).

The remainder of the burials commonly identified as being Scandinavian
consist of inhumations with grave goods, of which some were located under
mounds. For example, at Cambois, Bedlington (Northumb) two males and
a female were found in a cist beneath a mound, and were accompanied by an
enamelled disc-brooch and a bone comb; and at Camphill near Bedale
(Yorks) a burial in an artificial mound was accompanied by a sword and
spear.[7] An inhumation accompanied by a sword, spearhead, an axe, shield,
gold buckle and Carolingian-style strap-end was found placed within a stone
cist underneath a mound at Beacon Hill, Aspatria (Cumb), and a skeleton
accompanied by a sword, spearhead and possibly a ring-headed pin was
found beneath a mound at Eaglesfield (Cumb).[8] Again, these burials are
sufficiently distinctive to be assigned to the Scandinavians, although it
should be noted that a number of other mound burials that contained
weapons have been identified in Cumbria, and, although they are poorly
recorded, these could date to any point between the seventh and tenth centuries. Thus, it is possible that there was a tradition of periodic weapon
burials under mounds in the region prior to the Scandinavian settlements.[9]

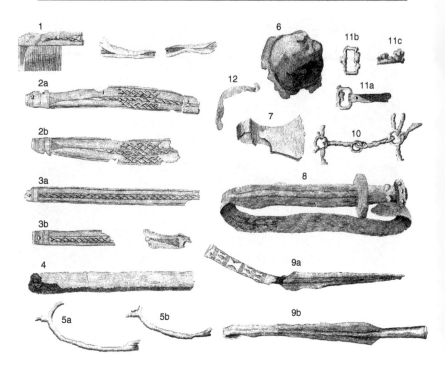

38   Grave goods excavated at Hesket-in-the-Forest (Cumb).
This illustration depicts fragments of antler combs (1–3), a whetstone (4),
spurs (5), a shield boss (6), an axe (7), a sword (8), spearheads (9),
a bridle (10), buckles (11) and an iron fragment (12).

At a handful of sites in the vicinity of churches, burials accompanied by
grave goods have been discovered. These include Kildale (Yorks), where
seven or eight inhumations accompanied by swords and other weapons;
spurs; the beam and pans of a set of scales; buckles; and a whetstone, were
discovered beneath the floor of the church; and Wensley (Yorks), where a
burial accompanied by a sword, spear, knife and sickle was found in
the churchyard.[10] A male buried to the north of the church of St Mary
Bishophill Junior in York had a coin dated c.905–15 in his hand, and was
accompanied by a schist whetstone and a copper-alloy buckle plate. Found
nearby was a skeleton of indeterminate sex which had a silver arm-ring on
the left arm.[11] At Santon Downham (Norf), a burial found to the north of
the church appears to have been accompanied by a sword and possibly a
pair of oval brooches, although the latter may have come from another
burial.[12] At Repton (Derbys) the burial of an adult male contained a

necklace with two beads and a Thor's hammer, a buckle, a sword, a knife, a key, the tusk of a wild boar, and the bone of a jackdaw.[13] A male with an iron knife was buried adjacent to grave 511, after which both graves were covered with a stone setting and a 30 cm-square post-hole centrally placed suggests that the two graves were marked above ground.[14] Also excavated at Repton were a male buried with a gold finger-ring and pennies of the mid-870s; another male with a copper-alloy ring on his finger; and the grave of a female buried a generation later contained an iron knife and a strike-a-light. It has also been suggested that an axehead and a spearhead discovered in the cemetery may have been disturbed from other graves.[15] Among the tenth-century burials from Repton located on and around the mound constructed over the former mausoleum (see pp. 13–14) one female was buried wearing cuffs or gloves with gold embroidery and accompanied by three spherical silver beads; a male had a long ribbon or braid embroidered with gold; and an unsexed adult had a leaf embroidered with gold on his chest, while several burials had iron knives. It has recently been suggested that these may be indicative of a continuing pagan presence at Repton, buried near to the mound covering the earlier mass burial, and that they were 'the burials of elite members of the Scandinavian population who looked back to the mound burial as a memorial of the foundation of their settlement'.[16] Burials accompanied by grave goods have also been excavated in established ceme-teries that were not certainly associated with a church. Examples include burials at Saffron Walden (Essex), where a female was wearing a necklace of silver, crystal, cornelian and glass beads, with three silver disc-shaped pen-dants, and accompanied by a knife. It is unclear whether a male buried with a horse is contemporary or much earlier, while a copper-alloy strap-end may have been disturbed from another burial.[17]

Seemingly isolated burials containing grave goods have been discovered at several sites. In 1851 two burials were discovered at Nottingham, accompa-nied by two swords and a spearhead. Interpretation of the evidence is com-plicated by the slight information recorded about their discovery, and the possibility that at least one of the swords dates to the later tenth or eleventh century.[18] A late Anglo-Saxon seax and knife were found in a burial at Wicken Fen (Cambs), and at Leigh-on-Sea (Essex) a burial with a horse and a sword contained coins deposited in c.895.[19] At Reading (Berks) a male was buried with a horse and a sword, and at Sonning (Berks) gravel-digging disturbed two male skeletons and a sword, a knife, a bronze ringed-pin and six arrow-heads.[20] At Middle Harling (Norf) the burial of a possible male was accom-panied by four knives, a whetstone, and a copper-alloy belt buckle, while a small iron buckle was found near the knees; an iron spur was recovered from near the feet; and a copper-alloy ear scoop was recovered from the grave fill. The burial was found in a ditch, possibly a boundary feature of some sort.[21] Excavation of a mid-later Anglo-Saxon cemetery at Sedgeford (Norf) encountered a female burial with the head over the burial of a horse, and this has recently entered into the corpus of viking burials, although the date of this burial is uncertain.[22] At Thetford (Norf), one burial was accompanied by a sword, while a second contained fragments of a socketed spearhead.[23] A recent re-analysis of an antiquarian discovery of a shield-boss, spearhead and axehead on the coastline at Meols (Ches) has concluded that these finds may have been from a grave, not least because the spearhead had been deliberately bent in a manner familiar from other contemporary graves.[24]

In recent years, the corpus of viking burials has been expanded by new discoveries. A female burial excavated in 2001 at Adwick-le-Street (Yorks) was accompanied by a pair of oval brooches, an iron knife, an iron key or latch-lifter and a decorated bronze bowl of 'Celtic' type dated to the seventh to tenth century.[25] Discoveries by metal-detectorists, reported in 2004, of clench nails, swords, weights, a belt buckle, strap-end, ring-headed pin and ninth-century coins, including an Arabic dirhem, at an as yet undisclosed location in Yorkshire, have been hailed as evidence of a viking boat burial, although in advance of excavation this remains a tentative conclusion.[26] Most recently, six Scandinavian burials were excavated at Cumwhitton (Cumb) (fig. 39). The site was identified by a metal-detectorist who recovered two oval brooches, which excavation subsequently confirmed as having come from a grave. The grave also contained an iron knife, a bead and a wooden chest with a weaving baton. A fragment of a trefoil brooch was found nearby in the topsoil, and this may have been disturbed from the grave by ploughing. A few metres away, five further burials were encountered. The grave of a second female contained a jet bracelet and a belt fitting. One of the male burials contained an iron knife, a copper pin and a spearhead; the second male grave contained a shield boss, sword, copper pin, and spearhead; a third grave contained a sword, beads, an iron knife and a strike-a-light; and the final male grave was accompanied by a sword, spurs, a spearhead, a strike-a-light and, possibly, a bridle. The latter grave was partly enclosed by a ditch.[27]

Finally, maps of viking burials often include sites where swords and other possible grave goods have been found in churchyards, although they were not securely associated with a skeleton. Examples include Ormside (Cumb), where a sword, a ninth-century shield boss, iron bar and knife were found during grave-digging in the churchyard, and where, on a separate occasion, a silver 'Celtic' style bowl, probably of eighth-century date, was found.[28] At both Rampside (Lancs) and Farndon (Notts), a sword was

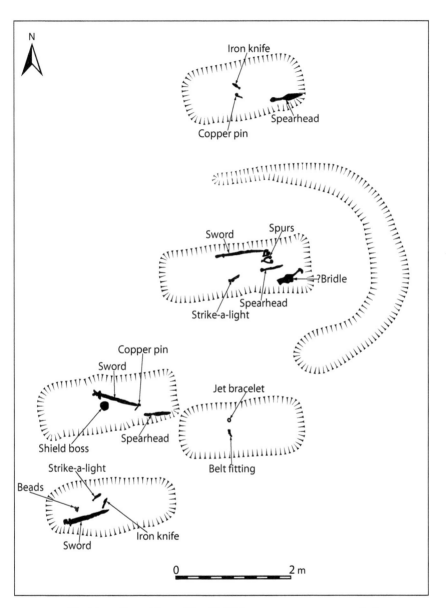

39 Burials at Cumwhitton (Cumb). This cemetery was excavated after a metal-detectorist discovered a pair of oval brooches. The grave from which they may have been disturbed was located to the south-west of five further graves depicted here, containing the burial of what appear, from the nature of the grave goods, to have been one female and four males.

recovered from the churchyard, and at West Seaton (Cumb) a sword was found near to the vicarage.[29] At Brigham (Cumb) a ring-headed cloak pin was found in the churchyard, and tenth-century buckles, strap-ends, and a pendant whetstone were found during excavations of the cemetery at Carlisle Cathedral.[30] At St Mary Bishophill Senior in York, a tenth-century strap-end and piece of silver appliqué ornament were found near the church, while a pair of oval brooches was found near the church at Bedale.[31] In all of these cases it has been presumed that the items concerned derived from disturbed Scandinavian burials.

This list of viking burials is not an extensive corpus, and problems are posed by the circumstances of excavation of many of the sites, the variability of available records, and the loss of some of the finds. It is also questionable whether these burials, most of which regularly appear in discussions of Scandinavian burials in England, really are representative of the funerary behaviour of the Scandinavian settlers. In order to appreciate the significance of the burials described above, we need to be clear about two things. First, we need to establish whether the evidence is diagnostic of Scandinavian burials, and second, we need to consider the possibility that there may be many other burials of Scandinavians in the archaeological record, but that they are present in forms that have not previously been recognised as diagnostic of Scandinavian influence.

Burial practices in England and Scandinavia in the ninth and tenth centuries

Discussions of Scandinavian burials in England are based on the premise that they are visible within the archaeological record because the Scandinavians both employed practices no longer found in Anglo-Saxon England, that is cremation and the deposition of grave goods, and, in some cases, chose distinctive locations, such as mounds, in which to bury their dead. Until recently, most accounts of Anglo-Saxon burials would have stated that by the eighth century the dead were buried in churchyards, in west–east aligned graves without grave goods. Some have gone further and suggested that the burial practices of the Christian Anglo-Saxons were egalitarian, and were perhaps deliberately intended to mask in death the social differences that had been apparent in life.[32] However, there is an ever-expanding body of archaeological material that has begun to change our impression of the characteristics of later Anglo-Saxon funerary practices, and which places the supposed Scandinavian influence in a new light. More recent studies have suggested that, although burial practices were no longer as elaborate as they had been in earlier centuries, from the eighth to eleventh centuries burials still exhibit diversity, and that social distinctions appear to have continued to inform burial display.[33] A brief review of the available archaeological evidence is instructive, and reveals that Scandinavian burial may not always have been as distinctive as is often thought.

By the eighth century, although few burials contained any artefacts other than coffin fittings, grave goods had not completely disappeared from burials. Most of the items found in graves of the eighth to eleventh centuries are either jewellery or the accoutrements of clothing, such as beads, small knives and dress-fasteners. Occasionally, however, graves yield artefacts that do not seem to be the products of clothed burial, and these appear to have been deposited deliberately. Few of the burials outlined below have been considered during discussions of Scandinavian burials, yet many of them are not dissimilar to some of the less elaborate of the burials already described. Two of the graves excavated beneath York Minster contained a coin, both of the mid-ninth century, while an adolescent burial from the same cemetery contained gold thread from a costume; earrings, finger-rings, a dress pin and gold thread were found in other graves.[34] Bone combs of later Anglo-Saxon date have been found in graves at Ripon (Yorks) and Swaby (Lincs).[35] In one grave at Caister-on-Sea (Norf), there was a silver coin of c.830–5; two graves included spearheads 'of Saxon type', and another contained a hairpin 'of late Saxon type'.[36] Later Anglo-Saxon burials at St Helen-on-the-Walls, York, have produced a pair of bronze tweezers, as well as a belt mount and finger-rings, while one burial in the cemetery at Swinegate in York produced a knife.[37] A dog was interred at the foot end of a burial in a mid-later Anglo-Saxon cemetery at Rivenhall (Essex), and a bronze pin was found in another grave.[38] Excavations of the church and cemetery built on the former Roman signal station at Scarborough (Yorks) revealed a ninth-century jet cross on the breast of one skeleton, and a ninth- or tenth-century bronze cross (possibly from a book cover), a ninth-century strap-end and a spearhead were also found during the excavations, and may have been associated with graves.[39] A wooden 'wand' and a glass bead were found in a tenth-century grave at Beverley (Yorks).[40] Ninth-century burials at Bedhampton (Hants) included combs, a hanging-bowl escutcheon, a ninth-century bronze strap-end, a bronze pin and iron knives and buckles.[41] A burial at Thwing (Yorks) contained beads of amber and glass and a knife, and was radiocarbon dated to the ninth or tenth century.[42] One of the individuals buried in the cemetery of a church subsequently subsumed within the bailey of Norwich castle wore a finger-ring; another finger-ring, a pair of iron tweezers and a comb fragment were found in other graves.[43] A late Anglo-Saxon grave at Exeter

Cathedral (Devon) contained a gold finger-ring, and a decorated copper-alloy plate was recovered from a grave in a mid-later Anglo-Saxon cemetery at Waltham Abbey (Essex).[44] A ninth- or tenth-century grave at Royston Heath (Cambs) contained a buckle and a penannular brooch.[45] Roman coins were found in the hands of later Anglo-Saxon burials at Staple Gardens in Winchester (Hants), and while these had probably been disturbed from Roman layers during grave-digging, the inclusion of them in the grave was deliberate.[46] Finally, we should remember that organic materials may also have been included in graves, but that they only survive occasionally in the archaeological record. At Barton-upon-Humber, where water-logged conditions resulted in good organic preservation, wooden rods (dubbed 'wands' by the excavators) were found in ten graves, and similar rods were also found in later Anglo-Saxon burials in a cemetery excavated at the Guildhall in London.[47]

There are significant numbers of Anglo-Saxon burials that contained only iron knives, and although these are often not closely datable, some may date to the ninth century or later. For example, a cemetery at Lewknor (Oxon) producing radiocarbon date-ranges between the mid-eighth and late ninth centuries included two burials containing knives, and a knife burial has been found in a cemetery at Chimney, near Bampton (Oxon), which has yielded radiocarbon date-ranges between the mid-tenth and mid-eleventh centuries.[48] In addition, coins, knives and jewellery of mid- to late Anglo-Saxon date have been found in churchyards with considerable frequency.[49] For example, tenth-century copper-alloy pins, a buckle, needle and strap-end were discovered during excavations of burials next to the church at Holton-le-Clay (Lincs).[50] The examples of finds from churchyards that have been cited as evidence of a disturbed Scandinavian burial (see p. 244), in fact, form a minority of the available evidence.

Thus, the occasional presence of artefacts in graves of the ninth to eleventh centuries across England presents problems for the establishment of a corpus of viking burials, requiring a chronological and ethnic divide to be established between what is likely to be attributable to Scandinavian influence; what pre-dates it; and what is contemporary with the period of Scandinavian settlement, but unaffected by it. Sometimes this leads to perplexing interpretations. For example, a burial with a bone comb at Heysham (Lancs) has been interpreted as being indicative of 'a pagan tradition in the Scandinavian manner', yet burials from Ripon also containing bone combs were assigned Christian connotations and described as the burials of priests.[51] The burials at York Minster containing coins, jewellery and gold costume adornments do not appear to be significantly different from similar burials at Repton, yet only the latter have been posited as pagan Scandinavian burials. Indeed burials containing only jewellery or iron knives are found widely across late Anglo-Saxon England, although only a few appear in the corpus of supposedly Scandinavian burials. The identification of Scandinavian burials does not even rest on the basis of whether the artefacts are of Scandinavian origin, since several of the supposedly Scandinavian-type graves contain a mixture of Scandinavian and Anglo-Saxon artefacts, while others include Carolingian and 'Celtic' material.[52]

The diversity evident in ninth- to eleventh-century burials extends beyond the occasional deposition of grave goods or evidence for clothed burial, to include various forms of coffin and grave-linings, which have been identified in cemeteries across the country, and which were doubtless partly intended as statements of wealth and social prominence. For example, at Black Gate, Newcastle-upon-Tyne (Northumb), over 660 burials have been excavated in a cemetery believed to have been in use from the eighth century until the post-Conquest period, and evidence for wooden coffins, stone-lined graves and graves with stones set around the skull has been found.[53] Excavation of the cemetery beneath York Minster has recovered evidence for wooden coffins with a diverse range of iron fittings; burial in reused wooden chests with locks; graves lined with stones, tiles and charcoal; and burials in which stones were set around the skull.[54] At Caister-on-Sea, twelve burials contained clench nails, implying that reused lapped planks, perhaps from a boat, were employed as grave-covers.[55] In Winchester, at both Old Minster and New Minster, there were numerous forms of burial employed in the tenth century (simple earth graves, wooden coffins, graves with stones set around the skull, charcoal graves, graves with yellow sand, graves with stone covers and burials within a monolithic stone coffin).[56] Arrangements of stones set around the skull have been found in many cemeteries of the tenth century, including those at Rivenhall and Raunds (Northants); Barnstaple (Devon); Trowbridge (Wilts); Fillingham (Lincs); and Cherry Hinton (Cambs).[57] Stones were also used in other ways in graves, including, for example, the inclusion of quartz pebbles, often white, in graves at Kellington (Yorks), Whithorn (Dumfries), Barnstaple (Devon), Llandough (Glamorgan) and Whitby (Yorks), and the placing of stones in the mouth or on the eyes of individuals at Fillingham, St Nicholas, Shambles in London and Raunds.[58]

In the light of this array of evidence, traditional discussions of Scandinavian burials appear to have a rather narrow focus, and one that fails to engage with the full range of available evidence. Moreover, it is now apparent that the Scandinavians not only came from an environment in which burial was a medium of social display, but that they also settled into regions in which burial fulfilled a similar function, even if the means were different. It has long been suspected that the small number of Scandinavian burials identified in England is a product both of the small number of excavated cemeteries of ninth- and tenth-century date, and the likelihood that many Scandinavian burials were near to churches, meaning that subsequent interments have reduced the likelihood of Scandinavian burials being found intact. However, in recent years the numbers of excavated burials of the later Anglo-Saxon period have increased significantly, but the numbers accompanied by weapons and other artefacts supposedly diagnostic of Scandinavian burial have not increased to anything like the same extent. This must surely lead to two conclusions. First, that few of the settlers were buried in elaborate fashion, accompanied by weapons and other artefacts, and, second, that it is certain that among the diverse range of burials in parts of northern and eastern England both settlers and those of indigenous stock are to be found. In sum, we are not faced with paucity of evidence, but rather with an abundance of evidence that is more diverse than is usually suggested.[59]

The implications of changing our focus from the traditional map of viking burials to a map of all known locations of burial, is demonstrated by consideration of the evidence from Lincolnshire. No Scandinavian burials have been identified there, yet a map of all burial sites in the ninth and tenth centuries includes a considerable number of excavated sites, and a host of other sites that have produced stone funerary sculptures of this date (fig. 40). Burials dating to the ninth to eleventh centuries have been identified at Fillingham, Barton-upon-Humber, Barrow-upon-Humber, Cumberworth, Stow, North Kelsey, Holton-le-Clay, Swinhope, Sleaford, Swaby, Thornton Curtis, Torksey, and on at least three sites in Lincoln (St Mark's, St Paul-in-the-Bail, and Saltergate).[60] The diversity of burial practices and forms of commemoration is striking. Stone-lined graves have been identified at Fillingham, Barrow-upon-Humber, Sleaford and Saltergate in Lincoln; and stone settings around the head have been found in graves from both Fillingham and Barton. Evidence for wooden coffins has been excavated at Barrow-upon-Humber, North Kelsey and Barton-upon-Humber, where waterlogged conditions permitted the identification of a diverse range, with some joined with wooden dowels, whereas others were held together with iron clenches and roves, implying a 'clinker-built' technique.[61] Charcoal layers have been identified in burials from St Mark's, Lincoln. An unusual example of burials in a mound at Swinhope has been radiocarbon dated to the tenth or eleventh century, and while

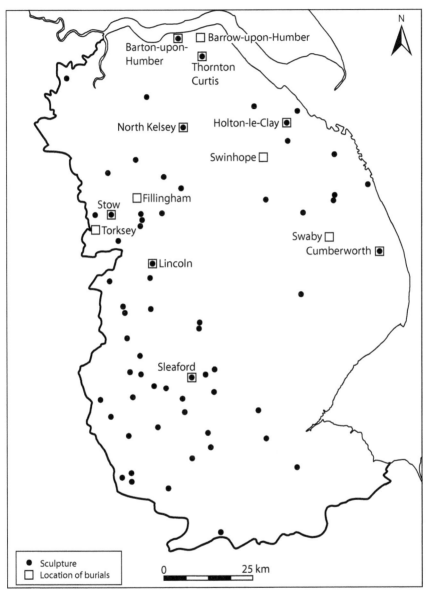

N

Barrow-upon-Humber

Barton-upon-
Humber

Thornton
Curtis

North Kelsey

Holton-le-Clay

Swinhope

Stow

Fillingham

Torksey

Swaby

Cumberworth

Lincoln

Sleaford

Sculpture
Location of burials

0   25 km

40   Locations of burials and sculpture in later Anglo-Saxon Lincolnshire.

such a practice has been identified elsewhere as a Scandinavian trait, it is also characteristic of execution cemeteries.[62] The stone funerary monuments from the region include grave-covers and also standing crosses, which appear to have marked graves. Indeed, a fragment of a cross-shaft has been excavated *in situ* above a grave in the cemetery at St Mark's in Lincoln.[63] In some parts of Lincolnshire, for example the area around Sleaford, up to two-thirds of the medieval parish churches have tenth-century sculptures, and most, if not all, of these are likely to have come from a contemporary cemetery. [64] In sum, the evidence for burial practices and funerary sculptures in later Anglo-Saxon Lincolnshire is extensive and diverse. Although the county does not feature in discussions of the funerary practices of Scandinavian settlers, it is difficult to escape the conclusion that the burials and funerary sculptures of the settlers, and their descendants, are to be found among the examples outlined here. The lack of what are deemed diagnostically Scandinavian burials in Lincolnshire is striking, given that other indicators of the influence of the settlers are abundant, including Scandinavian place-names (fig. 1) and jewellery displaying Scandinavian styles (figs 13, 14 and 18). Perhaps in a region seemingly heavily settled by Scandinavians, overt displays of Scandinavian identity were less necessary? Indeed, a paradox often found in the early medieval archaeological record is that small groups of newcomers, in a precarious position, attempting to assert their presence and status, may be more inclined to make dramatic funerary statements than in contexts where the newcomers are much more numerous.[65]

For each of the regions of Scandinavian settlement, one can find many more burials than those that typically come under the gaze of studies of Scandinavian burial practices. There is also a considerable body of stone sculpture, which was an important element of funerary display. As we saw in chapter 5, the production of stone sculpture was an indigenous tradition, scarcely known in Scandinavia, which proliferated in the tenth century in northern and eastern England. The innovative forms and decorative schemes of these monuments mean that they cannot be classified as either purely Anglo-Saxon or Scandinavian, and they represent a fusion of Anglo–Scandinavian influences, created in the context of new social circumstances.[66] The increasing secular influence on sculpture is suggested by the iconography (that both becomes increasingly diverse and displays many more 'secular' images), and by the range of churches with which sculpture is associated – both major religious communities and other seemingly ordinary local churches. A lot of tenth-century sculpture is much more explicitly funerary in nature than earlier sculptures, as grave-slabs and covers became more common in some regions.[67] A few sculptures of the later Anglo-Saxon period have been excavated *in situ* above a grave, for example at York Minster and St Mark's in Lincoln, confirming that such monuments were, indeed, sometimes used to mark individual graves.[68]

The need to broaden our perspective is also prompted by the diversity of burial practices in ninth- and tenth-century Scandinavia. They include both inhumation and cremation burials, with the two rites sometimes found contemporaneously in the same cemetery, as, for example, at Valsgärde, Vendel, Tuna in Alsike and Tuna in Badelunda (Sweden).[69] Cremation tends to be more common in Sweden and Norway than in Denmark, where the rite is mainly restricted to north Jutland. The form of cremation burial was regionally varied: in central Sweden, for example, after incineration the burnt remains were commonly placed in a pottery vessel and then buried, while elsewhere mounds were erected over the sites of funerary pyres.[70] The provision of grave goods varied from region to region and over time, and while research often focuses on the more elaborate burials, it should be noted that many graves had few or no grave goods. For example, among the cremation cemeteries of north Jutland grave goods are far less common or elaborate than among the cremation cemeteries of Sweden and Norway.[71] A recent survey of burial practices in southern Sweden in the period c.800–1100 revealed that elaborate assemblages of grave goods in both cremations and inhumations were restricted to a small number of burials, sometimes as few as a quarter, and that many burials contained few grave goods, typically a knife or beads, or none at all.[72] Burial in chambers and ships and under mounds is also found across Scandinavia. For example, ninth- and tenth-century ship burials under mounds have been excavated at Oseberg, Gokstad, Borre (Norway), and Ladby (Denmark).[73] Mounds are found above many other types of burial across Scandinavia, including both inhumations and cremations. Other forms of above-ground marking of burials include the arrangement of stones found at Lindholm Høje (Denmark), many of which are boat-shaped, while other shapes such as triangles, squares and circles are also found.[74] Burial in chambers – where a pit was dug and lined with timbers – seems to have been fairly common across Jutland (Denmark), but has also been found at Birka (Sweden), as has burial in wooden coffins.[75] Domestic storage chests were sometimes reused for burial, and examples have been excavated at Fyrkat, Forlev and Lejre on Sjælland (Denmark).[76]

The sheer diversity of burial practices in Viking Age Scandinavia, combined with the similarity of some of the burial forms with those found elsewhere in north-west Europe, means that even if the Scandinavian settlers simply transferred their customary burial practices, a good proportion of them would be archaeologically indistinguishable from the indigenous inhabitants of the places where they settled. Study of other early medieval migrating groups suggests, however, that there may be no simple correlation between burial form and place of origin, and that once migrants settle in new regions they often adopt new forms of burial ritual. Thus, we should not expect that the Scandinavian settlers necessarily employed, unaltered, the funerary rituals of their homelands.[77] Furthermore, even where burial rituals are similar to those found in the Scandinavian homelands, it is likely that this was because the ritual served a contemporary purpose in the context of settlement in a new region, rather than simply representing cultural conservatism.[78] Funerary rituals may also be modified or completely transformed by early medieval communities in response to changed political, economic, social and religious circumstances, and we should be alert to the possibility that the circumstances of settlement gave rise to new forms of burial rite and commemoration among the Scandinavian settlers.

In time, it may be possible to begin to distinguish individuals of Scandinavian stock from those of Anglo-Saxon origins by the application of scientific techniques. Such variables as skull size or stature are, however, incapable of identifying an individual Scandinavian or Anglo-Saxon, as they are generally too sensitive to a range of factors, including diet. The blood groups and other genetic characteristics of modern populations have excited recent interest, but while they may be able to indicate Scandinavian influences in some regions, they offer no possibility of distinguishing the origins of given individuals, or of identifying the scale or the impact of the Scandinavian settlements of over a thousand years ago.[79] A more promising possibility of identifying Scandinavian settlers comes from the analysis of oxygen and strontium isotopes, which are laid down in tooth enamel during infancy. These derive largely from drinking-water, and, thus, reflect the mineral content of groundwater and the local geology, which vary across northern Europe.[80] Yet some of those whom we think of as Scandinavian settlers did not come directly from Scandinavia, and they may, therefore, produce results more typical of western Britain. The most elaborate burial at Repton has been analysed in this manner, and the results revealed that he was, indeed, of north Scandinavian stock, yet similar results have been produced for a cemetery at Riccall (Yorks), where no grave goods were found, and this acts as important confirmation that the Scandinavians are not necessarily only identifiable in elaborate graves.[81] In assessing this scientific evidence, we must, however, remember that genetic evidence does not tell us what cultural characteristics an individual or a group displayed.

Funerary display in northern and eastern England in the later ninth and tenth centuries

By expanding our focus beyond those burials that are typically labelled as Scandinavian, we can begin to infer that the Scandinavian settlers engaged in a wide range of burial strategies, including the display of stone sculptures, where their influence was arguably more frequently – and certainly more visibly – expressed. Moreover, it is apparent that the factors that determined burial display, among both the settlers and the indigenous population, extended beyond matters of ethnic identity to incorporate other aspects of social identity, including family status, profession, gender identity, stage in the life cycle and social standing, although these were expressed sporadically and in a wide range of ways.

Only in recent years have the burial practices of later Anglo-Saxon England been subject to anything approaching the scrutiny afforded those of the earlier Anglo-Saxon centuries. Such studies reveal that elaborate burials (including various types of coffin or grave-lining, and those with evidence for above-ground markers) of the ninth and tenth centuries were not generally sensitive to either age or gender, unlike the burials of the earlier Anglo-Saxon centuries.[82] For example, at York Minster, tenth-century burials marked by stone sculptures include those of adult males, adult females and, on two occasions, infants; while an adolescent, a young adult male, a middle-aged female and an elderly male were among the burials in reused domestic chests.[83] Studies of many other later Anglo-Saxon cemeteries – including Black Gate in Newcastle, Swinegate in York, Barton-upon-Humber, Barrow-upon-Humber, Raunds, Caister-on-Sea, Barnstaple, Trowbridge and Rivenhall – have revealed that gendered distinctions among burials are rare, and although more elaborate burial provision sometimes becomes steadily more likely with increasing age, individuals of all ages are found with most grave variations.[84] Accordingly, it is difficult to escape the conclusion that family status was a significant factor determining burial rites. Another indication of the influence of family ties may be the clustering of distinctive grave types. For example, the aforementioned burials in reused domestic chests at York Minster were located close together. The burials of infants are sometimes found clustered near to the walls of churches, as has been demonstrated at Raunds, Whithorn and Cherry Hinton, and, although the significance of this is uncertain, it is probably another indication that all members of the family were accorded a similar level of care in the funerary context, which contrasts with earlier centuries and was doubtless a development to which the Church contributed.[85] The careful reopening of graves to accommodate subsequent interments, especially of infants, at Staple Gardens in Winchester, and at Raunds and Trowbridge, may be another indication of the influence of family ties on burial practices.[86]

Nonetheless, there is some slight evidence for the privileging of adult males in prominent burial locations. For example, a much higher proportion of male burials were excavated in the central zone around the church at Raunds (roughly 62% male burials compared with 38% female burials), while almost double the number of males were buried to the south of the church where a number of carved stone sculptures were found, in a sector also characterised by a greater number of coffins, grave-covers and markers.[87] Similar clusters of male burials have been noted near to Old Minster in Winchester, at Black Gate in Newcastle-upon-Tyne, and at the church excavated within the bailey at Norwich castle.[88] This suggests that access to desirable and prominent locations was slightly more readily available for males than females, but it was certainly far from an exclusive privilege.[89]

Despite the generally unelaborated nature of later Anglo-Saxon burials, it is clear that they were still capable of conveying messages about the status of a person, both by the manner and the location of burial, and the control of cemetery topography by the Church may have hinted at the post-mortem fate believed to await individuals. For example, burials located on the outskirts of Anglo-Saxon churchyards occasionally display unusual characteristics, indicating that the individual was either physically or socially distinctive, and these burials imply that some individuals were segregated from the rest of society in death. Examples include an adult male with a severely deformed leg buried just beyond the boundary wall at North Elmham (Norf), in the only burial with the head placed to the east rather than the west, and the adult male who had apparently met a violent death buried beneath the boundary wall of the same cemetery.[90] At Ripon, the last phase of burial at the Ailcy Hill cemetery (a former monastic burial ground), consisted of a number of distinctive burials, including a multiple burial and the burial of a severely deformed individual, and it has been suggested that by the tenth century the cemetery was being used to bury the socially excluded.[91] Later Anglo-Saxon law-codes stipulate that criminals and excommunicates should be denied burial in consecrated ground, and a small number of execution cemeteries have been identified on the basis of their unusual characteristics. They are typically located away from contemporary settlements and churchyards, and the burials are often disorderly: sometimes laid prone, in multiple graves or on diverse alignments, while the pathology of the interred is often distinctive, including evidence for decapitation and bodily mutilation. Execution cemeteries typically consist of a majority of adult male burials, and whether or not men were more inclined to criminality than women, it does suggest that they were more likely to be executed and hence excluded from burial in consecrated ground.[92]

Other factors that shaped burial rites in the tenth century include access to learned ideas about death and the afterlife. Victoria Thompson has recently suggested that the increasingly enclosed nature of later Anglo-Saxon graves may be a reflection of the concerns expressed in contemporary ecclesiastical writing about the desirability of maintaining bodily integrity after death, and the association of bodily decay with sin.[93] Thus, perhaps burials at Repton with evidence for gold costumes, and which were placed in coffins with comparatively complex iron fittings, may be as likely to have been those of elite members of a Christian population, whose burials were protected by manner and location of burial, as to have been the burials of a tenth-century pagan community (see p. 243).

Discussions of the burials that appear to be those of Scandinavians (i.e. cremations and those accompanied by grave goods) have usually focused on the ethnic identity of the deceased, but there are other dimensions to these burials, which are exposed by the foregoing review of the broader context of ninth- and tenth-century burials. Unlike the majority of the burials in ninth- and tenth-century cemeteries, the most elaborate burials of this period are mainly those of men, and they contain items strongly associated with early medieval masculinity and lordship. Examples include burials accompanied by weapons (as, for example, at Repton, Heath Wood, Hesket-in-the-Forest, Aspatria, Eaglesfield, Camphill, Thetford, Kildale, Cumwhitton and Wensley), equestrian equipment (such as the spurs and horse-bit at Hesket-in-the-Forest and the spurs and possible bridle at Cumwhitton) and perhaps even horses on occasion (as at Reading and Sedgeford, although the dating for the latter is inconclusive), and also items associated with agriculture (such as the sickles at Hesket-in-the-Forest and Wensley) or trade (such as a set of balances from a grave at Kildale).[94] It is, indeed, notable that although one of the mounds at Heath Wood included the burials of an adult female and a juvenile, they were accompanied by masculine items including a sword hilt guard and what appear to be clamps from a shield-rim. Whichever of the burials was given this mark of status, it is striking that the symbols were those associated with adult masculinity.[95] Thus, it appears that the most elaborate graves provided for the settlers were those of males, and it was through masculine display that claims to land and status were expressed. Clearly, Scandinavian women must have been buried somewhere, but if this corpus is representative, then there seems to have been less investment in their graves and they thus remain largely archaeologically invisible, as they are indistinguishable from Anglo-Saxon burials.[96]

Furnished graves were part of a short-lived practice, and the infrequency of such burials and the range of grave goods suggest that they were restricted to those of elite status. Many studies of early medieval society have argued that elaborate burial display is a transitory statement suited to the circumstances of social upheaval.[97] The turbulent political and military circumstances of northern and eastern England between the later ninth and the mid-tenth century can be plausibly adduced as the context for elaborate burial displays. Yet why were such burials so rare? It can hardly be claimed that the regions concerned experienced only short-lived social and political instability. Rather it seems more plausible to argue that lords, of whatever background, soon found other media for conspicuous display. One such medium was undoubtedly stone sculpture. Sculptures were expensive monuments, often painted and occasionally decorated with precious stones, and they seem unlikely to have been commissioned and manufactured during turbulent times without there being some potential for them to have a longer-term role in expressing and maintaining status. The employment of warrior images or scenes from heroic culture on sculptures may have served to commemorate the heroic, martial ethos of aristocratic society, perhaps even of specific individuals. Indeed, one sculpture from Chester-le-Street (Dur) bears an inscription of the name Eadmund set above a horseman with a shield, although the inscription may be a later addition.[98] A sculpture from Crowle (Lincs) depicts three men, one grasping a sword and another on horseback, and it bears an inscription, which, although much of it is lost due to subsequent cutting of the monument, was clearly commemorative, incorporating the element *līcbæcun*, 'corpse monument/memorial stone'.[99] It is likely that funerary sculptures were made for heads of households, who, according to documentary evidence, were normally male in this period, with women generally only having access to land when it suited family interests or in default of a male heir.[100] Indeed, the only clearly gendered secular images identifiable on the monuments largely involve masculine images and symbolism (see pp. 215–21). A rare secular female image appears on a cross-shaft at Weston (Yorks), and this may have something to reveal about the relative status of women in this artistic medium, and more generally about secular attitudes to lordship, as the woman is shown either being grabbed, or perhaps protected, by a male warrior brandishing his sword (fig. 41).[101]

There is a striking similarity between the funerary displays of weapons and other accoutrements of elite male lordship (see pp. 257–8) and the symbolism of some of the broadly contemporary stone funerary sculpture. Thus, it can be suggested that from the later ninth century onwards, both in graves and on stone sculpture, displays of elite masculinity, emphasising warrior

41   Sculpture at Weston (Yorks). This is a tenth-century sculpture depicting a warrior with his sword in one hand, while with the other hand he grabs, pushes, or perhaps protects, a woman (identifiable by the length of her skirt). On the reverse of this sculpture, the warrior is depicted alone with his sword and battle-axe. Height of section shown is 22 cm.

prowess, were used to negotiate local power politics in parts of northern and eastern England. This should not be surprising, since during moments of intense social stress, notions of masculinity were commonly re-evaluated in the early Middle Ages. In this respect, there is an interesting parallel between the period around 900 and the early years of Germanic settlement in the fifth century, when there was more signalling in burials of the masculine gender than of the feminine.[102] This doubtless reflects the fact that in times of social transformation it was typically to men that communities looked to ameliorate that disruption, to renegotiate local power structures, to make claims to land and to return the community to its status quo.[103]

Yet, if stone sculptures, as also elaborate funerary displays, were normally provided for men, we should remember that these men were also members of families. Stone monuments may often have been intended to serve as markers of the status of the whole family, and not simply of the status of the individual over whose grave they were placed. The symbolism of the house-shaped hogback monuments, in particular, may have reflected an emphasis on the family in burial strategies and forms of commemoration in the tenth century.[104] It is also likely that graveyard monuments became a focus for subsequent burials of family members and retainers. Excavation at Raunds, for example, reveals that the churchyard expanded outwards from a core of burials close to the church, two of which were elaborated with carved stone monuments – those of a middle-aged man buried in an exclusive plot, and an infant in a stone-lined grave.[105] Such monuments may have been as much family monuments as individual monuments; indeed, the sculpture placed over the infant had been recut and reused, perhaps from the disturbed adult male burial beneath. Tenth-century wills indicate that the deaths of individuals focused attention on the family unit, as they reveal a concern to dispose of family property, to provide for heirs, to place obligations regarding property and commemoration on future generations, and to carry out the wishes of already-deceased family members concerning both their property and the welfare of their soul.[106] Burial strategies – involving both location and the provision of monuments – may, then, have been a material manifestation of the contemporary concerns expressed in wills.

Many tenth-century sculptures are to be found at newly established churches, and may reflect local lords exercising a novel form of conspicuous display at the churches on their estate centres.[107] Such displays may have been particularly important to local lords during turbulent times. The sparse documentation for northern and eastern England during the tenth century provides only glimpses of the nature of lordship at this time, but what does emerge is the rapidity with which land changed hands. This suggests that it may have been difficult for prominent families to maintain their status locally by landownership alone, and they may have had to employ other strategies to maintain rank. Thus, in a study focusing on the comparatively better-documented East Anglia, Julia Barrow has suggested that the Church often had a vital role to play in local politics, because it provided careers for members of kin groups, who in turn could offer assistance to their relatives.[108] It can also be argued that the outward trappings of the Church must have helped to give these local lords some stability. Thus, the founding of local churches, which seems to have been much more advanced in eastern and some parts of northern England than elsewhere, and funerary stone sculptures both with and without heroic/warrior imagery, appear to have been symbols of a particular type of dynamic, but insecure, local lordship. It is also hardly surprising that secular lords should choose to proclaim their status and possession of land through local churches at their estate centres rather than at the old minsters, many of which had either failed to survive or had lost their communities of religious, landed endowments, saints' relics and aura of prestige.[109]

The difficulty of determining who commissioned stone sculpture has already been mentioned (see pp. 221–2), given the rarity of inscriptions and the absence of relevant documentary evidence, but it is worth reflecting on the historically attested role of early medieval aristocratic women in commemoration and in preserving dynastic memory, and their part in the transmission of cultural and artistic traditions through their marriages into new families.[110] As has already been suggested (see pp. 82–3), marriage strategies must have been a significant means by which the Scandinavian settlers, the majority of whom appear from available evidence to have been men, secured their position and authority in England, and marriage must also have been a context for the renegotiation of both ethnicity and religious affiliation. The stone sculptures and their role in expressing family status thus take on a new dimension, as they employ both indigenous and Scandinavian motifs, as well as innovative forms of secular display.

The role of sculpture in displays of lordly status and affiliations has attracted recent attention. For example, it is notable that sculptures from northern England not only combine Anglo-Saxon and Christian imagery with Scandinavian styles and motifs, but are also often influenced by Irish art, and this must derive from the clear links between the rulers of York and Dublin in the tenth century. Wheel-headed crosses in the Irish fashion are found in Yorkshire at North Frodingham, Hovingham, and St Mary

Bishophill Junior in York, while the cross at Kirby Grindalythe has an unperforated wheel-head with a Crucifixion on the arms, in the Irish manner.[111] A reciprocal influence has been identified between Castledermot (Kildare) and north Yorkshire: a panel showing Daniel between four lions from Castledermot is 'worked on exactly the same principles and units as the shafts at Kirklevington', while Castledermot has Ireland's only hogback and decoration on a cross incorporates a ring-twist pattern unique in Ireland but common in north Yorkshire.[112] This evidence serves as a reminder that at least some of the settlers in Northumbria operated in a cultural milieu that was not limited to England and Scandinavia.

In a recent survey of tenth-century sculpture in Yorkshire and Lincolnshire, David Stocker has observed that although most churches have sculpture from only a small number of monuments, in contrast there is a small number of churches with many more sculptures. The distinguishing factor does not appear to be that these were the mother churches of the region, but rather that these churches were located in trading places, usually on rivers or the coast. Examples include St Mark's and St Mary le Wigford in Lincoln (in what has been dubbed the 'strand' of this town); Marton-on-Trent; Bicker (on the fen edge) (Lincs); St Mary Bishophill Senior (in what has been identified as a beach market-place on the banks of the Ouse in York); Yarm; Kirklevington; and Lythe (Yorks). Stocker has argued that these graveyards with exceptional numbers of monuments may belong to unusual settlements with distinctive elite populations, with a sizeable number of newcomers in the form of merchants whose social competitiveness was played out, among other ways, through funerary display.[113] To this pattern one could add Little Shelford (Cambs), where fragments of between five and ten monuments have been found, and which appears to have earlier been the estate centre of a late ninth-century *jarl* who had coins minted there.[114] This suggests that in urban and trading environments of the later Anglo-Saxon period the social instability created by immigration and the presence of merchants was expressed, and presumably partly ameliorated, through elaborate display both within the grave and above ground.[115]

Conclusions

The ways in which communities bury and commemorate their dead have much to reveal about social organisation, lordship, politics, gender and the family. In the specific context of northern and eastern England, burial evidence also provides important insights into the impact of the settlers and the mutual responses of the settlers and the indigenous peoples, and our evidence suggests that the settlers quickly began to engage in indigenous burial strategies. Nonetheless, there is a small number of burials in which an overtly Scandinavian identity was expressed. For example, the cemetery at Heath Wood, Ingleby, with its combination of cremation, mound burial and sacrifice (of animals and weapons), has been interpreted as a statement of 'instability and insecurity of some sort . . . a statement of religious, political and military affiliation in unfamiliar and inhospitable surroundings'.[116] Here, for once, we probably can see the Scandinavian settlers behaving in a self-consciously 'Scandinavian' manner, and expressing an overt commitment to paganism, and similar conclusions have been drawn by David Griffiths about the mound burials in the north-west.[117]

Julian Richards has suggested that the burials at Heath Wood were of members of the 'great army', and that they may have been linked with the burials at Repton, just four kilometres away, which were for other members of the army: 'one explanation might be that the two cemeteries represent a division in the viking camp, the first group preferring legitimation through association with the Mercian site, the other preferring traditional pagan values'.[118] Richards adds that although we may propose other interpretations of these monuments, we cannot ignore 'the active role of monuments and visible cultural and ideological statements' in the establishment of relationships between members of the warring army.[119] Neither, it can be added, can we ignore the fact that this form of funerary display was not widely adopted. Rather, the settlers quickly demonstrated a willingness to adapt to the burial strategies of local people, including inhumation, largely unaccompanied by grave goods and involving a variety of types of coffin and grave-lining, burial near to churches, and the use of commemorative stone sculptures. This should not be surprising. Certainly, the Scandinavian settlers were initially distinctive elements within local society, pagan and with a separate ethnic identity, but they were also, of course, members of families; many were, or aspired to be, lords; and they had settled into a society in which the Church was an important element in expressions of status and the consolidation of power. We cannot easily use burial practices as an indication of the speed of the conversion of the Scandinavians to Christianity; many studies have demonstrated that there is no necessary contradiction between Christianity and grave goods, and at the same time it must be remembered that many burials among pagan communities were not elaborate.[120] Nonetheless, and irrespective of personal belief, the Church offered a more visible, permanent marker of status and forms of commemoration than the deposition of grave goods, and this may have been where investment was placed. Stone monuments in a church-yard provided a very visible, public statement, which permitted an individual, a family or community, to convey a distinctive political and cultural message through their form and decoration. It is notable that the stone sculpture of the tenth century did not simply mirror the interests and insignia of lords, but rather it was used to create new lordly ideals and images. In sum, while burial strategies initially, if apparently briefly, distinguished the settlers, they quickly provided a medium for the integration of the newcomers into the societies of the regions in which they settled.

Notes

1 J. D. Richards, *Viking Age England* (2nd edn, Stroud, 2000), p. 142.
2 On the earlier Germanic burial, see S. Lucy, *The Anglo-Saxon Way of Death* (Sutton, 2000), pp. 65-122.
3 J. D. Richards, M. Jecock, L. Richmond and C. Tuck, 'The Viking barrow cemetery at Heath Wood, Ingleby, Derbyshire', *Med. Arch.*, 39 (1995), 51-70; Richards, *Viking Age England*, pp. 146-9; *idem*, 'Excavations at the Viking barrow cemetery at Heath Wood, Ingleby, Derbyshire', *Antiq. J.*, 84 (2004), 23-116.
4 B. J. N. Edwards, *Vikings in North West England* (Lancaster, 1998), pp. 11-14.
5 *Ibid.*, pp. 14-16.
6 *Ibid.*, p. 20.
7 M. L. Alexander, 'A "Viking-Age" grave at Cambois, Bedlington, Northumberland', *Med. Arch.*, 31 (1987), 101-5; H. Shetelig, *Viking Antiquities in Great Britain and Ireland*, IV (Oslo, 1940), p. 15. Viking mound burials have also been reported at Silbury Hill (Wilts) and Hook Norton (Oxon), but the finds and the contexts are poorly recorded: J. Graham-Campbell, 'Pagan Scandinavian burial in the central and southern Danelaw', in J. Graham-Campbell, R. A. Hall, J. Jesch and D. Parsons (eds), *Vikings and the Danelaw. Select papers from the proceedings of the Thirteenth Viking Congress* (Oxford, 2001), pp. 105-23, at 115-18.
8 Edwards, *Vikings in North West England*, pp. 8-10, 19.
9 D. M. O'Sullivan, 'A group of pagan burials from Cumbria?', *ASSAH*, 9 (1996), 15-23; G. Halsall, 'The Viking presence in England? The burial evidence reconsidered', in D. M. Hadley and J. D. Richards (eds), *Cultures in Contact: Scandinavian settlement in England in the ninth and tenth centuries* (Turnhout, 2000), pp. 259-76, at 265.
10 F. Elgee, *Early Man in North-East Yorkshire* (Gloucester, 1930), p. 220; F. Elgee and H. W. Elgee, *The Archaeology of Yorkshire* (London, 1933), p. 214; J. D. Richards, 'The case of the missing Vikings: Scandinavian burial in the Danelaw', in S. Lucy and A. Reynolds (eds), *Burial in Early Medieval England and Wales* (London, 2002), pp. 156-70, at 160-1.
11 L. P. Wenham, R. A. Hall, C. M. Briden and D. Stocker, *St Mary Bishophill Junior and St Mary Castlegate*, The Archaeology of York, 8 (2) (York, 1987), p. 83.

12 Shetelig, *Viking Antiquities*, pp. 12–13; S. Margeson, *The Vikings in Norfolk* (Norwich, 1997), p. 15.

13 M. Biddle and B. Kjølbye-Biddle, 'Repton and the "great heathen army", 873–4', in Graham-Campbell, Hall, Jesch and Parsons (eds), *Vikings and the Danelaw*, pp. 45–96, at 60–5.

14 *Ibid.*

15 *Ibid.*, p. 65.

16 *Ibid.*, pp. 85–6.

17 S. Bassett, *Saffron Walden: excavations and research 1972–80*, CBA Research Rep. (London, 1982), p. 13; Richards, 'The case of the missing Vikings', p. 161.

18 Graham-Campbell, 'Pagan Scandinavian burial', pp. 105–6.

19 *Ibid.*, pp. 112, 114.

20 Shetelig, *Viking Antiquities*, p. 79; V. Evison, 'A Viking grave at Sonning, Berks', *Antiq. J.*, 49 (1969), 330–45.

21 A. Rogerson, *A Late Neolithic, Saxon and Medieval Site at Middle Harling, Norfolk*, EAA, 74 (Gressenhall, 1995), pp. 24–5, 79–80, 88–9; Graham-Campbell, 'Pagan Scandinavian burial', pp. 111–12.

22 A. Cox, J. Fox and G. Thomas, 'Sedgeford Historical and Archaeological Research Project, 1997 interim report', *Norfolk Arch.*, 43 (1998), 172–7, at 175; Graham-Campbell, 'Pagan Scandinavian burial', p. 112 and n. 5.

23 A. Rogerson and C. Dallas, *Excavations in Thetford, 1948–59 and 1973–80*, EAA, 22 (Gressenhall, 1984), pp. 53, 105–6.

24 D. Griffiths, 'Settlement and acculturation in the Irish Sea region', in J. Hines, A. Lane and M. Redknap (eds), *Land, Sea and Home* (London, 2004), pp. 125–38, at 135–6.

25 G. Speed and P. Walton Rogers, 'A burial of a viking woman at Adwick-le-Street, South Yorkshire', *Med. Arch.*, 48 (2004), 51–90.

26 Reported in *Curr. Arch.*, 191 (2004), 476–7.

27 M. Pitts, 'Cumbrian heritage', *British Arch.*, 79 (2004), 28–31.

28 J. D. Cowen, 'Viking burials in Cumbria', *TCWAAS*, new ser., 48 (1948), 73–6; Edwards, *Vikings in North West England*, pp. 17–18, 21–2.

29 Graham-Campbell, 'Pagan Scandinavian burial', pp. 106–8.

30 Cowen, 'Viking burials in Cumbria'; Edwards, *Vikings in North West England*, p. 20; Richards, 'The case of the missing Vikings', p. 161.

31 R. A. Hall, *Viking Age York* (London, 1994), p. 45; Richards, *Viking Age England*, pp. 151–2.

32 I. Hodder, 'Social structure and cemeteries: a critical appraisal', in P. Rahtz, T. M. Dickinson and L. Watts (eds), *Anglo-Saxon Cemeteries*, BAR Brit. Ser., 82 (Oxford, 1980), pp. 161–9, at 168; H. Geake, *The Use of Grave goods in Conversion-Period England, c.600–c.850*, BAR Brit. Ser., 261 (Oxford, 1997), p. 127; S. Tarlow, 'The dread of something after death: violation and desecration on the Isle of Man in the tenth century', in J. Carmen (ed.), *Material Harm: Archaeological studies of war and violence* (Skelmorlie, 1997), pp. 133–42, at 139; M. Carver, 'Cemetery and society at Sutton Hoo: five awkward questions and four contradictory answers', in C. Karkov, K. Wickham-Crowley and B. Young (eds),

Spaces of the Living and the Dead: an archaeological dialogue (Oxford, 1999), pp. 1–14, at 8.

33   D. M. Hadley, 'Burial practices in the Northern Danelaw, c.650–1100', *North. Hist.*, 36 (2) (2000), 199–216; G. Halsall, 'The Viking presence in England? The burial evidence reconsidered', in Hadley and Richards (eds), *Cultures in Contact*, pp. 259–76; D. M. Hadley, 'Burial practices in northern England in the tenth and eleventh centuries', in Lucy and Reynolds (eds), *Burial in Early Medieval England and Wales*, pp. 209–28.

34   D. Phillips, 'The pre-Norman cemetery', in D. Phillips and B. Heywood (eds), *Excavations at York Minster, Volume I* (2 parts) (London, 1995), pp. 75–92, at 90–2.

35   R. A. Hall and M. Whyman, 'Settlement and monasticism at Ripon, North Yorkshire, from the 7th to 11th centuries A.D.', *Med. Arch.*, 40 (1996), 62–150, at 127–8; N. Field, 'A possible Saxon cemetery at Swaby', *LHA*, 28 (1993), 45–6.

36   M. J. Darling and D. Gurney, *Caister-on-Sea: excavations by Charles Green 1951–55*, EAA, 60 (Gressenhall, 1993), p. 252.

37   J. Magilton, *The Church of St Helen-on-the-Walls, Aldwark*, The Archaeology of York 10 (1) (York, 1980), p. 15; Jo Buckberry, pers. comm.

38   W. Rodwell and K. Rodwell, *Rivenhall: investigations of a villa, church and village, 1950–1977*, CBA Research Rep., 55 (London, 1985), p. 82; the pin was Roman and had, perhaps, been found during grave-digging at this former villa.

39   A. Rowntree, *The History of Scarborough* (London, 1931), pp. 146–8.

40   M. Johnson, 'Beverley Minster', *Yorkshire Archaeology Today*, 6 (2004), 12.

41   Geake, *The Use of Grave Goods in Conversion-Period England*, p. 154.

42   *Ibid.*, p. 159.

43   B. Ayers, *Excavations Within the North-East Bailey of Norwich Castle*, EAA, 28 (Gressenhall, 1985), p. 27.

44   C. Henderson and P. Bidwell, ' The Saxon minster at Exeter', in S. Pearce (ed.), *The Early Church in Western Britain and Ireland*, BAR Brit. Ser., 102 (Oxford, 1982), pp. 145–75, at 154–5; P. J. Huggins, 'A note on a Viking-style plate from Waltham Abbey, Essex and its implications for a disputed Late-Viking building', *Arch. J.*, 141 (1984), 175–81.

45   Evison, 'A Viking grave at Sonning', 341.

46   R. Kipling and G. Scobie, 'Staple Gardens 1989', *Winchester Museums Service Newsletter*, 6 (1990), 8–9.

47   W. Rodwell and K. Rodwell, 'St Peter's church, Barton-upon-Humber: excavation and structural study, 1978–81', *Antiq. J.*, 62 (1982), 283–315, at 312; N. Bateman, 'The early 11th to mid 12th-century graveyard at Guildhall, City of London', in G. de Boe and F. Verhaeghe (eds), *Death and Burial in Medieval Europe* (Brugge, 1997), pp. 115–20.

48   J. Blair, *Anglo-Saxon Oxfordshire* (Stroud, 1994), pp. 72–3.

49   R. K. Morris, *The Church in British Archaeology*, CBA Research Rep., 47 (London, 1983), pp. 60–1.

50   J. Sills, 'St Peter's church, Holton-le-Clay', *LHA*, 17 (1982), 29–42.

51 T. W. Potter and R. D. Andrews, 'Excavation and survey at St Patrick's chapel and St Peter's church, Heysham, Lancs', *Antiq. J.*, 74 (1994), 55–134, at 124, 127; Hall and Whyman, 'Settlement and monasticism at Ripon', 130.

52 Halsall, 'The Viking presence in England?', pp. 268–9.

53 Reported in *Med. Arch.*, 37 (1993), 285–6.

54 Phillips, 'The pre-Norman cemetery', pp. 75–92.

55 Darling and Gurney, *Caister-on-Sea*, pp. 253–4.

56 B. Kjølbye-Biddle, 'The disposal of the Winchester dead over 2000 years', in S. Bassett (ed.), *Death in Towns. Urban responses to the dying and the dead, 100–1600* (London, 1992), pp. 210–47, at 227–31.

57 Rodwell and Rodwell, *Rivenhall*, p. 82; A. Boddington, *Raunds Furnells: the Anglo-Saxon church and churchyard* (London, 1996), pp. 38–42; T. J. Miles, 'The excavation of a Saxon cemetery and part of the Norman castle at North Walk, Barnstaple', *Proceedings of the Devon Archaeological Society*, hereafter: *PDAS*, 44 (1986), 59–84; J. L. Buckberry and D. M. Hadley, 'Fieldwork at Chapel Lane, Fillingham', *LHA*, 36 (2001), 11–18; A. Graham and S. Davies, *Excavations in Trowbridge, Wiltshire, 1977 and 1986–88*, Wessex Archaeological Report, 2 (Salisbury, 1993), pp. 38–41; Cherry Hinton was reported in *Med. Arch.*, 44 (2000), 252.

58 H. Mytum, 'Kellington church', *Curr. Arch.*, 133 (1993), 15–17; P. Hill, *Whithorn and St Ninian: the excavation of a monastic town, 1984–91* (Stroud, 1997), pp. 472–3; Miles, 'The excavation of a Viking cemetery', 66; A. Selkirk, 'Llandough', *Curr. Arch.*, 146 (1996), 73–7; Buckberry and Hadley, 'Fillingham', 15–16; W. White, *Skeletal Remains from the Cemetery of St Nicholas Shambles, City of London* (London, 1988), p. 24; Boddington *Raunds, Furnells*, p. 42.

59 See also Richards, 'Scandinavian burial', p. 170.

60 Buckberry and Hadley, 'Fillingham'; Rodwell and Rodwell, 'St Peter's Church Barton-upon-Humber'; J. M. Boden and J. B. Whitwell, 'Barrow-upon-Humber', *LHA*, 14 (1979), 66–7; F. J. Green, *St Helen's Cumberworth*, unpublished report by Hampshire Archaeology (1997); N. Field, 'Stow church', *LHA*, 19 (1984), 105–6; N. Field and I. George, 'Archaeology in Lincolnshire', *LHA*, 31 (1996), 49–68, at 59; Sills, 'St Peter's Church Holton-le-Clay'; P. Phillips, *Archaeology and Landscape Studies in North Lincolnshire*, BAR Brit. Ser., 208, 2 vols (1989), I, p. 5; G. Trimble, *Archaeological Investigation of a Pipeline along St Giles' Avenue, Sleaford, Lincolnshire*, unpublished report by Archaeological Project Services (1997); see Field, 'A possible Saxon cemetery at Swaby'; A. White, 'Archaeology in Lincolnshire and South Humberside', *LHA*, 13 (1978), 75–90, at 81–2; N. Field, *Castle Farm Torksey: exploratory excavations*, unpublished report by Lindsey Archaeological Services (1990); B. Gilmour and D. Stocker, *St Mark's Church and Cemetery*, The Archaeology of Lincoln 13 (1) (London, 1986); A. Vince, 'Lincoln in the early medieval era, between the 5th and 9th centuries', in D. Stocker (ed.), *The City by the Pool. Assessing the archaeology of the city of Lincoln* (Oxford, 2003), pp. 141–56, at 149–51, 154–5.

61 Rodwell and Rodwell, 'St Peter's Church Barton-upon-Humber', 291–2.

62 Phillips, *Archaeology and Landscape*, I, p. 5; A. Reynolds, *Later Anglo-Saxon England* (Stroud, 1999), pp. 105–8.

63 Gilmour and Stocker, *St Mark's Church*, pp. 20–1.

64 P. Everson and D. Stocker, *Corpus of Anglo-Saxon Stone Sculpture, Vol. 5. Lincolnshire* (Oxford, 1999), p. 77.

65 See, for example, L. Hedeager, 'Kingdoms, ethnicity and material culture: Denmark in a European perspective', in M. Carver (ed.), *The Age of Sutton Hoo* (Woodbridge, 1992), pp. 279–300.

66 R. Cramp, *Corpus of Anglo-Saxon Stone Sculpture, Vol. 1. County Durham and Northumberland* (Oxford, 1984), *passim*; R. N. Bailey and R. Cramp, *Corpus of Anglo-Saxon Stone Sculpture, Vol. 2. Cumberland, Westmorland and Lancashire North-of-the-Sands* (Oxford, 1988), *passim*; Everson and Stocker, *Corpus of Anglo-Saxon Sculpture: Lincolnshire*, *passim*; J. T. Lang, *Corpus of Anglo-Saxon Stone Sculpture, Vol. 3: York and Eastern Yorkshire* (Oxford, 1991), *passim*; *idem*, *Corpus of Anglo-Saxon Stone Sculpture, Vol. 6: Northern Yorkshire* (Oxford, 2001), *passim*.

67 D. Stocker, 'Monuments and merchants: irregularities in the distribution of stone sculpture in Lincolnshire and Yorkshire in the tenth century', in Hadley and Richards (eds), *Cultures in Contact*, pp. 179–212, at 179–80.

68 Gilmour and Stocker, *St Mark's Lincoln*, pp. 20–1; Phillips, 'The pre-Norman cemetery', p. 84.

69 P. H. Sawyer, *Kings and Vikings: Scandinavia and Europe AD 700–1100* (London, 1982), pp. 49–50.

70 T. Ramskou, 'Viking Age cremation graves in Denmark. A survey', *Acta Archaeologica*, 21 (1950), 137–82; Richards *et al.*, 'The Viking barrow cemetery at Heath Wood, Ingleby', 93–7.

71 See, for example, E. Roesdahl, *Viking Age Denmark* (London, 1982), pp. 164–71; L. Dommasnes, 'Male/female roles and ranks in late Iron Age Norway', in R. Bertelsen (ed.), *Were They All Men? An examination of sex roles in prehistoric society* (Stavanger, 1987), pp. 65–78; A. Pedersen, 'Similar finds – different meanings?', in C. K. Jensen and K. H. Nielsen (eds), *Burial and Society, The chronological and social analysis of archaeological burial data* (Aarhus, 1997), pp. 171–83.

72 F. Svanberg, *Death Rituals in South-East Scandinavia AD 800–1000* (Lund, 2003), pp. 20–4, 27–9, 39–41, 55–7, 70–3, 90–5, 98–101, 108–9, 117–21, 126–9.

73 A. C. Sørensen, 'Ladby: ship, cemetery and settlement', in Jensen and Nielsen (eds), *Burial and Society*, pp. 165–70; J. Graham-Campbell (ed.), *Cultural Atlas of the Viking World* (Oxford, 1994), pp. 34–5, 42–3, 68–73.

74 *Ibid.*, *Cultural Atlas of the Viking World*, pp. 68–72.

75 A.-S. Gräslund, *Birka IV: The Burial Customs, A Study of the Graves of Björkö* (Stockholm, 1980), pp. 7–49.

76 J. Brønsted, 'Danish inhumation graves of the Viking Age. A survey', *Acta Archaeologica*, 7 (1936), 81–228.

77 See, for example, N. Stoodley, *The Spindle and the Spear: a critical enquiry into the construction and meaning of gender in the early Anglo-Saxon burial rite*, BAR Brit. Ser., 288 (Oxford, 1999), pp. 8–10.

78 Griffiths, 'Settlement and acculturation', pp. 131–8.

79 M. P. Evison, ' "All in the bones": evaluating the biological evidence for contact and migration', in Hadley and Richards (eds), *Cultures in Contact*, pp. 277–94.

80 P. Budd, A. Millard, C. Chenery, S. Lucy and C. Roberts, 'Investigating popula-
    tion movement by stable isotope analysis: a report from Britain', *Antiquity*, 78
    (2004), 127–41.
81 *Ibid.*, 137–8 R. A. Hall, 'Blood of the Vikings – the riddle at Riccall', *Yorkshire
    Archaeology Today*, 2 (2002), 5.
82 For the earlier Anglo-Saxon period, see S. Lucy, 'Housewives, warriors and
    slaves? Sex and gender in Anglo-Saxon burials', in J. Moore and E. Scott (eds),
    *Invisible People and Processes: writing gender and childhood into European
    Archaeology*, (London, 1997), pp. 150–68; *idem*, *The Early Anglo-Saxon
    Cemeteries of East Yorkshire*, BAR Brit. Ser., 272 (Oxford, 1998); Stoodley, *The
    Spindle and the Spear*, pp. 105–18.
83 Phillips, 'The pre-Norman cemetery', pp. 83–4, 89–90; B. Kjølbye-Biddle, 'Iron-
    bound coffins and coffin-fittings from the pre-Norman cemetery', in Phillips and
    Heywood (eds), *Excavations at York Minster*, pp. 489–521, at 489–99.
84 Boddington, *Raunds Furnells*, pp. 38–48; Darling and Gurney, *Caister-on-Sea*,
    pp. 48–55, 253; Rodwell and Rodwell, *Rivenhall*, pp. 82–3; D. M. Hadley and
    J. L. Buckberry, 'Caring for the dead in the later Anglo-Saxon England', in F. Tinti
    (ed.), *Pastoral Care in Late Anglo-Saxon England* (Woodbridge, 2005),
    pp. 12–47.
85 Boddington, *Raunds Furnells*, pp. 55–7, 69; P. Hill (ed.), *Whithorn and
    St Ninian: the excavation of a monastic town 1984–91* (Stroud, 1997), pp. 164–72;
    S. Lucy and A. Reynolds, 'Burial in early medieval England and Wales: past,
    present and future', in Lucy and Reynolds (eds), *Burial in Early Medieval
    England and Wales*, pp. 1–23, on pp. 17–20.
86 Kipling and Scobie, 'Staple Gardens'; Boddington, *Raunds Furnells*, p. 52;
    Graham and Davies, *Excavations in Trowbridge*, p. 39.
87 Boddington, *Raunds Furnells*, pp. 55–7.
88 Kjølbye-Biddle, 'Winchester Dead', p. 227; D. M. Hadley, 'Engendering the grave
    in later Anglo-Saxon England' (forthcoming: 2004 Chacmool Conference); Ayers,
    Excavations Within the North-East Bailey of Norwich Castle, p. 51.
89 However, we have to be careful about interpretations of such evidence, as clusters
    of male burials in some cemeteries, such as those at Castle Green, Hereford and
    Beckery Chapel at Glastonbury (Som) were probably members of religious com-
    munities: see Hadley, 'Engendering the grave'.
90 P. Wade-Martins, *Excavations at North Elmham Park 1967–72*, EAA, 9, 2 vols
    (Gressenhall, 1980), I, p. 189.
91 Hall and Whyman, 'Settlement and monasticism', 112–13, 122.
92 J. Bartlett and R. Mackey, 'Excavations on Walkington Wold', *East Riding
    Archaeologist*, 1 (2), (1972), 1–93; G. Hayman, 'Further excavations at the former
    Goblin Works, Ashtead', *Surrey Archaeological Collections*, 81 (1991–2), 1–18;
    D. Liddell, 'Excavations at Meon Hill', *Proceedings of the Hampshire Field Club
    and Archaeological Society*, hereafter: *PHFCAS*, 12 (1933), 127–162; N. Hill,
    'Excavations on Stockbridge Down 1935–36', *PHFCAS*, 13 (1936–7), 247–259;
    J. Stone, 'Saxon interments on Roche Court Down, Winterslow', *Wiltshire
    Archaeological and Natural History Magazine*, hereafter: *WANHM*, 45 (1932),

568–99; Reynolds, *Late Anglo-Saxon England*, pp. 105–10; Hadley, 'Engendering the grave'.

93 V. Thompson, 'Constructing salvation: a homiletic and penitential context for late Anglo-Saxon burial practice', in Lucy and Reynolds (eds), *Burial in Early Medieval England and Wales*, pp. 229–40, at 230–4.

94 See also Halsall, 'The Viking presence in England?', pp. 270–1.

95 Richards, *et al.*, 'The Viking barrow cemetery at Heath Wood, Ingleby', 54–68.

96 D. M. Hadley, 'Gender and material culture in Viking-Age England' (forthcoming).

97 See, for example, G. Halsall, 'Female status and power in early Merovingian central Austrasia: the burial evidence', *EME*, 5 (1) (1996), 1–24; *idem*, 'Burial, ritual and Merovingian society', in J. Hill and M. Swan (eds), *The Community, the Family and the Saint: patterns of power in early medieval Europe* (Turnhout, 1998), pp. 325–38; Carver, 'Cemetery and society at Sutton Hoo'.

98 Cramp, *Corpus of Anglo-Saxon Stone Sculpture: County Durham and Northumberland*, pp. 31–2, 53–9.

99 Everson and Stocker, *Corpus of Anglo-Saxon Stone Sculpture: Lincolnshire*, pp. 147–52.

100 J. Crick, 'Women, posthumous benefaction and family strategy in pre-Conquest England', *J. Brit. Stud.*, 38 (1999), 399–42.

101 P. Addyman, 'The attackers return', in E. Roesdahl (ed.), *The Vikings in England* (London, 1982), pp. 55–68, at 61.

102 Stoodley, *The Spindle and the Spear*, pp. 80–1.

103 This argument was previously developed in D. M. Hadley, 'Negotiating gender, family and status in Anglo-Saxon burial practices, *c*.600–950', in J. Smith and L. Brubaker (eds), *Gender in the Early Medieval World. East and West, 300–900* (Cambridge, 2004), pp. 301–23.

104 J. T. Lang, 'The hogback: a Viking colonial monument', *ASSAH*, 3 (1983), 85–176; Stocker, 'Monuments and merchants', pp. 198–9; Hadley, 'Negotiating gender', p. 320.

105 Boddington, *Raunds Furnells*, p. 45.

106 J. Crick, 'Posthumous obligation and family identity', in W. O. Fraser and A. Tyrell (eds), *Social Identity in Early Medieval Britain* (London, 2000), pp. 193–208, at 199–205.

107 D. Stocker and P. Everson, 'Five towns funerals: decoding diversity in Danelaw stone sculpture', in Graham-Campbell, Hall, Jesch and Parsons (eds), *Vikings and the Danelaw*, pp. 223–43, at 225–7.

108 J. Barrow, 'Survival and mutation: ecclesiastical institutions in the Danelaw in the ninth and tenth centuries', in Hadley and Richards (eds), *Cultures in Contact*, pp. 155–76, at 170.

109 Hadley, 'Negotiating gender', pp. 318–19.

110 E. Van Houts, *Memory and Gender in Medieval Europe, 900–1200* (Basingstoke, 1999), pp. 65–120.

111 Lang, *Corpus of Anglo-Saxon Stone Sculpture: York and Eastern Yorkshire*, pp. 84–5, 145, 151, 187–9.

112 J. T. Lang, 'The distinctiveness of Viking colonial art', in P. Szarmarch (ed.), *Sources of Anglo-Saxon Culture* (Michigan, 1986), pp. 243–60, at 252 for the quotation.

113 Stocker, 'Monuments and merchants', pp. 200–6; see also Everson and Stocker, *Corpus of Anglo-Saxon Stone Sculpture: Lincolnshire*, pp. 76–9.

114 C. R. Hart, *The Danelaw* (London, 1992), pp. 11–12; D. Stocker and P. Everson, pers. comm.

115 Hadley and Buckberry, 'Caring for the dead'.

116 Richards *et al.*, 'The Viking barrow cemetery at Heath Wood, Ingleby', 66; Halsall, 'The Viking presence in England?', pp. 263, 272.

117 D. Griffiths, 'Settlement and acculturation' 131–8.

118 J. D. Richards, 'Boundaries and cult centres: Viking burial in Derbyshire', in Graham-Campbell, Hall, Jesch and Parsons (eds), *Vikings and the Danelaw*, pp. 97–104, at 102.

119 *Ibid.*

120 E. James, 'Burial and status in the early medieval West', *TRHS*, 5th ser., 29 (1989), 23–40; Halsall, 'The Viking presence in England?', pp. 264–7.

Epilogue

The focus of this volume has been on the Scandinavian impact on England, but in drawing the discussion to a close, it is important to set the subject in a broader context. It is apparent that the Scandinavian settlement in England proceeded along different lines from other regions of north-western Europe. It is important to bear this in mind, in part because it serves to highlight the potential diversity of Scandinavian impact on – and interaction with – other societies, and also because it seems likely that the more detailed documentary record from some other regions provides important parallels for events that are poorly documented in England. This broader context also serves to remind us that, while the Scandinavian settlements appear to have followed genuinely different trajectories in other regions, interpretations of the Scandinavian impact are also commonly shaped both by the diversity of the available evidence and also by historiographical biases.

In Frankia, while archaeological evidence for Scandinavian activity is scarce, there is copious documentary evidence for the Scandinavian raids and also for the diverse range of interaction between Scandinavian armies (and their leaders) and the Frankish secular and ecclesiastical elite.[1] While the Scandinavians have been accredited with all manner of calamities that befell the Carolingian Empire: from the destruction of churches and cities to the collapse of the authority of the monarchy and the rise of princely power, historians now more regularly stress the continuities with earlier institutions; the willingness with which many of the vikings 'opted in' to Frankish society; and the encouragement that they received to do this.[2] Frankish kings were sometimes, for example, inclined to employ raiders against rival raiding groups: as did Charles the Bald in 860 when he offered a certain Weland 3,000 pounds of silver to attack a viking group on the Seine, although, in the event, the two viking groups joined forces.[3] Raiders were also sometimes called upon to assist one or other side in an internecine dispute, as occurred when the Danish king Harald was employed by Lothar against his father Louis the Pious in 833.[4] Raiders were paid increasingly huge sums of silver during the course of the ninth century, to depart from Frankish territory or to desist from further destruction. For example, in 857 the churches of St-Denis, St-Stephen and St-Germain in Paris paid 'a great ransom in cash to save these churches from being burned' after several other churches in the city had been destroyed.[5] The Franks also sometimes responded to raiders by ceding them territory. In 841, Lothar granted the island of Walcheren off the coast of Frisia to the above-mentioned Harald, and in 911 Hrólfr (or Rollo), the defeated leader of a raiding party active in the Seine valley, was granted territory around Rouen by the West Frankish king Charles the Simple, in order that he would protect the maritime ports from other Scandinavian raiders.[6] This latter grant was to be the basis of the later duchy of Normandy. Yet, despite the fact that the descendants of Hrólfr remained as the rulers of this territory, there is very little that can be said to be Scandinavian about Normandy. Scandinavian place-names are clustered around Rouen, Cherbourg and Bayeux, and the presence of Celtic naming elements among these names suggests that the settlers included individuals who were native to Ireland or the western Isles of Scotland, or else individuals of Scandinavian descent who had settled in those regions.[7] Little Norse impact on the language can be identified.[8] The archaeological evidence for Scandinavian settlement in Normandy is also minimal. For example, funerary evidence amounts to little more than the burial of a woman at Pitres, a grave which contained two oval brooches of Scandinavian-type, and some ship-shaped stone settings found on the beach near Cherbourg, containing cremations.[9] As in England, one suspects that the remains of the settlers and their descendants are largely to be found in inhumation cemeteries without grave goods.[10]

In contrast, Brittany, which was under Scandinavian control for only around twenty years in the earlier tenth century, has produced considerably more archaeological evidence of Scandinavian settlement. Brittany had only been brought under Carolingian rule in the early ninth century, and became a main focus of viking assaults following the aforementioned settlement around Rouen. It was conquered by a Scandinavian force in 919, after which the Breton leaders fled, but in 939 the region was wrested back from the Scandinavians when the former rulers returned from exile.[11] Despite the short period of control, the archaeological evidence for

Scandinavian activity is considerably more visible than in Normandy.[12] Two fortifications excavated in Brittany, at Camp de Péran and Trans, were occupied, if not constructed, by the Scandinavians, to judge from the recovery of such items as a St Peter's penny from York at Péran.[13] An elaborate burial has been excavated on the island of Groix, off the western coast of Brittany, in which a longship was found with another smaller boat inside in a striking setting, approached by a processional way of standing stones. The burial included the bodies of an adult and an adolescent, accompanied by a rich assemblage of objects, including weapons, riding gear, gold and silver jewellery, ivory gaming pieces, smith's tools, and farming equipment. The ship was apparently surrounded by twenty-four shields, then set on fire, and eventually covered under a mound.[14]

The contrast between Brittany and Normandy reveals that the visibility of the Scandinavians in the archaeological record is not a straightforward guide to the extent or longevity of their impact; indeed, it is arguable that short-lived, insecure occupation of a region is likely to result in more dramatic material expressions of Scandinavian identity than in region of more well-established settlement. The difficulties of identifying specifically Scandinavian activity in the archaeological record are also highlighted by the written record, which reveals that items of Frankish manufacture were sought by the Scandinavian raiders: for example, legislation issued in 864 by Charles the Bald prohibited the sale of Frankish swords to the Northmen, who were apparently also keen to acquire Frankish horse-fittings.[15]

In Ireland, there is also extensive contemporary documentary evidence for the Scandinavian raids and settlement, particularly the impact on the Church – about which there has been considerable scholarly debate.[16] A recent survey concluded that although many raids on churches are documented in the ninth and tenth centuries in Ireland, nevertheless, the major early churches were still important churches after the Viking Age, while the departure of Irish clerics for the Carolingian court was not necessarily prompted only by the desire to escape viking assaults, but also by the lure of the intellectual and religious renaissance at the Carolingian court.[17] Archaeological evidence for the settlers is overwhelmingly located in urban contexts, and, as a consequence, debate about the Scandinavian impact has focused on the contribution of the settlers to the development of urbanisation in Ireland. For a long time, towns were regarded as specifically non-Irish developments, and the Scandinavian settlements were considered as the catalyst for urban development, prompted in part by the experiences of the settlers of the towns of other parts of western Europe. Whether tenth-century Irish towns were genuinely towns or 'colonial way-stations' – more dependent on long-distance trade than links with the rural hinterlands – has also been extensively debated.[18] More recently, however, the Irish contribution to urbanisation has been stressed, in particular the role of monasteries as centres of manufacture and trade.[19] In contrast, archaeological traces of Scandinavian settlement in a rural context have proved more elusive, although, as John Bradley has argued, it is inconceivable that the Norse could have retained control of Dublin without at least some Scandinavian settlement in the surrounding hinterland.[20] A recent study by John Sheehan, of hoards, largely from rural contexts, has suggested that they reflect a variety of types of contact between the Scandinavians and the Irish, with silver ornaments (including Scandinavian-type arm-rings) being particularly associated with hill-forts, and interpreted as items of social display, while ingots and hacksilver are commonly found on crannogs and at ecclesiastical sites (especially in the vicinity of Dublin) and are deemed representative of economic activity.[21]

Written evidence for Scandinavian settlement in Scotland is far less plentiful than that for Frankia and Ireland, and much of it is contained in the later and problematic sagas.[22] Thus, it is the archaeological record that has driven debate about the Scandinavian impact on Scotland and its isles. The archaeological evidence for Scandinavian influence is overwhelmingly to be found in rural contexts, and, unlike in other parts of the British Isles, both settlements and cemeteries that reveal evidence for Scandinavian activity have been excavated.[23] Examples include the elaborate burials at Càrn a'Bharraich (Oronsay), Kiloran Bay (Colonsay), Ballinaby (Islay) and Westness (Rousay), where burials in boats and in oval-shaped graves lined with stones, perhaps intended to represent ships, have been excavated at the site of a pre-viking cemetery.[24] Settlements deemed indicative of Scandinavian occupation, on the basis of new house forms and Scandinavian-style artefacts, include Jarlshof (Shetland), Buckquoy (Orkney) and the Brough of Birsay (Orkney).[25] Indeed, such is the abundance of evidence that a recent review observed that 'Viking-age Scotland must provide one of the clearest examples of population movement into previously occupied territory known to archaeology'.[26] On some of the Scottish islands the Scandinavian influence is deemed so overwhelming that there has been considerable debate over the possibility that the indigenous populations were not only overwhelmed but even eradicated in some regions by the settlers.[27] Yet, a number of sites of apparent Scandinavian settlement have produced indigenous-style material culture, including pins and pottery, and these suggest some level of interaction with the local population, as does the fact that a number of these sites occupy the locations of earlier settlements.[28] The study of the Scandinavian settlements in Scotland routinely encompasses a much longer time-frame (often expanding into the fourteenth century) than do studies of Scandinavians in other regions, in part because of evidence for ongoing contact with Norway, and in part because of the continuing political significance of the earldom of Orkney, created during the period of Norse domination.[29] It has recently been argued by James Barrett that many of the divergent interpretations of the Scandinavian impact on Scotland have arisen, in part, from competing historiographical traditions, but he cautions that in seeking new ways of approaching the available evidence we must be aware not only of previous historiographical preoccupations, but also of the range of variables that undoubtedly underpinned the Scandinavian impact (including the scale of the population movement), but also issues relating to power and social status and the diverse ways in which this is manifest in the archaeological record.[30]

Scandinavian impact on the Isle of Man is similarly not well-documented in contemporary sources, but archaeological and place-name evidence indicate that it was substantial. Scandinavian influence is indicated by burials accompanied by grave goods, such as seven burials at St Patrick's Isle, Peel, including the burial of a female accompanied by two knives, a bone comb, a work bag, needles and shears, and a necklace. However, the possibility that the Scandinavians adopted existing burial grounds is raised by this evidence. For example, in the case of the Peel burials, they are scattered among a larger cemetery consisting of around 300 burials in stone cists, which suggests that the settlers used a pre-existing cemetery.[31] Meanwhile, at Balladoole, a boat burial including a male and a female and a lavish array of grave goods was placed on top of a pre-existing cemetery, and in this case although the Scandinavian impact was dramatic, whether it was an act of assimilation or a slighting of the earlier cemetery is debatable.[32] Place-names on the Isle of Man contain elements from various parts of Scandinavia, but also suggest that some of the settlers came via England, given the prevalence of names formed with the element -by, which are also common in northern England, but not in other regions of western Britain that seem to have been settled largely from northern Scandinavia.[33] Around twenty hoards dating to between the late ninth and early eleventh centuries are known from Man, including those from Ballaquayle (Douglas) and Ballacamaish (Andreas). These hoards include coins from England, Dublin and Frankia, and also a number of silver arm-rings similar to examples from the western Isles of Scotland and Ireland. While varying in design, these arm-rings are typically of a similar weight and, accordingly, these have been interpreted as a form of currency, which reflects the economic links between the various regions surrounding the Irish Sea.[34] These economic links are also reflected in the distribution of silver 'ball-brooches', which have been found in Shetland, Orkney, Cumbria and Ireland, and which are thought to have been manufactured in Man – given the similarity of design with some of the sculptures from the island. Accordingly, it is the Irish Sea dimension of the Scandinavian settlement in Man that has accorded much recent discussion. Sculptures carved on slate incorporate both Christian and Scandinavian imagery, and provide a strong indication of interaction between the settlers and the indigenous peoples, although other indications of the fate of the Christian Church on Man are elusive, since the rough-built chapels, or 'keeils', are difficult to date closely.[35] A number of rectangular and bow-sided buildings have been interpreted as evidence for Scandinavian impact, such as those from Vowlan and The Braaid. However, there is little associated material culture or dating evidence, and, in this respect, studies of these remains are faced with a range of interpretative issues that are familiar to the study of the visibility of the Scandinavian imprint in the archaeology of rural settlement elsewhere in Britain.[36]

The Scandinavian impact on the various kingdoms of Wales has generally been deemed to have been slight.[37] A series of raids and battles are recorded in accounts preserved in later medieval chronicles, and there is a handful of place-names, largely in coastal districts, that are indicative of Scandinavian influence. Scandinavian activity has, until recently, proven elusive in the archaeological record, and was limited to a handful of burials accompanied by grave goods, including a burial in a stone-lined grave accompanied by a knife and a spearhead at Talacre (Flintshire) and the burial of a female accompanied by a bone comb at Benllech on Anglesey; a number of coin hoards, such as those from Bangor and from Red Wharf Bay on Anglesey; and sculptures displaying Scandinavian influence, such as those from Penmon on Anglesey.[38] However, recent excavations at Llanbedrgoch on Anglesey have transformed our picture, as they have revealed Scandinavian influence on a pre-existing manufacturing site. The enclosure boundary was rebuilt in stone during the ninth century, and new types of buildings, utilising the sill-beam construction method, appeared in the late ninth or tenth centuries. Artefacts indicative of Scandinavian influence include hacksilver, a fragment of an oval brooch, and a copper-alloy belt buckle decorated with Borre-style ring-chain ornament. A range of other items reflect trading contacts with the wider Irish Sea territory, including a lead trial-piece, which appears to have been for manufacturing an arm-ring of the type already mentioned as being common in this region;

lead weights of a type found in Man, Ireland and the western Isles; fragments of the aforementioned arm-rings; and decorated ring-headed pins.[39]
While it is difficult to know whether Scandinavians settled in or even took
over the Llanbedrgoch settlement, the recent excavations have reinforced
the importance of considering the Scandinavian impact on Wales in its
broader Irish Sea context.[40]

   This all-too-brief survey of the evidence for, and debates about, the
Scandinavian impact on other regions highlights the variability of that
impact, the inconsistent nature of the evidence and also the differing preoccupations of students of the Viking Age across north-western Europe.
This broader context also reinforces the notion that there was nothing predictable about the Scandinavian impact on England, or about the ways in
which the Scandinavians constructed and expressed their identities following settlement. There was clearly no single experience of settlement or
of interaction with the local population and their leaders – rather it is
apparent that the Scandinavian impact was expressed differently among
diverse social groups and within differing settlement contexts. We have
seen that the imprint of the settlers can rarely be found anywhere in
England in an undiluted fashion, and it has been argued that the major
dynamic visible in the written, linguistic and archaeological record is the
interaction of the settlers with native peoples and institutions. This is not
to imply that the Scandinavian settlement was conducted in a harmonious
fashion, but it does suggest that the Scandinavians frequently responded to
the circumstances of conquest and settlement by appropriating aspects of
local society, economy, culture and behaviour. What has also emerged from
this study is the enormous potential for interrogating familiar bodies of
data in new and exciting fashion, and also the potential that archaeology holds for exposing new sites that can transform the study of the
Scandinavian impact. It can be concluded that it is only through an interdisciplinary approach that we can enhance our understanding of the
Scandinavian impact on Anglo-Saxon England.

   Throughout this volume, the vikings of popular stereotype have been
absent, not because of any desire to deny the damage caused and terror
engendered by these undoubtedly fearsome raiders, but because in seeking
to understand the impact of the Scandinavians, particularly once settlement
had commenced, we need to consider not only the 'otherness' of the settlers, but also what they had in common with the local population and the
ways in which interaction proceeded. As Janet Nelson has recently, and
aptly, observed of the Scandinavians who travelled to and settled in other
parts of Europe 'the ties that bound were not age-old inborn solidarities but

man-made lordship and fidelity . . . differentiated levels of social power and of rank and status . . . partnerships of mutual interest'.[41] Scandinavian settlers of the later ninth and tenth centuries have been addressed in this study not simply as people from a different ethnic and cultural background, but also as groups and individuals of differing social status and with diverse roles in society. It is to be hoped that future study of Anglo–Scandinavian interaction will not lose sight of the need to be sensitive to the multiplicity of identities that the settlers and the local populations possessed.

Notes

1 P. H. Sawyer, 'Conquest and colonisation: Scandinavians in the Danelaw and in Normandy', in H. Bekker-Nielsen, P. Foote and O. Olsen (eds), *Proceedings of the Eighth Viking Congress* (Odense, 1981), pp. 123–31; *idem*, *Kings and Vikings. Scandinavia and Europe AD700–1100* (London, 1982), pp. 78–92; J. Graham-Campbell (ed.), *Cultural Atlas of the Viking World* (New York, 1994), pp. 142–6.

2 A recent summary is J. L. Nelson, 'England and the continent in the ninth century: II, the Vikings and the others', *TRHS*, 13 (2003), 1–28.

3 J. L. Nelson, *The Annals of St-Bertin* (Manchester, 1991), pp. 95–6, 98–9, 110–11; *idem*, 'The Frankish Empire', in P. H. Sawyer (ed.), *The Oxford Illustrated History of the Vikings* (Oxford, 1997), pp. 19–47, at 36.

4 *Ibid.*, pp. 23–4.

5 Nelson, *The Annals of St-Bertin*, p. 85.

6 *Ibid.*, p. 51; Nelson, 'The Frankish Empire', pp. 30–1; D. Bates, *Normandy Before 1066* (London, 1982), pp. 2–43.

7 G. Fellows-Jensen, 'Scandinavian place-names and Viking settlement in Normandy: a review', *Namn och Bygd*, 76 (1988), 113–37; Graham-Campbell (ed.), *Cultural Atlas of the Viking World*, p. 145.

8 Sawyer, 'Conquest and colonisation', p. 124.

9 Graham-Campbell (ed.), *Cultural Atlas of the Viking World*, p. 145.

10 For excavated examples, see E. Zadora-Rio, 'The making of churchyards and parish territories in the early-medieval landscape of France and England in the 7th–12th centuries: a reconsideration', *Med. Arch.*, 47 (2003), 1–19.

11 N. Price, *The Vikings in Brittany* (London, 1989), pp. 39–51.

12 *Ibid.*, pp. 54–85.

13 *Ibid.*, pp. 55–8.

14 *Ibid.*, pp. 64–74.

15 Nelson, 'The Frankish Empire', pp. 37–8.

16 A. T. Lucas, 'The plundering and burning of churches in Ireland, 7th to 16th century', in E. Rynne (ed.), *North Munster Studies. Essays in commemoration of Monsignor Michael Moloney* (Limerick, 1967), pp. 172–229; Sawyer, *Kings and Vikings*, pp. 95–6.

17 D. Ó Corráin, 'Ireland, Wales, Man and the Hebrides', in Sawyer (ed.), *History of the Vikings*, pp. 83–109, at 83–97.

18 Summarised in J. Bradley, 'The interpretation of Scandinavian settlement in Ireland', in J. Bradley (ed.), *Settlement and Society in Medieval Ireland* (Dublin, 1988), pp. 49–78.

19 H. Clarke, 'The topographical development of early medieval Dublin', in H. Clarke (ed.), *Medieval Dublin: the making of a metropolis* (Blackrock, 1990), pp. 52–69; P. Wallace, 'The origins of Dublin', in *ibid.*, pp. 70–97.

20 Bradley, 'The interpretation of Scandinavian settlement in Ireland'.

21 J. Sheehan, 'Social and economic integration in Viking-Age Ireland: the evidence of the hoards', in J. Hines, A. Lane and M. Redknap (eds), *Land, Sea and Home* (Leeds, 2004), pp. 177–88.

22 J. Graham-Campbell and C. Batey, *Vikings in Scotland: an archaeological survey* (Edinburgh, 1998), pp. 43–6.

23 *Ibid.*, pp. 113–78.

24 *Ibid.*, pp. 113–25, 135–8.

25 *Ibid.*, pp. 155–67.

26 J. H. Barrett, 'Beyond war or peace: the study of culture contact in Viking-Age Scotland', in Hines, Lane and Redknap (eds), *Land, Sea and Home*, pp. 207–18, at 207.

27 *Ibid.*, pp. 209–13; B. Crawford, *Scandinavian Scotland* (Leicester, 1987), pp. 25–30.

28 Graham-Campbell and Batey, *Vikings in Scotland*, pp. 171–8 for discussion of Pool (Orkney) and The Udal (North Uist).

29 See, for example, Graham-Campbell (ed.), *Cultural Atlas of the Viking World*, pp. 148–54; M. Parker Pearson, H. Smith, J. Mulville and M. Brennand, 'Cille Pheadair: the life and times of a Norse-period farmstead c.1000–1300', in Hines, Lane and Redknap (eds), *Land, Sea and Home*, pp. 235–54.

30 Barrett, 'Beyond war or peace', pp. 213–17.

31 Graham-Campbell (ed.), *Cultural Atlas of the Viking World*, pp. 157–8.

32 M. Cubbon, 'The archaeology of the vikings in the Isle of Man', in C. Fell, P. Foote, J. Graham-Campbell and R. Thomson (eds), *The Viking Age in the Isle of Man. Select papers from the Ninth Viking Congress* (London, 1983), pp. 13–26, at 16–18; S. Tarlow, 'The dread of something after death: violation and desecration on the Isle of Man in the tenth century', in J. Carman (ed.), *Material Harm: Archaeological Studies of War and Violence* (Skelmorlie, 1997), pp. 133–42.

33 G. Fellows-Jensen, 'Scandinavian settlement in the Isle of Man and north-west England: the place-name evidence', in Fell, Foote, Graham-Campbell and Thomson (eds), *The Viking Age in the Isle of Man*, pp. 37–52, on pp. 46–9.

34 J. Graham-Campbell, 'Viking-Age silver hoards from Man', in Fell, Foote, Graham-Campbell and Thomson (eds), *The Viking Age in the Isle of Man*, pp. 53–80, at 62–70.

35 S. Margeson, 'On the iconography of the Manx crosses', in Fell, Foote, Graham-Campbell and Thomson (eds), *The Viking Age in the Isle of Man*, pp. 95–106; R. I. Page, 'The Manx rune-stones', in *ibid.*, pp. 133–46; D. M. Wilson, 'The art of the Manx crosses of the Viking Age', in *ibid.*, pp. 175–87; C. D. Morris, 'The survey and excavations at Keeill Vael, Druidale in their context', in *ibid.*, pp. 107–31.

36 M. Cubbon, 'The archaeology of the Vikings in the Isle of Man', in C. Fell, P. Foote, J. Graham-Campbell and R. Thomson (eds), *The Viking Age in the Isle of Man*.

Select papers from the Ninth Viking Congress (London, 1983), pp. 13–26, at 18–19;
J. D. Richards, 'Identifying Anglo-Scandinavian settlements', in D. M. Hadley and
J. D. Richards (eds), *Cultures in Contact: Scandinavian settlement in England in
the ninth and tenth centuries* (Turnhout, 2000), pp. 295–309, on pp. 298–9.

37 H. Loyn, *The Vikings in Britain* (London, 1977), p. 112.

38 M. Redknap, *Vikings in Wales: an archaeological quest* (Cardiff, 2000).

39 M. Redknap, 'Viking-age settlement in Wales and the evidence from
Llanbedrgoch', in Hines, Lane and Redknap (eds), *Land, Sea and Home*,
pp. 139–75, at 147–73.

40 *Ibid.*, pp. 172–3.

41 Nelson, 'England and the continent in the ninth century', p. 28.

SELECT BIBLIOGRAPHY

This bibliography is arranged thematically, and is restricted to books and papers that focus specifically on the Scandinavians in England.

The Vikings in England: general

Brooks, N. P., 'England in the ninth century: the crucible of defeat', *TRHS*, 5th ser., 29 (1979), 1–20

Edwards, B. J. N., *Vikings in North West England* (Lancaster, 1998)

Graham-Campbell, J. (ed.), *Cultural Atlas of the Vikings* (New York, 1994)

Graham-Campbell, J., Hall, R. A., Jesch, J. and Parsons, D. (eds), *Vikings and the Danelaw: Select papers from the proceedings of the Thirteenth Viking Congress* (Oxford, 2001)

Hadley, D. M., ' "And they proceeded to plough and to support themselves": the Scandinavian settlement of England', *ANS*, 19 (1997), 69–96

Hadley, D. M. and Richards, J. D. (eds), *Cultures in Contact: Scandinavian settlement in England in the ninth and tenth centuries* (Turnhout, 2000)

Hines, J., Lane, A. and Redknap, M. (eds), *Land, Sea and Home* (London, 2004)

Jones, G., *A History of the Vikings* (2nd edn, Oxford, 1984)

Keynes, S., 'The Vikings in England, c.790–1016', in P. H. Sawyer (ed.), *The Oxford Illustrated History of the Vikings* (Oxford, 1997), pp. 48–82

Sawyer, P. H., *The Age of the Vikings* (2nd edn, London, 1971)

——, *Kings and Vikings: Scandinavia and Europe AD 700–1100* (London, 1982)

Stafford, P. A., 'The Danes and the Danelaw', *Hist. Today*, 36 (1986), 17–23

Smyth, A., *Scandinavian York and Dublin. The history and archaeology of two related Viking kingdoms*, 2 vols (Dublin, 1975–8)

Wormald, P., 'Viking studies: whence and whither', in R. T. Farrell (ed.), *The Vikings* (Chichester, 1982), pp. 128–53

Documentary sources relevant to the period of Scandinavian settlement

Campbell, A. (ed.), *The Chronicle of Æthelweard* (Edinburgh, 1962)

Keynes, S. and Lapidge, M., *Alfred the Great. Asser's* Life of King Alfred *and other contemporary sources* (Harmondsworth, 1983)

Rollason, D. W., *Sources for York History to AD 1100*, The Archaeology of York, 1 (York, 1998)

South, T. J., *Historia de Sancto Cuthberto: a history of Saint Cuthbert and a record of his patrimony* (Cambridge, 2002)

Whitelock, D. (ed.), *English Historical Documents, vol. I, c.500–1042* (2nd edn, London, 1979)

Lordship and kingship in northern and eastern England after the Scandinavian settlement

Davidson, M., 'The (non)submission of the northern kings in 920', in N. J. Higham and D. H. Hill (eds), *Edward the Elder 899–924* (Manchester, 2001), pp. 200–11

Dumville, D. N., *Wessex and England From Alfred to Edgar* (Woodbridge, 1992)

Hadley, D. M., ' "Hamlet and the princes of Denmark": lordship in the Danelaw, c.860–954', in Hadley and Richards (eds), *Cultures in Contact*, pp. 107–32

——, 'Viking and native: rethinking identity in the Danelaw', *EME*, 11 (1) (2002), 45–70

Innes, M., 'Danelaw identities: ethnicity, regionalism and political allegiance', Hadley and Richards (eds), *Cultures in Contact*, pp. 65–88

Kershaw, P., 'The Alfred–Guthrum treaty: scripting accommodation and interaction in Viking Age England', in Hadley and Richards (eds), *Cultures in Contact*, pp. 43–64

Lund, N., 'King Edgar and the Danelaw', *Mediaeval Scandinavia*, 9 (1976), 181–95

Whitelock, D., 'The dealings of the kings of England with Northumbria in the tenth and eleventh centuries', in P. Clemoes (ed.), *The Anglo-Saxons: studies presented to Bruce Dickins* (London, 1959), pp. 70–88

Numismatic evidence for Scandinavian settlement and lordship

Blackburn, M. A. S., 'Expansion and control: aspects of Anglo–Scandinavian minting south of the Humber', in Graham-Campbell, Hall, Jesch and Parsons, *Vikings and the Danelaw*, pp. 125–41

——, 'The coinage of Scandinavian York', in Hall (ed.), *Aspects of Anglo–Scandinavian York*, pp. 325–49

Blunt, C. E., Stewart, B. H. I. H. and Lyon, C. S. S., *Coinage in Tenth-Century England: from Edward the Elder to Edgar's Reform* (Oxford, 1989)

Dolley, M., 'The Anglo-Danish and Anglo-Norse coinages of York', in R. A. Hall (ed.), *Viking Age York and the North*, CBA Research Rep., 27 (London, 1978), pp. 26–31

Smart, V., 'Scandinavians, Celts and Germans in Anglo-Saxon England: the evidence of moneyers' names', in M. A. S. Blackburn (ed.), *Anglo-Saxon Monetary History* (Leicester, 1986), pp. 171–84

Rural settlement in northern and eastern England in the ninth and tenth centuries

Cabot, S., Davies, G. and Hoggett, R., 'Sedgeford: excavations of a rural settlement in Norfolk', in Hines, Lane and Redknap (eds), *Land, Sea and Home*, pp. 313–23

Coggins, D., 'Simy Folds: twenty years on', in Hines, Lane and Redknap (eds), *Land, Sea and Home*, pp. 326–34

Coggins, D., Fairless, K. J. and Batey, C. E., 'Simy Folds: an early medieval settlement in Upper Teesdale, Co. Durham', *Med. Arch.*, 27 (1983), 1–26

Davis, R. H. C., 'East Anglia and the Danelaw', *TRHS*, 5th ser., 5 (1955), 23–39

Dickinson, S., 'Bryant's Gill, Kentmere: another "viking-period" Ribblehead?', in J. R. Baldwin and I. D. Whyte (eds), *The Scandinavians in Cumbria* (Edinburgh, 1985), pp. 83–8

Griffiths, D., 'Settlement and acculturation in the Irish Sea region', in Hines, Lane and Redknap (eds), *Land, Sea and Home*, pp. 125–38

Higham, N., 'Viking-Age settlement in the north-western countryside: lifting the veil?', in Hines, Lane and Redknap (eds), *Land, Sea and Home*, pp. 297–311

Jones, G. R. J., 'Early territorial organization in Northern England and its bearing on the Scandinavian settlement', in A. Small (ed.), *The Fourth Viking Congress* (Edinburgh, 1965), pp. 67–84

King, A., 'Gauber high pasture, Ribblehead – an interim report', in R. A. Hall (ed.), *Viking Age York and the North*, CBA Research Rep., 27 (London, 1978), pp. 21–5

——, 'Post-Roman upland architecture in the Craven dales and the dating evidence', in Hines, Lane and Redknap (eds), *Land, Sea and Home*, pp. 335–44

Morris, C. D., 'Viking and native in northern England: a case-study', in H. Bekker-Nielsen, P. Foote and O. Olsen (eds), *Proceedings of the Eighth Viking Congress* (Odense, 1981), pp. 223–44

——, 'Aspects of Scandinavian settlement in northern England: a review', *Northern Hist.*, 20 (1984), 1–22

Richards, J. D., 'Cottam: an Anglian and Anglo–Scandinavian settlement in the Yorkshire Wolds', *Arch. J.*, 156 (1999), 1–110

——, 'Identifying Anglo–Scandinavian settlements', in Hadley and Richards (eds), *Cultures in Contact*, pp. 295–309

——, 'The Anglo-Saxon and Anglo–Scandinavian evidence', in P. Stamper and R. Croft (eds), *Wharram: a Study of Settlement in the Yorkshire Wolds. VIII: the South Manor*, York University Archaeological Publications, 10 (York, 2000), pp. 195–200

Stone sculptures

Bailey, R. N., *Viking Age Sculpture in Northern England* (London, 1980)

——, *England's Earliest Sculptors* (Toronto, 1997)

Bailey, R. N. and Cramp, R., *Corpus of Anglo-Saxon Stone Sculpture, Vol. 2. Cumberland, Westmorland and Lancashire North-of-the-Sands* (Oxford, 1988)

Cramp, R., *Corpus of Anglo-Saxon Stone Sculpture, Vol. 1. County Durham and Northumberland* (Oxford, 1984)

Everson, P. and Stocker, D., *Corpus of Anglo-Saxon Stone Sculpture, Vol. 5. Lincolnshire* (Oxford, 1999)

Lang, J. T., 'Sigurd and Weland in pre-Conquest carving from northern England', *YAJ*, 48 (1976), 83–94

——, 'The hogback: a viking colonial monument', *ASSAH*, 3 (1984), 85–176

Lang, J. T., 'The distinctiveness of Viking colonial art', in P. Szarmarch (ed.), *Sources of Anglo-Saxon Culture* (Michigan, 1986), pp. 243–60

——, *Corpus of Anglo-Saxon Stone Sculpture, Volume: 3: York and Eastern Yorkshire* (Oxford, 1991)

Sidebottom, P., 'Viking Age stone monuments and social identity', in Hadley and Richards (eds), *Cultures in Contact*, pp. 213–35

Stocker, D., 'Monuments and merchants: irregularities in the distribution of stone sculpture in Lincolnshire and Yorkshire in the tenth century', in Hadley and Richards (eds), *Cultures in Contact*, pp. 179–212

Stocker, D. and Everson, P., 'Five towns funerals: decoding diversity in Danelaw stone sculpture', in Graham-Campbell, Hall, Jesch and Parsons, *Vikings and the Danelaw*, pp. 223–43

Linguistic evidence for Scandinavian settlement

Barnes, M., 'Norse in the British Isles', in A. Faulkes and R. Perkins (eds), *Viking Revaluations* (London, 1993), pp. 65–84

Ekwall, E., 'How long did the Scandinavian language survive in England?', in N. Bøgholm, A. Brusendorff and C. Bodelsen (eds), *A Grammatical Miscellany Offered to Otto Jespersen on His Seventieth Birthday* (London and Copenhagen, 1930), pp. 17–30

Geipel, J., *The Viking Legacy: the Scandinavian influence on the English and Gaelic languages* (Newton Abbot, 1971)

Hansen, B., 'The historical implications of the Scandinavian element in English: a theoretical valuation', *Nowele*, 4 (1984), 53–95

Hines, J., 'Scandinavian English: a creole in context', in P. S. Ureland and G. Broderick (eds), *Language Contact in the British Isles* (Tübingen, 1991), pp. 403–27

——, 'Focus and boundary in linguistic varieties in the north-west Germanic continuum', in V. Faltings, A. Walker and O. Wilts (eds), *Friesische Studien II* (Odense, 1995), pp. 35–62

Holman, K., *Scandinavian Runic Inscriptions in the British Isles: their historical context* (Trondheim, 1996)

Kastovsky, D., 'Semantics and vocabulary', in R. M. Hogg (ed.), *The Cambridge History of the English Language*, vol. 1 (Cambridge, 1992), pp. 290–408

Page, R. I., 'How long did the Scandinavian language survive in England? The epigraphical evidence', in P. Clemoes and K. Hughes (eds), *England before the Conquest: studies in primary sources presented to Dorothy Whitelock* (Cambridge, 1971), pp. 165–81

Parsons, D., 'How long did the Scandinavian language survive in England? Again', in Graham-Campbell, Hall, Jesch and Parsons (eds), *Vikings and the Danelaw*, pp. 299–312

Townend, M., 'Viking Age England as a bilingual society', in Hadley and Richards (eds), *Cultures in Contact*, pp. 89–105

——, *Language and History in Viking Age England. Linguistic relations between speakers of Old Norse and Old English* (Turnhout, 2002)

Scandinavian place-names

Abrams, L. and Parsons, D. N., 'Place-names and the history of Scandinavian settlement in England', in Hines, Lane and Redknap (eds), *Land, Sea and Home*, pp. 379–431

Cameron, K., *Scandinavian Settlement in the Territory of the Five Boroughs: the place-name evidence* (Nottingham, 1965)

——, 'Scandinavian settlement in the territory of the Five Boroughs: the place-name evidence, part II, place-names in thorp', *Mediaeval Scandinavia*, III (1970), 35–49

——, 'Scandinavian settlement in the territory of the Five Boroughs: the place-name evidence, part III, the Grimston-hybrids', in P. Clemoes and K. Hughes (eds), *England Before the Conquest: studies in primary sources presented to Dorothy Whitelock* (Cambridge, 1971), pp. 147–63

Fellows-Jensen, G., 'Of Danes – and thanes – and Domesday Book', in I. Wood and N. Lund (eds), *People and Places in Northern Europe, 500–1600* (Woodbridge, 1991), pp. 107–21

——, 'Scandinavian place-names of the Irish Sea province', in J. Graham-Campbell (ed.), *Viking Treasure from the North-West: the Cuerdale Hoard in its context* (Liverpool, 1992), pp. 31–42

——, 'Scandinavian settlement in Yorkshire – through the rear-view mirror', in B. E. Crawford (ed.), *Scandinavian Settlement in Northern Britain* (London, 1995), pp. 170–86

Lund, N., 'The settlers: where do we get them from – and do we need them?', in H. Bekker-Nielsen, P. Foote and O. Olsen (eds), *Proceedings of the Eighth Viking Congress* (Odense, 1981), pp. 147–71

Anglo-Scandinavian metalwork

Leahy, K. and Paterson, C., 'New light on the Viking presence in Lincolnshire: the artefactual evidence', in Graham-Campbell, Hall, Jesch and Parsons, *Vikings and the Danelaw*, pp. 181–202

Margeson, S., 'Viking settlement in Norfolk: a study of new evidence', in S. Margeson, B. Ayres and S. Heywood (eds), *A Festival of Norfolk Archaeology* (Hunstanton, 1996), pp. 47–57

——, *The Vikings in Norfolk* (Norwich, 1997)

Thomas, G., 'Anglo-Scandinavian metalwork from the Danelaw: exploring social and cultural interaction', in Hadley and Richards (eds), *Cultures in Contact*, pp. 237–55

Urban centres and the Scandinavian settlements

Baker, D., Baker, E., Hassall, J. and Simco, A., 'Excavations in Bedford', *Bedfordshire Archaeological Journal, hereafter: BAJ*, 13 (1979)

Barley, M. W., 'The medieval borough of Torksey: excavations 1963–8', *Antiq. J.*, 61 (1981), 264–91

Carter, A., 'The Anglo-Saxon origins of Norwich: the problems and approaches', *ASE*, 7 (1978), 175–204

Courtney, P., 'Saxon and medieval Leicester: the making of an urban landscape', *TLAHS*, 73 (1998), 110–45

Crummy, P., *Aspects of Anglo-Saxon and Norman Colchester*, CBA Research Rep., 39 (London, 1981)

Dallas, C., *Excavations in Thetford by B. K. Davison between 1964 and 1970*, EAA, 62 (Gressenhall, 1993)

Griffiths, D., ' The coastal trading ports of the Irish Sea', in J. Graham-Campbell (ed.), *Viking Treasure From the North-West: the Cuerdale Hoard in its context* (Liverpool, 1992), pp. 63–72

Hall, R. A., *The Viking Dig* (London, 1984)

——, 'The Five Boroughs of the Danelaw: a review of present knowledge', *ASE*, 18 (1989), 149–206

——, 'Anglo–Scandinavian attitudes: archaeological ambiguities in late ninth- to mid-eleventh-century York', in Hadley and Richards (eds), *Cultures in Contact*, pp. 311–24

——, *Aspects of Anglo–Scandinavian York*, The Archaeology of York, 8 (York, 2004)

Mahany, C. and Roffe, D., 'Stamford: the development of an Anglo–Scandinavian borough', *ANS*, 5 (1985), 197–219

Mahany, C., Burchard, A. and Simpson, G., *Excavations in Stamford Lincolnshire 1963–1969*, (London, 1982)

Perring, D., *Early Medieval Occupation at Flaxengate, Lincoln*, The Archaeology of Lincoln, 9 (1), (London, 1981)

Rogerson, A. and Dallas, C., *Excavations in Thetford, 1948–59 and 1973–80*, EAA, 22 (Gressenhall, 1984)

Vince, A., 'Lincoln in the Viking Age', in Graham-Campbell, Hall, Jesch and Parsons (eds), *Vikings and the Danelaw*, pp. 157–80

——, 'The new town: Lincoln in the high medieval era (c.900 to c.1350)', in D. Stocker (ed.), *The City By the Pool: assessing the archaeology of the city of Lincoln* (Oxford, 2003), pp. 159–296

Pottery production in eastern England

Kilmurry, K., *The Pottery Industry of Stamford, Lincs*, BAR Brit. Ser., 84 (Oxford, 1980)

Miles, P., Young, J. and Wacher, J., *A Late Saxon Kiln Site at Silver Street, Lincoln*, The Archaeology of Lincoln, 12 (3), (London, 1989)

Symonds, L., *Landscape and Social Practice: the production and consumption of pottery in 10th-century Lincolnshire*, BAR Brit. Ser., 345 (Oxford, 2003)

——, 'Territories in transition: the construction of boundaries in in Anglo–Scandinavian Lincolnshire', D. Griffiths, A. Reynolds and S. Semple (eds), *Boundaries in Early Medieval Britain* (Oxford, 2003), pp. 28–37

Churches and churchmen

Abrams, L., 'The conversion of the Danelaw', in Graham-Campbell, Hall, Jesch and Parsons (eds), *Vikings and the Danelaw*, pp. 31–44

Abrams, L., 'Conversion and assimilation', in Hadley and Richards (eds), *Cultures in Contact*, pp. 135–53

Barrow, J., 'Survival and mutation: ecclesiastical institutions in the Danelaw in the ninth and tenth centuries', in Hadley and Richards (eds), *Cultures in Contact*, pp. 155–76

Fleming, R., 'Monastic lands and England's defence in the Viking Age', *EHR*, 100 (1985), 247–65

Foot, S., 'Violence against Christians', *Med. Hist.*, 1 (1991), 3–16

Halsall, G., 'Playing by whose rules? The Vikings and the Church in ninth-century England', *Med. Hist.*, 2 (1992), 2–12

Rollason, D. W., 'The wanderings of St Cuthbert', in D. W. Rollason (ed.), *Cuthbert, Saint and Patron* (Durham, 1987), pp. 45–59

——, 'St Cuthbert and Wessex: the evidence of Cambridge, Corpus Christi College MS 183', in G. Bonner, D. Rollason and C. Stancliffe (eds), *St Cuthbert, His Cult and His Community to AD 1200* (Woodbridge, 1989), pp. 413–24

Smyth, A., 'The effect of Scandinavian raiders on the English and Irish churches: a preliminary reassessment', in B. Smith (ed.), *Britain and Ireland 900–1300. Insular responses to medieval European change* (Cambridge, 1999), pp. 1–38

Whitelock, D., 'The conversion of the eastern Danelaw', *Saga-Book of the Viking Society*, 12 (1937–45), 159–76

Wilson, D. M., 'The vikings' relationship with Christianity in northern England', *JBAA*, 3rd ser., 30 (1967), 37–46

Scandinavian burials and their context

Biddle, M. and Kjølbye-Biddle, B., 'Repton and the "great heathen army", 873–4', in Graham-Campbell, Hall, Jesch and Parsons (eds), *Vikings and the Danelaw*, pp. 45–96

Graham-Campbell, J., 'Pagan Scandinavian burial in the central and southern Danelaw', in Graham-Campbell, Hall, Jesch and Parsons (eds), *Vikings and the Danelaw*, pp. 105–23

Hadley, D. M., 'Burial practices in the Northern Danelaw, c.650–1100', *North. Hist.*, 36 (2) (2000), 199–216

——, 'Negotiating gender, family and status in Anglo-Saxon burial practices, c.600–950', in J. Smith and L. Brubaker (eds), *Gender in the Early Medieval World. East and West, 300–900* (Cambridge, 2004), pp. 301–23

Halsall, G., 'The Viking presence in England? The burial evidence reconsidered', in Hadley and Richards (eds), *Cultures in Contact*, pp. 259–76

Phillips, D., 'The pre-Norman cemetery', in D. Phillips and B. Heywood (eds), *Excavations at York Minster, Volume I* (2 parts) (London, 1995), pp. 75–92

Pitts, M., 'Cumbrian heritage', *British Arch.*, 79 (2004), 28–31

Richards, J. D., 'Boundaries and cult centres: viking burial in Derbyshire', in Graham-Campbell, Hall, Jesch and Parsons (eds), *Vikings and the Danelaw*, pp. 97–104

Richards, J. D., 'The case of the missing Vikings: Scandinavian burial in the Danelaw', in S. Lucy and A. Reynolds (eds), *Burial in Early Medieval England and Wales* (London, 2002), pp. 156–70

—— 'Excavations at the Viking barrow cemetery at Heath Wood, Ingleby, Derbyshire', *Antiq. J.*, 84 (2004), 23–116

Speed, G. and Walton, P., 'A burial of a viking woman at Adwick-le-Street, South Yorkshire', *Med. Arch.*, 48 (2004), 51–90

INDEX

Abbo of Fleury 11
Abrams, Lesley 102-3, 225-6
acculturation 98, 127, 131, 179, 215, 219
Addingham 206
administrative organisation, local 89-92,
    130, 174
Adwick-le-Street 244
Ælfgar 213
Ælfgifu 83
Ælfhelm 199
Ælfred 93
Ælfric of Eynsham 94-5
Ælfweard 63-4
Ælfwold, King 16
Ælla, King 40, 209
Ælstan 85
Aethelbert, St 161
Æthelflaed 55-7, 62, 87, 128, 162, 166,
    170, 202, 210
Æthelfrith 65
Æthelhelm 213
Æthelred, King of East Anglia 11-12
Æthelred II 68-9, 83, 128, 214
Æthelred (ealdorman) 55-6
Æthelthryth, St 199-200, 207
Æthelweard, King 12
Æthelweard (chronicler) 15, 40-1, 85,
    94-5, 155, 174
Æthelwold (nephew of King
    Alfred) 54-5
Æthelwold, Bishop 60, 199
Æthelwulf (ealdorman) 94, 155
Aidan, St 198, 210
Alcuin 16, 148-9, 196-7, 209
Aldgyth 83
Alfred, King 12, 16, 29, 33, 54, 66, 93,
    208, 210, 226
    treaty with Guthrum 30-7, 67

Alkmund, St see Ealhmund, St
Anglo-Saxon Chronicle 1, 4, 12, 28-31,
    34-7, 51-64, 68, 82, 85, 87, 94, 155,
    159-63, 169-70, 174, 193, 196, 200,
    203, 213, 224
Annales Cambriae 62
Annals of St-Bertin 82
Annals of Ulster 61
Anound, King of Sweden 19
archaeological record 5, 12-20, 52, 82,
    95-6, 104-18, 131-2, 149-50, 179-81,
    246, 252, 274-8; see also
    excavations
Asser 29-30, 37, 209, 224
Athelney 224
Athelstan, King 48, 50, 56,
    59-65 passim, 83, 172-3, 202, 214,
    224, 227
Athelstan, Half-King 65, 213
Augustine, St 156
Aycliffe 44

Bailey, Richard 7, 211-12, 216, 218,
    223
Bakewell 204-5
Bamburgh, earls of 64, 67, 71
baptism 29-30, 64
Barrett, James 276
Barrow, Julia 214, 261
barter 128
Barton-upon-Humber 248, 250-1
Batey, Coleen 107-8
Beacon Hill, Aspatria 241, 257
Bedale 246
Bede 157, 200, 205
Bedford 161, 173
Bedhampton 247
bells 112

Beorhtwulf 55
Beornheah 11
Beornoth (atheling) 55
Beowulf 221
berewicks 214
Beverley 202-3, 247
Biddle, Martin 14, 146
bilingualism 95
bishoprics, establishment and
    disappearance of 207-8, 225, 227
Blackburn, Mark 12, 31, 33, 46, 48-9
Blæcca 158
Blair, John 160, 198-9
Bleasby 102
Blinkhorn, Paul 179
Bloodaxe, Eric 51
Bluntisham 129
boat burial 276
Boga of Hemingford 60
Borre style 110-11, 122-4, 152, 176-7,
    277
Bossall 128
bow-shaped buildings 106-8, 277
Bradley, John 275
Bradley, Richard 15
Brigham 246
Brihtsige 55
Brittany 273-4
Brompton 222
brooches 122-7, 152-3, 176-7, 239, 245,
    277
Brooks, Nicholas 4, 208
Brunanburh, Battle of 51, 63, 65
Brut y Tywysogion 62
Bryant's Gill 104-5
Buckden 106
building styles 106-8, 154, 277
Burgred, King 12
burhs 54, 56, 59, 62, 100, 181-2, 211
    early history of 155-62
    following West Saxon conquest
        169-74
    under Scandinavian control 162-9
burial practices 5, 13-15, 201-7, 212,
    224-5, 237-64

in Scandinavia 253-4
    see also funerary displays
Burrow Hill 194
Bury St Edmunds 213

Caister-on-Sea 247, 249
Cambois 241
Cambridge 161, 171
Cambridge, Eric 39
Cameron, Kenneth 4, 99
Campbell, James 36-7
Camphill 241
Canterbury 208
Carlisle 246
Catholme 106, 111
Cenwulf, King 90, 155
Ceolfrith, St 210
Ceolred, Bishop 207
Ceolwulf, King 12, 15, 30
Charles the Bald 19, 30, 82, 272-4
Charles the Simple 45, 47, 273
charters 59-61, 208, 210, 224
Cheddar 106
Cherry Hinton 206, 249, 255
Chester 62, 106, 161-2, 170-4, 181
Chester-le-Street 38-9, 42, 198, 258
Chimney 248
Christianisation 225-6
Christianity
    aristocratic ethos of 221
    conversion to 7, 29, 35, 40, 82, 215,
        219, 222-7
    fears for the fate of 210
    imagery and symbolism of 48-9, 53,
        62-3, 215-19, 223, 261, 277
    influence of 46-7, 127
    promotion of 36, 212
Chronicle of the Archbishops of York 62
churches 7, 49, 173-7, 180, 192, 227, 256,
        260-1, 274
    circumstancial evidence on fortunes
        of 207-14, 227
    during period of Scandinavian raids
        and settlement 193-6
    protection of 225

sculptural evidence on fortunes of 214-23
and social status 263-4
see also Christianity; land-holdings; mother churches
Clark, Cecily 6
Claughton Hall 239
clergy, recruitment and training of 226
Cnut, King 45, 68-9, 83, 96, 227
Coddenham 180
Coenwald 200
coffins 249-50, 255, 263
coinage see minting of coin; numismatic evidence; St Edmund's coinage; St Martin's coinage; St Peter's coinage
Colchester 161-2, 173
Coldingham 194
Columba, St 156
Congham 180
Constantin, king of the Scots 58, 64-5, 83
conversion see Christianity
Cottam 110-12, 118
Cox, Barrie 92
craft-working 150-3, 163-6, 169, 172
Cramp, Rosemary 194-5, 199
cremation 5, 212, 237-41, 246, 253, 263
Crowland Abbey 213
Croyden 127
Cuerdale hoard 128
cultural influences 130-1, 152-3, 179-81, 222; see also acculturation
Cumbria, kings of 62, 71
Cumwhitton 244-5
Cuthbert, St 37-42, 198-9
community of 37-44, 64, 66, 84-8 passim, 198, 201, 209, 227
see also History of St Cuthbert
Cynewaru, Abbess 206

Danelaw 9, 29, 32-3, 69
Davidson, Michael 58-9
Davis, R.H.C. 2-4
Davison, Brian 175

Derby 155-7, 162-3, 166-9, 172-3, 201-2
diplomatic negotiations 67
Dolley, Michael 50
Domesday Book 4, 85, 88, 90, 92, 99-100, 116, 118, 146-7, 159, 173-8 passim, 195, 202-3, 209
Dommoc, bishopric of 207
Dublin 181, 261, 275
Dumville, David 30, 59-60, 226

Eadred, Abbot of Carlisle 38-43
Eadred, King 51, 66-7, 203-5
Eadwig, King 68
Eaglesfield 241
Ealdred, lord of Bamburgh 56, 58, 64
Ealhmund, St 155, 210
Eardwulf, Bishop 38
Eardwulf, King 155
Ecclesiastical History 200
Ecgred, Bishop 198
Edgar, King 67-9, 173, 226
Edington, Battle of 29
Edmund, King 11, 35-6, 51, 63, 65-6, 162, 213
Edward the Elder 36, 47-8, 54-63 passim, 67, 69, 161-2, 165, 169-73, 210
Edwin, King 147
Egbert, King 11, 40
Egbert, St 203
Egils's Saga 19
Ekwall, Eilert 95-7
Ely 193-4, 199-200, 207
Emma, Queen to Cnut 83
English Place-Names Society 2
Englishness, concept of 32
Eohric 55
Eowils, King 55
Eric Bloodaxe 66-7
Esbrid 85
estate structures 84-8, 130, 211, 214
ethnic identities and ethnic solidarity 9, 83-4, 112, 114, 118, 128-31, 257, 261, 263
ethnographic studies 226

evangelisation 225
Everson, Paul 7, 52–3
excavations 12–15, 37, 151–77 *passim*, 194–5, 199–204, 239–50
execution cemeteries 91, 250–2, 256–7
Exeter 247–8
Exeter law-code 67

Faith, Rosamond 116
De Falsis Diis 94
family relationships 255–61
Farndon 244
Fellows-Jensen, Gillian 6, 100
Flegg 36–7
Fleming, Robin 209
Flixborough 113, 180
'Florence' of Worcester 129
Flores Historiarum 194
Folcard 148–9
Foot, Sarah 200
Frankia 272–4
Frankish Royal Annals 82
Frithegod 203
funerary displays 70–1, 127, 237, 252–63
fusion of styles 223

Gainford 43–4, 88
Gainsborough 128–9
gender distinctions 255–61
gender imbalances 83
genetic identification 254–5
Glastonbury 210
Godfred, King of Denmark 17, 19
Godmanchester 161, 170–1
'Golden Gospels' 93
Goldsborough 128
Goltho 106, 113, 116–17
Gosforth 215–16, 218, 221, 223
Graham-Campbell, James 106
grave goods 5, 18, 212, 237, 241–58, 263, 276–7
Griffiths, David 63, 181, 263
Gundbert 36
Guthfrith, King 41, 48, 51, 64

Guthfrithson, Olaf 48–50, 70–1, 83, 169, 172, 224
Guthfrithson, Ragnall 42–4, 47–8, 51, 58, 64–5, 84–5
Guthred 37–43, 87–8, 227
Guthrum 29–37, 93, 118–19, 212–14, 227

Hadcock, Neville 193
Haddr 60
Hæsten 82
Halfdan, King 55–6, 85
Halfdene 60
Hall, Richard 50, 150, 153
Harald, King of Denmark 19, 30, 273
Haslam, Jeremy 161
Heath Wood 239–41, 257–8, 263
Heimskringla 19
Hemming 19
Hesket-in-the-Forest 239, 242, 257
Hexham, bishopric of 207–8
Heysham 206, 248
Hild, St 210
Hines, John 6–7, 98
Historiarum adversum Paganos Libri Septem 94, 210
History of St Cuthbert 38, 40, 42, 62, 64, 66, 84, 100, 198, 209, 211
hoards 127–8, 149, 158, 165, 202, 275–7
hogback monuments 222–3, 260, 262
Holton-le-Clay 248, 250
Horningsea 200, 212
Hovingham 206, 261
Hrólfr 273
Hubba 194
Hunberht, Bishop of 207
hundreds 89–92, 146
Huntingdon 161, 170, 173

iconography 215, 224, 227, 252
Iguuar 15
Ingimund 61–2, 87
Inguar 194
inhumation 237–42 *passim*, 253, 263, 273
Innes, Matthew 67, 69, 129

Inskip 239
Insley, John 6
institutions, role of 9
Iona 18
Ipswich 174, 177-8
Ireland 261-2, 274-8
iron-working 172, 176
Isle of Man 97, 108, 112, 182, 276-9
Ivar, King 55

Jelling style 111, 122, 152, 223
Jeremiah (the prophet) 16
jewellery 18, 61, 110-11, 120-6, 247, 252
John, Bishop 203
John X, Pope 226

Kershaw, Paul 32
Keynes, Simon 70
Kildale 242, 257
kingship, nature and styles of 44, 70-1,
    154
Kirklevington 219, 262
Kjølbye-Biddle, Birthe 14
Klak, Harald 82
Knowles, David 193

land acquisition, methods of 87-8, 93,
    210, 260-1
land-holdings, ecclesiastical 209-11
Lang, James 7, 222
language and language change
    6, 92-102, 131, 278
Launditch Hundred 115, 117
law-codes 67-9, 90, 129, 256
'Laws of Edward and Guthrum' 69
Leahy, Kevin 120
Leeds 216, 220
Leicester 156-7, 162, 167-73
    bishopric of 207
Leigh-on-Sea 243
Lewknor 248
Libellus Æthelwoldi episcopi 199-200,
    212
Liber Eliensis 60, 194, 199
Liber miraculorum beate virginis 199

liberi homines 88
libraries, ecclesiastical 208, 227
Life of John of Beverley 148-9
Life of King Alfred 29, 37, 224
Life of Oda 212-13
Life of St Anskar 19
Life of St Wilfrid 203
Lincoln 157-8, 162-74, 225, 250-3
Lincolnshire 250-2
Lindisfarne 18, 37-9, 42, 196-9
Lindsey, bishopric of 207
linguistics see language
literacy, standards of 208-9
Little Shelford 36, 262
London 248
    bishopric of 207
lordly status and styles of lordship 7, 70,
    112-13, 116-18, 126, 131, 182, 221,
    225, 258-61, 264
Lothar, son of Louis the Pious 19,
    273
Louis the Pious 19, 30, 273

Maccus, Earl 67
Malcolm, king of the Scots 63
Malmesbury, William of 210
Mammen style 177
Margeson, Sue 120
marriage 83, 98, 127, 225, 261
meeting-places 91-2
Meols 181, 244
metal-detecting 120, 180, 244-5
metalwork 5, 14, 120-7, 131, 212, 239
Middle Harling 243-4
minting of coin 33-7, 45-7, 50, 56-64
    passim, 70, 119, 147, 165-9, 172-8
    passim, 262
monetary economy 128, 149
moneyers see minting
Monkwearmouth 194-5, 201
mother churches 207, 211, 214
mound burials 241, 243, 246, 253, 263
multiple estates 84; see also estate
    structures
Myrhe, Björn 18

naming practices *see* personal names; place-names
Nelson, Janet 278–9
Newark 170–3
Newcastle-upon-Tyne 229, 256
Normandy 273–4
Norse language 94–8, 131
Norse mythology 215–16, 219–21
North Elmham 256
Northampton 160–1, 168, 173
Norwich 174–7, 247
Nottingham 57, 158–9, 162–3, 167–72 *passim*, 243
numismatic evidence 11–14, 29–37, 45–63 *passim*, 119, 127–8, 154, 159, 165–6, 214, 224–5
Nunburnholme 217, 223
nunneries 200

Oda, Archbishop 212–13
Offa, King 161
Ohthere 94
Olaf Cuarán 51, 65, 67, 173
Onlafbal 42–3, 85
onomastics 6
Orkney 276–7
Orm, Earl 83
Ormside 244
Orosius 210
Osbert, King 40, 209
Oscytel, Bishop 119–20
Oswald, King 11–12
Oswald, St 48, 210
Oswald, Archbishop of York 203
Oswulf, Earl of Bamburgh 67
Otley 206
Oundle 213
Owain, King of Cumbria 63
Oxford 129
oxygen isotopes 254

pagan artefacts and practices 212–15, 223–6, 243, 248–9, 263
Page, Raymond 97
Parsons, David 6, 96–8, 102–3, 117

Pastoral Care 208–9
patrons, preferences of 221–2
Paulinus, Bishop 157–8
peasants, status of 88–9
personal names 2–6, 118–20
Peterborough 193
place-names 2–7, 36–7, 42, 61, 88, 92–104 *passim*, 120–1, 131, 212, 224, 252, 276–7
pottery 108, 115, 165–79

radiocarbon dating 14, 91, 105, 157, 160–1, 168, 248, 250
raiding 16–20, 34–5, 55, 61, 83, 192, 195, 208, 227, 272–3, 278
Ralegh Radford, C.A. 201–2
Rampside 244
ransom 273
Raunds 256, 260
Reading 243
Reginald (monk of Durham) 198–9
Regino of Prüm 83
regional identities 61, 67, 69, 71, 178
relics 207, 210–13
Repton 12–15, 37, 203–4, 242–3, 248–9, 254, 257, 263
Ribblehead 104–5
Riccall 254
Richards, Julian 15, 106–7, 110–12, 237, 241, 263
Richardson, Caroline 120
Ricsige 11
Ripon 51, 203, 206, 247–8, 256
ritual, funerary 254–5
Rivenhall 247
Roger of Wendover 63–4, 67, 85, 194
Rollason, David 39, 66, 154, 203
Royston Heath 248
runestones 16

Saffron Walden 243
St Edmund coinage 36, 56, 59, 65, 166, 168, 172–3, 212, 227
St Martin's coinage 59, 165, 227
St Peter's coinage 47–9, 165, 227, 274

Santon Downham 242
Sawyer, Peter 4–6, 20, 85, 87, 100
Scarborough 247
Scotland 275–6
Scula 85
Scule 60
Scull, Christopher 146
secular influences 221–2, 252, 258–9
Sedgeford 114, 244
Sheehan, John 275
Sherburn 223
Sigefrid 4
Sigered 11
Sigurd legend 53, 216–17
Sihtric, Earl 56
Sihtric, King 48
Sihtric Caoch, King 48, 59, 64, 83, 165
Simpson, Luisella 66
Simy Folds 104–5
Smyth, Alfred 50
social interaction and social distinctions
   120, 131–2, 225, 246–50, 255–6
Sockburn 220
sokemen 88, 121
solskifte 109
Sonning 243
South Acre 91
Stainmore 102
Stamford 158–74 *passim*
Stenton, Sir Frank 2, 89, 98, 193
Stocker, David 7, 52–3, 222, 262
Stoke-by-Nayland 213
stone sculpture 7, 39, 42–4, 52–3, 61, 70,
   89–90, 96–100, 120–1, 130, 154,
   173–4, 195, 198, 200, 204–6, 211–27,
   252–5, 258–64
   as evidence on the fate of churches
   214–23
Stonegrave 206, 222
strap-ends 110–11, 123–6, 152
Stukeley, William 166
Swaby 247–8
Swein Forkbeard 128–9
Symeon of Durham 38, 206
Symonds, Leigh 178

Theodred, Bishop 213
Thetford 106, 174–6, 213, 244, 257
Thomas, Gabor 120–3, 126
Thompson, Victoria 257
'Three Fragments of Irish Annals' 61–2
Thurcaston 128
Thurcytel 56, 61
Thurferth 56, 60
Thwing 247
Tilred, Abbot of Heversham 211
Torksey 159–60, 167–74
town-planning 153–4, 165
town status, definition of 145–6
Townend, Matthew 6–7, 50, 93–6,
   99–102
trading activities 19, 82, 180–2, 225, 262
Trafford, Simon 5–6
Turner, Sam 91
Tynemouth 205

Uhtred 56, 58, 205
Ulfcytel 119–20
urban settlements, origins of 145–7
Urnes style 177

village nucleation 109, 114–18
vills 90, 100
Vince, Alan 165
'The Voyages of Ohthere and Wulfstan'
   94

Wales 277–8
Walkington Wold 91
Waltham Abbey 105–6, 248
Wantage law-code 68–9
wapentakes 89–92, 146
Wensley 242, 257
Werburg 93
Werburgh, St 162
West Seaton 246
Weston 258–9
Wharram Percy 110–12, 115–18
Whitby 205
Whitelock, Dorothy 201, 212–13
Whithorn, bishopric of 207

Wicken Fen 243
wics 146, 180
Wihberht, St 203
Wilfrid, St 203
William the Conqueror 116
Williams, Ann 112
Williams, John 160
wills 213, 260
Wilson, David 224
Winchester 129, 248–9
Winwick 223
Wirksworth 206
Witham 57
Wormald, Patrick 7, 19–20, 69–70,
    207–8, 221

Wulfhere, Archbishop 11, 45–6, 206
Wulfsige the Black 66
Wulfstan, Archbishop 50–2, 65, 68,
    213
Wulfstan II, Archbishop 69
Wystan, St 204

York 5, 11, 36, 40, 44–55, 58–61, 64–6,
    71, 147–54, 168, 179–81, 223–7, 242,
    246–9, 253, 255, 261–2
    archbishopric of 53–4, 62, 68, 147,
    206
Yorke, Barbara 90

zoomorphic designs 52, 123, 223